Between Solidarity and Economic Constraints

Rethinking the Cold War

Edited by
Kirsten Bönker and Jane Curry

Volume 12

Between Solidarity and Economic Constraints

Global Entanglements of Socialist Architecture and Planning in the Cold War Period

Edited by
Christoph Bernhardt, Andreas Butter
and Monika Motylińska

DE GRUYTER
OLDENBOURG

This publication was financially supported by the Leibniz Institute for Research on Society and Space (IRS), Erkner/Germany and is a result of the research project "Architekturprojekte der DDR im Ausland", which was generously funded by the Gerda Henkel Stiftung, Düsseldorf/Germany.

ISBN 978-3-11-065406-6
e-ISBN (PDF) 978-3-11-065849-1
e-ISBN (EPUB) 978-3-11-065423-3
ISSN 2567-5311

Library of Congress Control Number: 2022949972

Bibliographic information published by the Deutsche Nationalbibliothek
The Deutsche Nationalbibliothek lists this publication in the Deutsche Nationalbibliografie; detailed bibliographic data are available on the internet at http://dnb.dnb.de.

Cover image: "Produktion im Zementanlagenbau Dessau", colour woodcut, Benno Butter (1914–1985), ca. 1975, photo and copyright: Andreas Butter.
Typesetting: Integra Software Services Pvt. Ltd.
Printing and binding: CPI books GmbH, Leck

www.degruyter.com

Contents

Christoph Bernhardt, Monika Motylińska
Global Entanglements of Socialist Architecture and Planning in the Cold War Period – Approaches and Perspectives —— 1

I Soviet Transfer: Strategies and Limits

Susanne Stein
Between 'Self-Sovietisation' and Soviet Assistance: Urban Planning and Design in China, 1950s–1960s —— 21

Nikolay Erofeev, Łukasz Stanek
Integrate, Adapt, Collaborate: Concerns of Comecon's Technical Assistance to Mongolia during the Cold War —— 43

Mariya Petrova, Jonas van der Straeten
Prefabricating Uzbekistan? Discourses and Realities of Urban Redevelopment in Tashkent and Samarkand under Soviet Rule —— 73

II Networks: Comecon, GDR and the "Global South"

Monika Motylińska
A Cuban Nickel Plant made in the GDR? The Architecture of a Comecon Joint Venture —— 103

Anne-Kristin Hartmetz
Between Factory and Fiction – Planning and Implementation of Agro-Industrial Development Projects in Ghana in Cooperation with CMEA Countries, 1960–1966 —— 123

Rachel Lee
Of Mobility and Earth: Hannah Schreckenbach's Engagements with Indigenous Architectures in Ghana —— 143

Franziska Klemstein
Stralsund – More than Exchange of Experiences —— 165

III Media, Perceptions and Afterlives of Socialist Architecture and Planning

Jasna Galjer
Architecture of International Zagreb Fair between the East and West —— 189

Andreas Butter
Shell Sheds for China: Exported Industrial Architecture from the GDR – Intentions and Reception —— 211

Paul Sprute
Settlements of Post-Socialist Development? Reconstructing East German Solidarity through Housing Projects in the Global South after 1990 —— 241

Christina Schwenkel
The Afterlife of Architectural Aid to Vietnam: A View from the Global South —— 267

About the Authors —— 289

Christoph Bernhardt, Monika Motylińska

Global Entanglements of Socialist Architecture and Planning in the Cold War Period – Approaches and Perspectives

Global entanglements in the fields of architecture, planning and building have played a rather minor role in the historiography of globalisation, if compared to the flows of natural resources, manufactured goods, technologies, labour, migration, or the transfer of institutions.[1] However, within the more general and long-term process of globalisation circulations of architecture and planning became relevant in at least three ways. Firstly, colonial planning and building generated a large number of facilities worldwide, like harbours, roads, forts, settlements and other infrastructures of colonial power which played a decisive role in the maintenance of imperial regimes.[2] Secondly, multilayered global circulations of planning concepts interconnected societies and cities across and far beyond colonial contexts. As a result, an extensive legacy of urban layouts, military engineering as well as public, religious and private buildings are preserved worldwide, which until nowadays, refer to each other and document material and cultural ties across the globe.[3] Thirdly, many 'transfer agents' like architects, engineers and planning institutions who designed and directed the construction of buildings created multipolar professional networks and personal relations, triggering economic exploitation and cultural exchange.[4]

Following a long-term perspective also helps to reflect the specific historical place of global entanglements in the field of architecture and planning between the

1 See Sven Beckert, *Empire of Cotton. A Global History* (New York, NY: Knopf, 2015); Jürgen Osterhammel, *Die Verwandlung der Welt. Eine Geschichte des 19. Jahrhunderts* (München: C.H. Beck, 2009).

2 Robert Home, *Of Planting and Planning. The Making of British Colonial Cities* (London and New York, NY: Routledge, 2013); Matthew Gandy, *The Fabric of Space. Water, Modernity and the Urban Imagination* (Cambridge, MA and London: MIT Press, 2014).

3 ICOMOS ed., *Moderne neu denken. Architektur und Städtebau des 20. Jahrhunderts* (Stuttgart: Karl Krämer Verlag, 2019); Hans-Jürgen Lüsebrink and Sylvère Mbondobari, eds., *Villes coloniales/métropoles postcoloniales. Représentations littéraires, images médiatiques et regards croisés* (Tübingen: narr Verlag 2015); Horst Gründer and Peter Johanek, eds., *Kolonialstädte – europäische Enklaven oder Schmelztiegel der Kulturen?* (Münster: LIT-Verlag 2001).

4 Aymone Nicolas, *L'apogée des concours internationaux d'architecture: l'action de l'UIA, 1948–1975* (Paris: Picard, 2007); Martin Kohlrausch, *Brokers of Modernity. East Central Europe and the Rise of Modernist Architects, 1910–1950* (Leuven: Leuven University Press, 2019).

https://doi.org/10.1515/9783110658491-001

Socialist Bloc and the "Global South" in the post-World War Two period. In this edited volume, we connect this perspective to a conceptual approach that puts the study of global flows of capital, labour, know-how, visions and ideas, as well as institutions and materialities, centre stage.[5] Each of these flows could follow, as historical analyses have shown, a different intrinsic logic and undergo periods of rise, stagnation and fall. Consequently, the notion of a linear trend of a long-term growing transnational cooperation or one-dimensional ideas of ubiquitous antagonist confrontation during the Cold War become obsolete. In nineteenth-century Europe, for example, the transnational flows of capital strongly increased in the context of industrialisation, driven by investment in railways and other transport infrastructures and fuelled by the rise of modern imperialism. On the other hand, expertise in building and planning in the first decades of the nineteenth century became increasingly "nationalised" in many newly founded Technical Universities so that early modern patterns of the transnational migration of experts gradually expired.[6] At the same time, departments for building and planning or public works within state administrations were expanded and powerful corps of engineers constructed large national infrastructural networks. Some decades later, rapid urbanisation paved the way for the emergence of urban design as a new academic discipline and triggered the transnational circulation of ideas and cooperation, culminating between 1900 and World War One.

Globalisation of building and planning in the twentieth century

Until 1910 intensive transnational communication on architecture and planning and solid professional networks had been established. Leading professional journals like the British "Journal of the Royal Institute of Architects", the French "L'Architecture" or the "Deutsche Bauzeitung" in Germany continuously presented key projects of planning and building in the five continents – if still with a strong Western bias – to experts in a growing number of building authorities and universities. Early multilateral associations such as the "International Federation for Housing

5 Anthony D. King, *Writing the Global City* (London: Routledge, 2016).

6 Christoph Bernhardt, "Europäische Wasserbau-Ingenieure im 18. und 19. Jahrhundert. Wanderungen und Wissenszirkulation," in *Migration und Baukultur. Transformation des Bauens durch individuelle und kollektive Einwanderung*, edited by Heiderose Kilper, 259–270 (Basel: Birkhäuser, 2019).

and Town Planning" (IFHTP),[7] large international conferences like the RIBA conference in London 1910 and planning competitions like "Wettbewerb Groß-Berlin" 1908 to 1910 served as platforms for the exchange of ideas.[8] At the same time, powerful construction companies like Balfour Beatty Pic (GB), Société générale d'entreprises (F), Philipp Holzmann AG or Grün & Bilfinger (G) and others sent numerous engineers to many parts of the world, where they, together with local subcontractors and workers constructed bridges, railways and roads.[9]

Within this multipolar process, two modes of professional exchange and communication were given special attention by scholarly research until recently: On the one hand, rapidly growing "Atlantic crossings" (D. Rodgers) of concepts and experts indicated strong mutual interest and increasing cooperation between European and US-American experts and authorities.[10] As a result, key innovations like the Chicago Plan of 1908/10 and the Greater Berlin competition of 1908/10 were intensively discussed on both sides of the Atlantic.[11] On the other hand leading US-American and European experts, and private enterprises transferred technologies and concepts to the East and the South. Siemens delivered projects for underground railways to Moscow, Edo (Tokyo) and Buenos Aires,[12] and German Engineering company G. Polysius supplied machinery and cement plants to clients in Egypt, Belgian Congo and Iran, for instance. The French Compagnie des Eaux de Constantinople constructed modern Western sanitary infrastructure in Istanbul,[13]

7 Philipp Wagner, *Stadtplanung für die Welt? Internationales Expertenwissen 1900–1960* (Göttingen: Vandenhoek & Ruprecht, 2016).

8 Christoph Bernhardt and Harald Bodenschatz, eds., "Der Wettbewerb Groß-Berlin 1910 im internationalen Kontext." *Informationen zur modernen Stadtgeschichte* 41 (2010): special issue no. 1.

9 Bernhard Stier and Martin Krauß, *Drei Wurzeln – ein Unternehmen. 125 Jahre Bilfinger Berger AG* (Ubstadt-Weiher: ifu – Institut für Unternehmensgeschichte, 2005); Monika Motylińska and her research group are currently investigating the role of construction companies in the ongoing research project "Conquering (with) Concrete. German Construction Companies as Global Players in Local Contexts" (Freigeist Fellowship fund, edited by Volkswagen Stiftung, 2020–2024).

10 Shane Ewen and Pierre-Yves Saunier, *Another Global City. Historical Explorations into the Transnational Municipal Moment 1850–2000* (Basingstoke: Palgrave, 2008); Daniel T. Rodgers, *Atlantic Crossings: Social Politics in a Progressive Age* (Cambridge, MA: Harvard University Press, 1998).

11 Carl Smith, *The Plan of Chicago: Daniel Burnham and the Remaking of the American City* (Chicago: University of Chicago Press, 2006).

12 Dietmar Neutatz, *Die Moskauer Metro. Von den ersten Plänen bis zur Großbaustelle des Stalinismus (1897–1935)* (Köln: Böhlau Verlag, 2001); Dennis Kirchberg, *Analyse der internationalen Unternehmenstätigkeit des Hauses Siemens in Ostasien vor dem Zweiten Weltkrieg*. Diss. Friedrich-Alexander-Universität Erlangen-Nürnberg, 2010, d-nb.info/1056018593/34 (accessed 20 October 2021).

13 Noyan Dinckal, *Istanbul und das Wasser. Zur Geschichte der Wasserversorgung und Abwasserentsorgung von der Mitte des 19. Jahrhunderts bis 1966* (München: Oldenbourg, 2004).

and colonial authorities imposed urban planning in Delhi/India, Tanganyika (now Tanzania) and elsewhere.[14] For a long time, these forms of cooperation were mainly perceived as a one-way transfer of knowledge and benefits from North to South within the framework of imperial exploitation. They were also condensed into narratives and genealogies of Western architectural styles and pioneering figures (predominantly those of "white men", more reciprocal concerning East Asia). But this cliché of a one-way-transfer from North to South which dominated teaching, research and popular media and made invisible the active role of local actors and governments as well as the expertise of planners from the "Global South,"[15] has been increasingly replaced by the notion of a global "circulation and appropriation" of ideas, as Hard/Misa put it.[16] The knowledge of the manifold interferences and transnational diffusion of concepts of planning and building, which went far beyond the US-American and European exchange, has been strongly developed in the last years.

In the aftermath of the revolutions in Russia (1917), Germany and Austria (both 1918), the emergence of socialism as a state order in a growing number of national states in the Eastern hemisphere fueled concepts of socialist planning and building, which had previously been marginalised, and new modes of transnational professional communication. Between 1920 and 1935, a new transnational order of antagonist cooperation in planning and architecture was established, in which contradicting trends of transfer, appropriation and conflict arose. When in the late 1920s, the Soviet regime launched campaigns of rapid and brutal industrialisation as a key strategy in its first five-years-plan, some of the largest US-American capitalist companies, like Ford, were hired to build factories and company towns in the USSR.[17] At the same time, West-European left-wing modern architects and planners like former Frankfurt councillor for building, Ernst

14 Jane Ridley and Edwin Lutyens, "New Delhi, and the Architecture of Imperialism." *The Journal of Imperial and Commonwealth history* 26, no. 2 (1998): 67–83; Jochen Monstadt and Sophie Schramm, "Toward the Networked City? Translating Technological Ideals and Planning Models in Water and Sanitation Systems in Dar es Salaam." *International Journal of Urban and Regional Research* 41, no. 1 (2017): 104–125.

15 Greg Grandin, *Fordlandia. The Rise and Fall of Henry Ford's Forgotten Jungle City* (London and New York, NY: Picador, 2009); Smitri Pant, "Capital Planning and State Formation: Examples Outside Europe," in *Moderne neu denken. Architektur und Städtebau des 20. Jahrhunderts*, edited by ICOMOS, 59–67 (Stuttgart: Karl Krämer Verlag, 2019).

16 Mikael Hard and Thomas J. Misa, "Modernizing European Cities: Technological Uniformity and Cultural Distinction", in *Urban Machinery. Inside Modern European Cities*, edited by Mikael Hard and Thomas J. Misa, 1–22 (Cambridge, MA and London: MIT Press, 2008).

17 Harald Bodenschatz, and Christiane Post, eds., *Städtebau im Schatten Stalins. Die internationale Suche nach der sozialistischen Stadt in der Sowjetunion* (Berlin: Verlagshaus Braun, 2003).

May, were invited to create blueprints for large-scale urbanisation of the USSR.[18] Against this background, the well-established scholarly narrative of a decline and collapse of transnational cooperation in "the age of extremes" (Hobsbawm)[19] has to be modified and specified for the field of architecture and planning. On the one hand, in the early 1930s, the USSR became a hub and hotspot of international professional debate. It was only in 1935 when the Stalinist turn in architectural doctrine towards socialist realism provoked a fundamental clash between the socialist and the modern Western approach to architecture and planning which would last until 1955. On the other hand, it has been largely overlooked that German National socialism or fascist Italy did not strictly follow a strategy of national autarchy and isolation but developed a kind of imperialistic internationalism, in which spatial planning and transnational policies prepared and accompanied the deadly political and military concepts of occupation, exploitation, and genocide.[20]

Transnational relations in planning and architecture in the Cold War period: A "blind spot" of research?

In 2012, one of the leading experts in the field, Łukasz Stanek, considered the history of the transfer of architecture and planning between the socialist countries and the "Global South" a "major blind-spot of current architectural historiography of the post-war period".[21] In a special issue of the *Journal of Architecture*, he addressed five key questions to pursue: the modes of multiple cooperation, the role of organisations and collective actors, the "export beyond modernism", architecture as self-representation of political systems, and the important role of "socialist-inspired modernisation processes" in the history of the "Global South".[22] Since

18 Claudia Quiring, ed., *Ernst May, 1886–1970. Neue Städte auf drei Kontinenten* (München: Prestel, 2011).
19 Eric Hobsbawm, *The Age of Extremes. The Short Twentieth Century* (London: Michael Joseph, 1994).
20 Isabel Heinemann, and PatrickWagner, eds., *Wissenschaft – Planung – Vertreibung. Neuordnungskonzepte und Umsiedlungspolitik im 20. Jahrhundert* (Stuttgart: Franz Steiner Verlag, 2006); Phillip Wagner, "Between National Socialism and Expert Internationalism: Karl Strölin and Transnationalism in Urban Planning, 1938–45." *European Review of History: Revue européenne d'histoire* 25, nos. 3/4 (2018): 512–534.
21 Łukasz Stanek, "Introduction: the 'Second World's' Architecture and Planning in the 'Third World.'" *The Journal of Architecture* 17 (2012) no. 3: 299–307, 299.
22 Stanek, "Introduction," 299.

then, the state of research has considerably progressed, not least as a result of Stanek's own work. In his seminal book on "Architecture in Global Socialism", published in 2020, Stanek investigated the triangular cooperation between the Socialist Bloc, the Middle East and the (anglophone) West Africa, delivering fundamental insights into this world of collaboration, encounters and experiences.[23] His study makes clear that the built environment in cities like Accra, Lagos or Baghdad was strongly shaped by actors from the Eastern Bloc – and that ideological and economic differences were negotiated in particular, seemingly remote locations. Stanek also demonstrates how the experiences abroad impacted particular actors and their later projects in Eastern Europe.

However, his contribution is by far not a singular occurrence, but rather part of a larger shift in scholarly attention towards the "Second World" and its global entanglements. Jonathan Bach and Michał Murawski have recently proposed considering different case studies of the urban planning from the "Global East" not only in their historical development – which follows a longer trajectory of research on the history of the built environment in Eastern Europe after World War Two – but also to look at their appropriation and transmutations in a variety of spatial, both urban and more peripheral contexts.[24] A considerable number of other architectural and urban historians participated in the debate which seeks to overcome binary narratives of antagonist competition between the "First" and the "Second World" and their role in the so-called "Third World".[25]

Within the realm of social and cultural anthropology, the material and social dimensions of the built socialism have gained momentum in the work of Christina Schwenkel.[26] The author has managed to bridge the gap between the (often rather abstract) planning imaginaries proposed by the architects from the GDR, for instance, and the labourers who actually built the settlements in Vietnam. Moreover, she has investigated memories of the socialist planning in the context of the current functioning of the towns like Vinh, countering the all-too-easy perception of ruination and decay of the socialist heritage.

---

23 Łukasz Stanek: *Architecture in Global Socialism. Eastern Europe, West Africa, and the Middle East in the Cold War* (Princeton and Oxford: Princeton University Press, 2020).

24 Jonathan Bach, and Michal Murawski, *Re-Centring the City Global Mutations of Socialist Modernity* (London: UCL Press, 2020).

25 E.g. Andreas Butter, "Showcase and Window to the World: East German Architecture abroad 1949–1990." *Planning Perspectives* 33, no. 2 (2018): 249–269. For the agenda of the actors from the "Global South" see Duanfang Lu, ed., *Third World Modernism* (London: Routledge, 2011).

26 Especially in her most recent monograph, Christina Schwenkel, *Building Socialism: The Afterlife of East German Architecture in Urban Vietnam* (Durham: Duke University Press, 2021).

In the field of economic history Oscar Sanchez-Sibony and Max Trecker analysed the economic frameworks as well as decision-making processes on the ground, for instance in joint-venture projects of the Council for Mutual Economic Assistance (Comecon) in Syria or India.[27] These multi-scalar studies followed up on the institutional histories, such as the monograph about Comecon by Ralf Ahrens.[28] Both Sanchez-Sibony and Trecker investigated the agency of various stakeholders. As Trecker observes, "the cooperation between East and South during the Cold War was underpinned by ideological as well as pragmatic political considerations".[29] The attention to those pragmatical considerations is something that resonates with the contributions gathered in this volume.

The role of the actors from the Socialist Bloc has also recently been investigated by historians of development aid who took an interest in their complex entanglements in different settings in the "Global South".[30] The strategies and activities of the GDR in various campaigns of solidarity were reconstructed in a volume on "Comrades of Color", which was edited by Quinn Slobodian.[31] The contributors offered a nuanced analysis of clashes between the official political discourse of socialist solidarity and actual encounters among students and planners from Cuba, Vietnam, the GDR and Mozambique. Within the history of diplomacy, for instance, similar striving for a more differentiated approach towards the historiography of the Cold War has been visible – with a sensitivity towards the variety of specific vantage points and local contexts instead of larger narratives of a bipolar confrontation.[32]

---

27 Oscar Sanchez-Sibony, *Red Globalization: The Political Economy of the Soviet Cold War from Stalin to Khrushchev. New Studies in European History* (Cambridge: Cambridge University Press, 2014); Max Trecker, *Red Money for the Global South: East-South Economic Relations in the Cold War*, Routledge Studies in Modern History (London: Routledge, 2020).

28 Ralf Ahrens, *Gegenseitige Wirtschaftshilfe? Die DDR im RGW – Strukturen und handelspolitische Strategien 1963–1976*, Schriften des Hannah-Arendt-Instituts für Totalitarismusforschung, vol. 15 (Köln: Böhlau, 2000).

29 Ahrens, *Gegenseitige Wirtschaftshilfe?*, 228.

30 E.g. Marc E. Frey, Sönke Kunkel, and Nancy H. Kwak, "Introduction. Transforming Cities: Urbanization and International Development in Africa and Latin America since 1945." *Comparativ* 30, nos. 1/2 (2020): 10–19; specifically for Germany: Young-sun Hong, *Cold War Germany, the Third World, and the Global Humanitarian Regime*, Human Rights in History (Cambridge: Cambridge University Press, 2015).

31 Quinn Slobodian, ed., *Comrades of Color: East Germany in the Cold War World*, Protest, Culture and Society, vol. 14 (New York, NY and Oxford: Berghahn Books, 2015).

32 E.g. Simo Mikkonen, Jari Parkkinen, and Giles Scott-Smith, eds., *Entangled East and West: Rethinking the Cold War Cultural Diplomacy and Artistic Interaction during the Cold War*, Rethinking the Cold War, vol. 4 (Berlin: De Gruyter Oldenbourg, 2019).

All of these research strands converge into a handful of interdisciplinary anthologies, like the series "Rethinking the Cold War". In this regard, the notion of "alternative globalisations" as proposed by James Mark, Artemy M. Kalinovsky and Steffi Marung resonates with our understanding of circulations of architecture, and urban planning under global conditions – neither as a streamlined process of the spread of Western ideas of 'modernity' and 'progress', nor as a straightforward opposition to it, but rather as a larger cluster 'globalising projects'.[33] As this short overview shows, in the last decade substantial contributions have been made to complicate the history of the Cold War period, thus drawing closer to fulfilling Stanek's plea for investigations of modes of multiple cooperation, the role of collective actors, or "socialist-inspired modernisation processes" in the history of the "Global South".

Key aspects and guiding questions

Recent critical research on twentieth-century globalisation, development and modernity largely agrees that traditional categories of centre and periphery, of a linear modernity, and of simple bipolar relations between a dominating "North" and a subaltern "South" in contexts of colonialism or globalisation are not productive anymore, as they obscure the complex dynamics of processes which developed under global conditions. Thus, they have been replaced by inquiries on the "coproduction of modernity",[34] "multipolar historical relationships" and "variations of colonialism".[35]

Building on these calls for more diversified approaches and in line with multidisciplinary investigations of alternative globalisations as discussed above, we are interested in revealing the nuanced global entanglements during the Cold War era, especially with regard to interactions between the actors from the "Second" and "Third World" – and also within the respective blocs. However, rather than proposing one definition of "socialist architecture and planning", we use this term as a broad indicator, denoting activities in countries that were

---

33 James Mark, Artemy M. Kalinovsky, and Steffi Marung, eds., *Alternative Globalizations: Eastern Europe and the Postcolonial World* (Bloomington, IN: Indiana University Press 2020).

34 Thomas Schwinn, "Globalisation and Regional Variety: Problems of Theorisation," in *World Culture Re-Contextualised. Meaning Constellations and Path Dependencies in Comparative and International Research* edited by Jürgen Schriewer, 119–138 (London: Routledge 2016).

35 "Empires of Knowledge: Expertise and Imperial Power across the Long Twentieth Century," conference at University of British Columbia, Vancouver/Canada, 15–16 September 2017, conveners: Axel Jansen (GHI), John Krige (Georgia Institute of Technology) and Jessica Wang (UBC).

either identifying themselves as socialist or in which socialist-leaning tendencies occurred throughout the time, as was the case in Ghana. In order to conduct multifaceted analyses of circulations of socialist planning and architecture, it is our aim to further interrogate personal experiences of actors involved but also to observe how diverse constraints denoted the challenges with which architects, urbanists, clients or users were confronted through planning, construction and appropriation of the built environment. Moreover, this focus resonates with reflections of architectural historians looking at the links between architecture and economy.[36] However, so far very little attention has been paid to non-capitalist economies and their impact on the built environment.

The notion of economic constraints is a helpful lens through which to analyse multi-scalar processes of global circulations of the Cold War period in architecture and planning, as it enables us to observe ways in which room for manoeuvre was frequently restricted.[37] However, we define constraints broadly, taking into account a variety of factors limiting the scope of activities in the domain of the built environment. Thus, we want to address the perceived or actual scarcity of (economic) means, for instance lack of construction materials, capital, (skilled) labour or know-how, but also to restraints of legal frameworks or bureaucratic practice, limiting the possibility of travel for the actors from the "second" and "third world". These constraints strongly shaped the outcome of architectural and urban projects that were often either not realized at all or strongly modified. In the long term, potential for conflict arose from the often bureaucratic, centralised nature of project management plus travel/contact restrictions, which led to a delayed perception of feasibility deficits (e.g. due to inefficient transport routes) and technological incompatibility with foreign partners – such as different voltages for electrical appliances. Moreover, the target countries had their own ideas of modernity, which could differ from those of the foreign experts – and those models were born out of the encouraging spirit of helping people to help themselves.

Yet it would be too simple to draw a general causal link between the socialist economies and scarcity. Instead, we prefer a notion of economic constraints

36 E.g. Aggregate Group, ed., *Governing by Design: Architecture, Economy, and Politics in the Twentieth Century* (Pittsburgh, PA: University of Pittsburgh Press, 2012); Jo Odgers, Mhairi McVicar, and Stephen Kite, eds., *Economy and Architecture* (London and New York, NY: Routledge, 2015); Peggy Deamer, ed., *Architecture and Capitalism: 1845 to the Present* (London and New York, NY: Routledge, 2014).

37 The concept of economic constraints has permeated developmentalists discourses from the Cold War period (e.g. Charles Elliott, *Constraints on the Economic Development of Zambia* [Oxford: Oxford University Press, 1971]) – in this regard, this an attempt to overcome the limitations of this vantage point.

which builds on the perceptions and experiences of contemporary witnesses – or is depicted by the protagonists in the sources.[38] This also applies to the concept of solidarity, not specifically defined here, but rather observed as another recurring theme for the actors from the Socialist Bloc, especially in their encounters with their counterparts from the "Third World".[39] Repeatedly we at least see tensions between those two poles – of solidarity and economic constraints – and conflicts between (supposedly) noble ambitions and challenging circumstances on the ground.

However, even if attempts to overcome those constraints did not prove satisfactory in many cases, Max Trecker's observation holds true that "the state socialist countries of the East may not have been able to provide the other side with the latest technology of the world but the technology they could provide was sufficient for the purposes it had to serve".[40]

In order to pursue such an analysis, we are also interested in various scales related to the built environment. Starting with the micro-perspectives of biographically-oriented investigations, we intend to contribute to a better understanding of personal motivations in the field of construction, including gender aspects. This means, for instance, paying attention to professional and private challenges that female architects such as the German planner Hannah Schreckenbach in Ghana were confronted with during their international careers. On an individual level, the Cold War might not have been perceived by the protagonists as the dominant context of their acting – and yet the sheer fact of being associated with the Western or Eastern Bloc often had a direct or indirect impact on their room for manoeuvre.[41]

As transnational activities of architects and planners – especially those from Eastern Europe due to politically imposed limitations to individual mobility – took place mostly in institutionalised contexts, we pay particular attention to the role of collective actors such as construction companies and state Design Institutes. Moreover, we take a closer look at platforms of exchange such as trade fairs and professional media. All these institutions which were not something

38 Cf. Monika Motylińska and Phuong Phan, "'Not the usual way?' On the Involvement of an East German Couple with the Planning of the Ethiopian Capital." *Architecture Beyond Europe (ABE)* 8, no. 19 (2019). *journals.openedition.org/abe/6997* (accessed 2 July 2021).

39 Slobodian, ed., *Comrades of Color*.

40 Trecker, *Red Money for the Global South*, 228.

41 Jadwiga E. Pieper Mooney, and Fabio Lanza, eds., *De-Centering Cold War History: Local and Global Change* (London and New York, NY: Routledge, 2013); Eric Burton, Anne Dietrich, Immanuel R. Harisch, and Marcia C. Schenck, eds., *Navigating Socialist Encounters: Moorings and (Dis)Entanglements between Africa and East Germany during the Cold War* (Berlin: De Gruyter, 2021).

particular for the Cold War period but part of a longer trajectory across the twentieth century, played a crucial role in negotiating, brokering and bartering building projects.[42] International fairs in Zagreb and elsewhere and strategies of specialised enterprises from socialist states, which are analysed in this volume, provided contemporary architects and planners with alternative spaces of interaction in times when more direct collaborations across political, ideological or economic divisions were more difficult to realise than after the political turn of 1989 to 1991 and the collapse of the Eastern Bloc.

On the organisational macro-level, we address questions on the role of multilateral institutions and global networks and flows. One of the specific socialist institutions of paramount transnational importance was the already mentioned Council for Mutual Economic Assistance (Comecon). In 1959, the Permanent Commission for Building of the Comecon was created; its conferences were regularly held in different member states, such as the 37th conference in the Czechoslovakian capital of Prague.[43] Main themes discussed during meetings of the Permanent Commission were strategies of standardisation and methods of prefabrication, with a focus on industrial architecture and mass housing. Yet, apart from producing a large body of (grey) literature, this administration does not seem to have had a strong direct impact on the realities of international construction processes. Far more relevant in this regard was the system of barter, which means the mutual exchange of goods and services as an alternative to financial credits. This system was widely used among members of Comecon and sometimes in joint projects with states in the Middle East or Africa.[44] Shaped by particular interests, strategies and actors' constellations, it also materialised through architecture and infrastructure.

We are combining attempts to contribute to the more nuanced history of the Cold War era with the particular attention to narratives of dealing with constraints, not only in political terms but also related to economic and material aspects of construction processes. We address the need for complex global histories of the built environment post-1945. In doing so, we are aware of the imbalances between different vantage points, as those centring the actors from the Eastern Bloc feature more prominently in this volume. However, instead of exclusively focusing on competitions between the "East" and the "West", or tensions within the Soviet Bloc, or tracing links between the "Second" and "Third" world, we

---

42 For the role of construction companies: Marc Linder, *Projecting Capitalism: A History of the Internationalization of the Construction Industry*, Contributions in Economics and Economic History, vol. 158 (Westport, CT: Greenwood Press, 1994).

43 Ministerium für Bauwesen der DDR, ed., *Zusammenarbeit der Mitgliedsländer des RGW auf dem Gebiet des Bauwesens* (Berlin 1975: Bauakademie der DDR), 5.

44 Stanek, *Architecture in Global Socialism*.

prefer to move beyond those preset geographies, focusing instead on different *modi operandi* of diverse actors and construction of the built environment under the conditions of global socialism. For us, the Cold War is, first of all, a temporal framework delimiting the scope of the investigations, even if some of the studies from the volume also deal with its aftermath until the present. In this regard, we are venturing rather far from Westad's political history of the Cold War "as a confrontation between capitalism and socialism",[45] looking for cases of collaboration across the divides or tensions within the socialist bloc, for instance. At the same time, this is an attempt at "writing about the politics of architecture" – and urban planning – without reducing the architectural and the urban to politics, to paraphrase Sibel Bozdogan's question.[46]

These observations on the multilayered and multiscalar circulations of architecture and planning during the Cold War lead to five sets of guiding questions for our volume. The first set of questions addresses the actors and institutions on the micro, meso and macro-scale. Who set the rules, and which persons, professions and roles were present in the complex histories of construction projects? Far beyond architects and planners, we have to include a variety of political institutions such as ministries, foreign trade institutions, and different economic actors, for instance, Publicly Owned Enterprises, labourers or even singular personalities that acted as brokers in the processes of exchange into our perspective. Second, to better understand the circulation of knowledge, practices and material, the geographies and temporalities of these mutual exchanges, we are focusing on essential arenas and particular spatial settings, such as trade fairs as hubs for construction industries, but also in a more narrow sense on their role in the circulation of design solutions which has been largely overlooked.[47] Third, we inquire into how the architectural projects were shaped by the actual context of the Cold War, antagonist ideologies and economic interests. To what extent could political (and personal) solidarity be reconciled with economic interests, both strong and often conflicting motives of the "export" of built socialism? Fourth, we are analysing conflicts and supposed "failures" of projects and their far-reaching consequences, sometimes also on the diplomatic level, far away from the construction site. Finally, and perhaps most importantly, we are interested in different patterns of appropriation of the built environment, and consider how users adapted the buildings once they

45 Odd Arne Westad, *The Cold War. A World History* (London: Allen Lane, 2017), 1.
46 Sibel Bozdogan, "Architectural History in Professional Education: Reflections on Postcolonial Challenges to the Modern Survey." *Journal of Architectural Education* 52, no. 4 (1999): 207–221.
47 Apart from rare exemptions such as the study by Anoma Pieris ("Modernity and Revolution: The Architecture of Ceylon's Twentieth-Century Exhibitions," in *Third World Modernism*, edited by Duanfang Lu, 141–164 [London and New York, NY: Routledge, 2010]).

had been erected and inhabited, and what labels and meanings were associated with them, in political discourses and daily practices.

This book is derived from the contributions to an international workshop and an international conference which were held in the Leibniz Institute for Research on Society and Space in Erkner (near Berlin) in July 2017 and June 2018. The editors organised these events in the context of the research project "Architectural projects of the GDR abroad. Buildings, actors, and cultural transfers", which was financed by the Gerda Henkel foundation from 2016 to 2018.[48] Delayed by the Covid pandemic and related problems, authors updated and revised their contributions in spring 2022.[49] A related publication from the same research project which is edited by Andreas Butter and Thomas Flierl offers additional insights on architectural projects of the GDR abroad.[50]

Contributions

The book's first part reflects the basic model of socialist international planning and building. From its beginnings, it was characterised by transferring Soviet concepts to foreign partners in a bilateral, mostly hierarchical cooperation. At the same time, in any of these bilateral projects, the adaptation of Soviet blueprints and recipes was fundamentally shaped by the USSR's partners, as Susanne Stein reveals along the process of the "self-Sovietisation" of China in the 1950s. Despite its status as a developing country, China was undoubtedly the most important socialist nation-state outside the USSR. In the long run, it developed its imperial strategy (culminating, as we know, in the early twenty-first century). Framed by large Soviet loans and military support, the education of planners and the diffusion of manuals and reference books were, as Stein shows, critical strategies shaping professional cultures and standards of building in China. This was especially true for Chinese economic and urban planning along Soviet guidelines,

48 Out of this project, articles and an interactive website were published. See the references in the footnotes to this introduction and the website: ddr-planungsgeschichte.de/auslandsprojekte/ (accessed 15 January 2022).

49 We are very thankful for the kind and extremely helpful cooperation with series editor Kerstin Bönker and Verena Deutsch and for the comments of the unknown reviewers which helped to improve the manuscript.

50 Andreas Butter, and Thomas Flierl, eds., *Der Architekturexport der DDR: Von Sansibar bis Halensee* (Berlin, Lukas Verlag 2022). Besides a number of essays, the volume presents a catalogue of 110 buildings and ensembles as well as a facsimile of the "Tropenbaubriefe" publication by the Weimar University from the 1980s.

directed by many planners, engineers and other experts from the USSR. But, as Stein underlines, the Chinese adaptation of Soviet concepts was very selective and guided by intrinsic interests and modes of appropriation.

The pathway of the socialist state of Mongolia has a similar significance, especially concerning its role as one of the few non-European member states of Comecon, which the country joined in 1962. Nikolaj Erofeev and Łukasz Stanek discuss the dominant role of Soviet and Comecon capital for economic development and urbanisation and the fusion of bilateral and multilateral cooperation of experts within this organisation. They reconstruct in detail how, following a mechanism of "imperatives", the Mongolian capital city of Ulan Bator was developed with the help of Soviet and Comecon concepts, loans and close institutional cooperation with key domestic organisations, like the Mongolian state Design Institute. As in many others cases, a strong logic of permanent negotiation and conflict fundamentally shaped this fraternal socialist cooperation.

The basic mission and origin of the Soviet model of imperial development was the execution of Moscow's rule in the Soviet republics, as Petrova and van der Straeten demonstrate in the prominent case of Uzbekistan. Even in areas representing the inner periphery of the USSR, the regime's fundamental philosophy of imposing a socialist model of modernisation with mass housing as its key strategy could only be partially realised. Besides the ubiquitous tensions between Moscow's central authorities and planners on the one hand and their local partners on the other, the lack of resources for Soviet prefabricated mass housing gave place to local initiatives for individual private homes, which corresponded to the local housing traditions. Mismatches between the Chruschtschev housing program, local climate and family patterns triggered a critical debate on the deficits and a potential co-evolution of modern and vernacular architecture.

The book's second part widens the perspective beyond the USSR, its member states and its closest neighbour China to the GDR and the "Global South", exploring the multipolar and tangential character of socialist globalisation in architecture and planning. This part reflects the fact that since the 1960s, parallel to the USSR, other socialist countries increasingly developed global engagement strategies and inner-socialist cooperation. As a result, the role of the Soviet Union changed from being a headquarters to a key critical player amongst others in an increasingly multilateral setting. Along with a nickel plant planned for Cuba from 1975 onwards, Monika Motylińska reveals the complex interaction between various stakeholders, from state authorities through large enterprises to local administrations and individual planners, which repeatedly changed their roles over time. By addressing the shift of GDR's architectural "export" from inner-European to global networks in the early 1970s, Motylińska demarcates this period as a significant turning point in the long-term development of socialist architectural circulations that this book reconstructs. The Comecon and its different sub-units were strongly dominated by the USSR and other European countries and helped to coordinate many partners, which represented eight national states in the case of the Cuban nickel plant.

From a "Global South" perspective of African countries which had achieved independence in the early 1960s, agreements with Comecon countries seemed to promise economic development plus public welfare. They often pursued concepts of Pan-Africanism and Non-alignment, as Anne-Kristin Hartmetz shows in her chapter on Ghana's agro-industrial cooperation with Comecon. Hartmetz demonstrates that Ghana's option for state socialism as an institutional model did not prevent close collaboration with Israel or Western public and private organisations. This multifaceted cooperation called for several strategic decisions, like intense public supervision, control and coordination of foreign trade and economic exchange. Industrialising agricultural production strongly stimulated collaboration with countries like Czechoslovakia or Poland to construct sugar plants and other industrial factories. Still, it proved very complicated to realise and to do so for all partners.

A large number of adventurous experts often carried out such joint transnational projects. Amongst these, female planners and architects have been largely overlooked, as Rachel Lee demonstrates highlighting the case of the West German planner Hannah Schreckenbach in socialist Ghana. Schreckenbach's career reflected typical patterns of multicultural education and mobility in the post-World War Two period when she studied both in parts of Germany and London. Having become an expert in tropical architecture, she moved to Africa and achieved top positions in the Ghanaian public works department and tropical architecture; she then moved to Africa and earned top posts in the Ghanaian public works department and higher education. Schreckenbach was part of a particular multinational network of engineers and architects in Ghana, together with other foreign experts and Ghanaian specialists. Some of them had been trained in the US and Great Britain. By documenting and promoting indigenous mud architecture, Schreckenbach raised awareness of special traditional building techniques that most modern architects at the time overlooked or even despised.

Most building projects in transnational socialist cooperation were certainly realised in Europe. Franziska Klemstein shows the work of Polish experts for urban reconstruction and historic preservation in the Northern German city of Stralsund and the various layers of cooperation in this field. Here, Polish specialists counted among the leading international experts, since they had realised the reconstruction of the heavily destroyed cities in Poland after World War Two. The Stralsund case reflects in detail the substantial challenges that the attempt of socialist planning ideology to transform a sizeable pre-socialist building stock to the demands of a "socialist urban society" was confronted with. As a result, the East-German public "Peoples own enterprises" (VEB) often followed a kind of Potemkin strategy of modernising apartments behind historical facades. For the mission to mix renovation and new construction of buildings, the Polish Enterprise of PKZ Szczecin offered a multidisciplinary team of experts with unique experience which was active in many parts of the world, from Paris to Egypt and beyond.

The third part of the book reflects the patterns and channels of perception and communication in which the visions and concepts of socialist architecture were publicly presented. Here a multitude of media and modes of perception becomes apparent. International Fairs, like those of the 1950s and 1960s in Zagreb, functioned as hubs for exchanging new ideas on "modern" architecture and planning. At the same time, they resented the Yugoslavian state as an intermediary and "translator" between East and West, as Jasna Galjer's chapter shows.

Cooperation between socialist architects and planners from different countries could build on close political and institutional relations within the Comecon block and on common visions for prefabricated housing and friendship associations. This was clearly the case in the cooperation between the GDR and China, which Andreas Butter examines in his chapter. Here, economic cooperation was framed by ideas of political solidarity in which the export of factories and specific technologies, like thin concrete shells, were part of the more general idea to stabilise the socialist world as part of the Cold War confrontation. Projects like "factory 718" in Bejing were constructed with the help of an extensive network of GDR specialists and functioned as an experimental field for prefabrication in industrial construction. They were highly valued by officials because of their functional features but also conformed to Chinese ideas of beauty. Some of these factories are still producing today; others became architectural icons in the course of postmodern urban transformation.

Socialist transnational solidarity policies were based on interstate cooperation but also relied on the work of semi-public mass organisations, associations and campaigns, as Paul Sprute shows in the case of the East-German solidarity committee ("Solidaritätskomitee"). By collecting donations and organising work camps in the "Global South", the committee created strong support for local projects and personal ties between the persons involved. Losing its official status after the collapse of the GDR, the committee continued its activities as a private association in several parts of the world so that the socialist political legacy was transformed into a post-socialist NGO.

The transformation of East-German architecture that had been constructed in the Vietnamese city of Vinh in the post-World War Two period is reflected on by Christina Schwenkel as a case of "travelling architecture" and its re-interpretation in everyday life. She shows that from the beginning, the housing projects proposed by the Germans were negotiated in a kind of "co-production" with Vietnamese representatives and were rooted in different cultures of space, especially regarding the design of apartments. Moreover, many tenants remodelled their living space to maintain domestic traditions of family life and specific spatial arrangements of the basic functions of cooking, sleeping and sanitation.

The observation that the built environment in the so-called "developing countries" was co-produced by actors from the "Global South" and the "Global North" among tensions, imbalances and inequalities as well as collaborations and was strongly transformed by various groups of local actors is one of the main messages that this book wants to transmit.

I Soviet Transfer: Strategies and Limits

Susanne Stein

Between 'Self-Sovietisation' and Soviet Assistance: Urban Planning and Design in China, 1950s–1960s

"News from China is scarce, particularly regarding the field of architecture," the renowned German architectural journal *Bauwelt* observed in November 1957, adding that since the People's Republic of China (PRC) had shut itself off from the unwelcome gaze of Western foreigners behind the "silk curtain" some ten years ago "hardly any European or American knows what is really going on in this country".[1]

Despite the acknowledged lack of reliable information on contemporary China and Chinese architecture, it was taken for granted that the country had actively followed the example of its closest political ally since 1949. For the author of the *Bauwelt* report a sample of drawings and layout plans chosen at random from the 1957 February and April issues of the Chinese language periodical *Architectural Journal*[2] sufficed to corroborate the assumption of an ongoing Chinese self-Sovietisation: "By chance we got hold of some issues of a Chinese journal of construction from the beginning of this year. They allow us to draw certain conclusions. [. . .]. Examples of industrial construction convey a plain and functional impression – but when it comes to 'design' the pervasive influence of the Russians who still adhere to ideas dating far back into the 19th century is conspicuous".[3]

The travel accounts of a group of Western architects who had only recently returned from a "Journey to Peking" organised by the Architectural Society of China seem to have told a different story.[4] Among the delegates were several high-

1 G. K., "Die Reise nach Peking. Zu Zeichnungen von Werner Hebebrand." *Bauwelt* 47 (1957): 1246–1249, 1246. The author of the article could not be identified beyond their initials.

2 The *Architectural Journal* (*Jianzhu xuebao* 建筑学报) has been published monthly since 1954. It was the PRC's first periodical on construction that covered a broad range of issues from architectural theory, building practice and design to questions of urban planning. See www.aj.org.cn/en/about.aspx (accessed 19 June 2022).

3 G. K., "Reise nach Peking," 1246.

4 The Architectural Society of China (ASC; Zhongguo jianzhu xuehui 中国建筑学会) was founded in October 1953 with US-educated architects Liang Sicheng 梁思成 (1901–1972) and Yang Tingbao 杨廷宝 (1901–1982) successively serving as the society's first directors. In 1955, the ASC became a

Note: I wish to thank Fabian Fechner for his comments on the manuscript and Andreas Seifert and Christoph Piechotta for image editing.

https://doi.org/10.1515/9783110658491-002

ranking professionals from East and West Germany such as Hamburg's senior city planner and architect Werner Hebebrand (1899–1966), senior architect Rudolf Hillebrecht (1910–1999) from Hannover and Hans Hopp (1890–1971), president of the German Academy of Construction in East Berlin. The author of the *Bauwelt* article mentions that the German "China travellers" had witnessed "attempts at new forms" and the use of a "rejuvenated and genuinely Chinese style of construction" during their stay. But he immediately downplays their first-hand observations. From his point of view, Chinese construction professionals were "still showing a strong predilection for the ideas of their Soviet Russian colleagues" and continued to be preoccupied with designing "classical representative facades and decorative city plans" instead of finding ways to cope with the lack of "modern building materials" and alleviate the severe housing shortage in Chinese cities.[5] Was this criticism justified or just another example of Cold War pigeonholing?

From the early 1950s onwards, enthusiastic Chinese self-portrayals had indeed nourished the notion of a pervasive Soviet impact on post-war reconstruction in the People's Republic. State propaganda emphasised that "Today's Soviet Union is our tomorrow".[6] The slogan became ubiquitous around 1954 and was frequently illustrated by a set of motifs showing Soviet-style skyscrapers amidst agro-industrial landscapes. (Fig. 1) These stereotypical projections of New China's future were circulated through the various genres of the period's print media, ranging from comic books, propaganda posters and popular readers to newspapers and academic journals.[7]

The imagery of socialist reconstruction did not just materialise on paper. A multitude of built structures emerging in China during the 1950s bore the hallmarks of "Soviet influence". The architectural design and spatial layout of newly constructed administrative buildings, exhibition halls, industrial complexes, residential areas and various other public facilities unmistakably followed the principles of neo-classical Socialist Realism – the "other" International Style of modernity that seemed to characterise all "Cities of the Stalinist Empire", regardless of their specific cultural con-

member of the International Union of Architects (UIA), an international non-governmental organisation uniting architects around the globe through a federation of their national organisations. See http://www.chinaasc.org.cn/en/; and https://www.uia-architectes.org/en/about/about-the-uia/ (accessed 19 June 2022).

5 See G. K., "Die Reise nach Peking," 1247.

6 *Sulian de jintian shi women de mingtian* 苏联的今天是我们的明天. The origin of this catchphrase remains obscure.

7 See, for example, the website chineseposters.net (accessed 19 June 2022) and Andreas Seifert, *Bildgeschichten für Chinas Massen. Comic und Comicproduktion im 20. Jahrhundert* (Köln: Böhlau, 2008).

Fig. 1: China Reconstructs – "Learning from the Advanced Knowledge of the Soviet Union". (Sources: Hua Sanchuan (Cartoonist), *Qianjin ba, zuguo!* [Forward, fatherland!] (Shanghai: Xin meishu chubanshe, 1955): picture 63; vignette from the journal *Jianzhu* [Construction] 2, 1954: 39).

texts.[8] Within China, arguably the most outstanding buildings in this respect were the four exhibition halls built in Beijing, Shanghai, Guangzhou and Wuhan between 1954 and 1956 to display the "Economic and Cultural Achievements of the Soviet Union" to the Chinese people.[9] (Fig. 2) Equally noteworthy were the country's key construction projects of heavy industry including their new residential areas. Most of them were designed and built during the period of the PRC's first and second Five-Year-Plans (FYP, 1953–1957 and 1958–1962) with substantial

8 Greg Castillo, "Cities of the Stalinist Empire," in *Forms of Dominance. On the Architecture of the Colonial Enterprise*, edited by Nezar AlSayyad, 261–287 (Aldershot: Avesbury, 1992). As Wolfgang Schivelbusch argues, monumentalist neo-classicism was "no less an 'international style'" as modernism during the 1930s. See Schivelbusch, *Entfernte Verwandtschaft. Faschismus, Nationalsozialismus, New Deal, 1933–1939* (München: Hanser, 2005): 8–10.

9 The "Exhibition of the Economic and Cultural Achievements of the Soviet Union" (Sulian jingji ji wenhua jianshe chengjiu zhanlanhui 苏联经济及文化建设成就展览会) was staged to commemorate the fifth anniversary of the "Sino-Soviet Treaty of Friendship, Alliance and Mutual Assistance" (Zhong-Su youhao tongmeng huzhu tiaoyue 中苏友好同盟互助条约) signed on 14 February 1950. Starting in Beijing, the exhibition subsequently travelled from north to south. The Guangzhou exhibition hall was a "native" building designed by the city's chief architect Lin Keming 林克明 (1901–1999), whereas the other three were built in cooperation with Soviet architects. See Sun Haigang 孙海刚, Zhong-Su youhao dasha. Guangzhou di-yi zuo 'Sushi' zhanlanguan 中苏友好大厦. 广州第一座"苏式"展览馆. www.gzzxws.gov.cn/gxsl/gzwb/lsjq/201703/t20170310_40550.htm (accessed 27 September 2019).

Fig. 2: Beijing Exhibition Hall (Beijing zhanlanguan).
(Source: Andreas Seifert 2001, private photo).

help from "Soviet experts".[10] To this day the industrial complexes of the era, among them the Changchun No. 1 Motor Works or the Luoyang No. 1 Tractor

10 According to the most prominent Chinese Cold War historian Shen Zhihua, there is still no exact data available concerning the total number of Soviet experts working in China between 1949 and 1960. Among other reasons this may be attributed to the variety of Chinese terms used to designate "Soviet experts". Before "expert" (*zhuanjia* 专家) became the umbrella term for the various professionals and political functionaries from the Soviet Union (and other socialist countries) around 1957, those working in administration, management and the military were usually called "advisors" (*guwen* 顾问), whereas foreign experts in educational institutions were called

Factory, are considered historical landmarks.[11] They demonstrate how the Chinese leadership's political directive to "lean to one side" only and "learn from the Soviet Union" had been translated into urban planning and design during the formative years of the People's Republic.[12]

While the physical evidence of Chinese "Self-Sovietisation" and Soviet assistance to China has become an object of closer scrutiny in debates on modern Chinese architecture and urban planning history over the past two decades, comparatively little has been revealed about the ways the policy of "leaning" and "learning" had been received among various groups of Chinese construction professionals at that time.[13] What can be retrieved from the period's sources about the appropriation, adaptation and possibly also the rejection of the "advanced Soviet experiences" by the first and second generation of Chinese architects and planners?

Much of what we know to date about the acquisition of Soviet ideas on architectural design and socialist city planning during the first decade of the PRC derives from contemporary Chinese periodicals and, more recently, also from Chinese planners' personal memoirs.[14] In several of these accounts, direct interaction and

---

"professors" or simply "teachers" (*jiaoshou* 教授, *jiaoshi* 教师, *laoshi* 老师). See Shen Zhihua 沈志华, "Dui zai Hua Sulian zhuanjia wenti de lishi kaocha. Jiben zhuangkuang ji zhengce bianhua 对在华苏联专家问题的历史考察 (An Historical Investigation of Soviet Experts in China. Circumstances and Policy Changes)." *Dangdai Zhongguo shi yanjiu* 9, no. 1 (2002): 24–37, 26.

11 Several of these sites have attained national heritage status and are included in one of the Twentieth-Century Architectural Heritage Lists that have been released by the Chinese Society of Cultural Relics and the Architectural Society of China since 2016.

12 On the origins of this decision and on the policies resulting from "leaning to one side" (*yibiandao* 一边倒) and "learning from the Soviet Union" (*xuexi Sulian* 学习苏联) see contributions compiled by Hua-Yu Li and Thomas Bernstein, eds., *China Learns from the Soviet Union, 1949–Present* (Lanham: Lexington Books, 2010).

13 An exception is the controversy about the future development of the city of Beijing after 1949. One of the most detailed studies on the period's conflicting visions for the reconstruction of the Chinese capital is Jun Wang, *Beijing Record. A Physical and Political History of Planning Modern Beijing* (Singapore, London: World Scientific, 2011).

14 The latest collection of memoirs was published by Chen Bochao 陈伯超, Liu Siduo 刘思铎, eds., *Zhongguo jianzhu koushushi wenku (Di-yi ji). Qiangjiu jiyi zhong de lishi* 中国建筑口述史文库 (第一辑)。抢救记忆中的历史 [Oral History Library of Chinese Architecture (Vol. 1). Rescuing historical recollections] (Shanghai: Tongji daxue, 2018). Another five-volume compilation of personal recollections was published by Li Hao 李浩 ed., *Cheng. Shi. Ren. Xin Zhongguo di-yi dai chengshi guihua gongzuozhe fangtanlu* 城.事.人.新中国第一代城市规划工作者访谈录 [Cities, planning activities and witnesses. Records of interviews with New China's urban planning professionals of the first generation] (Beijing: Zhongguo jianzhu gongye, 2017).

exchange with experts from the Soviet Union is mentioned but apart from some more specific examples, the overall picture remains vague.[15]

This chapter focuses on an aspect of knowledge circulation that was closely connected to the engagement of Soviet experts in China but has not yet been studied systematically. By exploring to what extent instructional and reference media from the Soviet Union had facilitated and framed Chinese urban planning and design as a distinct field of knowledge and application during the first decade of the country's "socialist reconstruction", the study aims to expand the scope of previous research on the ambiguous role of the so-called "Soviet model" in the PRC's early planning history.[16]

Based on a sample of manuals and reference books originating from the Soviet Union, I will describe what kinds of texts were chosen for translation and how they were annotated, circulated and received among the community of Chinese construction professionals, as far as this can be traced from the accessible sources to date. Given the fragmentary nature of information on the topic and the limited availability of archival documents, an appraisal of the workings and the extent of "Soviet influence" via these media will inevitably remain provisional.[17] Preliminary findings, however, do not suggest that the policy of "learning from the Soviet Union" had resulted in an unqualified copying or imposition of "*the* Soviet model" in the field of urban planning and building design all over China. As the Sino-French architect Hua Lanhong (Léon Hoa, 1912–2012), one of New China's famed and also temporarily disgraced planning professionals, had noted in his recollections, Soviet influence on Chinese reconstruction did not make itself felt everywhere in the same manner.[18]

The essay begins with a brief outline of the Soviet Union's economic aid programme for China that was the outcome of extended negotiations between the

15 See for example Liu Shixun 刘诗峋, "Qimeng laoshi bu neng wang 启蒙老师不能忘 [The first teacher is unforgettable]," in *Wushi nian huimou. Xin Zhongguo de chengshi guihua* 五十年回眸。新中国的城市规划 [Looking back on 50 years. New China's city planning], edited by Zhongguo chengshi guihua xuehui, 142–147 (Beijing: Shangwu yinshuguan, 1999).

16 See Li Hao 李浩, "Yi wu shiqi de chengshi guihua shi zhaoban Sulian moshi ma? 一五时期的城市规划是照搬苏联模式吗? [Did urban planning during the period of the first FYP imitate the Soviet model?]." *Chengshi fazhan yanjiu* 22, no. 9 (2015): C1–C5. For an overview see Hou Li, "Six Decades of Planning Education in China. Those Planned and Unplanned," in *Urban Planning Education. Beginnings, Global Movement and Future Prospects*, edited by Andrea I. Frank, Christopher Silver, 81–99 (Cham: Springer, 2018); and Daniel B. Abramson, "The Uses of Planning History in China," in *The Routledge Handbook of Planning History*, edited by Carola Hein, 260–272 (New York, London: Routledge, 2018), 266.

17 This is an impediment for Chinese colleagues working on contemporary architectural and planning history as well.

18 Léon Hoa, *Reconstruire la Chine. Trente ans d'urbanisme, 1949–1979* (Paris: Éditions du Moniteurs, 1981), 76. A Chinese edition of the book was not published before 2006.

Chinese and Soviet leaderships after the inception of the PRC in 1949. It then proceeds to the issues of knowledge circulation and acquisition via Soviet instructional and reference media against the backdrop of the PRC's institutional restructuring of the early to mid-1950s. The final section is devoted to one of New China's industrial showcase projects and illustrates how Chinese practitioners tried to build "by the book" during the first FYP and how theirs attempts to implement Soviet norms and guidelines were evaluated over time.

1 Importing socialism: New China's "156 key construction projects"

On 1 July 1949, the *People's Daily* front-paged Mao Zedong's (1893–1976) speech "On the People's Democratic Dictatorship", in which the CCP chairman elaborated on the policy of "leaning to one side" and "learning from the Soviet Union":

> The serious task of economic construction lies before us. We shall soon [. . .] be compelled to do things we don't know well. This means difficulties. [. . .]. We must overcome difficulties, we must learn what we do not know. We must learn to do economic work from all who know how, no matter who they are. We must esteem them as teachers, learning from them respectfully and conscientiously.

Despite its conciliatory tone in the beginning, the speech eventually culminates in an appeal for Chinese self-Sovietisation, for emulating – first and foremost – the Soviet example: "The Communist Party of the Soviet Union is our best teacher and we must learn from it."[19]

If this enunciation can be read as the strategic roadmap for New China's reconstruction in the years to follow, it was the "Sino-Soviet Treaty of Friendship, Alliance and Mutual Assistance" concluded eight months later that eventually provided the economic and technological framework necessary for getting the country started again after decades of political turmoil, disintegration and war. The Soviet Union was the first foreign state to recognise the PRC upon its establishment.[20] Equally important was the Soviet government's provision of a 300 million US dollar loan granted over a period of five years that laid the foundation for China's economic recovery and

19 Mao Zedong, "Lun renmin minzhu zhuanzheng 论人民民主专政 (On the People's Democratic Dictatorship)." *Renmin ribao* (1 July 1949): 1. An English translation of this speech held in commemoration of the CCP's 28th anniversary is reprinted in Mao Tsetung, *Selected Readings From the Work of Mao Tsetung* (Peking: Foreign Languages Press, 1971): 371–386.

20 On the part of the Western countries only followed by Great Britain, Sweden and Switzerland.

rapid industrialisation during the next decade. The PRC's international isolation further increased in October 1950, when China entered the Korean War (1950–1953) to assist the North Korean military in fighting the United States and its United Nations allies for control of the Korean peninsula. The Soviet Union not only supported the Chinese People's Volunteer Army in Korea with military equipment and air force units, but at the same time arranged for a large-scale transfer of technology, building materials, know-how and manpower to the Chinese "home front".[21]

Soviet aid to China was mainly channeled into industrial construction schemes related to heavy industry, resource extraction and military purposes, in retrospect summarised as the "156 key construction projects". For their realisation the PRC heavily relied on the technical and strategic advice of experts from the Soviet Union working in China. Since 1950, the Chinese Ministry of Industry had commissioned various land surveys in order to find appropriate locations for the new industrial enterprises. Groups of Chinese engineers, party cadres and Soviet experts were jointly touring the country prospecting potential construction sites.[22] By 1951, 42 teams of Soviet construction engineers and planners had been sent to China to carry out surveying work and draft construction plans in tandem with their Chinese colleagues. Most teams were dispatched to north-eastern China where the "residual benefits of the Japanese Empire"[23] – a solid infrastructural basis in terms of railway transport, roads, electric power grids and water supply systems – facilitated rapid industrial reconstruction despite the destruction and dismantling of factories and infrastructures between 1945 and 1949.[24] Until 1960 when the Sino-Soviet split materialised and led to the withdrawal of all Soviet experts from the PRC,

21 For more details see Shen Zhihua, *Mao, Stalin and the Korean War. Trilateral Communist Relations in the 1950s* (Milton Park, Abingdon: Routledge, 2012); and by the same author: *Sulian zhuanjia zai Zhongguo* 苏联专家在中国 (1948–1960) [Soviet Experts in China (1948–1960)] (Beijing: Xinhua, 2009): 49–62.

22 On the so-called "156 key construction projects" (*156 xiang zhongdian gongcheng* 156 项重点工程) that became the backbone of the PRC's industrialisation see Li Baihao 李百浩, Peng Xiutao 彭秀涛, Huang Li 黄立, "Zhongguo xiandai xinxing gongye chengshi guihua de lishi yanjiu. Yi Sulian yuanzhu de 156 zhongdian gongcheng wei zhongxin 中国现代新兴工业城市规划的历史研究。以苏联援助的 156 重点工程为中心 [Historical research on city planning for China's newly built modern industrial cities – with a focus on the 156 key projects supported by the Soviet Union]," *Chengshi guihua xuekan* 4 (2006): 84–92, 85.

23 Daqing Yang, "Resurrecting the Empire? Japanese Technicians in Postwar China, 1945–49," in *The Japanese Empire in East Asia and its Postwar Legacy*, edited by Harald Fuess, 185–205 (München: Iudicium-Verlag, 1998): 201.

24 The dismantling of industrial facilities in north-eastern China by Soviet troops is mentioned by Alfred Schinz, *Cities in China* (Berlin, Stuttgart: Gebrüder Borntraeger, 1989), 408.

150 of the originally scheduled 156 projects had been built throughout the country, with the majority located along major railway lines and in the vicinity of existing cities.[25] (Map 1)

Map 1: Distribution of the PRC's Key Construction Projects.
(Source: Map by Andreas Seifert, adapted from: *First Five-Year Plan for Development of the National Economy of the People's Republic of China in 1953–1957 (Illustrated)* (Peking: Foreign Language Press, 1956) [unpaginated]).

The emulation of the Soviet model of economic planning inevitably influenced the trajectory of urban development in China. In keeping with the motto "serving

25 See Shen Zhihua, "Dui zai Hua Sulian zhuanjia," 27; Li Baihao, Peng Xiutao, Huang Li, "Zhongguo xiandai xinxing gongye chengshi guihua," 84–85; and Zhang Baichun 张柏春, Zhang Jiuchun 张久春, Yao Fang 姚芳, Sulian jishu xiang Zhongguo zhuanyi de tedian ji qi yingxiang 苏联技术向中国转移的特点及其影响 [Characteristics and impact of the technology transfer from the Soviet Union to China]. *Kexuexue yanjiu* 3 (2004): 278–283.

production [first], serving the people [second]", cities were conceptualised as "bases" of (industrial) production in the first place, whereas living conditions were considered to be of minor importance. Senior planner Zou Deci (1934–2020) was one of Tongji University's first urban planning graduates who became immediately involved in the country's key construction projects in 1955. He recalled that New China's urban development was seen as driven by, closely correlated to and instrumental in industrial construction. Urban planning, in turn, was officially defined as "the continuation and concretisation of the national economic plan".[26] This definition (and its institutional implementation) stressed the profession's practical relevance for China's "national reconstruction" but, as first-generation planner Chen Zhanxiang (1916–2001) sharply criticised in his "big-character poster" in 1957, at the same time reduced its practitioners to brainless "drawing machines".[27]

The economic logic of the period's urban planning approach was mirrored by a strictly hierarchical allocation of resources. (See Map 1) Greatest emphasis was placed on the expansion and development of China's eight designated centres of heavy industry (Xi'an, Taiyuan, Baotou, Luoyang, Lanzhou, Wuhan, Chengdu and Datong) that would each be home to several of the PRC's key construction projects.[28]

Another group of 14 cities would experience a "relatively high percentage of industrial development" during the first FYP, like Anshan, Taiyuan, Zhengzhou and Wuhan. A third category – made up of China's "old" (and formerly colonial) harbour and railway cities like Shanghai, Tianjin and Changchun – would be

---

26 See Zou Deci 邹德慈, "Zou xiang zhudongshi de chengshi guihua 走向主动式的城市规划 [Moving towards active urban planning]." *Chengshi guihua* 29, no. 2 (2005): 20–22. Since the early 2000s, Zou has been actively promoting research on the PRC's urban planning history. For further biographical details, see www.thepaper.cn/newsDetail_forward_2150620 (accessed 19 June 2022); an overview of Chinese planning history research is provided by Zou's former staff member Li Hao 李浩, "Xin Zhongguo chengshi guihua fazhanshi sikao 新中国城市规划发展史思考 (China's urban planning history research since 1949)." *Guihuashi* 9 (2011): 102–107.

27 Chen Zhanxiang 陈占祥 voiced his criticism during the Hundred Flower Campaign (1956–1957) at the Beijing Architectural Design Institute (Beijing shi jianzhu shejiyuan 北京市建筑设计院). As a result, he was labelled a "Rightist" and was no longer involved in the institute's practical work. In 1962, after intermittent periods of physical labour, he was transferred to work at the institute's technical information office where he translated foreign works and technical reference materials on architecture and urban planning into Chinese. Further (auto-) biographical details and contemporary documents on Chen can be retrieved from Chen Yanqing 陈衍庆, Wang Ruizhi 王瑞智, eds., *Jianzhushi bu shi miaotu jiqi* 建筑师不是描图机器 [An Architect is not a drawing machine] (Shenyang: Liaoning jiaoyu, 2005).

28 A recent monograph on the planning history of the eight industrial key cities is Li Hao 李浩, *Ba da zhongdian chengshi guihua. Xin Zhongguo chengli chuqi de chengshi guihua lishi yanjiu* 八大重点城市规划. 新中国成立初期的城市规划历史研究 [The planning of the eight big key cities. Research on the urban planning history of the early period of New China] (Beijing: Jianzhu gongcheng, 2016).

assigned just one or two smaller industrial projects each. In terms of spatial layout and construction activities, these places were to be reorganized only to a lesser degree. The fourth category comprised the country's non-industrial cities. Given their minor contribution to the national economy in terms of industrial output, they would remain largely unchanged except for basic measures of infrastructural maintenance, sanitation and public hygiene.[29] With regard to these fundamental tasks of municipal management, urban planning and design were also conceptualised as indispensable tools of social transformation: "Rational" spatial structures would benefit production and at the same time help to generate and shape the new socialist man.[30]

2 Bourgeois specialists, Soviet manuals: Restructuring higher education

Recognition as a relevant field of knowledge within the PRC's development strategy as well as the acute shortage of qualified "reconstruction personnel" compelled the new Chinese administration to draw on all architects, planners and engineers available and willing to cooperate with the Communist Party and government. Most of these "old experts" had received their education and professional training abroad or at foreign institutions of higher learning in China during the Republican period (1911–1949).[31]

Broadly speaking, the professionals who had promoted and influenced the development of modern urban planning and design in China can be divided into two groups. First, there was a circle of about 50 planner-architects who had graduated from the University of Pennsylvania and other North American Universities and returned to China during the 1920s and 1930s. Most of them were trained in the

29 See Zhou Rongxin 周荣鑫, Song Yuhe 宋裕和, "Jianzhu gongchengbu dangzu guanyu chengshi jianshe zuotanhui de baogao 建筑工程部党组关于城市建设座谈会的报告 [Report of the Ministry of Construction's leading Party group on the Urban Construction Symposium]," in *1949–1952 Zhonghua Renmin Gongheguo jingji dang'an ziliao xuanbian. Jiben jianshe touzi he jianzhuye juan* [Collection of archival materials on the economy of the PRC, 1949–1952. Investment in capital construction and the building industry], edited by Zhongguo shehui kexueyuan, Zhongyang dang'anguan, 610–614 (Beijing: Zhongguo chengshi jingji shehui, 1989).

30 On aspects of social engineering in New China's reconstruction and urban planning, see Susanne Stein, *Von der Konsumenten- zur Produktionsstadt. Aufbauvisionen und Städtebau im Neuen China, 1949–1957* (München: Oldenbourg, 2010): 341–343.

31 Such as the Anglican St. John's University founded in 1879 by American missionaries in Shanghai.

neoclassical Beaux-Arts tradition that favoured grand vistas, monumental designs and "national styles". Well-known representatives of this group were Liang Sicheng, Yang Tingbao, Wang Dingzeng (1912–2014) and Wang Huabin (1907–1988).[32]

Second, there was a group of graduates from various European universities, such as the already mentioned Chen Zhanxiang, student of the British planner Patrick Abercrombie at the University of Liverpool, Lin Keming, a graduate of the Institut d'Architecture in Lyon,[33] and Hua Lanhong who had graduated from the École Nationale Supérieure des Beaux-Arts in Paris. Jin Jingchang (1910–2000) and Feng Jizhong (1915–2009) who both became professors at the Tongji University School of Architecture in Shanghai, had studied at TU Darmstadt and the University of Vienna respectively. Compared to their peers trained in the US, the members of this latter group were more strongly influenced by modernist principles of architecture and urban planning.[34]

From the late 1920s onwards, the first generation of foreign-educated Chinese architects began to establish private architectural firms in Republican China's major cities; a number of them became engaged in architectural education within various Chinese universities, others also participated in the work of the Republic's municipal planning institutions.[35] Zhang Qinnan (1931–?), a graduate from the Massachusetts Institute of Technology who returned to Shanghai in 1951, relates in his memoirs that most of his peers and colleagues were highly motivated to engage in China's reconstruction after the Communists took power in 1949. But Zhang notes that even though their know-how was badly needed, they repeatedly became the targets of "ideological reeducation" during the PRC's early mass campaigns.[36] Their pre-revolutionary inventory of knowledge and their political reliability would be continuously challenged in the years to follow.

32 See Jeffrey W. Cody, "Introduction," in *Chinese Architecture and the Beaux-Arts*, edited by Tony Atkin, Nancy Shatzman Steinhardt, Jeffrey W. Cody, xi–xxi (Honolulu: University of Hawaii, 2011).

33 On Lin Keming, see www.bm-lyon.fr/nos-blogs/le-fonds-chinois/documents-et-ressources/institut-franco-chinois-de-lyon-ifcl/presentation-de-l-institut-franco-chinois/les-etudes-suivies/article/lin-keming-1901–1999 (accessed 19 June 2022).

34 Ke Song, "Political Ideology and the Production of Architectural Theories in Mao's China (1949–1976)." *Architectural Histories* 6, no. 1 (2018): 1–15, 2.

35 On the pre-revolutionary careers of Chinese architects and planners, see, for example, Daqing Gu, "An Outline of Beaux-Arts Education in China. Transplantation, Localization, and Entrenchment," in *Chinese Architecture and the Beaux-Arts*, edited by Tony Atkin, Nancy Shatzman Steinhardt, Jeffrey W. Cody, 73–90 (Honolulu: University of Hawaii, 2011).

36 Ideological allegations and political persecution during the "Three- and Five-Anti" campaigns (1951–1952) resulted in a number of suicides among Chinese construction professionals; see Zhang Qinnan 张钦楠, "Wushi nian cangsang. Huigu guojia jianzhu shejiyuan de lishi 五十年沧桑。回顾国家建筑设计院的历史 [Fifty Years' Vicissitudes. The history of state-owned design institutes in

At the PRC's first national conference on urban development held in October 1952, the expertise of the "old" construction professionals was openly called into question. They were reproached of being unable "to build cities of the people that would represent the new era and way of life in China correctly".[37] About the same time, China's private architectural firms were closed down one by one and merged into smaller collective enterprises before they were finally replaced by large state-owned design institutes that would cater to the needs of the huge industrial construction projects of the first FYP.[38]

Moreover, in order to raise a "new type" of expert and train large numbers of ideologically reliable reconstruction personnel, the Chinese government embarked on a reorganisation of its universities that was closely modelled on the Soviet system of tertiary education and stipulated the extensive use of Soviet curricula and teaching materials.[39] Between 1952 and 1953 this so-called "restructuring of colleges and departments" resulted in a concentration of architectural education within eight universities and technical institutes mainly situated in the eastern and central parts of China.[40] The government's directive to use and adapt Soviet curricula was not generally perceived as an imposition. For some of the foreign educated "bourgeois" construction professionals it was a convenient

retrospect]," in *Jianzhu baijia huiyilu xubian* 建筑百家回忆录续编 [Sequel of One Hundred Architectural Memoirs], edited by Yang Yongsheng 杨永生, 100–106 (Beijing: Zhongguo shuili shuidian, 2003).

37 Zhou Rongxin, Song Yuhe, "Zuotanhui de baogao," 614; also see Susanne Stein, *Konsumentenstadt*, 195–197.

38 See Xue, Charlie Q.L. and Guanghui Ding, *A History of Design Institutes in China. From Mao to Market* (London/New York: Routledge, 2018), 9, 24; on Soviet assistance provided to the PRC's design institutes during the first FYP, see Shen Zhihua, *Sulian zhuanjia*, 90.

39 Zuo hao yuanxi tiaozheng gongzuo, youxiao de peiyang guojia jianshe ganbu 做好院系调整工作, 有效得培养国家建设干部 [Successfully complete the restructuring of colleges and departments, effectively train cadres for national reconstruction] *Renmin ribao* (24 Sept. 1952): 1. See Douglas A. Stiffler, "Der Widerstand gegen die Sowjetisierung der Universitäten und die Umstrukturierung der Hochschulen in China (1949–1952)," in *Zwischen Autonomie und Anpassung. Universitäten in den Diktaturen des 20. Jahrhunderts*, edited by John Connelly, Michael Grüttner, 199–227 (Paderborn: Schöningh, 2003).

40 The eight schools were located at Tsinghua University (Beijing), Tongji University (Shanghai), Tianjin University, the Nanjing Institute of Technology, the South China Institute of Technology (Guangzhou), the Chongqing Institute of Construction and Engineering, the Harbin Institute of Construction and Engineering, and the Xi'an Institute of Metallurgical Construction (The last five institutions changed their names later on). In the process of reorganisation, St. John's University was also closed and its faculty members and students were transferred to other universities. On the administrative and educational restructuring of 1952, see K. Sizheng Fan, "A Classicist Architecture for Utopia," in *Chinese Architecture and the Beaux-Arts*, edited by Tony Atkin, Nancy Shatzman Steinhardt, Jeffrey W. Cody, 91–126 (Honolulu: University of Hawaii, 2011), 94–95.

opportunity to modify and modernise existing study programmes by integrating urban planning and design into the course catalogues of their home institutions.[41]

The ideologically appropriate teaching materials, however, were still in short supply. Senior planners Zou Deci and Chen Baorong remembered that their university education had been based on a mixture of Western (mostly English) and Soviet (Russian) textbooks and manuals during the early and mid-1950s, even though Chinese students had increasingly rejected the use of "capitalist" reference books at that time.[42] The following publications of Soviet origin, either Chinese translations of manuals and reference materials from the Soviet Union or mimeographed lectures given by Soviet experts in China, were available in the library at the Qinghua University School of Architecture, one of New China's key institutions for architecture and urban planning.[43] (Tab. 1)

While this list may not be exhaustive, it conveys an impression of the kind of "foreign" knowledge circulated among Chinese professionals and students. Further insights are provided by the synopses that each of these translations contains. Apart from summarising the content of the respective publication, the editors' comments usually contain information about the target readership of the book and its function within the specific context of the PRC's "national reconstruction". Taken as a whole, they reveal what the Chinese side wanted to import and adopt from their Soviet ally: Systematically organised scientific findings and up-to-date technological know-how illustrated with drawings and examples that could be readily applied in New China's urban-industrial reconstruction.[44]

Among the earliest translations of Soviet reference books on urban planning, the library kept two different editions of J.P. Levchenko's manual *City Planning.*

41 This is what Tongji University emeriti Dong Jianhong 董鉴泓 (*1926; Tongji University, 1951) and Li Dehua 李德华 (*1924; St. John's, 1945) observed retrospectively in their article "Chengshi guihua zhuanye 45 nian de zuji 城市规划专业 45 年的足迹 [Traces of 45 Years of Urban Planning Education]" in *Chengshi guihua lishi yu lilun yanjiu* 城市规划历史与理论研究 (Historical & Theoretical Research of Urban Planning), edited by Dong Jianhong, 92–95 (Shanghai: Tongji Daxue, 1999); also see Hou Li, "Six Decades," 86–87.

42 Interviews with Prof. Chen Baorong 陈保荣 (Qinghua University, 26 May 2005) and Prof. Zou Deci 邹德慈 (China Institute of Urban Planning and Design, 16 Nov. 2000); for more details, see Stein, *Konsumentenstadt*, 228–229.

43 The school houses an extensive collection of national and international publications on architecture and urban planning ranging from the late nineteenth century to the present. During several visits to Qinghua University in the early 2000s, I had the privilege of personal access to the stack-room of the library where I could freely use the school's collection of "old books" published before and after 1949.

44 On the content and style of the period's synopses (*neirong tiyao* 内容提要), see Stein, *Konsumentenstadt*, 229.

Tab. 1: Translated Soviet Manuals and Teaching Materials, 1953–1956 (Qinghua School of Architecture).

1953
Liefuqinke (**J.P. Levchenko**). *Chengshi guihua. Jishu jingji zhi zhibiao ji jisuan* [**City Planning. Technical-economic norms and calculations**]. Beijing: Shidai, 1953.
Sulian chengshi jianshebu chengshi guihuaju [**Bureau of Urban Planning, Soviet Ministry of Urban Construction**] (ed.). *Chengshi dixia wangdao. Bushe yu celiang* [**The urban underground network. Layout and Measurement**]. Shanghai: Longmen lianhe shuju, 1953.
1954
Liefuqinke (**J.P. Levchenko**). *Chengshi guihua. Jishu jingji zhi zhibiao ji jisuan* [**City Planning. Technical-economic norms and calculations**]. Beijing: Jianzhu gongcheng, 1954.
Aoxipofu [**Osipov**], *Jianzhuxue* [**Architecture**], Beijing: Zhonggongye, 1954.
Axiefukefu [**Ashchepkov**], *Gongye jianzhu* [**Industrial architecture**], Beijing: Zhongyang jianzhu gongchengbu shejiyuan, 1954. [Mimeographed lecture, Qinghua University]
1955
Alieshen [**Aleshin**], Malinqinke [**Marinchenko**], Keliesinigefu [**Koletsnikov**], *Xuexiao jianzhu* [**School architecture**], Beijing: Jianzhu gongcheng, 1955.
1956
Shasi [**Shass**], *Zhuzhai jianzhu* [**Residential architecture**], Beijing: Chengshi jianshe, 1956.
Kelielikefu [**Korenkov**], Chalisiman [**Zaltsman**], Gelibie'erge [**Gelberg**] (eds), *2–5 ceng zhuzhai biaozhun sheji* [**Standardized design of 2–5-floor housing**], Beijing: Jianzhu gongcheng, 1956.

Technical-economic norms and calculations. The first Chinese edition was published in Beijing in January 1953 with Shidai [Epoch] publishers, a publishing house that belonged to the Soviet news agency TASS.[45] The Chinese synopsis focuses on the handbook's usefulness for New China's urban planning in conjunction with the country's industrial development. There is no reference to the origin of the book and, rather surprisingly, also no word of praise for the "advanced Soviet knowledge" or the Soviet Union's great achievements in socialist city planning as one might have expected.[46] In a very sober manner it was stated that

45 The Shidai chubanshe 时代出版社 was liquidated in February 1953 and merged into the People's Literature publishing house (Renmin wenxue chubanshe 人民文学出版社), one of the PRC's earliest publishers.

46 This stands in marked contrast to the foreword Kurt W. Leucht, member of the GDR's Ministry of Construction under Lothar Bolz, wrote for the East German edition of Levchenko's book in the same year. See Lewtschenko, *Die Stadtplanung. Technisch-wirtschaftliche Richtzahlen und Berechnungen*, (Berlin: VEB Verlag Technik, 1953).

> [t]his book provides a systematic account of the most prominent questions often encountered in urban planning work and all kinds of economic-technical norms related to them, for example how to calculate the urban population, how to select the site of the city (proper) and estimate land-use, as well as the quotas for all kinds of public facilities within the residential quarters, the costs of urban construction etc. These research materials are an invaluable reference for our urban planning.[47]

Who had access to this "invaluable reference"? There is no reliable evidence on the distribution of the manual. Data concerning the number of copies printed of the first edition is missing.[48] But anecdotal information on its circulation shows how difficult it could be to get hold of such basic materials – even if you were a professor at one of New China's key universities. According to Dong Jianhong, a manuscript of the Chinese translation of Levchenko's book was brought to Shanghai early in 1953 by a member of the Shanghai municipal administration, who happened to be connected to Jin Jingchang, then dean of the Tongji University School of Architecture. Jin was able to borrow the manuscript provided that he brought it back to Beijing on the following day. So he and three of his colleagues (including Dong himself) eventually copied the whole manuscript by hand during their ride on the night train from Shanghai to Beijing, including the numerous drawings that it contained. Dong related that this hand-copied manual subsequently became the "planning bible" for faculty and students at Tongji University. He stressed that many of the terms and concepts he and his peers used in practical urban planning later on were also derived from this translation of Levchenko's book.[49]

The scarcity of approved reference materials on urban planning and design lasted throughout the 1950s. It took another eight years until the first national textbook on *Urban and Rural Planning* was commissioned by the PRC's Ministry of Construction and Engineering. It was to be written and compiled within six months by a small group of "old" and new professionals from Tongji University, Nanjing Institute of Technology and Chongqing Institute of Construction and Engineering under the leadership of Wu Liangyong (*1922) from Qinghua University. As one of the contributors recalled, the two-volume work was mainly based on mimeographed lectures on urban planning, teaching materials used within the

47 Liefuqinke 列甫琴柯 (J.P. Levchenko), *Chengshi guihua. Jishu jingji zhi zhibiao ji jisuan* 城市规划。技术经济之指标及计算 [City Planning. Technical-economic norms and calculations] (Beijing: Shidai, 1953) (unpaginated).

48 The second edition published with Jianzhu gongcheng [Construction and Engineering] Press amounted to 3,000 copies.

49 See Dong Jianhong 董鉴泓, "Ji jian jiyi youxin de wangshi 几件记忆犹新的往事 [Some past events still fresh in memory]," in *Wushi nian huimou* 五十年回眸 [Looking back on 50 years], edited by Zhongguo chengshi guihua xuehui, 664–669 (Beijing: Shangwu yinshuguan, 1999), 664–665.

above-mentioned institutions, excerpts of translated Soviet manuals and reference materials issued by the Chinese Ministry of Construction and Engineering.[50]

In this context it is also very instructive to survey publications and periodicals that used to be circulated among the staff of the state-owned design institutes for "internal use". Their contents indicate that the tide of exclusive learning from the Soviet Union was already turning by the mid-1950s. The 1955 book series "Collection on Urban Construction" edited by the Chinese Ministry of Construction and Engineering for instance includes a great variety of translated essays and speeches not only from the Soviet Union but also from other "People's Democracies". All of them are presented as valuable reference materials for China.[51] Another example is the periodical *Collection of Translations on Construction* which was founded in 1954 explicitly to disseminate knowledge on Soviet science and technology, a mission the editors – hardly accidentally – updated in late 1955 to include an increasing number of translations from Poland, the GDR and Hungary.[52] This trend of opening up, first to other socialist countries (that were considered relatively "progressive"), and then, although to a lesser degree, also to the "capitalist West" becomes more pronounced during the latter half of the 1950s. A closer look at the reference materials translated during this time reveals that the adjective "foreign", which had previously been almost a synonym for "Soviet", acquired new meaning in the course of the 1950s – to the point that the original hierarchy of "learning from the Soviet Union first" was tacitly turned upside down by the end of the decade, despite official declarations that "active and correct" learning from the "elder brother" should be continued.[53] While Soviet influence on Chinese urban planning and design persisted and lasted well beyond the political split of the late 1950s, the scope of the PRC's "learning from others" broadened at the same time. The Chinese leadership itself had set the tone for this reorientation by the end of the first FYP.

---

50 "Chengxiang guihua" jiaocai xuanbian xiaozu "城乡规划"教材选编小组, ed., *Chengxiang guihua* 城乡规划 [Urban and rural planning] (2 Vol.) (Beijing: Zhongguo gongye, 1961): 1; and Huang Guangyu 黄光宇, "Woguo chengshi guihua zhuanye jiaocai jianshe er san shi 我国城市规划专业教材建设二三事 [Some recollections on the compilation of teaching materials for our city planning programmes]," in *Wushi nian huimou* 五十年回眸 [Looking back on 50 years], edited by Zhongguo chengshi guihua xuehui, 126–135 (Beijing: Shangwu yinshuguan, 1999), 126–128. Even though the work group had accomplished its task in time, the printing of the first issue was eventually delayed until fall 1961 due to issues of censorship after the Sino-Soviet split. The delay was allegedly caused by the mentioning of a Soviet planning example connected to Nikita Khrushchev.

51 For a detailed description of the "Chengshi jianshe wenji" series, see Stein, *Konsumentenstadt*, 225–226.

52 The Chinese title of the periodical is *Jianzhu yicong* 建筑译丛. Compare the editor's mission statements of July 1954 and December 1955.

53 Lan Tian 蓝田, "Jiji zhengque de jixu xiang Sulian xuexi 积极正确地继续向苏联学习 [Continue to learn actively and correctly from the Soviet Union]." *Chengshi jianshe* 11 (1957): 7–9.

3 From conscious copying to creative application? Residential construction in Changchun

In spring 1957, Mao Zedong reaffirmed the need to learn from the Soviet Union by reminding his audience of the generous Soviet assistance the PRC had received since 1949. Yet he also called for a more selective, focused and self-confident acquisition of "foreign experience" than he did in 1949:

> It is perfectly true that we should learn from the good experience of all countries, socialist or capitalist, about this there is no argument. But the main thing is still to learn from the Soviet Union. Now there are two different attitudes towards learning from others. One is the dogmatic attitude of transplanting everything, whether or not it is suited to our conditions. This is no good. The other attitude is to use our heads and learn those things which suit our conditions, that is, to absorb whatever experience is useful to us. That is the attitude we should adopt.[54]

How his admonition affected Chinese urban planning and design is reflected in the example of the Changchun No. 1 Motor Works. Within just a few years this much publicised socialist construction project had been intermittently praised and discredited for being the result of consciously copying Soviet building norms and aesthetic self-Sovietisation – the latter, however, was usually indicated by using the term "traditionalism".[55]

China's new "motor city", as the whole scheme was dubbed in contemporary propaganda, was among the first 50 of the PRC's "156 key construction projects". The plant itself was closely modelled on the example of the Stalin Motor Works near Moscow: Most of the production facilities had been imported from the Soviet Union and were set up according to Soviet blueprints under Soviet guidance at a site recommended (if not chosen) by Soviet advisors.[56]

---

54 Mao Zedong 毛泽东, Guanyu zhengque chuli renmin neibu maodun de wenti 关于正确处理人民内部矛盾的问题 (On the correct handling of contradictions among the people). *Renmin ribao* (19 June 1957): 1. The original speech was held on 27 February 1957. The English translation is reprinted in Mao, *Selected Readings*, 432–479.

55 The Chinese term *fuguzhuyi* 复古主义 is sometimes also translated as "classical revivalism" or "renaissance" but has clearly negative connotations. In the context of the PRC's 1950s construction activities it usually denotes those designs that emphasized "national forms."

56 On Soviet experts working in Changchun, see Shen, *Sulian zhuanjia*, 89; Cao Lin 曹麟, Wang Suyang 王苏阳, "Ban ge shiji yuan yi meng. Zhongguo qiche gongye chuangjian licheng huigu 半个世纪圆一梦。中国汽车工业创建历程回顾 [Fulfillment of a fifty-year-old dream. The founding of the Chinese motor industry in retrospect]." *Qiche weixiu* 12 (1999): 4–7. Meng Shaonong 孟少农, "Zhongguo qiche gongye de chuangjian 中国汽车工业的创建 [The founding of the Chinese motor industry]." *Zhongguo keji shiliao* 8, no. 1 (1987): 12–13.

On commission of the Chinese side, the general plan of the construction site at Mengjiatun, a location on the southwestern outskirts of Changchun, was provided by Soviet planners in Moscow and sent to Changchun in April 1953. Based upon this blueprint, the detailed plan of the factory's residential quarters was drawn up by a team of construction professionals from the state-owned East China Industrial Architecture Design Institute in Shanghai under the leadership of chief architect Wang Huabin, one of the Penn State graduates who were well-versed in neoclassical design.[57] By and large, the layout that he and his colleagues fleshed out conformed to the technical standards and norms laid down in Levchenko's manual. The plan was defined by a strictly geometrical grid of streets – the hallmark of centralized planning[58] – and featured a central axis that was oriented towards the imposing gateway of the "pulsating" Changchun motor works, the "heart of the new city", as a popular description of the building site read in 1955.[59]

The factory's residential compounds conveyed an orderly and homogeneous impression. They consisted of standardised three- to four-story apartment houses built up along the perimeter of the street blocks, thus forming courtyards and central spaces in the rear. (Fig. 3) In terms of architectural style, workers' houses as well as the factory's main buildings both displayed the distinctive features of (Chinese) Socialist Realism: Entrances and facades were decorated with a variety of stylized ornaments derived from classical Chinese architecture, all buildings were capped by pitched roofs, the more prominent ones having Chinese-style "big roofs" or turrets. (Fig. 4)

Even though this was one of the showcase projects of Sino-Soviet cooperation, the whole area came under attack before construction was completed. Viewed in the light of the PRC's reconstruction efforts throughout the country, the motor works' facilities were deemed to be prematurely well, too luxurious, and too exclusive. Criticism in the *People's Daily* targeted the "well-spaced" layout of the residential area, featuring wide streets (with almost no traffic on them), large squares, large tracts of greenery and lavishly embellished apartment buildings equipped with private shower rooms and many other amenities. What had initially been praised as an expression of the Communist leadership's "concern for the people"

57 See Yishi Liu, "Competing Visions of the Modern. Urban Transformation and Social Change of Changchun, 1932–1957" (Diss., Berkeley: University of California, 2011): 121–122; 128–132 (on Wang Huabin) escholarship.org/uc/item/0149581v (accessed 19 June 2022); and Zhang Baichun 张柏春, Zhang Jiuchun 张久春, Yao Fang 姚芳, "20 shiji 50 niandai Sulian yuanjian di-yi qiche zhizaochang gaishu 20 世纪 50 年代苏联援建第一汽车制造厂概述 (The Soviet Union's aid in building the First Automobile Factory in the 1950s)." *Ha'erbin gongye daxue xuebao* 4 (2004): 11–20.

58 On the origins of the street grid and its interpretations, see plannersweb.com/2010/03/origins-of-the-street-grid/ (accessed 19 June 2022).

59 Hsu Chih, "The Dawn of a Great Project. On the Construction Site of No.1 Motor Works." *People's China* 4 (1955): 26–29, 26.

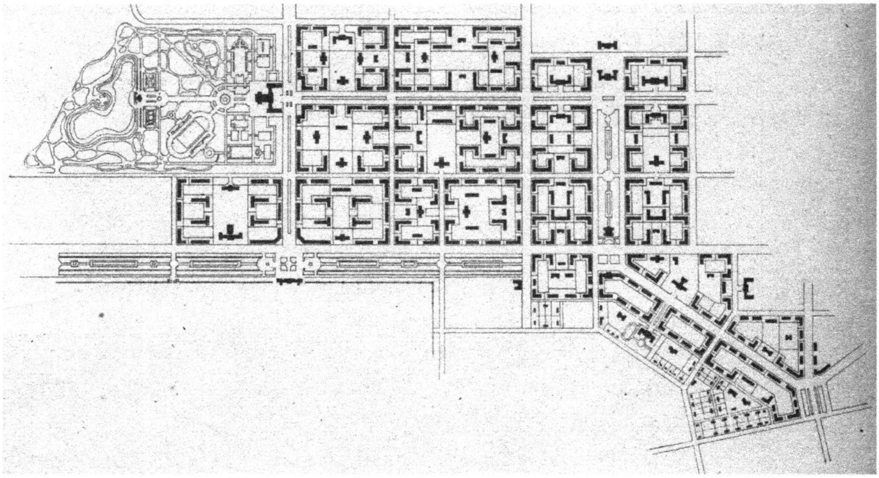

Fig. 3: Layout plan of residential area, Changchun No. 1 Motor Works.
(Source: Jianzhu gongcheng bu jianzhu liaoxue yanjiuyuan (ed.), *Jianzhu shi nian: Zhonghua Renmin Gongeheguo jianguo shi nian zhounian jinian 1949–1959* [Ten years of construction: In commemoration of the 10th anniversary of the founding of the PRC, 1949–1959] (Beijing 1959): picture 265 [unpaginated]).

(at least temporarily) became the epitome of "waste".[60] Moreover, official accounts highlighted that it was inappropriate for New China to hide a brand-new factory equipped with modern machinery behind the historicising facade of traditional Chinese palace and temple architecture.[61]

This turn of events was the result of the CCP's 1955 directive to "Practice strict economy and oppose waste" that eventually developed into a full-fledged critique of the allegedly "blind appropriation" of the Soviet model in Chinese industrial and urban construction. As Wang Huabin's elaborate self-criticism of his own design for the residential blocks of the "motor city" illustrates, Soviet norms and styles were rejected for "not being compatible with the overall situation in China". The catchphrase signalled the emergence of a new Chinese attitude towards or a

60 On housing allocation as the "most practical reward and the most powerful piece of propaganda for ordinary people" see Miin-ling Yu, "'Labor Is Glorious.' Model Laborers in the PRC," in *China Learns from the Soviet Union, 1949–Present*, edited by Hua-Yu Li, Thomas Bernstein, 231–258 (Lanham: Lexington Books, 2010), 242–243.
61 Lin Li 林里, "Zhongdian gongcheng bixu lixing jieyue 重点工程必须厉行节约 [The key projects have to practice strict economy]." *Renmin ribao* (13 August 1955): 3.

Fig. 4: Residential blocks, Changchun No. 1 Motor Works.
(Source: Jianzhu gongcheng bu jianzhu liaoxue yanjiuyuan (ed.), *Jianzhu shi nian: Zhonghua Renmin Gongeheguo jianguo shi nian zhounian jinian 1949–1959* [Ten years of construction: In commemoration of the 10th anniversary of the founding of the PRC, 1949–1959] (Beijing 1959): pictures 265–266 [unpaginated]).

different interpretation of "learning from the Soviet Union" in the wake of various attempts at de-Stalinisation within the eastern bloc.[62]

62 See Wang Huabin 王华彬, "Women dui Dongbei mou chang juzhuqu guihua sheji gongzuo de jiancha 我们对东北某厂居住区规划设计工作的检查 [Our review of residential planning and design work for a certain factory in the north-east]." *Jianzhu xuebao* 2 (1955): 20–23.

More modernist-minded Chinese professionals used the so-called "anti-waste campaign" of the mid-1950s as an opportunity to voice their criticism of Soviet, or more precisely, Stalinist urban planning and design as being too rigid, too uniform, backward-looking and expensive. They pointed out that large amounts of resources were spent on an imposing outward appearance, even though the inflexible spatial layout of the perimeter block was almost impossible to adapt to the diverse climatic and geographical conditions throughout the country.[63] In the end their arguments facilitated a reappraisal of other types of layouts and building styles and enabled China's urban planners in all parts of the country to draw on a greater variety of forms during the latter half of the 1950s – as long as they could be presented as the most economical solution for an industrialising country striving to build "more, faster and better with less".

This trend had not only been ignored by contemporary observers, as for example the report in the German *Bauwelt* illustrates. In Western scholarship, the Soviet aid programme for China has often been described in terms of a "tool of influence" or dominance, portraying the PRC as the passive recipient of "foreign" assistance. Recent findings, by contrast, present a different reading. They indicate that the Chinese leadership's foreign policy decision to rely on the Soviet "older brother" was a strategy closely connected to the long-cherished aim of economic self-reliance as the main driver behind China's industrialisation.[64] It is an assumption one should keep in mind for further explorations of Chinese planner-architects' appropriation of the "advanced Soviet experiences" and their implementation within the various geographical, socio-economic and academic contexts of the People's Republic. It had never been as wholesale as officially stated as recently published oral history materials confirm: It had been a rather selective process from the start and was decisively shaped by the educational backgrounds of all involved.[65]

---

63 The debate on urban layout plans (especially for residential areas) is reflected in several articles published in *The Architectural Journal* in 1956. See, among others, Ji Ping 纪平, "Guanyu juzhu jianzhu buzhi fang'an de taolun 关于居住建筑布置方案的讨论 [On the discussion of the layout plans for residential architecture]." *Jianzhu xuebao* 2 (1956): 103–107; and Wang Hua 汪骅, "Guanyu juzhuqu guihua sheji xingshi de taolun 关于居住区规划设计形式的讨论 [On the discussion of the forms of residential area planning and design]." *Jianzhu xuebao* 5 (1956): 51–57.

64 Izabella Goikhman convincingly argues in this direction: "Soviet-Chinese Academic Interactions in the 1950s. Questioning the 'Impact-Response' Approach," in *China Learns from the Soviet Union, 1949–Present*, edited by Hua-Yu Li, Thomas Bernstein, 143–157 (Lanham: Lexington Books, 2010).

65 For a long-term perspective also see Zhao Chunlan, Socio-Spatial Transformation in Mao's China. Settlement Planning and Dwelling Architecture Revisited (1950s–1970s) (Leuven: KU Leuven, 2007).

Nikolay Erofeev, Łukasz Stanek

Integrate, Adapt, Collaborate: Concerns of Comecon's Technical Assistance to Mongolia during the Cold War

Introduction

The BUK-1 factory of prefabricated concrete panels is a large compound located in the south-western part of Ulaanbaatar, the capital of Mongolia. Constructed in 1963 by the Soviet Union, by the time of our visit in April 2018 the factory was about to reopen after more than 25 years of idleness.[1] Under the new ownership of the Erel Group, it had been renovated and equipped with machinery from Belgian, German, and Italian manufacturers. Jargalan Erdenebat, the executive director of the Erel Group, argued that high-quality, large-scale, prefabricated concrete technology was a solution to Mongolia's housing shortage, and instrumental for the government's attempt to modernise the informal settlements, or ger districts, in Ulaanbaatar and other Mongolian cities.[2] As he explained, the revived factory would assume its former role as an essential supplier of construction materials for the city: according to Erdenebat, "eighty percent of buildings in Ulaanbaatar were built with precast elements manufactured in this plant".[3]

This example alone demonstrates the importance of the Soviet Union for the urbanization processes in Mongolia during the twentieth century. Yet the BUK-1 factory was just one of many components of what the Soviets called the "material-technical base" for construction, or the network of organisations that included building-materials producers, construction companies, design institutes,

1 The first version of this chapter was published in: N. Erofeev and Ł. Stanek, "Integrate, Adapt, Collaborate: Comecon Architecture in Socialist Mongolia." *ABE Journal* 19 (2021), DOI: 10.4000/abe.12604.

2 Jargalan Erdenebat, interview by Nikolay Erofeev and Łukasz Stanek (Ulaanbaatar, 13 April 2018); see also: "New Living Space for the Mongolian Population – Precast Plant Successfully Opened." *Concrete Plant International* 4 (2018): 176–180, https://www.ebawe.de/fileadmin/user_upload/Pdf-Ebawe/Artikel_Erel_en.pdf. (accessed 10 June 2022). We would like to thank Togos Khosbayar and Bolor Enkhbat for their invaluable assistance during our research in Mongolia, and Badruun Gardi for assisting us with the transliteration from the Mongolian language. Archival research at the Mongolian National Central Archives in Ulaanbaatar and translation of archival documents from Mongolian was supported by a Research Support Grant from The University of Manchester, UK.

3 Jargalan Erdenebat, interview by Nikolay Erofeev and Łukasz Stanek (Ulaanbaatar, 13 April 2018).

https://doi.org/10.1515/9783110658491-003

and education and research centres. From the creation of the Mongolian People's Republic (MPR) in 1924 until the end of the Cold War, this material-technical base in Mongolia was established and advanced with "technical assistance" from the socialist countries. They included the Soviet Union, followed after World War Two by the People's Republic of China (until the mid-1960s) and the socialist states in Eastern Europe. By the 1960s, a significant part of this technical assistance was coordinated by the Comecon (Council for the Mutual Economic Assistance): the economic organisation of the socialist states under Soviet hegemony, of which Mongolia became the first non-European member in 1962. This vast movement of people and resources – including construction materials, machinery, individual and type designs, and regulatory documents, standards, and building codes – shaped Mongolia's path "from feudalism to socialism, bypassing capitalism".[4]

Our investigation of the involvement of Comecon in Mongolia is situated at the intersection of two bodies of literature: one focused on architectural mobilities during the Cold War and the other on "global socialism", or the multiple, evolving, and often contradictory exchanges between socialist countries and the newly independent countries after 1945.[5] While Comecon's support for Mongolia's material-technical base for construction was part of the architectural mobilities between the "Second" and the "Third" worlds, its dynamics were distinct in three important ways. First, the uninterrupted presence of the Soviets in the MPR lasted from the 1920s until the end of the Cold War. In a difference to many other developing countries which accepted Soviet assistance, the Soviet presence in the MPR was rarely challenged, in particular after the country severed its relations with the People's Republic of China in the wake of the Sino-Soviet split. Second, the overall share of Comecon technical assistance in Mongolia's investments in the construction industry was unprecedented. This assistance decisively shaped the industrialisation and urbanisation of the country from the interwar period until the end of the Cold War, and by the 1970s the share of the Comecon states and, above all, the Soviet Union, was still estimated at 80 percent of the overall investments in the

4 Sh. Bira, *Mongolia's Road to Socialism* (Ulaanbaatar: Montsame, 1981), 8.

5 Ł. Stanek, *Architecture in Global Socialism. Eastern Europe, West Africa, and the Middle East in the Cold War* (Princeton: Princeton University Press, 2020); Mark, James, and Paul Betts. *Socialism Goes Global: The Soviet Union and Eastern Europe in the Age of Decolonisation* (Oxford: Oxford University Press, 2022). Oscar Sanchez-Sibony, *Red Globalization: The Political Economy of the Soviet Cold War from Stalin to Khrushchev* (Cambridge University Press, 2016). For a longer literature review, see Erofeev and Stanek, "Integrate, Adapt, Collaborate: Comecon Architecture in Socialist Mongolia."

MPR's economy.[6] Third, once the Eastern Europeans joined the Soviets in providing technical assistance to Mongolia, this assistance was coordinated to a much larger extent than was the case in other newly independent countries during the Khrushchev and the Brezhnev years. This coordination included bilateral agreements between the countries concerned, as well as multilateral coordination by Comecon institutions. Among them, a key role was played by the Permanent Commission for Construction (PCC), created in 1958 in East Berlin with the aim of stimulating and coordinating inter-socialist division of labour in architecture, engineering, and construction, prepared by the standardisation of construction materials, nomenclature, and regulations.[7]

The study of this long, intense, multilateral, and coordinated mobilisation and implementation of architectural resources in socialist Mongolia offers an opportunity to advance current historical scholarship by looking beyond singular designs and construction projects and by considering instead the longer dynamics of state-socialist architectural mobilities in the MPR. These dynamics were conditioned by the broader political economy of the Comecon which, as scholars have pointed out, was evolving from the Soviet exploitation of the satellite countries during the immediate post-war years to their subsidisation in later periods.[8] In the course of this process, the Soviet objective of international economic integration often failed in view of the satellites' resistance and evasion. While much of this dynamic is confirmed by the archival material we discuss, our approach differs from that of political and economic historians. Instead of focusing on political leaders and high-ranking bureaucrats, we concentrate on mid-level professionals, in particular architects, planners, engineers, managers, and administrators in charge of the material-technical base for construction. In so doing, we study how these actors followed, exploited, and sometimes challenged the political economy of Comecon's technical assistance and negotiated it with feedback from design institutes and construction sites.

In what follows, we study the work of Mongolian, Soviet and other Comecon actors by introducing the concept of "concern". Using this concept we aim to capture long-term directives, guidelines, and obligations (whether they were formulated explicitly or implicitly), that conveyed the priorities, motivations, and aspirations of

6 L. Minjuurdorj, "Bnmau-yn barilgazhilt, sotsialist èdyn zasgyn integrats." *Èdyn zasgyn asuudal* 6 (1977): 21–25. The scale of the developmental projects in Mongolia was comparable with Soviet Tajikistan; see Artemy M. Kalinovsky, *Laboratory of Socialist Development.*

7 Gerhard Kraft, *Die Zusammenarbeit der Mitgliedsländer des RWG auf dem Gebiet der Investitionen* (Berlin: Akademie-Verlag, 1977).

8 Randall W. Stone, *Satellites and Commissars. Strategy and Conflict in the Politics of Soviet-Bloc Trade* (Princeton, NJ: Princeton University Press, 1996), 115.

Comecon actors and institutions and their counterparts in the MPR. We reconstruct their "concerns" based on documents from Russian, German, Polish, and Mongolian archives, extended by interviews with Mongolian and Russian professionals. The archival sources include discursive documents, such as policy outlines, as well as technical material, such as architectural and urban drawings, norms and standards that guided the work of Mongolian and Comecon actors. On their basis we construct the concept of concern and employ it as a framework to understand the dynamics of work of foreign and local professionals in Mongolia across the political, economic, ideological, technological, and professional coordinates of Comecon's technical assistance.

After an overview of the impact of architectural exchanges between the Comecon countries and Mongolia on the development of Ulaanbaatar, we argue that the work of Comecon actors in Mongolia was informed by three concerns. They included, first, the concern for integrating Mongolian design and construction industries into a comprehensive network of organizations in charge of the urbanization processes; second, the concern for adapting foreign resources to the conditions on the ground; and, third, the concern for an increasing collaboration between Mongolian and other Comecon actors. We will show how these actors referred to the three concerns – although not always explicitly nor unambiguously – in order to prioritize, substantiate, evaluate, evidence, and explain their work. While the concerns were referred to by the Soviets, Eastern Europeans, and Mongolians in order to build a consensus between the actors on the ground, Mongolian decision-makers sometimes proposed interpretations of the concerns in ways that gave them leverage in their negotiation with other Comecon professionals and institutions.

By studying how the three concerns informed the architectural production in the MPR, but also by accounting for conflicts around their interpretation and implementation, this chapter complements the perspective of political and economic historians. At the same time, it expands a more common focus of architectural historians on individual buildings and singular designs. Beyond advancing the scholarship on Mongolian architecture and urbanisation from the 1960s to the 1980s, we argue that the concept of concern may be of use to scholars who study the mobilities of architecture within various scales of global socialism, as well as those interested in worldwide urbanization processes across competing developmental regimes during the twentieth century.

Ulaanbaatar in the socialist world

Laid out in the valleys of the Tuul and the Selbe rivers, Ulaanbaatar emerged from a monastery town of Khüree, also called Örgöö (or Urga) which largely consisted of felt houses (called gers or yurts) grouped around Buddhist monasteries, temples, and markets.[9] After the foundation of the Soviet-dependent MPR (1924), the first master plan of the city, by then renamed Ulaanbaatar ('red hero'), was delivered by the Moscow-based Giprogor (State Institute of Urban Planning, 1954). The Peace Avenue, laid out parallel to the Tuul River and the trans Mongolian railway line (completed in 1956), was planned as the city's backbone, connecting most of its districts (referred as *khoroolol* in Mongolian or *mikroraion*, plural: *mikroraiony* in Soviet documents).[10] The size of the city envisaged by the plan for the 1970s was already surpassed by the late 1950s, at which time most of Ulaanbaatar's population of 152,000 still lived in ger districts, in spite of the accelerated production of new housing.[11] Subsequent plans provided by Giprogor with varying levels of Mongolian participation (1963, 1971, 1986) laid out a further extension of the city along the Tuul river valley, maintaining the general decision to assign areas around the railway line for industrial development, and northwards of the line for housing, with additional residential neighbourhoods on the southern bank of the Dund Gol river (a section of the Selbe river). They accommodated a large portion of the city's expanding population, even if ger districts continued to grow in Ulaanbaatar (Fig. 1).[12]

A drive down the city's main road, Peace Avenue, reads like a timeline of socialist architecture and urban planning. Its point zero is Sükhbaatar Square, once the site of the mausoleum (now demolished) of the Communist leaders Damdin

9 Valentin Tkachev, *Istoriia mongol'skoi arkhitektury* (Moscow: MGSU Izd-vo Assots. stroit. vuzov, 2009), Chapter 6. See also D. Maidar, *Arkhitektura i gradostroitel'stvo Mongolii* (Moscow: Stroiizdat, 1971).

10 In order to avoid ambiguity with later nomenclature, and reflecting the majority of our sources, we are using the socialist-period names of the districts and refer to them with the term mikroraiony.

11 Balazs Szalontai, "From the Demolition of Monasteries to the Installation of Neon Lights: The Politics of Urban Construction in the Mongolian People's Republic," in *Sites of Modernity: Asian Cities in the Transitory Moments of Trade, Colonialism, and Nationalism*, edited by Wasana Wongsurawat, 161–179 (Berlin, Heidelberg: Springer, 2016), 169.

12 On Ulaanbaatar's urban development, see S. Munkhjargal, D. Tsedev and S. Luvsangombo, *Ulaanbaatar: Hotyn hogjil, buteen baiguulalt, tuhen zamnal* (Ulaanbaatar, 2006); on ger districts, see Alexander C. Diener and Joshua Hagen, "City of Felt and Concrete: Negotiating Cultural Hybridity in Mongolia's Capital of Ulaanbaatar." *Nationalities Papers* 41, no. 4 (2013): 622–650.

Fig. 1: General plan of Ulaanbaatar. Giprogor (Moscow), 1971.
Source: S. Munkhjargal, D. Tsedev and S. Luvsangombo, *Ulaanbaatar: Hotyn hogjil, buteen baiguulalt, tuhen zamnal*, Ulaanbaatar, 2006, p. 78.

Sükhbaatar and Khorloo Choibalsan. Inspired by Lenin's mausoleum in Moscow, it was designed after Sükhbaatar's death (1922) by Mongolian architect B. Chimed and Soviet architect B. Bezencev.[13] Added to the mausoleum were the Government Palace and the National Academic Theater of Opera and Ballet, the latter designed during World War Two by Gerhard Kosel, a German architect who worked in the Soviet Union and later became the head of the PCC (with M. S. Shirov, 1942) (Fig. 2).[14]

Reflecting the turn of Soviet architecture to modernism and its subsequent revisions, buildings constructed from the 1960s to the 1980s abandoned the socialist realist idiom of the Theater. Those in the city centre and its vicinity include the Palace of Culture, the House of Young Technicians, the Pioneer Palace, and the Wedding Palace (D. Lur'e, N. Stuzhin).[15] Besides the Soviets, architects and engineers from other Comecon countries also contributed to the urban landscape of Ulaanbaatar, with a hospital designed by a Czechoslovak team (Zdeněk Přáda, Karel Hauer, Jan Řídký, design 1960s) (Fig. 3) and the Romanian-designed circus (Proiect București, 1970s) being among the most visible.[16] By the late 1960s, Mongolian

13 A. Khishigt, "Mongol-Zövlöltyn zoorag töslyn baigoollaga hamtyn ajillagaa." *Barilgachin* 4 (1971): 4–7.

14 Gerhard Kosel, "Intermezzo im Großen Vaterländischen Krieg – Das Theater für Ulan-Bator." *Architektur der DDR* 34, no. 5 (1985): 297–300.

15 Other buildings in the idiom of socialist realism include the Ministry of Foreign Affairs (V. Shul'gina) and the Choibalsan University (N. Shchepetel'nikov).

16 "Nemocnice s poliklinikou v Ulán-bátaru, Mongolská lidová republika." *Architektura ČSSR* 6 (1963): 347–348; National Central Archives of Mongolia (Ulaanbaatar, Mongolia, later: UTA), f. 288, o. 1, d. 329, l. 1.

Fig. 2: Sükhbaatar Square in Ulaanbaatar. On the left: the Palace of Culture, TsNIIEP im. B. Mezentseva, Moscow (1988); on the right: National Academic Theater of Opera and Ballet, Gerhard Kosel, M. Shirov (1942).
Source: Photo by Łukasz Stanek, 2018.

architects with Soviet collaborators employed the modernist idiom in the design of the Museum of the Revolution (A. Khishigt, 1971), the Zaisan Mount Memorial (A. Khishigt, 1971–1979), and the Lenin Museum (G. Luvsandorj, design 1970s) (Fig. 4). Some of these buildings were clustered with structures designed by Chinese architects and built by Chinese workers during the 1950s and early 1960s, among them the Central Department Store, the Bayangol Hotel, and the 5th housing district (Fig. 5).[17]

Like the development of public buildings, the expansion of Ulaanbaatar's housing districts reflected the general tendencies of Soviet and Eastern European architecture and planning. Designed by Soviet institutes, joined by Chinese (until the mid-1960s) and Eastern European architects, and increasingly planned by Mongolian professionals, the evolution of these districts followed the typological shift from the *kvartal* layout to that of the mikroraion. The former was employed in the areas around the Sükhbaatar Square, while the latter typology, itself evolving,

17 The Beijing Industrial Design Institute also designed the Central Stadium, the Bogd Khan Mountain Hotel (1959), and the Bogd Khan Mountain Guesthouse (1960), constructed by Chinese workers. See Guanghui Ding and Charlie Q. L. Xue, "China's Architectural Aid: Exporting a Transformational Modernism." *Habitat International* 47 (2015): 137. On the Chinese involvement in Mongolia, see Sergey Radchenko, "New Documents on Mongolia and the Cold War." *Cold War International History Project Bulletin* 16 (2007): 341–446.

Fig. 3: Hospital in Ulaanbaatar constructed with technical assistance of Czechoslovakia, Zdeněk Přáda, Karel Hauer, Jan Řídký (mid-1960s).
Source: Photo by Łukasz Stanek, 2018.

Fig. 4: The Lenin Museum, Ulaanbaatar, G. Luvsandorj (design 1970s).
Source: Photo by Łukasz Stanek, 2018.

Fig. 5: Central Department Store, Gong Deshun, Beijing Industrial Design Institute (completed 1960). Source: Photo by Łukasz Stanek, 2018.

guided the expansion of the city to the east, including mikroraiony 12, 13, 14 and 15 (1965–1970), and to the west, the 3rd and 4th mikroraiony (1975–1983).[18] The latter two were together referred to in the Soviet documentation as the "Gandan district", as they were adjacent to the Gandan monastery, one of the few that survived the demolition of Buddhist monasteries in Mongolia by Communist authorities in 1937 to 1938.[19] These residential areas reflected the development of the Soviet prefabrication systems and housing typologies. For example, both mikroraiony 12 and 15 began with the construction of five-story prefabricated blocks and later were extended by nine- and 12-story towers with more complex volumes. They were equipped with social facilities distributed according to a normalised system of

18 For commission documents of mikroraiony 3, 4, and 12 see: UTA f. 288, o. 1, d. 820, 1017, f. 288, o. 1, d. 60–106; on mikroraion 5, see: Russian State Archive for Economy (Russian Federation, Moscow) (later, RGAE), d. 5, o. 1, l. 687, l. 73.

19 Balazs Szalontai, "From the Demolition of Monasteries".

catchment areas, and they occasionally included a unique building, such as the Palace of Science and Culture in the 12th mikroraion (Mosproekt II, 1975).[20] By the 1970s, urban layouts and apartment plans became more flexible and differentiated, as evidenced by the Gandan district. It included five 12-story buildings, laid out on a shamrock plan, and connected by a lower building that housed shops and services.[21]

Not only were these structures designed and built with the assistance of the Soviet Union and its satellites, but the socialist countries provided much of the financing, materials, technologies, expertise, training, and labour that made these investments possible. While the most visible and most celebrated instances of Comecon's technical assistance in Ulaanbaatar were buildings gifted by the Soviet Union, such as the Wedding Palace or the 12th mikroraion, the majority of projects were funded by loans granted by the Soviet Union and its satellites. In line with Comecon's foreign trade practice, many of them were repaid with Mongolia's export products, including foodstuffs and raw materials. Based on loan agreements, intergovernmental commissions formulated guidelines concerning specific investments, which were then implemented by the responsible ministries in Ulaanbaatar and their counterparts in Eastern Europe.[22] These guidelines were followed by detailed contracts between state enterprises and foreign trade organisations in the respective socialist country and Mongolia.[23] Since the 1960s, Comecon's PCC had played a decisive role in these negotiations. In particular, Commission experts wrote up proposals concerning the distribution among Comecon member states of particular tasks, including design, construction, and modernization of buildings and ensembles in Mongolia, their expansion, and the training of their personnel.[24]

Communication between Mongolian and Eastern European institutions was facilitated by the fact that Mongolian organisations in charge of architecture, planning, and construction were based on Soviet models. The main planning

20 In 1965, type designs constituted 90% of the total of residential construction in Mongolia, *Desiat' let raboty postoiannoi komissii SEV po stroitel'stvu* (Moscow: TSINIS Gosstroia SSSR, 1968), 19.

21 On the Gandan district, see RGAE, f. 5, o. 5, d. 116, l. 73–78.

22 In order to reduce travel and communication costs, several Soviet organisations established branches in Mongolia, including the Gosstroi, the Gosgrazhdanstroi (State Committee for Civil Construction and Architecture), and the GKES (Committee for Foreign Economic Relations). See Dashiin Bat, *Zurag tosol* (Ulaanbaatar: Munkhyn useg, 2016), 58.

23 On Mongolian-Soviet agreements concerning the construction of agricultural buildings, see UTA f. 288, o. 2, d. 7, l. 49; on Mongolian-Polish agreement concerning repair workshops, see Archiwum Akt Nowych (Poland, Warsaw) (later, AAN), 2/2309/0/-/353; on Mongolian-Soviet agreement on economic aid and the construction of residential, agricultural, and industrial objects, see RGAE, f. 339, o. 3, d. 2302, l. 273–279.

24 "Protokoll der Spezialistenberatung [. . .]," March–April 1973, Bundesarchiv (Germany, Berlin) (later, BA), DH1: 25038, 2 von 2.

institution was the State Planning Commission in Ulaanbaatar (the equivalent of the Soviet Gosplan), which produced investment plans and passed them on to the branch ministries, among them the State Committee for Construction (equivalent to the Soviet Gosstroi). The investment plans laid out by central institutions were executed by a network of state organisations which, together, constituted the material-technical base for construction in Mongolia.

Within this network, the Mongolian State Design Institute played a key role in terms of architectural and urban planning. The Institute emerged from a string of organisations established with the close assistance of the Soviets, starting with the foundation in 1929 of a drafting office in charge of construction plans executed by the first Mongolian construction cooperative (founded in 1926). From the 1930s, Mongolian planning institutions played an increasing role in the production of design documentation, they employed a growing number of Mongolians, and accelerated the standardization and typification of designs.[25] The Institute was divided into specialised sections, including housing, urban planning, industrial architecture, rural architecture, as well as their supporting sections in charge of budgeting and surveys.[26] By the 1960s, it employed more than 500 people, including over 150 foreign specialists and experts, above all from the Soviet Union and Bulgaria, but also from China, East Germany, Hungary, and Poland (Fig. 6).[27] While many among them travelled to the MPR early in their careers, some were already successful professionals before coming to Mongolia. For example, Volia Kossarzhevskii, the head designer of the 15th mikroraion in Ulaanbaatar, had been chief architect at a Moscow-based design institute specializing in public buildings (TsNIIEP im. Mezentseva).[28]

During the first decades of the Institute's operations, most of its staff were trained in the framework of Soviet, and later Eastern European technical assistance. Some among them were recruited from other professions: a case in point was the career of D. Tsultem, presented in the Mongolian press as "an exemplary Communist".[29] After graduating from a teachers' college in 1943 and working as a teacher for

25 A. Khishigt, "Barilgyn zoorag töslyn baigoollaga 50 zhild." *Èdyn zasgyn asuudal* 5 (1979): 35–37; Khishigt, "Mongol-Zövlöltyn zoorag töslyn baigoollaga hamtyn ajillagaa," 4–7.

26 Wincenty Szober, "Architekci polscy w Mongolii," 473; J. Zukhaa, "Barilgyn zoorag tösöl." *Unèn* 308 (22 December 1976): 2; L. Tserendondog, "Zoorag töslyn baigoollaga 50 zhild." *Barilgachin* 1 (1971): 2–4; "Barilgyn zoorag tösvyn tovcho." *Unèn* no. 56 (25 February 1978): 1; B. Baatarjav, "Zoorag töslyn baigoollaga, tèrguun turshlaga." *Unèn*, no. 4 (4 January 1980): 35–37; D. Sain-Er, "Zoorag töslyn baigoollaga 50 zhild." *Barilgachin* no. 1 (1971): 8–11.

27 Wincenty Szober, "Architekci polscy w Mongolii," 473; for the history of the institute, see Dashiin Bat, *Zurag tosol*, 196. Interview with Dagshigdorj Chimed by Nikolay Erofeev and Łukasz Stanek (Ulaanbaatar, 10 April 2018).

28 RGAE, f. 5, o. 1, d. 687, l. 70a.

29 N. Tsevegmid, "Duurialtai komunist." *Unèn* 287 (14 October 1979): 3.

Fig. 6: Experts at Mongolian State Design Institute: S. Munkhjargal, Dashiin Bat and others, 1968. Source: Dashiin Bat, *Zurag Tosol*, Ulaanbaatar: Munkhyn useg, 2016, p. 252.

several years, Tsultem was trained by Soviet specialists in the financial planning of construction projects. He was then put in charge of budgeting several large investments at the Mongolian State Design Institute. Other paths to a professional career at the Institute led through scholarships that allowed Mongolians to study at architectural schools in the socialist countries, above all in the Soviet Union, but also in Bulgaria, Czechoslovakia, East Germany, Poland, and Romania.[30] In order to facilitate architectural education in Mongolia, in 1973 the School of Architecture was established at the University of Mongolia in Ulaanbaatar. The first head of the architectural school, Mongolian architect Bandi Dambiinyam (himself trained in Moscow), explained in an article published in 1979 that the school's curriculum was modelled according to the five-year specialist training at the Moscow State University of Civil Engineering.[31] After the School's foundation, the numbers of architects in Mongolia began to rise quickly, and by 1987 Mongolia's architectural union counted at least 150 members, trained either locally or in other socialist countries.[32]

30 See, for example, UTA, f. 288, o. 2–29, d. 69.

31 B. Dambiiniam, "Arkhitekturnoe obrazovanie v MNR." *Arkhitektura SSSR* 9 (1979): 15–17.

32 Werner Rietdorf, "Bauen und Wohnen in der Mongolischen VR." *Architektur der DDR* 7 (1988): 19.

Soviet and Eastern European technical assistance was also decisive for the creation of the construction industry in the MPR. Since the formation of the first state building organisation in 1926, the Soviets had supported the development of the Mongolian construction industry and supplied it with experts, machinery, construction materials, and mobile, mechanised construction brigades.[33] Central for this process was the foundation and advancement of Mongolian construction-materials industry and its supporting plants. For example, among more than 150 industrial facilities constructed with Soviet assistance between 1961 and 1973 were mining facilities and processing plants based on mineral raw materials, as well as factories, several among them in the new industrial towns of Erdenet and Darkhan.[34] Besides the Soviets, other Comecon countries contributed too, including a Czechoslovak cement factory in Darkhan; a silicate factory in the same city and lightweight concrete and wooden-element factories in Ulaanbaatar, all three from Poland; and several Bulgarian brick factories.[35]

Integration and adaptation

The duration and intensity of Comecon's technical assistance in Mongolia, along with its multilateral and coordinated character, give us an opportunity to examine several questions that would be difficult to answer in any other location. What were the priorities, motivations, and aspirations of foreign and local architects, planners, engineers, managers, and administrators who worked within the uneven and unequal dynamics of Comecon's technical assistance from the 1960s to the 1980s? How did these priorities, motivations and aspirations respond to the shifting political and economic directives across the chains of command of the respective party organizations and ministries in the MPR and abroad? How did Mongolian and other Comecon professionals and bureaucrats negotiate these directives with their experience on construction sites and in design offices in Ulaanbaatar during the three decades of their exchanges? What was the role of distinct and evolving bodies of architectural and planning knowledge in these negotiations? How were specific design concepts, methods,

33 S. Budsuren, "ZHU-aas manai orny barilgyn uildverleld uzuulsen tuslamj." *Barilgachin* 1 (1971): 8–10; Wincenty Szober, "Architekci polscy w Mongolii," 471.

34 Ministerium für Bauwesen, *Zusammenarbeit der Mitgliedsländer des RGW auf dem Gebiet des Bauwesens. Zum 25. Jahrestag d. Rates für Gegenseitige Wirtschaftshilfe* (Berlin: Bauinformation, 1975), 29–33.

35 Ministerium für Bauwesen, *Zusammenarbeit der Mitgliedsländer des RGW auf dem Gebiet des Bauwesens*, 29–33.

and guidelines introduced and implemented, and how were they shaped and re-shaped in a confrontation with the differing professional traditions of the Comecon countries involved?

We begin answering these questions by advancing the concept of "concern", inspired by debates in philosophy and anthropology.[36] In what follows, we argue that three areas of concern – integration, adaptation, and collaboration – consistently informed the work of foreign and local professionals and mid-level administrators involved in Comecon's technical assistance to Mongolia. While the concept of concern is ours, Mongolians, Soviets, and Eastern Europeans often referred to "integration", "adaptation", and "collaboration", although not always explicitly or unambiguously. The term "collaboration" was discussed frequently and explicitly, while "integration" and "adaptation" were used interchangeably with several other terms with similar connotations, often in reference to more general principles of architectural practice in the socialist countries. "Integration" reverberates with the Russian adjective *kompleksnyi* (*kompleksowy* in Polish, *komplex* in German), which in Comecon's architectural discourse referred to the tendency towards "holistic integration and [. . .] comprehensiveness".[37] Beyond the architectural scale, this term conveyed a vision of socialist urbanisation informed by what Kimberly E. Zarecor calls "infrastructural thinking", or the design and construction of territorial systems (infrastructure, production, transport, social services, recreation) at all scales, from architectural, through urban and regional, to international.[38] In turn, the term "adaptation" encompasses the architectural procedure of modifying type designs to local conditions (*priviazka*), which was at the core of Soviet design culture, and in itself conveyed the broad consensus within this culture that architecture and urban planning needed to be adequate to the local conditions.

We reconstruct the three areas of concern based on a range of archival documents, including policy outlines, professional publications, press accounts, official

---

36 The concept of concern, referring to Martin Heidegger's concept of *Sorge* (care or concern), has been much debated in philosophy and anthropology; see, for example, Tatjana Thelen, "Care as Social Organization: Creating, Maintaining and Dissolving Significant Relations." *Anthropological Theory* 15, no. 4 (2015): 497–515, DOI: 10.1177/1463499615600893. Our discussion is inspired by but distinct from these debates.

37 Michał Murawski, "Actually-Existing Success: Economics, Aesthetics, and the Specificity of (Still-) Socialist Urbanism." *Comparative Studies in Society and History* 60, no. 4 (2018): 924–927.

38 Kimberly Elman Zarecor, "Infrastructural Thinking: Urban Housing in Former Czechoslovakia from the Stalin Era to EU Accession," in *The Housing Question: Tensions, Continuities, and Contingencies in the Modern City*, edited by Edward Murphy, Najib B. Hourani, 57–78 (Farnham: Ashgate, 2013); see also: Kimberly Elman Zarecor, "What Was So Socialist about the Socialist City? Second World Urbanity in Europe." *Journal of Urban History* 44, no. 1 (2018): 95–117, DOI: //doi.org/10.1177/0096144217710229.

communications, reports from construction sites, and minutes of professional meetings, complemented by interviews with Mongolian and Russian professionals. We extend these discursive sources with technical documentation: architectural drawings and urban plans; and regulatory documents for architectural and construction practices, including building norms, construction standards, and procedures for the division of labour between the actors involved. In this sense, rather than as a means to analyse the discourse of Comecon actors in Mongolia,[39] we use the concept of concern to understand the broader dynamics of their professional practices. In order to mitigate the fragmentation of archival sources, our basic procedure is that of juxtaposing texts and drawings from various archives in ways that allow for comparisons across longer timespans.

In what follows, we read these documents by focusing on how the professionals and administrators involved prioritised and substantiated investments, evaluated and evidenced design decisions, extracted resources across the chains of command, and made sense of their own work. We will show that, more often than not, the concern to integrate, adapt, and collaborate reverberated across these practices – even if the actors involved were not always able to agree on the specific interpretation of the three concerns, and often struggled to deliver on them. The aspirational dimension of the three concerns made them often ambiguous, and their specific meaning was subject to negotiation and disagreement. By the end of this chapter, the review of a few of such disagreements will show how Mongolian professionals and administrators aimed to obviate the obstacles and exploit the opportunities of the political economy of Comecon's technical assistance.

A starting point for evidencing these arguments is the 1966 report by a delegation of Soviet architects led by Mikhail Posokhin, chief architect of Moscow and head of the design institute Mosproekt II. After his inspection of Soviet architectural work in Ulaanbaatar, Posokhin was not impressed. Addressing the Department of Construction Abroad at the Soviet Gosstroi, he described the Soviet-designed and constructed 12th mikroraion (Fig. 7) and compared it unfavourably with the Chinese-designed and built 5th mikroraion (Fig. 8).

Posokhin pointed out the poor quality of the Soviet housing when compared with Chinese buildings in Ulaanbaatar.[40] Such a comparison was a sensitive matter in the wake of the Sino-Soviet split, when both countries competed for the status of the progressive force in world politics, and actively sought to promote their paths

39 On (late) Soviet discourse, see Alexei Yurchak, *Everything Was Forever, until It Was No More: The Last Soviet Generation* (Princeton NJ: Princeton University Press), 2005.
40 RGAE, f. 5, o. 1, d. 687, l. 73–80.

Fig. 7: Mikroraion 12 in Ulaanbaatar (1960s), to which the Palace of Science and Culture II (on the left) was added in 1975, Mosproekt II, Moscow.
Source: *Information Mongolia: The Comprehensive Reference Source of the People's Republic of Mongolia*, Oxford, 1990, plate 10.

to socialism among governments of decolonising countries in Africa and Asia.[41] In order to distinguish the Soviet approach to technical assistance from the Chinese one, a Soviet author argued in the early 1970s that Chinese development aid aimed at an incremental transformation of the national economy, in contrast to the vision of structural change that underlay the Soviet developmental approach.[42] This contrast appears plausible when buildings constructed in the course of the 1960s in Ulaanbaatar are considered: whereas the Chinese-designed buildings were constructed by means of conventional methods, many of the Soviet ones were based on an industrialised system of construction.

41 See Susanne Stein's contribution to this volume. See also Jeremy Scott Friedman, *Shadow Cold War: The Sino-Soviet Split and the Third World* (Chapel Hill: University of North Carolina Press, 2015); Sergey Radchenko, 'Sino-Russian Competition in Mongolia,' in *International Relations and Asia's Northern Tier: Sino-Russia Relations, North Korea, and Mongolia*, edited by Gilbert Rozman and Sergey Radchenko, 111–126 (Singapore: Palgrave Macmillan, 2018).
42 "Chinese Aid Criticised." *West Africa* (December 2, 1974): 1466.

Fig. 8: Mikroraion 5 in Ulaanbaatar, with a kindergarten, five-story residential buildings and two towers of Bayangol hotel. Gong Deshun, Beijing Industrial Design Institute (design 1964). Source: D. Maidar, *Arkhitektura i gradostroitel'stvo Mongolii,* Moscow: Stroiizdat, 1971, p. 71.

The cornerstone of this system was the house-building factory in Ulaanbaatar, which we described in the opening vignette of this chapter. Donated by the Soviet Union as a gift to Mongolia in early 1960s, the factory was designed by the Moscow-based design institute *Giprostroiindustriia* to prefabricate elements of the I-464 building system – one of the most widespread large-panel technologies used in the Soviet Union.[43] The factory was conceived as an essential node within an integrated network of institutions in charge of the urbanisation of the country, some of which already existed, while others were to be established in the future. Due to this factory's central role in Mongolia's material-technical base for construction, it was prioritised by decision-makers in Moscow and Ulaanbaatar over more spectacular buildings and more urgently needed facilities. The development of the factory during the 1970s and 1980s continued to be informed by the concern for integration. After its expansion and modernisation in 1972,[44] the network

43 Nikolay Erofeev, "The I-464 Housing Delivery System: A Tool for Urban Modernisation in the Socialist World and Beyond." *Fabrications* 29, no. 2 (2019): 207–230.

44 The prefabrication technology was modernised by the Moscow-based TsNIIEP Zhilishcha, see Archive of TsNIIEP Zhilishcha (Archive of the Central scientific-research institute for experimental

of industrial plants centered on this facility included two other plants of prefabricated elements constructed by then, and their supporting industries and infrastructures. This network was instrumental in the government's programme to rehouse much of the country's population to new residences.[45]

At the same time, the Soviets pointed out that the factory's integrative role in the development of Mongolia's material-technical base was predicated upon the adaptation of its technology to the local conditions. In the MPR, Soviet engineers performed such adaptation either by applying solutions from regions of the Soviet Union claimed to be similar to Mongolia, such as Soviet Buriatia, or by directly adapting Soviet technological systems to Mongolia. The latter path was chosen for the design of the Ulaanbaatar factory, based on the procedure of trying-in (*privїazka*). Following this procedure, Soviet engineers adapted the factory's standard design to seismic and soil conditions in Ulaanbaatar. Because it was one of the first attempts to export the I-464 system abroad, this adaptation process was long and challenging, resulting in delays in the operation of the plant.[46]

The construction and expansion of the factory in Ulaanbaatar from the 1960s to the 1980s not only exemplified the persistent concerns for integration and adaptation by Soviet and Mongolian decision-makers and professionals, but also their conviction that both concerns were interdependent. Yet rather than being limited to a singular project, however large, we argue that both concerns were constitutive for the overarching vision of urbanisation supported by the Soviet Union and other socialist countries in the MPR.

Particularly useful in understanding this vision is the document titled "Unified technical conditions for the design of plants and other buildings constructed in the MPR with the technical assistance of the member states of the Comecon".[47] Published in 1976 by the PCC, thus in the midst of the accelerated involvement of Comecon's member-states in Mongolia, the "Conditions" were made obligatory for all Comecon actors working in the MPR. The "Conditions" prescribed the application of a range of planning procedures, including standardisation, modularisation, typification, and, ultimately, industrialisation. The document listed such

and typical design of housing, Russian Federation, Moscow), inv. 2620 "92–07S-1-UB," inv. 2131 "92–016S-1-UB."

45 Ayuushiyn Davaa, "Osnovnoi rychag razvitiia stroitel'nogo proizvodstva MNR." *Ekonomicheskoe sotrudnichestvo stran-chlenov SEV* 2 (1977): 48–52, 50.

46 Gosstroi identified technical adaptations to Mongolian realities as the main concern in the delivery of Soviet housing to the MPR: RGAE, f. 5, o. 1, d. 139, l. 149; d. 522, l. 55; RGAE, f. 339, o. 3, d. 2302, l. 36.

47 *Einheitliche technische Bedingungen für die Projektierung von Betrieben und anderen Objekten, die in der Mongolischen Volksrepublik mit technischer Hilfe der Mitgliedsländer des RGW errichtet werden* (Berlin: Bauakademie der DDR, 1976).

general principles of modern planning as zoning and division of traffic, as well as more specifically Soviet and Eastern European planning procedures of coordinating economic and spatial planning in longer time spans (perspective plans) and larger scales (regional plans). Based on earlier Soviet norms for Mongolia, the "Conditions" also prescribed the typology of the mikroraion as the basic unit within a nested hierarchy of settlements and their respective social facilities, as applied in the urban design of the 15th mikroraion in Ulaanbaatar (Fig. 9).[48]

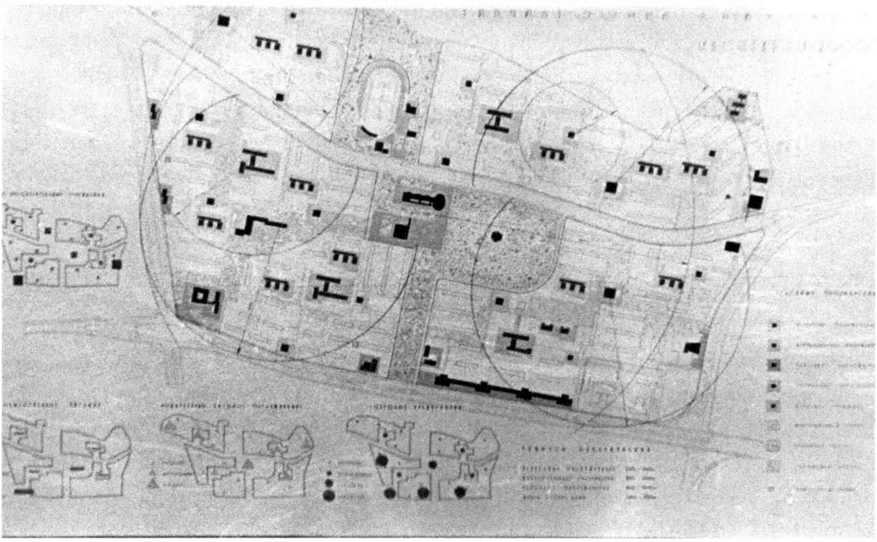

Fig. 9: Schematic map of social facilities in mikroraion 15 in Ulaanbaatar, Mongolian State Design Institute, 1966.
Source: RGAE, f. P-149, o. 1–1, d. 3238, l. 45.

As was the case with the house-building factory in Ulaanbaatar, the concern for integration went hand in hand with the concern for adaptation. The urban and architectural norms stipulated in the "Conditions" convey both concerns in specific and concrete terms. These norms were introduced in order to facilitate an urbanism designed in an "integrated" or "comprehensive" (*komplex*) manner.[49] They were expected to coordinate "the spatial, constructive, sanitary and electrical

48 *Einheitliche technische Bedingungen*; see also: *Edinye tekhnicheskie usloviia na proektirovanie predpriiatii i drugikh ob"ektov, stroiashchikhsia v Mongol'skoi Narodnoi Respublike pri tekhnicheskom sodeistvii SSSR* (Moscow: Glavstroiproekt, Promstroiproekt, 1965).
49 *Einheitliche technische Bedingungen*, 31.

solutions with a high standard of technology" and to guarantee a unified system of supply of social services on all scales and in all locations.[50] The introduction of such norms responded to the advice of Soviet professionals who listed the lack of universal standards among the main hindrances for the advancement of Mongolia's construction industry.[51] At the same time, the prescription of building standards and type projects was intended to enforce the adaptation of Eastern European designs to the climatic, seismic, economic, and technological specificity of the MPR, and the ways of life of the country's inhabitants. The "Conditions" required type housing projects to be responsive to "local climatic and living conditions, and the demographic composition of the population", while urban centres were to be designed as compact, "in order to account for the continental climate of the MPR".[52] Furthermore, and adding a third concern to those of integration and adaptation, the use of the "Conditions" by all actors in Mongolia, both local and foreign, would facilitate collaboration between them.

Collaboration and its discontents

In 1974, Orony Tleyhan, Mongolian minister for the construction and construction-materials industries, addressed the participants of the PCC meeting in Prague. Tleyhan expressed gratitude for the technical assistance provided by the Soviet Union and other Comecon countries to Mongolia. Yet his phrasing stressed the local agency in these exchanges. He argued that with Comecon's support "the Mongolian people [. . .] led by the Mongolian Revolutionary People's Party transformed [. . .] a backward country based on livestock farming into a socialist country with a fast-growing, modern industry and large collective farms".[53]

These statements conformed to the Comecon discourse, which stressed collaboration as its core premise and the defining experience of socialist internationalism. The principle of collaboration was referred to by the Soviets to distinguish their technical assistance from Western "development aid", which Soviet propaganda accused of prolonging colonial-era economic dependencies. By contrast, collaboration between the Comecon and less advanced countries would allow the latter to achieve socialist development goals and to fully participate in the economic exchanges within

50 *Einheitliche technische Bedingungen*, 9.

51 RGAE, f. 339, o. 3, d. 2100, l. 65.

52 *Einheitliche technische Bedingungen*, 36. See also, *Edinye tekhnicheskie usloviia*, 1–4.

53 Ministerium für Bauwesen, *Zusammenarbeit*, 29. The name is spelled "Tleichan" in the East German sources.

the socialist world[54] – even if the negotiation of their specific roles in these exchanges and the division of labour within this world led to tensions among Comecon member-states. For example, while the Soviets encouraged Mongolia to develop its traditional areas of export (livestock farming and mining), the leadership of the MPR often contested this advice as leading to a perpetuated "backwardness" of their country, and instead requested technical assistance for industrial development.[55]

Writing in 1977, Luujugin Lhamsurem, director of the State Planning Commission of the MPR, distinguished three modes of Mongolia's collaboration with other Comecon countries in architecture, planning, and construction. The first was the provision of machinery, equipment, technical documentation and design manuals by the socialist countries, as well as the training of Mongolian specialists in these countries, and the work of Eastern European experts in the MPR. As the second mode, he named turn-key projects constructed by socialist countries in Mongolia, in particular the Soviet Union, and handed over to the Mongolian authorities. The third mode of collaboration was construction projects, designed, built, and operated jointly by Eastern Europeans and Mongolians, in particular in the industrial towns of Darkhan and Erdenet.[56]

Dashiin Bat, the former head of the Industrial Construction Department at the Mongolian State Design Institute, largely confirmed that these modes of collaboration were applicable to the work of the Institute, too. He pointed out that the provision of complete buildings by the Soviets as turn-key projects was the most efficient but also the most expensive mode of collaboration. While it was preferred by Mongolian officials, the Soviets reserved this approach mostly for exceptional and highly visible projects, such as gifted buildings.[57]

Bat's comments make it clear that beyond political and ideological objectives, the concern for collaboration was also motivated economically. The Soviets required that Mongolians participate in the provision of resources for technical assistance projects, above all labour. This included the agreement about the construction of Ulaanbaatar's house-building factory, according to which Mongolia agreed to provide up to 65 percent of the labourers. However, the authorities were unable to deliver on this obligation,[58] and labour shortages became a huge challenge after China withdrew most of its workers from the MPR in the

54 Leonid S. Yagodovsky, *The World Socialist System – Its Role in the World Today* (Moscow: Novosti Press Agency Publishing House), 1975.

55 See Balazs Szalontai, "From the Demolition of Monasteries," 173.

56 Luujugin Lkhamsurien, "Pomoshch bratskikh stran v uskorenii razvitiia i povyshenii effektivnosti ekonomiki MNR." *Ekonomicheskoe sotrudnichestvo stran-chlenov SEV* 1 (1977): 25–30.

57 Dashiin Bat, interview by Nikolay Erofeev and Łukasz Stanek (Ulaanbaatar, 10 April 2018).

58 RGAE, f. 339, o. 3, d. 2100, l. 65.

wake of the Sino-Soviet split.[59] Accordingly, by the 1960s, Soviet and Mongolian officials discussed various measures to train and involve Mongolians in the housing delivery process.[60] Following an agreement signed in 1965, the Soviets stepped in to train local construction cadres. They opened training centres for the building trades at Mongolian construction sites and at the house-building factory in Ulaanbaatar. Training sessions were also offered by the joint Soviet-Mongolian brigades.[61]

Training was a priority of Comecon's technical assistance to the MPR more generally. This priority was reflected in individual contracts of Eastern European architects, technicians, and foremen. For example, the contract signed by Józef Musiał, a Polish bricklayer-foreman, who worked in Mongolia in 1968 and 1969, listed the supervision and training of Mongolian workers among his chief duties.[62] Accordingly, knowledge of Russian – the language in which Comecon's organisations delivered the documentation of technical assistance projects[63] – was an essential criterion in recruiting Eastern European staff for contracts in the country. Since the 1970s, their communication with each other and with their Mongolian counterparts was facilitated by various publications issued by the PCC, notably the monumental *Dictionary of Civil Engineering in Twelve Languages*, including Mongolian.[64]

In addition to linguistic obstacles, Mongolians and foreigners also faced other challenges which reveal the uneven and unequal character of their collaboration. For example, in 1964 the joint Soviet-Mongolian brigades were able to account for only 47 percent of the expected construction output.[65] In order to catch up with the plan, Soviet military labour was tasked with helping out on the construction sites.[66] Accordingly, by 1965 almost 3,000 military labourers contributed to the construction of Soviet projects, among them both mikroraiony 12 and 15 in Ulaanbaatar.[67] Soviet soldiers and labourers often lived in military camps, which limited their opportunities for everyday contacts with Mongolians, thus contradicting Comecon's

59 Balazs Szalontai, "From the Demolition of Monasteries," 169–170.

60 RGAE, f. 339, o. 3, d. 2302, l. 161–64, 273–279.

61 RGAE, f. 339, o. 3, d. 2302, l. 33.

62 AAN 2/2309/0/-/362, p. 2–5, see also: AAN 2/1154/0/25/526.

63 *Einheitliche technische Bedingungen*, 9.

64 *Dvenadcatijazyčnyj stroitel'nyj slovar'* (Moscow: Izd. Rus. Jazyk, 1981); for the list of all volumes and discussion, see Łukasz Stanek, "Paper Cybernetics. Notes on Comecon's Dictionary of Civil Engineering in Twelve Languages (1979)." *Pidgin (Princeton University School of Architecture)* 25 (2019): 80–90.

65 RGAE, f. 339, o. 3, d. 2100, l. 66.

66 On Soviet soldiers in Mongolia, see Ram Rahul, *Afghanistan, Mongolia, and USSR* (New Delhi: Vikas Pub. House, 1987), 65–67; Sergei Radchenko, "The Soviets' Best Friend in Asia: The Mongolian Dimension of the Sino-Soviet Split." *Wilson Center Working Papers* 42 (2003).

67 RGAE, f. 339, o. 3, d. 2302, l. 37, 129.

propaganda that such contacts were a core experience of socialist technical assistance. This was confirmed by Ludmila Samsonova, an engineer from Leningrad, who was employed by a builders' brigade of a military organisation in charge of the implementation of type-housing projects for both military and civilian uses in Mongolia.[68] Further tensions in daily contacts between Soviet and local experts stemmed from the fact that the former enjoyed access to consumer goods distributed in special shops and social services which were not available to ordinary Mongolians.[69]

The challenges of collaboration notwithstanding, a review of the design and construction of Ulaanbaatar's housing projects supported by socialist countries shows a growing involvement of Mongolians. This included workers and technicians, but also architects, engineers, and planners. A comparison between the design processes of mikroraiony 12 and 15 illustrates this point. The 12th mikroraion was planned by the design institute Mosproekt II and the role of the Mongolian State Design Institute was limited to the provision of topographical, geological, and engineering data for Soviet experts.[70] The mikroraion was constructed as "turn-key", fully equipped and operational, by workers from Soviet construction firms, supervised by Moscow-based institutions.[71] By contrast, the design of the 15th mikroraion was delivered by planners at the Mongolian State Design Institute, who were advised by Soviet experts.

Such experiences of collaboration and feedback from completed buildings resulted in lessons for both Soviet and Mongolian architects. The Gandan district evidences several such lessons. Its designers at Mosproekt and Giprogor drew larger kitchens, additional storage rooms, and a balcony which was used to freeze meat supplies during winter. The prefabricated system used for the construction of these buildings was expanded to include ornamental slabs that referred to vernacular decoration, based on studies of ornamental motifs and the architectural heritage of Mongolia, carried out by Soviet and Mongolian scholars (Fig. 10).[72] By the 1980s, the Mongolian architectural critic Niamosoryn Tsultem was arguing that MPR architects were capable of taking over. He criticised several buildings

68 Ludmila Samsonova worked in 1985–88 in the military unit "73 939". Interview with Ludmila Samsonova, by Nikolay Erofeev (over Skype, 18 June 2018).

69 Alexey V. Mikhalev, "Soviet Experts in Mongolia: Between International Mission and Colonial Practices." *Sensus Historiae* 10, no. 1 (2013): 177–194.

70 RGAE, f. 5, o. 1, d. 686, l. 66.

71 The construction was supervised by the Moscow City Hall Administration, RGAE, f. 339, o. 3, d. 2302, l. 37.

72 See, for example, D. Maidar and J. Piurev, *Ot kochevoi do mobil'noi arkhitektury* (Moscow: Stroiizdat, 1980), 41–50.

Fig. 10: A residential building in the Gandan district, 1978–1983.
Source: Photo by Łukasz Stanek, 2018.

designed by Soviet specialists in Ulaanbaatar's city center during the earlier periods for not paying attention to the "national character" of the country.[73] Yet this critique in itself testified to the impact of Soviet architectural culture, in which the concept of "national character" (or "national tradition") was a central criterion of geographical difference, particularly relevant for the development of architectural and planning practices in Soviet Central Asia.[74]

---

73 Niamosoryn Tsultem, *Arkhitektura Mongolii – Mongolian architecture – Architecture de la Mongolie – La arquitectura de Mongolia* (Ulaanbaatar: State Publishing House, 1988); quoted in Balazs Szalontai, "From the Demolition of Monasteries," 175.

74 Igor Demchenko, "Critical Post-functionalism in the Architecture of Late Soviet Central Asia." *ABE Journal* 13 (2018), DOI: 10.4000/abe.4509. Boris Chukhovich, "Orientalist Modes of Modernism in Architecture: Colonial/ Postcolonial/Soviet." *Études de Lettres* 2–3 (2014): 263–294, DOI: 10.4000/edl.728; see also, Łukasz Stanek, "Socialist Worldmaking: The Political Economy of Urban Comparison in the Global Cold War." *Urban Studies* 59, no. 8 (2022): 1575–1596, DOI: 10.1177/00420980211050178.

This brief overview of the housing districts in Ulaanbaatar points at the ways in which their designers and builders across three decades largely shared an overarching concern for integration, adaptation, and collaboration. At the same time, this overview makes it clear that the three concerns did not describe a static ideal but rather a dynamic process. Such a process was implied by the previously discussed "Unified technical conditions", which suggested that with the increasing modernisation of Mongolian cities, new architectural typologies would need to be designed. A comparison of Ulaanbaatar's housing layouts confirms this tendency: while in the 1960s the layouts of buildings designed with the I-464 system had been adapted for the use of solid fuel cast-iron stoves to cope with Mongolia's lack of centralised heating and electricity infrastructure, apartments in the Gandan district built during the following decade were fully integrated into such infrastructural networks.[75] Comecon decision-makers were aware that such advancement of design and construction required that the professionals involved be given opportunities for innovation and experimentation. This was the role of "experimental designs" which, in line with the Soviet practice, allowed planners to test new construction methods, building materials, and architectural layouts. Experimental designs were one more area in which Mongolian professionals were increasingly taking over from the Soviets: while in the early 1960s experiments were carried out in the Soviet Union prior to their implementation in Mongolia, by the next decade most of them were conducted in the country.

The narrative that accompanied Comecon's technical assistance to Mongolia often suggested that the three concerns were intertwined and reinforced each other: collaboration between professionals from socialist countries was expected both to facilitate the integration of the Mongolian construction industry and to allow for a "better consideration of national and other features of the country".[76] However, the interpretation of the three concerns and of the principles of their implementation was subject of negotiation and, sometimes, led to disagreements between Mongolian, Soviet, and Eastern European actors. When requesting funding from the Comecon for extension, adjustment, and modernization projects, Mongolian bureaucrats pointed out the need to integrate new investments into the existing network of institutions and their better adaptation to the conditions on the ground. These arguments were substantiated by the language of the Comecon documents and the authority of Soviet experts – and yet they were sometimes challenged by representatives of Eastern European countries.

---

75 TsNIIEP Zhilishcha developed an amended system I-464-UB for Ulaanbaatar. See: RGAE, f. 339, o. 3, d. 2302, l. 70; RGAE, f. 5, o. 1, d. 139, l. 85, 111.

76 RGAE, f. 339, o. 3, d. 2302, l. 206.

A case in point was a document titled "Proposals and fundamental measures for a perspective development of the construction and construction-materials industry as well as design and research capacities of the MPR in the period until 1990", prepared in 1973 by the Mongolian Ministry of Construction.[77] The document, which referred to a previous Soviet report on the same subject, included a vision of a massive expansion of Mongolia's construction industry, and a "shopping list" of plants which the Mongolians requested the Comecon countries to construct. The list specified six plants to be requested from the Soviet Union, three from Czechoslovakia, two from East Germany, and one from Poland. In a letter sent to the East German Ministry of Construction, Gerhard Kosel argued that the "Proposals" misrepresented the report of the Soviet experts who had recommended that the future collaboration with the MPR was based on decreased rather than expanded transfers from Comecon countries.[78] In this and other instances, professionals and decision-makers from socialist countries often resisted Mongolian proposals for developing the material-technical base for construction in the country, even if these proposals were framed in the language of the Comecon and were based on the interpretations of the three concerns. Comecon's experts sometimes saw Mongolian requests as unreasonable and motivated by the will to "impress".[79] Such orientalising perceptions revealed a racialised gaze cast by some Soviet and Eastern European professionals on their Mongolian counterparts.

Resistance to the increase in requests from MPR officials was particularly strong among managers of Eastern European companies. They were under pressure from state and party leaderships to fulfil production plans in their home countries and, by the 1970s, to deliver on the export quotas and the obligatory "hard currency plans", introduced in response to the debt crisis in Eastern Europe. For example, in March 1970 one of East Germany's combines refused a request from the Ministry of Construction in East Berlin to send 17 specialists to a meat processing plant in Ulaanbaatar and argued that their enterprise's capacities were already stretched to breaking point by the deployment of personnel to a carpet factory in Mongolia's capital.[80]

Conflicts around resources continued after their allocation. The Mongolian authorities were in charge of budgeting and financial management of each investment, and Eastern European representatives in Ulaanbaatar were eager to dispel any ambiguity in this respect. A case in point was the experience of a group of ten Polish

77 "Zu einigen Problemen des Bauwesens der MRV [. . .]," BA DH1: 25038, 2 von 2, 4.

78 "Zu einigen Problemen des Bauwesens der MRV [. . .]," 4–5.

79 Balazs Szalontai, "From the Demolition of Monasteries," 17; see also, Alexey V. Mikhalev, "Soviet Experts in Mongolia."

80 Letter from Eichstädt to Junker, 24 March 1970, BA DH1: 25038, 2 von 2, 1.

architects who arrived to Mongolia in 1962 to work, initially, as one team. Yet when several of their designs were rejected by Mongolian institutions and Soviet advisors, the architects were distributed across various sections of the Mongolian State Design Institute.[81] The architects objected to this decision, and yet the Polish embassy refused to support them, in particular as this reorganization meant that all responsibility for the design decisions of the Polish architects was ceded to the Mongolians.[82] In several other cases, when Mongolian authorities modified the design documentation delivered by Eastern European countries, their representatives used these changes as an excuse to withdraw from the investment in question.[83]

These examples suggest that while the three concerns were generally shared by Mongolian and Comecon actors, they often interpreted them in diverging ways in order to request more resources or, on the contrary, to resist such requests. The margins of these interpretations were flexible, but they were not open ended, as they were restricted by the patterns of industrial and urban development promoted by the Comecon and the Soviets in particular. In other words, while accepting that the three concepts came as a leverage for Mongolian professionals and decision-makers in their negotiations within the Comecon, it also resulted in limiting their visions for the country to what was achievable within Comecon's developmental frameworks.

Conclusions

The city of Ulaanbaatar was reshaped beyond recognition during the socialist period. Yet the growth of new housing neighbourhoods and social and technical infrastructure was accompanied by an even faster expansion of the ger districts, and the living conditions in many parts of the city remained poor. In 1983, a report by the Central Committee Secretary P. Damdin offered a shocking picture of several districts where poor sanitation resulted in a constant danger of epidemics and high infant mortality, while public transport, and water and power supply were often insufficient and low quality.[84] As scholars have shown, Damdin's report testified not only to rivalry within the Communist Mongolian Revolutionary

81 AAN 2/1154/0/25/526, 106–103 [sic]. Their work included the design of the 4th and 5th mikrorai-ony, planned where a decade later the Soviet-designed the Gandan district was constructed.
82 AAN 2/1154/0/25/526, 106–103 [sic].
83 AAN 2/2309/0/353, 21.
84 This is how the Hungarian embassy in Ulaanbaatar summarised the report; quoted in Balazs Szalontai, "From the Demolition of Monasteries," 176.

People's Party, but also reflected broader dissatisfaction of the inhabitants of Ulaanbaatar who voiced their anger in demonstrations against the regime in 1990, followed by the end of socialism in the country.[85]

This chapter argued that the urbanisation of Ulaanbaatar during socialism cannot be understood without accounting for the exchanges in architecture, planning, and construction between the Soviet Union, Eastern Europe, and Mongolia. By reviewing a range of buildings as well as design, regulatory, and bureaucratic paperwork circulating between professionals and decision-makers from the MPR and other Comecon countries, we conceptualised their priorities, motivations, and aspirations as informed by three concerns. These concerns included, first, that of integrating all elements of the material-technical base for construction with the goal of producing a system of functionally synchronized scales of urbanization. Second, the concern for dynamic adaptation of foreign precedents to local conditions, in particular climatic and geological. Third, the concern for collaboration, which included a progressive delegation and devolution of tasks to Mongolians. Not always complementary and rarely unambiguous, these three concerns were interpreted by Mongolian actors within the uneven dynamics of subsidy and exploitation that characterised the political economy of the Comecon.

As we understand them, the three concerns bypassed the conventional dichotomies of the historiography of architecture and urban planning in socialism. Beyond the opposition between "pragmatic" and "ideological" motivations often attributed to state-socialist decision-makers, the concept of concern shows how professionals and administrators translated, interpreted, negotiated, exploited, and sometimes challenged the political, economic, technological, ideological, and professional coordinates of Comecon's technical assistance in Mongolia. At the same time, beyond the dichotomy between "creative freedom" and "political decision", often invoked by critics of socialist architecture, we argue that technological know-how, professional knowledge, and disciplinary cultures played an important role in these exchanges. In particular, we suggest that procedures of typification, standardisation, and industrialisation were a means not simply to deliver on the three concerns, but rather to formulate, specify, and negotiate them. Finally, the three concerns conveyed a normative vision of urbanisation in the socialist world in ways that bypassed the Western-Marxist dichotomy between "bureaucracy" and "utopia". However restricted, this vision of socialist urbanisation as integrated, adapted, and collaborative was dynamic, since the need to account for existing conditions was constantly confronted with the need to respond to shifting levels of economic resources and the evolution of everyday life in socialism.

85 Szalontai, "From the Demolition of Monasteries," 176.

While we have formulated the three concerns based on research on Cold War Mongolia, this conceptualisation may provide a useful framework for the analysis of long-term trajectories and path-dependencies of architectural mobilities during the Cold War, and their roles in developmental projects more generally. We would like to end with two suggestions for such uses. The first relates to the scholarship about architectural mobilities between the "Second" and "Third" worlds during the Cold War. These mobilities straddled a wide spectrum: beyond the southern members of the Comecon (Mongolia, Vietnam, Cuba) they also included countries which pursued specific versions of socialist development, such as Ghana under Kwame Nkrumah (1957–1966); countries belonging to the "World Socialist System", such as Ba'athist Iraq that benefited from preferential foreign trade agreements with Eastern Europe; and even countries with elites hostile to socialism, such as Nigeria or the Gulf states.[86] The concept of the three concerns suggests a way to differentiate these exchanges based on an analysis of chains of investment projects which unfolded in longer time spans. Rather than building upon broadbrush geopolitical and geoeconomic distinctions, the three concerns open a possibility of a fine-grained analysis of decision-making processes from the perspective of mid-level administrators and professionals, and their shifting priorities in the provision of assistance in design, planning, and construction. This concept may be particularly useful for studies of architectural exchanges in countries where the Soviet presence was interrupted because of a regime change, such as Ghana in 1966, and thus where the priorities and motivations of the parties involved may be difficult to understand on the basis of only partially realised investments.

Secondly, the three concerns may be useful for studying architectural mobilities not only across global socialism, but also across other developmental regimes during the Cold War. While the Soviets contrasted their approach to colonial developmentalism, the three concerns often resembled the declared aims of colonial governments after World War Two. These similarities included the belief that new investments needed to be planned as part of an economy integrated both locally and with the colonial metropole; the understanding that architecture and urban planning needed to be adapted to the specificity of the local conditions (exemplified by the British "tropical architecture"); and the commitment to the "indigenisation" of the colonial economies and governments through an expanding collaboration with the local elites. Yet the dynamics of these processes were distinct from the practices of integration, adaptation, and collaboration as discussed in this chapter, as they differed in terms of political economies, positionalities,

86 Stanek, *Architecture in Global Socialism.*

and modes of interaction available to local and foreign actors. Unpacking these similarities and differences in architectural, planning, and construction mobilities may offer a more diversified perspective on twentieth-century developmental regimes and the specific spectra of welfare and violence that they entailed. Contrary to many Eastern European protagonists in this chapter, who perceived the MPR as isolated and peripheral, we argue that as a crucial node of Comecon's technical assistance, Mongolia offers a vantage point for a more comparative understanding of the urbanisation processes during the Cold War, and of their architecture.

List of abbreviations

MPR	Mongolian People's Republic
PCC	Permanent Commission for Construction
Comecon	Council for the Mutual Economic Assistance

Mariya Petrova, Jonas van der Straeten

Prefabricating Uzbekistan? Discourses and Realities of Urban Redevelopment in Tashkent and Samarkand under Soviet Rule

Introduction

In the opening scene of one the most popular Soviet Uzbek films *The whole mahalla talks about it* (*Mahallada duv duv gap*, 1960) the camera flies over the central squares and parks of Tashkent. An off-camera narrator praises the modern cityscape that has only recently replaced what is here referred to as "narrow and dusty alleyways and ramshackle mud huts".[1] The plot itself takes place in the remnants of one of Tashkent's old *mahallas*, the traditional Islamic neighbourhoods. Modernisation looms large, as these remnants are already enclosed by the loud and dusty construction site of new multistorey houses. There, the male dwellers of the mahalla have found work. The women, for their part, are engaged with the tedious chores indispensable to housekeeping in a *mahalla*: chopping wood, cooking on an open fire, fetching water in buckets and washing dishes with water from an irrigation drain.

Another scene shows the daydreams of an elderly woman who imagines herself living in one of the new apartments. The advancing change, as goes the message to the audience, is what Uzbeks are striving for. And so it happens. In the lively comedy, the progressive prevails over the backward. With the help of their friends, a young couple that works on the construction site finally manages to marry and thus evades an arranged marriage planned by the parents. The mud walls give way to apartment houses with balconies and all necessary amenities. In the final scene, happy families move into the newly built apartment house. The elderly woman marvels at the water tap in the light-flooded kitchen, and the first pieces of furniture, which the younger generation brings into the apartment are European-style chairs.[2]

1 The film can be watched in full on Youtube both in Russian and in Uzbek versions: www.youtube.com/watch?v=KUxcI0ZguNM. Accessed 4 July 2022.

2 The traditional sitting furniture in many Central Asian households consists of carpets, specific thin mattresses and pillows placed on the floor or, outside the house, on different types of platforms (wooden or earthen).

https://doi.org/10.1515/9783110658491-004

The film provides a fascinating glimpse into the *zeitgeist* in the Uzbek SSR of the 1960s. At the same time, it depicts the official Soviet vision of the imminent modernisation path that Uzbek society was believed to follow. In this narrative, the traditional *mahallas* were inadequate and unsanitary, not only in a physical sense. What was more, the low-rise adobe brick courtyard houses and the dense network of narrow alleyways were regarded as an urban environment in which backward traditions could persist in the face of modernisation and socialist enlightenment. In turn, the transformation of physical spaces both within households and the cityscape as a whole was expected to bring about social change and facilitate the creation of the new socialist woman, man, and family.[3]

If this transformation could be achieved in Central Asia, many planners and politicians believed, it could be achieved elsewhere too. Under Khrushchev in the 1950s, the Soviet Union had just enhanced its engagement with the former colonies, many of which had now joined the Comecon or the Non-Aligned Movement. For the export of both Soviet technology and communist ideology to these countries, the "Soviet South" was now of pivotal importance. In his recent book on Tajikistan, Kalinovsky meticulously traces how Central Asia became the Soviet Union's "laboratory of socialist development".[4] Experiences and knowledge gathered in the construction and redevelopment of multiple cities in the region found their way into the blueprints for similar projects in Cuba or Afghanistan.[5] Tashkent became Central Asia's socialist showcase city. For the visitors from the "developing countries", the city was to give evidence of the narrative of Soviet urban planners that came, saw, and transformed the Islamic cities of Central Asia into the socialist cityscapes of the future.

This narrative has survived until today, not only in popular history. The fascination with the Soviet mass housing programme has informed much of the academic research on urban transformation in (post-)socialist countries in general.[6]

3 Paul Stronski, *Tashkent. Forging a Soviet City, 1930–1966* (Pittsburgh: University of Pittsburgh Press, 2010), 3.

4 Artemy Kalinovsky, *Laboratory of Socialist Development: Cold War Politics and Decolonization in Soviet Tajikistan* (Ithaca: Cornell University Press, 2018).

5 Hugo Palmarola, and Pedro Ignacio Alonso, "Tropical Assemblage: The Soviet Large Panel in Cuba," in *Beyond Imported Magic: Essays on Science, Technology, and Society in Latin America*, edited by Eden Medina, Ivan da Costa Marques, and Christina Holmes, 159–179 (Cambridge, Mass.: MIT Press, 2014); Elke Beyer, "Competitive Coexistence: Soviet Town Planning and Housing Projects in Kabul in the 1960s." *The Journal of Architecture* 17 (2012): 309–332.

6 Cf. Ernst Giese, "Transformation of Islamic Cities in Soviet Middle Asia into Socialist Cities," in *The Socialist City: Spatial Structure and Urban Policy*, edited by Richard A. French and F.E. Ian Hamilton, 145–166 (Chichester et. al.: Wiley, 1979); Jonas van der Straeten, and Mariya Petrova, "The Soviet City as a Landscape in the Making: Planning, Building and Appropriating Samarkand,

True enough, the program for the industrial prefabrication of apartment houses was unprecedented in the scale of housing construction it achieved. The programme has become a prism through which historians attempt to understand the Soviet Union after the Stalin-Khrushchev break, as it was "one of the most revealing and extensive of the resulting Soviet welfare measures".[7] At the same time, the hastily built *khrushchevki* with their poor quality building fabric, their small flats and lack of elevators have been used to illustrate the deficits of the Soviet command economy.[8] Whatever their verdict may be, few authors put into question the notion that mass housing "shaped the culture and everyday life of nearly all Soviet citizens".[9]

Such generalisations need to be carefully tested, however, especially for the Soviet periphery. The few historical studies that exist on Central Asia have already put into question the narrative of Soviet mass housing as a swift and all-encompassing urban modernisation programme – as regards the process, the distribution of agency, as well as the outcome. Even in the showcase city of Tashkent, building the Soviet city was a contingent and at times messy and disorganised process that often defied the Soviet officials' belief in rational planning. It was also no one-way street. While seldomly being involved directly, local residents left their imprint on the urban redevelopment through a multitude of actions, complaints or responses.[10] The comprehensive study by Paul Stronski on Tashkent, however, ends with the earthquake of 1966, which – in a quite literal sense – cleared the way for the surge in the construction of prefabricated apartment buildings that followed immediately afterwards.

If Soviet urban planning reached its limits in the capital, it did much more so in the second-tier cities that were structurally disadvantaged when it came to the distribution of scarce building resources. For the city of Samarkand in the Uzbek SSR, for example, we have recently demonstrated a degree of (ethno)cultural and material persistence in the cityscape that seems strikingly high, compared to Soviet planners' own ambitions for the city's redevelopment. By and large, Samarkand remained a city of adobe bricks throughout Soviet rule, with prefabricated concrete

---

C. 1960s–80s." *Central Asian Survey* 41 (2022): 297–321. For a review of relevant literature, see Jonas van der Straeten, "Borderlands of Modernity: Explorations into the History of Technology in Central Asia, 1850–2000." *Technology and Culture* 60 (2019): 659–687.

7 Mark B. Smith, *Property of Communists: The Urban Housing Program from Stalin to Khrushchev* (DeKalb: Northern Illinois University Press, 2010), 4.

8 Gregory D. Andrusz, *Housing and Urban Development in the USSR* (London: Macmillan, 1984); Alfred John DiMaio, *Soviet Urban Housing: Problems and Policies* (New York: Praeger, 1974).

9 Philipp Meuser, and Dimitrij Zadorin, *Towards a Typology of Soviet Mass Housing: Prefabrication in the USSR 1955–1991* (Berlin: DOM Publishers, 2015).

10 Stronski, *Tashkent*, 13.

apartment blocks at its fringes only. The self-help construction of private homes not only continued after the start of the mass housing campaign in the late 1950s but was even supported by state authorities. It is traditional courtyard houses and not prefabricated apartment blocks that cover most of the city's space until today.[11] Samarkand is no exceptional case. In 1980, 40 percent of urban housing spaces was still in private hands in the Uzbek SSR and figures in other Central Asian SSRs did not differ significantly.[12] According to a study by Tulaganov et al., 60 to 80 percent of Central Asian dwellings were made of soil in the early 2000s.[13]

Contrary to what our introductory example suggests, the persistence of Central Asia's cultural and architectural legacy in face of the Soviet urbanisation programme created a tension that was never fully resolved. This notion forms the point of departure for this chapter on the Uzbek SSR. Our study focuses on the discussions between those Soviet architects and urban planners who faced the formidable task of producing not only visions but also concrete plans of housing that, despite all systemic limits and constraints, would comply with a complex set of ideological and practical requirements. Certainly, like all architects and planners in the Soviet Union, they were "torn between promises of plenty and rationalizations for scarcity" but the pitfalls of the command economy was not the only tension they had to deal with.[14] They had to negotiate the very notion of Soviet Central Asian urban modernity between "national" identities that were themselves ideological "prefabrications" of Soviet ethnographers, and reconcile this idea with the realities of everyday life and necessity to comply with conceptions of the socialist city and the directive of mass production and standardisation.

Our analysis of professional discourses shows the different and changing strategies that architects adopted for this task. The chapter reveals a broad toolset of approaches, including climatic and demographic studies, to experimental projects for low-rise housing, and attempts to translate elements of local housing culture or the idiosyncrasies of Central Asian family life into the metrics of Soviet

11 Jonas van der Straeten, and Mariya Petrova, "Mud Bricks in a Concrete State: Building, Maintaining and Improving One's Own House in Soviet Samarkand, 1957–1991," in *Histories of Technology's Persistence: Repair, Reuse, and Disposal*, edited by Stefan Krebs, and Heike Weber, 111–137 (Bielefeld: transcript, 2021).

12 Andrusz: *Housing and Urban Development in the USSR*, 291.

13 A. Tulaganov et al., "Housing Construction with Use of Clay Materials in Uzbekistan," in *Kerpic – Living in Earthen Cities* (Istanbul: Istanbul Technical University, 2005) cited in Enrico Fodde, "Traditional Earthen Building Techniques in Central Asia," in *International Journal of Architectural Heritage 3* (2009). 145–168.

14 Greg Castillo, *Cold War on the Home Front: The Soft Power of Midcentury Design* (Minneapolis: University of Minnesota Press, 2010), 204.

urban planning. At the same time, it gives reasons for the inability of planners and architects to develop solutions for redevelopment of the old central quarters that would be both gradual, feasible and accepted among the existing dwellers. Ultimately, except for a handful of small-scale, singular experimental projects, urban planners were stuck with an all-or-nothing approach, that played out very differently in Tashkent in Samarkand. While major parts of old *mahallas* were submerged by high-rise apartment buildings in the capital city, they remained almost entirely untouched in Samarkand.

Our study primarily draws on a textual analysis of the journal *Stroitel'stvo I Arkhitektura Uzbekistana* (Construction and Architecture in Uzbekistan, in the following referred to as SIA) and focuses on the two decades after 1957, when Khrushchev formalised his all-union mass housing policy.[15] The journal articles are complemented with files from the Central State Archive in Tashkent, including, for example, minutes of the Architects Association, and from the City Archive of Samarkand. We furthermore conducted in-depth oral history interviews with architects and owners of houses and apartments in a variety of neighbourhoods and their corresponding modes of housing in Samarkand.

Building, sovietizing, and standardising the Uzbek city: A historical overview, 1924–late 1950s

In the years after the establishment of Soviet rule in Central Asia in 1924, its imprint on the cityscapes of Tashkent and Samarkand remained limited by the construction of singular administrative, public and housing buildings. These buildings featured a mixture of constructivist and oriental styles.[16] Samarkand was the first capital of the young Uzbek SSR until 1930 when Tashkent became the new capital. Both cities featured a dual structure, that included an old Islamic city centre and a colonial city which had been built next to it under Tsarist Russian administration. The construction of new buildings largely remained limited to the latter part of the

15 We have analyzed all issues between 1960 and 1980. The journal's foundation in 1960 was intimately connected with the expansion of the construction industry and different architectural institutions for urban planning in the Uzbek SSR. The journal served as a joint organ of the State Committee for Construction (Gosstroy), the Scientific and Technical Society of the construction industry and the Architects Association of the Uzbek republic.

16 The most comprehensive overview of the architectural heritage from the 1920s to 1930s period is provided by the alerteheritage.org project.

city. In the 1930s, the institutional capacities for urban planning grew considerably after the foundation of several new planning organisations in Tashkent, and the Uzbek branch of the Architects' Union in which ethnic Uzbek architects initially remained rare though.[17] In the course of the decade, urban planners created ambitious general plans for the redevelopment of Tashkent and Samarkand. What these plans had in common was a vision of overcoming the dual structure by demolishing the old Islamic city centres except for their central monuments, and creating entirely new, unified and geometrically arranged structures.[18] The sweeping masterplans of the 1930s were created with few concerns about costs and feasibility. As a result, their imprint on Tashkent, and even more so on Samarkand before World War Two remained relatively benign. Beyond a number of individual residential and public buildings scattered across the city, the construction of entire building ensembles remained a rare exception.[19]

While the shortage of housing space had been one of the most pressing social issues in the Soviet Union since its inception, World War Two came as a major rupture. Not only did the war cause the destruction of housing space in the European frontline cities, but the evacuation and deportation of millions of people also transferred the housing crisis to the Asian periphery of the Soviet Union. The Uzbek Soviet Socialist Republic was not an exception in that regard. Within a short time, its major cities had to accommodate hundreds of thousands of new arrivals from other parts of the Union, along with industries that had been relocated there from the frontlines to save them from the advancing German troops. The hasty and uncoordinated industrialisation thwarted the carefully drafted masterplans as the evacuated enterprises were placed on the first available plots with access to the electric grid and infrastructure.[20]

In the first post-war decade, the Uzbek SSR struggled with a massive housing crisis. After the rapid increase of Uzbekistan's urban population during the war, the figure continued to grow in the first post-war decade due to a high natural population growth rate. According to the census of 1960, the population of Tashkent had grown by a staggering 314,000 people in only ten years to a total of

---

17 See also Stronski, *Tashkent*, 6. Sergej Abashin, *Nacionalizmy V Srednej Azii V Poiskach Identičnosti* (St. Petersburg: Ateleya, 2007); Francine Hirsch, *Empire of Nations: Ethnographic Knowledge and the Making of the Soviet Union, Culture and Society after Socialism* (Ithaca: Cornell University Press, 2005).

18 Stronski, *Tashkent*, 56.

19 For Samarkand, see Christa Diener, and Anette Gangler, *Städte Usbekistans zwischen Tradition und Fortschritt: Städtische Transformationsprozesse der zentralasiatischen Städte Taschkent und Samarkand* (Cottbus: Technische Univ, 2006), 210, 219.

20 Mariya Petrova, *Nah am Boden: Privater Hausbau zwischen Wohnungsnot und Landkonflikt im Samarkand der 1950er- und 60er-Jahre* (Berlin/Boston: DeGruyter, 2021), 36.

879,000 inhabitants. The city of Samarkand had grown at a similar rate from 120,000 to 190,000 inhabitants during the same period.[21] With a per capita living space only 6.3 sqm, the Uzbek SSR ranked well below the Union-wide average in the official statistics.[22] Only 20 percent of state-owned housing space in the Uzbek republic were connected to the water or sewage infrastructures, compared to an average for the Soviet Union of around 50 percent.[23] Under Stalin, heavy industry remained the top priority of economic policy, at the expense of investments in housing and service provision. Investments in housing furthermore remained relatively inefficient regarding the housing space they created. Moreover, a significant share of available resources went into the construction of original, relatively expensive residential buildings of neoclassical grandeur along representative avenues.[24]

It was only after Khrushchev's ascent to power in 1953, that the nascent efforts to address the housing crisis in the more focused and systematic way of the last two Stalin years reached a new level.[25] The necessity to reduce costs for construction became the mayor guiding principle. A decree of 1955 that proclaimed the fight against "excessive decoration on buildings" set a new tone in the discourse on urban housing in the Soviet Union.[26] When including elements that did not serve an immediate functional purpose, architects and urban planners exposed themselves to the risk of being accused of wastefulness. During the mid-1950s, the development of a mass housing programme gained traction and culminated in the decree of 1957, in which the leadership committed to solve the housing crisis once and for all. Within ten to 12 years, the decree stated, every family in the Soviet Union would be provided with a separate and enclosed living space.[27] To achieve this goal, Soviet planners believed, large quantities of housing space would need to be produced at the lowest possible cost. The Soviet administration therefore embarked on a programme for the industrial-scale prefabrication of standardised multistorey apartment buildings.[28]

---

21 Central State Archive of the Republic of Uzbekistan/ Tsentral'nyj Gosudarstvennyj arkhiv Respubliki Uzbekistan (TsGARUz) f. 1619 (Central Department for Statistics/ Tsentral'noe statisticheskoe upravlenie), op.16, d. 4, l. 25.

22 Mitkhat Bulatov, "Zadachi gradostroitelej Uzbekistana." *SIA* 1 (January 1962): 12.

23 TsGARUz, f. 1619, op. 16, d. 4, l. 14.

24 Smith, *Property of Communists*, 32–42.

25 Smith, *Property of Communists*, 21.

26 Decree by the Central Committee of the Communist Party of the USSR from 04.11.1955. "On removal of superfluities in construction." Available online at: www.libussr.ru/doc_ussr/ussr_5043.htm. Accessed 4 July 2022.

27 Decree by the Central Committee of the Communist Party of the USSR from 03.07.1957. Available online at www.libussr.ru/doc_ussr/ussr_5213.htm. Accessed 4 July 2022.

28 Smith, *Property of Communists*, 60.

The mass housing programme under Khrushchev came with an ambitious agenda of Union-wide standardisation under the banner of rationality and social progress. It was a de facto transfer (one might say, an export) of norms of standards from the Soviet Union's European core to its periphery. The decree made the use of a standardised design, called *tipovoi proekt* (literal translation: type project), in each project for new housing construction compulsory.[29] Starting with 1953, the Central Institute for Standardised Planning (Tsentral'nyi institut tipovogo planirovaniya. TsITP), an agency of Gosstroy, was tasked with developing, collecting, systematising these designs and publishing them in catalogues for every existing type of construction: apartment houses, kindergartens, shopping centres, elements for playgrounds, boiler-rooms, etc. Between 1955 and 1966 branches of the institute were created in several regions. The branch responsible for the Central Asian republics was located in Kazakhstan. The type projects themselves were then designed in the institutions of the respective Soviet republics and approved by the regional branch. Local planning organisations could then choose appropriate variants for particular construction project as blueprints. Their ability to choose, however, was usually limited by the capacities and the particular setup of the large-scale factories where prefabricated panels would be produced (*Domostroitel'nyj Kombinat, DSK*).

The so-called sanitary norm of 9 sqm living space per person became the basis for the planning of further type projects.[30] Standardised formulas were used to calculate averages for key parameters in housing: the size of the families, the respective size of apartments and the individual rooms, or the residents' demands for goods and service. Other parameters such as distance to the public services, for example transport, came into play for the planning of entire neighbourhoods, the micro-districts (*mikroraion*) which had become the basic unit for urban planning. In these ideal-typical self-contained neighbourhoods, Soviet planners expected to reconcile the directive of maximising of housing production, the promise of providing separate family apartments and the communist idea of communal living.[31]

---

29 The idea for standardized projects to save costs for new planning dated back to the late 1920s and early 1930s: with several decrees that ordered various measures for standardization and first steps of industrialization of construction. Exchange and cooperation with European architects, like Ernst May left a strong imprint on urban planning practices. Cf. Yulia Kosenkova, ed. *Sovetskoe gradostroitel'stvo 1917–1941. Kniga vtoraya* (Moscow: Progress-Traditsiya, 2018), 1079.

30 Soviet statistics on housing differentiated between living space and overall space. The former did not include utility-rooms (*khozyaistvennye pomeshcheniya*) like toilets, baths and kitchens.

31 Smith, *Property of Communists*, 116–117.

In the Uzbek SSR, the construction of the first type projects started in 1956 in Chilanzar, a model district for the new form of socialist housing in Tashkent. Chilanzar provided a taste of the monotone sight of apartment blocks that became characteristic for the new micro-districts. Only four different type projects with a similar layout were produced by Uzgosproekt for the micro-district; three types were for brick construction and only one type for panel construction.[32] The fact that these type projects had not undergone any adaptation to local social or environmental conditions was not of concern to responsible municipal planners and architects in the Uzbek SSR of the late 1950s. The decree of 1957 had further increased the pressure to create new housing space at a fast rate, leaving little leeway for adaptation. What was more, the planning of the type projects was based on the premise that all peoples of the Soviet Union would undergo a similar path of societal modernisation in the future. Rather than providing location-specific solutions, planners and architects were focused on the provision of amenities they considered appropriate for the different stages of socialist development.

After the completion of the first mass housing projects, however, some of the downsides of this approach became too apparent to be ignored. People began complaining publicly, for example in readers' letters, about monotonous views, the poor quality of assembly, the lack of greenery and of maintenance facilities. For the typical Central Asian household, that consisted of large, often multigenerational families, the two- and three-room apartments proved to be too small.[33] During the extreme heat of the Central Asian summer concrete walls and roofs turned the flats into veritable stone ovens and even in case the apartments featured small balconies, the latter proved to be unsuited to providing outdoor living space in the summer (*letnee pomeshchenie*).[34] Soon after moving in, people began closing their balconies, using self-made window-frames, bricks or plywood in order to expand their living space.[35] This practise did not go unnoticed among architects and active readers – the journal reacted with caricatures and published a reader's letter that proposed establishing a central supply of prefabricated window frames that residents could use – at their own cost – to close balconies

32 Inna Gordeeva, "Proshlo chetyre goda." *SIA* 2 (1960): 36–39. Uzgosproekt was the central planning agency/institution of the Uzbek ministry for construction (Gosstroi).

33 Until 1963, no four room flats were built at all and later only on very low scale; see Lyudmila Rusanova, "Demografiya I zhilishche na primere Samarkanda." *SIA* 3 (1968): 30.

34 Stronski, *Tashkent*, 227–228.

35 For similar practices in Vietnam, see Christina Schwenkel, *Building Socialism: The Afterlife of East German Architecture in Urban Vietnam* (Durham, London: Duke University Press, 2020).

without disturbing the character of the building facade.[36] Not surprisingly, many Central Asian families were unwilling to move into the new apartments. Leonid Volynskii, a Russian traveller and journalist to Uzbekistan in 1961 who published his experiences in an article in the journal *Novyi Mir*, noted that in summer, the temperature in the traditional mud-brick homes in Tashkent was four or five degrees cooler than elsewhere in the city – including the Chilanzar district, for which he had only harsh criticism.[37]

Against clay and climate: The functional dilemma of mass housing in Uzbekistan in the early 1960s

At the turn of the 1950s and 1960s, the shortcomings of the first mass-housing projects in the Uzbek SSR had become a widely accepted diagnosis among architects and urban planners. This diagnosis prompted lively discussions at the meetings of the Architects' Association and in the newly founded journal *Stroitel'stvo I Arkhitektura Uzbekistana*. The debate unfolded in the context of the political thaw under Khrushchev that would allow – within certain boundaries – for a relatively open and, at times, critical professional discourse on housing.

During one of the conferences of the Architects' union, for example, Alexander Yakushev criticised the methods of planning type projects in the republic. Without questioning the concept of the type project per se, he criticised the lack of a proper scientific basis for planning and the uncritical acceptance of standards that had not been tested and approved for the local conditions in the Uzbek SSR. With a sarcastic undertone, he praised the success in reducing the costs of construction, while pointing out that this had led to neglect of aesthetic considerations in architecture and housing construction.[38] In an article in the journal that summarised the first four years of mass housing construction in Tashkent, Inna Gordeeva, an architect from one of the numerous planning institutions in Tashkent, issued an unveiled criticism of "inexpressive and monotonous" designs and poor assembling quality that "exacerbated the overall impression", and neglected residential and public infrastructure like public greenery and recreational areas.[39] Mitkhat Bulatov, the head architect of Tashkent, addressed the same problems at domestic and union-level conferences.

36 I. Irkutov, "Protiv samodeyatel'nykh krasot." *Stroitel'stvo i Arkhitektura Srednei Azii* 9 (September 1964): 17.
37 Leonid Volynskij, "Doroga k novoi zemle." *Novyi Mir* 12 (December 1961): 121–127.
38 TsGARUz, f.2532, op. 1, d. 256, ll. 46–49.
39 Gordeeva, "Proshlo chetyre goda".

He also lamented the delays in the construction of public infrastructure in newly build micro-districts, most notably social infrastructure, that left the newly built apartment buildings poorly serviced.[40] The criticism, however, never put into question the political administration and its housing policy as such. Sober assessments of the overall situation were expressed together with commitments to the targets – the calculated optimism of the party directives could not be objected.

Until the mid-1960s, the debate was characterised by a highly ambivalent stance towards the architectural legacy of Uzbek cities. Many authors shared a pronounced aversion to vernacular architecture. In their eyes, the modest and lacklustre aesthetics and the profane materiality of the mud-brick courtyard houses were incompatible with the idea of a modern socialist city. In the leading article on urban redevelopment of April 1960, an anonymous author claimed that "the necessity of reconstructing of the old city centres is beyond doubt, as the primitive, unhygienic and ramshackle housing is not appropriate to enter the era of communism".[41] Even though a reconstruction of the city centre would first require the demolition of old housing space that amounted to 30 or even 50 percent of the newly created space, the author saw it as the "most urgent political task for promoting hygiene and health", regardless of the costs. In the same manner, Mitkhat Bulatov, declared 9 out of 17 million square metres of existing housing unworthy of preservation in 1962.[42] Proponents of the demolition of old Islamic city centres also argued with the moral imperative of improving what they assumed to be appalling living conditions in the old quarters. In the dense network of narrow alleyways, they put forward, it would be almost impossible to provide networked infrastructure services such as water, sewerage or gas.[43]

The assumed backwardness of vernacular architecture offered a supposedly easy answer to a fundamental decision that architects, urban planners and state officials had to make: Should building resources be directed to the more cost-efficient construction of apartment buildings on the cities' outskirts, or to the reconstruction of the traditional, low-rise, Islamic city centres? After all, both types of housing competed for scarce building land. The rapid territorial expansion of Uzbekistan's major cities already caused concern among Soviet administrators as it came at the expense of the surrounding *kolkhozes*. The fertile land in the oases accounted for only 6 percent of the republic's whole territory.[44] The problem of

---

40 See the report from the 3rd Forum of Soviet Architects, Moscow, May 1961 in Konstantin Babievskij, "Tretij forum sovetskikh arkhitektorov." *SIA* 2 (1961): 34.

41 N. a., "Sostoyanie i zadachi gradostroitel'stva v Uzbekistane." *SIA* 2 (1960): 1–3.

42 Mitkhat Bulatov, "Zadachi gradostroitelej Uzbekistana," 12.

43 N. a., "Sostoyanie i zadachi gradostroitel'stva v Uzbekistane."

44 Mitkhat Bulatov, "Zadachi gradostroitelej Uzbekistana."

territorial expansion was exacerbated by extensive individual construction, which was intensively supported by the state between 1957 and 1962. The municipal administration issued plots and housing loans to those willing to build houses on their own and for those people who had been evicted to make space for state projects. This form of construction remained controversial, yet its treatment by the authorities continued to be very inconsistent as the recurring bans were compromised by various exceptions and de facto toleration of self-help building.[45]

Furthermore, the land shortage and insufficient capacities to house evicted dwellers put serious constraints on the possibilities of large-scale demolition, especially in Samarkand. These issues, however, were never addressed in the discussions printed in the journal. In a combination of detachment from what was happening on the ground and ignorance, planning institutions continued drawing up ambitious plans for the reconstruction of city centres as a photo from 1963 shows. In this architectural model of the prospective socialist transformation of the city centre of Samarkand old Islamic neighborhoods would be entirely replaced by multistorey, prefabricated residential buildings that lined roads radiating from the historical Registan complex (Fig. 1).[46]

While dismissing most of the existing housing stock in the cities as unworthy of preservation, architects were directed to identify the "progressive" elements of traditional architecture and incorporate them into the design for these new projects alongside the imperative of national in form, socialist in content. As it had become apparent that the existing prefabricated apartment buildings were ill-suited to local conditions, especially to the hot summer in Uzbekistan, many authors suggested that the traditional architecture of the region had to offer practical and "rational" solutions to alleviate the effects of the summer heat. In several articles, they discussed different technical elements for sun protection on windows, ventilation in the houses, and for the creation of an agreeable microclimate and of shaded outdoor space beyond the small, standardised balconies that turned out to be useless during the hot summer.[47] In the early 1960s, however, these discussions mostly revolved around functional aspects of the prefabricated apartment buildings. While architects consented to the need to adjust their layouts and building standards of these multistorey apartment houses, their primacy as the most rational type of housing remained unchallenged as it was declared to be the cheapest and the question of cost was a pivotal factor.

45 Petrova, *Nah am Boden*, 53–87.

46 Printed in *SIA* 1 (1964): 34.

47 Pulat Zakhidov, "Arkhitektura shiipana I voprosy proevetrivaniya." *SIA* 5 (1961): 28–29; J. Sulejmanov, "Diskussiya po voprosam organizatsii zhil'ya." *SIA* 4 (1962): 32–33.

Fig. 1: A model for the redevelopment of Samarkand's city centre.
Source: *Stroitel'stvo I Arkhitektura Srednei Azii, 01/1964, p.34.*

The contradictory nature of this assumption was hard to ignore, given the broad consensus among architects that low-rise housing (two to three stories) with shaded courtyards or small garden plots was best suited for the local climate. As families in the old city centres remained reluctant to move into the new apartments, architectural research institutions acknowledged the necessity of building neighbourhoods that were better suited to the social structure of the local Central Asian population. In the mid-1960s, researchers from these institutions therefore set out to explore a physical and social space that had been largely arcane to them: the Uzbek *mahalla*.

Measuring the *mahalla*: Making sense of "Uzbek" people and spaces in the mid-1960s

In 1965, the Tashkent Zonal Research Institute for Experimental Planning (*Tashkentskij zonal'nyj nauchno-issledovatel'skij institut eksperimental'nogo planirovaniya*, TASHZNIIEP) began developing proposals for an experimental project in the old city centre of Tashkent. Named after the "mahalla", the Uzbek term for a traditional neighbourhood, the project was aimed at reconstructing one of the districts while taking account of the area's "specific features" – for example, its demographic structure, daily life and microclimate.[48] Results from the project, that were presented and discussed in several journal articles in the late 1960s and early 1970s, revealed a relatively benign and culturally sensitive approach towards urban modernisation. Tellingly, a report on the project in the 1968 issue by the project leader Zlata Chebotareva would remain the only one by an author throughout the journal's history who explicitly reflected on the interests and concerns of the mahalla's dwellers.[49] As one of the most important conditions for the project's success, for example, Chebotareva named a sequential process of construction and resettlement, that would ensure that residents could continue living within the district boundaries. She justified this condition with the observation that the "local population values neighbourhood and family ties that have developed over the course of several generations and it is not prone to migration".[50]

The project offers detailed insight into how planners and architects tried to render the complex social and material conditions in the *mahalla* legible and translate them into the terms, concepts and metrics of their own professional discourse.[51] For this purpose, the institute's scientific department conducted studies of the population's demographic structure, field surveys to study the dwellers' everyday habits and analyses of the spatial composition of the existing neighbourhood. Articles by the project's members now recognised that the demographic reality in the Uzbek SSR was a far cry from the figures that the planners had taken as a basis for the first mass housing projects. For calculating the size of flats for the Uzbek families, the planners had assumed an average family size that was only a slight adjustment of the Union-wide average family size of 3.2 persons. In an article from 1968, Rusanova lamented the uselessness of the average figures for the planning of urban housing schemes, calling attention to the high variation of family sizes across different cities and the districts within these

48 See Zlata Chebotareva, "Opyt proektirovaniya eksperimental'nykh mikroraionov-mahlla v Tashkente." *SIA* 7 (1968): 11–15. For another aspect of the study, see Svetlana Moiseeva, "Organizatsiya kul'turno-bytovogo obsluzhivaniya pri rekonstrukcii gorodov Uzbekistana." *SIA* 10 (1966): 32–36.

49 I. Vukolova, "Zhenshchiny-Arkhitektory i stroiteli Uzbekistana." *SIA* 1 (1976): 3–4.

50 Chebotareva, "Opyt proektirovaniya," 11.

51 For the concept of legibility, see James C. Scott, *Seeing Like a State: How Certain Schemes to Improve the Human Condition Have Failed* (New Haven, Conn.: Yale University Press, 1998). For a more detailed account on how Soviet architects in the Uzbek SSR attempted to incorporate traditional and practical knowledge into their planning practice, see Mariya Petrova, and Jonas van der Straeten, "Wissen, Bauen und urbaner Wandel im sowjetischen Usbekistan der 1960er Jahre." *Moderne Stadtgeschichte* 1 (2021): 83–101.

cities. Especially in the old city, larger families with more than a half of all children under seven years in the old parts dominated the picture.[52]

Other authors had already outlined the challenges this type of family presented to the planning of housing projects. In the census for the Uzbek SSR of 1959, 17 percent of families had been classified as "big families" which consisted of more than six family members. The census differentiated between two types of big family that both came with their own requirements for urban housing. The first type of big family were parents with many children. Most planners agreed that they could not be housed adequately in the relatively small apartments of the multistorey buildings but only in one-two storey townhouses with a courtyard, that were specifically designed for this type of family. The second type was the 'complex' or 'conglomerate' family that included several elements of an extended family – a typical case was a household that consisted of a married couple, its children, and the husband's parents. The composition of these families was in constant flux, the authors claimed. According to a survey conducted in 1965, 94 percent of conglomerate families intended to split up once the housing situation improved.[53]

Another element of rendering the *mahallas* legible was an assessment of their spatial composition. As the project members found, this composition hardly complied with the functional requirements that the authors regarded as essential for a modern neighbourhood. Almost all the territory was built with privately owned one- or two-storey houses and 6 to 7 percent of the total space was covered by roads with a width of only 6 to 8 metres. Spaces for public use were almost absent (about 1 sqm per person on average). The same applied to public greenery. At the same time, the author acknowledged the advantages that this kind of spatial arrangement offered in the hot climate: narrow streets were protected by the shadow of the walls, blind walls of densely built houses protected the living space from dust and sound of the street. Small, shaded courtyards with an average size of 60 sqm served as an outdoor living space during the seven to eight warm months of the year and provided for temperatures that were 4 to 5 degrees lower than inside the houses.[54]

Notably, Chebotareva did not make any mention of preserving the existing housing stock. On the contrary, much like her colleagues, she saw an "urgent necessity to reconstruct those areas where the adobe housing of the local type was predominant".[55] The self-proclaimed goal for the experimental project was to

---

52 Rusanova, "Demografiya I zhilishche," 28–30.
53 Rusanova "Demografiya I zhilishche," 30.
54 Chebotareva, "Opyt proektirovaniya," 11.
55 Chebotareva, "Opyt proektirovaniya."

develop new housing that would make provisions for the specific demographics of the old districts in the city centres and incorporate in the designs for modern houses the "positive aspects of a traditional Uzbek town house".[56] Accordingly, on the level of the neighbourhood, the project aimed at developing concepts that would reconcile the social and spatial composition of the *mahalla* with the requirements of the 'micro-district' (*mikroraion*).

After some preparatory work on a rather conceptual level, the project team presented its first five versions of the *mahalla-mikroraion*.[57] All models featured a combination of high-rise apartment buildings of four, nine and up to 16 stories and of two-story buildings with flats on both levels and small courtyards for families with many children. It was, however, only the model created by Chebotareva herself that favoured these low-rise buildings as the dominant form of housing that would take up 80 percent of the territory. In her model, houses would be arranged in a block wise and dense way, thus replicating the existing spatial structure of the neighbourhood.[58] Chebotareva would remain a vocal proponent of low-rise housing in the journal throughout the 1970s.

Eventually, the *mahalla* project would remain without having any substantial material impact on the cityscape of Tashkent. The construction of the first building series was due in 1969 but did not materialise in the proposed form. A likely reason lies in the earthquake of 1966, that opened the possibility of reconstructing the city centre on a much larger scale.[59] But even after 1966, experimental schemes in Tashkent were only implemented on a very small scale. Nonetheless, the TASHZNIIEP project was among the most important initiatives for creating a consciousness about local forms and types of houses that would give rise to a broader debate on the topic in the 1970s.

Imaginaries of the new, comforts of the old: Interpretations of low-rise housing in Tashkent in the 1970s

In the early 1970s, the number of articles in the journal that discussed a specific Uzbek pathway of urban modernisation surged. The increase in publications

56 Chebotareva, "Opyt proektirovaniya."
57 For the preparatory work, see Moiseeva, "Organizatsiya kul'turno-bytovogo obsluzhivaniya."
58 Chebotareva, "Opyt proektirovaniya," 13.
59 Stronski, *Tashkent*.

reflected the growing research capacities and the number of institutes involved in urban planning, most of which were based in Tashkent.[60]

Some of the authors continued to discuss how certain technical or constructional elements of the 'traditional' local architecture could be abstracted and incorporated into the standardised design of prefabricated apartment buildings for mass housing. These articles revolved, for example, around ventilation methods and allocation of special rooms inside the buildings.[61] Other authors presented concepts for high-rise apartment buildings with courtyards.[62] Iosif Notkin, architect and art historian, and head of the section for the reconstruction of the cities in UZNIIP *gradostroitel'stva*[63] dedicated several articles to the search for an optimal geometric form of an inner courtyard – including an attempt to find a formula for an ideal *Aiwan*, a mixture between a roofed pergola and a terrace that formed the centerepiece of a traditional Uzbek courtyard house.[64] While reflecting the official requirement to provide "correct" and "scientifically approved" solutions, these authors were criticised by some of their colleagues for being too theoretical.[65]

After all, the architects and planners could now draw on a considerably expanding knowledge base, for example regarding the demography of Uzbek cities. While the lack of local statistical data, had caused planners in the 1960s to extrapolate demographic figures based on union-wide general data, new studies now provided differentiated insights into the demographic structure of different cities in the republic, down to the ethnic composition of the different districts in the cities.[66] Researchers increasingly paid attention to the "peculiarities of every-day

60 Isaak Israilov, "Uzbekskij nauchno-issledovatel'skij I proektnyj institut po gradostroitel'stvu I ego razvitie." *SIA* 1 (1974): 35. The organigram shows the growth and expansion of numerous planning and construction institutions from 1925 till 1969.

61 Ozkhon Dzhabbar, "Skvoznoe provetrivanie kvartir v mnogoetazhnykh zhylykh domakh vertikal'nymi tokami vozdukha cherez shakhtu sposobom 'hashtaka.'" *SIA* 9 (1969): 17–20.; Ozkhon Dzhabbar, "Tipy planirovochnykh struktur kvartir mnogoetazhnykh domov Tashkenta." *SIA* 2 (1975): 15–19.

62 See, for example, Savelij Rozenblum, and Irina Shakhnazarova, "Prikvartirnye dvoriki v mnogoetazhnom zhilishche." *SIA* 1 (1973); Tamara Isaeva, and Zlata Chebotareva, "Planirovochnye vozmozhnosti eksperimental'nogo zhilogo doma s blokirovannymi letnimi pomeshcheniyami." *SIA* 3 (1973): 19–22.

63 Uzbek Research Institute for Urban Planning.

64 Iosif Notkin, "Klassifikatsiya letnikh pomeshchenij v narodnom zhilishche Uzbekistana (Khiva i Tashkent)." *SIA* 6 (1968): 30–33; Iosif Notkin, and L.P. Makarova, "Prostranstvennaya sruktura I prognoz mikroklimata vnutrennikh dvorikov v maloetazhnom zhil'e Uzbekistana." *SIA* 7 (1971): 36–39.

65 Quoted in Il'ya Merport, "K voprosu o preemstvennosti v arkhitekture." *SIA* 3 (1969): 18–20.

66 Lyudmila Rusanova, "Zhilishche I demograficheskie faktory." *SIA* 2 (1973): 24–26.

life" (*osobennosti mestnogo byta*) and their spatial implications in order to improve the planning of micro-districts and the provision of services in them.[67]

TASHZNIIEP, for example, conducted sociological studies on the space utilisation and everyday demands of dwellers in the newly built micro districts. When publishing their results in the journal, the authors highlighted the "everyday household traditions" of the different ethnic groups in the micro districts and the respective requirements towards the apartments these traditions implied.[68] The studies furthermore tried to quantify the gender-specific amount of household work with the goal of planning a service infrastructure that would 'liberate' the housewives.[69] Seemingly astonished, the authors noted that the "local population tends to maintain the established and habitual [*privychnye*] household traditions and means of communication even after moving into modern housing". By interpreting some of these traditions as 'progressive' forms of collectivism and mutual help (*vzaimopomoshch*), they displayed at the same time astonishing ideological flexibility but also a superficial understanding of the social and cultural reality in the micro districts.[70]

The discussion on adequate housing in the urban centre reached a new level after the completion of the first experimental projects allowing for first-hand observations and comparisons. What the researchers found, however, was not always easy to reconcile with their preconceptions about the role of housing for societal progress. An article on the housing of families with many children by Roman Kontorer, a researcher for TASHZNIIEP, is a case in point. His article begins with the observation that these families, after learning about the inconveniences of the multistorey apartment houses, had become generally reluctant to move into comfortable (*blagoustroennye*) houses.[71] This observation had led TASHZNIIEP to conduct a study comparing the suitability of different housing forms for big families: The researchers visited and surveyed: a *mahalla* (Fig. 2); an area that featured more recently built private houses; the area where the experimental project with prefabricated townhouses had recently been completed, and an area with prefabricated multistorey apartment buildings.

67 Svetlana Moiseeva, Tat'yana Zimakova, "Nekotorye osobennosti perspektivnogo razvitiya kul'turno-bytovogo obsluzhivaniya v Srednei Azii." *SIA* 6 (1972): 24–27.
68 Margarita Budagova, Tat'yana Zimakova, and Lyudmila Rusanova, "Zhilye kompleksy s obsluzhivaniem dlya IV zony." *SIA* 4 (1973): 36–38.
69 Budagova, et al., "Zhilye kompleksy s obsluzhivaniem dlya IV zony," 36–38.
70 Budagova, et al., "Zhilye kompleksy s obsluzhivaniem dlya IV zony," 36–38.
71 Roman Kontorer, "Rasselenie mnogodetnykh semei v usloviyakh Uzbekistana." *SIA* 8 (1971): 34.

Fig. 2: Street scene of a traditional mahalla as depicted in the article by Kontorer.
Source*: Stroitel'stvo I Arkhitektura Usbekistana,* 08/ 1971, p. 35.

What the researchers had observed in the *mahalla,* seems to have jumbled up the tidy timelines of societal progress that constituted the underlying narrative for his article:

> The apartments are electrified, equipped with radios, and many families have TV's and so on. Nonetheless, in spite of the desire for the improvement of public services [*blagoustroistvo*] and an increased level of domestic culture and comfort, the very existence of a primitive housing structure and the crowded, uncomfortable housing in itself, which has evolved as result of the influence of outdated socio-economic factors, [. . .] not just delays the natural improvement of the everyday culture in the households [*povyshenie kul'tury byta*], but contributes to the persistence of certain reactionary traits and remnants of the traditional everyday life.[72]

72 Kontorer, "Rasselenie mnogodetnykh semej," 35.

The impression in the quote of a cognitive dissonance is further supported by his detailed description of the grapevines in the yard, of the "wooden platforms that are arranged for eating, relaxing and sleeping" in the summer, and of the small canals that were running through the yards. None of these observations convinced Kontorer to reconsider his outright dismissal of the old cities as inherently backwards and uncomfortable.

From residents of the experimental "modern" townhouses, in turn, Kontorer cited several complaints. The researchers had studied an area where the houses had been arranged in a checkerboard pattern to create courtyards in the empty spaces between them (Fig. 3). The dense arrangement of two-storey buildings, however, prevented a proper circulation of air, so residents lamented the bad ventilation in the yards. What was more, people in the courtyards – particularly women – were exposed to the views of neighbours, a fact that presented a major issue for traditional Muslim families. A linear allocation of the houses and plots received a higher approval by the residents. The requirements of big families, Kontorer concluded, were still not addressed adequately in the experimental housing schemes. The apartments' maximum number of four rooms was still insufficient for families consist of seven to 12 people. Low-rise housing, he insisted, should only be implemented as a niche solution for those very large families with preschool children. For them, the respective micro districts should consist of two-storey apartments with five to six rooms, built on plots of not less than 70 sqm that were aligned in a linear fashion.[73]

Kontorer's article illustrates why most Soviet architects, in their attempts to appropriate the idea of standardised and mass-produced urban housing to the requirements of big families in Uzbekistan, remained stuck in their own preconceptions of hygiene, comfort, and service provision. Their interpretations of existing conditions, and hence their designs for new housing reflected a preconceived notion about which ensemble of technologies, materials and practises qualified as signifiers of societal progressiveness in a linear conception of urban modernisation. The coexistence of what was perceived as "old" and "new" technologies had no place in their interpretation – and hence no gradualist approaches to urban development were adopted. Furthermore, the understanding of housing remained an almost exclusively functionalist one, even when it came to local "traditions and particularities of everyday life". In terms of its specific housing cultures, social organisation, or the ideas and ethics of family and household organisation, the Uzbek *mahalla* remained an opaque place for the architects, almost none of whom were of Central Asian origin.

73 Kontorer, "Rasselenie mnogodetnykh semej," 35.

Fig. 3: Aerial view of the experimental schemes for low-rise housing as part of the mahalla project. Source: *Stroitel'stvo I Arkhitektura Usbekistana* 08/ 1971, p. 36.

Tellingly, the sole voice that drew attention to the cultural meaning of different spaces in an Uzbek house, was the only architect with an Uzbek surname to participate in the discussion. In his contribution from September 1971, Khairulla Pulatov describes in detail the organisation of an Uzbek house, highlighting the cultural importance of hospitality and the necessity of a courtyard for family events, and of sizeable rooms to sleep guests or their own children.[74]

In the end, those voices who argued that low-rise housing should remain a niche solution for large families within the wider redevelopment of Uzbek cities maintained the upper hand in the debate, while the majority of such projects anyway remained on paper. In 1974, Chebotareva complained that respective pilot projects for low-rise housing based on her teams' proposals from 1966 were insufficient in design and scope to be able to prove their value. In the article she repeats her demand for more low-rise housing in cities with a hotter climate, lower infrastructural capacities and in historical city centres.[75] Her demand was to no avail. At the same time, the idea of building low-rise houses in the historical

74 Khairulla Pulatov, "Planirovochnaya struktura narodnogo zhil'ya Tashkentskoi oblasti." *SIA* 9 (1971): 17–19.

75 Zlata Chebotareva, "V zashchitu plotnoi maloetazhnoi zastroiki." *SIA* 11 (1974): 14–18.

centeres connected to another big discussion that concerned architectural heritage that presented another large challenge for urban redevelopment.

Dealing with heritage, staging Uzbek history: The redevelopment of Samarkand in the 1960s and 1970s

If creating the modern Uzbek city was an endeavour that came with many contradictions on the functional level, it was even more so on the level of aesthetics. While a union-wide decree of 1955 had banned the "excessive decoration" of buildings, the central doctrine for architectural projects that were "national in form and socialist in content" remained in place – now refined with the appeal to extract the inherent logic of traditional architecture instead of just superficially copying it.[76] In the journal and at conferences, architects tried to solve the riddle presented to them by this double bind, as Boris Chukhovich describes it.[77] In practice, the directive instead provided architects in the Uzbek SSR with a welcome excuse to deviate from those standards that their colleagues in the European part of the Soviet Union were still "abiding by to the letter."[78]

When it came to the reconstruction of entire inner cities with their dual core consisting of a colonial and an old Islamic part, the tensions between modernisation and the "national form" became increasingly difficult to resolve, especially in cities like Samarkand and Bukhara that were renowned for their rich cultural and architectural heritage. The Venice Charta of 1964 and the subsequent foundation of ICOMOS (International Council on Monuments and Sites) in 1965, a professional organisation that the Soviet Union had joined, put the topic on the international agenda and probably contributed to the start of a critical discussion among local architects.[79] At the meeting of the Architects' Union in May and June 1964, the participants controversially discussed proposals for an internal contest for the redevelopment of the historical city centre around the Registan Square in Samarkand in connection to the masterplan for the city. Now, the project presented a year earlier (Fig. 1) drew fierce criticism for

76 For the decree, see www.libussr.ru/doc_ussr/ussr_5043.htm. Accessed 4 July 2022.
77 Boris Chukhovich, "Orientalist modes of modernism in architecture: Colonial/Postcolonial/Soviet." *Études de lettres* 2–3 (2014): 266.
78 Boris Chukhovich, "Building the 'living East,'" in *Soviet Modernism. 1955–1991 Unkhown History*, edited by Katharina Ritter, and Waltraud Bayer, 214–237 (Vienna: Park Books, 2012), 217.
79 Galina Pugachenkova, "K sozdaniyu regional'noi initsiativnoi gruppy respublik Srednei Azii sovetskogo komiteta ICOMOSA." *SIA* 6 (1982): 31–33.

placing new housing in the "monumental zone" (*zona pamyatnikov*). As construction works had already started, the discussants exchanged different opinions on how to proceed. Finally, the meeting resolved that the Architects' Union would request that Gosstroi stop the project and call for a new all-union tender.[80]

While the minutes of the meetings provide only a rough summary of the discussion, two years later in 1966 Il'ya Notkin and Konstantin Kryukow provide a more elaborated argument for the concerns regarding the practises of reconstructing historical cities.[81] Not only individual monuments like mosques and mausoleums deserve preservation, they argue, but the whole architectural ensemble, including old residential houses, bazaar streets and the like. They explicitly criticise the construction of five-storey apartment blocks just opposite Samarkand's historical Registan square – the part of the project that obviously could not been stopped. These apartment blocks would cause harm to the monuments' "dominating role" and distort the existing proportions of the whole ensemble. The monuments would "lose their natural backdrop, of the material surrounding, that is formally not protected by the state".[82] The article marked the point of departure for a discussion in the journal on how to modernise existing urban structures while maintaining their "charm of antiquity".

The quote shows that Notkin and Krukow, along with other participants of this discussion, primarily argued along lines of architectural aesthetics and the "best possible visual perception".[83] As far as the materiality of the old neighbourhoods was concerned, they shared their colleagues' aversion to clay. While admitting that the preservation of the existing housing stock, coupled with a reduction of the population density, would present an ideal solution to the aesthetic problem, they considered it technically unfeasible. The adobe construction, they argued, was not durable, vulnerable to earthquakes, too dark, lacked amenities, and was therefore not modern. Thus, the authors called for a type of housing that would be modern on the inside but emulate the "traditional" exterior of the traditional adobe-brick houses. Unlike the parallel discussion on the experimental projects in Tashkent, this debate remained entirely detached from those people living in the respective neighbourhood and their requirements and interests. In the eyes of the authors, the old city centres should primarily serve as tourist attractions, renovated in a way that would please the sight of visitors.[84]

80 TsGARUz, f. 2532, op. 2, d. 21, ll. 61–72.
81 Il'ya Notkin, and Konstantin Kryukov, "Rekonstruktsiya drevnikh gorodov i problemy sokhraneniya pamyatnikov arkhitektury Uzbekistana." *SIA* 11 (1966): 27–30.
82 Notkin, and Kryukov, "Rekonstruktsiya," 28.
83 Notkin, and Kryukov, "Rekonstruktsiya," 26.
84 Notkin, and Kryukov, "Rekonstruktsiya," 26.

This perspective brought together the growing consciousness of the touristic potential that the historical heritage of many cities throughout the Soviet Union could have and the concern for the preservation of this heritage. Architects and art-historians started to raise questions about the criteria and rules for construction in the historical city centres and monument preservation areas, criticised the lack of coordination and a regulatory basis to determine the value of existing architecture. They further argued for the necessity of scientifically based planning and the need for studies on historical urban centres that would provide help and orientation for the reconstruction plans.[85]

One of the most comprehensive contributions to this debate is presented in the July issue of the journal in 1972 that was completely dedicated to the topic. It contained another critique of current practises of urban redevelopment co-authored by Notkin. In addition to the earlier argument about the existing adobe-brick housing as a part of the architectural ensemble, the authors now paid attention to the fact that the old city was "being constantly regenerated", referring to the local practises of maintenance and periodical reconstruction.[86] While admitting that living and adjusting the house to the needs of its dwellers is the best preservation they also complain that these reconstruction works or the installation of electricity and networked infrastructure services, "distort the originality" of the houses. Here the ambivalence about the target conflict of preserving the historical and art value (*hudozhestvennaya tsennost'*) of the city center on the one side, and the urge to either modernise or musealise them on the other becomes especially obvious.

The rest of the issue was dedicated to a comprehensive report on a study of Samarkand's historical zone by TASHZNIIEP that had been conducted with the goal of equipping urban planners with detailed information on the architectonical composition and historical value of existing buildings.[87] The study presented an inventory of the existing structure of the old city – the streets and alleyways, the irrigation system, traditional water reservoirs (*hauz*), small district mosques and service infrastructure. The report furthermore contained proposals for establishing a touristic zone which some authors termed an 'ethnographic protection zone' (*etnograficheskij zapovednik*) and advocated the introduction of an urban heritage zone in the centre to protect the building stock that formed the backdrop to the city's key monuments.

85 Liya Man'kovskaya, "O rabote sektsii istorii arkhitektury, restavratsii i okhrany pamyatnikov (1967–1971)." *SIA* 8 (1971): 20–21.

86 Il'ya Notkin, and Inna Gordeeva, "Pamyatniki arkhitektury i rekonstruktsiya gorodov Uzbekistana." *SIA* 7 (1972): 7–11.

87 "Issledovanie istoricheskoi zony Samarkanda." *SIA* 7 (1972): 12–24.

Again, in line with the entire discourse on urban heritage, existing traditional housing was almost exclusively discussed in terms of its aesthetic appearance, completely detached not only from its social and cultural context, but even from its main function as a place where people live. Boris Chukhovich compares this orientalist and voyeuristic desire of the architects to turn the homes of people and their lives into an "ethnographic museum" and draws parallels with the attitude of the European architects in the colonial Maghrib and India.[88] For the majority of actively publishing architects, traditional *mahalas* and housing still represented a picturesque orient.

The subsequent years did not see a major shift in the debate as architects, oftentimes the same protagonists as in the 1960s and 1970s, now increasingly acknowledged the persistence of the traditional housing or even the fact that its dwellers did not want to change their housing practises and places.[89] In 1985, at the dawn of *perestroika*, two authors pointed out in a critical retrospective on Samarkand's urban development that the "'old town' is not a museum piece, but lives an active life, full of context and demands preservation and maintenance".[90] Now the plan for the historical parts of the city still included the development of the touristic infrastructure, while existing traditional housing was to be maintained and provided with infrastructural services.

In the end, the block just opposite the Registan complex, built in the mid-1960s remained the only one state-built housing project in the 'historical' area of the city. While some parts of the *mahallas* in the direct proximity of Registan square had to make way for a museum, a cinema and a restaurant, most of the old town remained. Constrained by a lack of both financial resources and organisational capacities, the implementation of the comprehensive master plans almost always lagged behind the construction activities and other changes on the ground.

The failure of the planned redevelopment of Samarkand's central *mahallas* left a gap that was filled by the initiative of local residents, as we showed elsewhere Somewhat ironically, the long-established technique of building with adobe bricks remained vital for the creation and maintenance of housing space in Samarkand. Not only in the old *mahallas* in the city centre but also in the newly emerging private residential areas, people resorted to traditional materials and collective practises

88 Boris Chukhovich, "Orientalist modes of modernism in architecture: Colonial/Postcolonial/ Soviet." *Études de lettres* 2–3 (2014): 263–294.

89 Mitkhat Bulatov, and Il'ya Notkin, "Praktika i problemy rekonstruktsii istoricheskikh gorodov Srednei Azii." *SIA* 9 (1978): 10–12; Shukur Askarov, "Istoricheskij gorod kak ob'ekt turizma." *SIA* 10 (1978): 27.

90 Ne'mat Sadykov, and P. Tarasenko, "Samarkand Stupeni rosta." *SIA* 1 (1985): 13–24.

of labour mobilisation, locally known as *hashar*, for building and improving private houses. By doing so, they maintained a high degree of independence from the Soviet housing economy and the state's social engineering attempts. And while state architects discussed how the advantages of the courtyard house could be incorporated into mass-housing projects, countless dwellers of single-family houses took matters into their own hands.[91]

Conclusion

Central Asia has recently attracted the attention of architectural historians who have taken an interest both in the functionalist forms of mass housing, but also in the region-specific architecture which Soviet modernism created there.[92] Yet neither the mass housing nor singular and exceptional modernistic projects cover the full experience in Central Asian cities or professional discourses or of their material legacy.

This chapter has aimed for a more nuanced account of how architects and planners negotiated a Central Asian blend of socialist urban modernity after the inception of the mass-housing campaign under Khrushchev in the region after 1960. We show that this debate, while ideologically framing urban redevelopment as a triumph of progressiveness over backwardness, left considerable scope for reflections on the shortcomings of prefabricated multistorey apartment buildings vis-à-vis the environmental conditions, social structure and architectural legacy of Uzbek cities. Among the major target conflicts and inherent contradictions of urban modernisation in the Soviet Union, we have focused on those that concerned the material constitution of the old Uzbek oasis cities. One major tension arose from the recognition that the very architectural legacy that the discussants unanimously deemed unworthy of preservation in its materiality, namely the traditional adobe-brick courtyard house, provided adequate solutions for the major challenges that mass-housing in multistorey apartment buildings faced in Central Asia: Hot indoor temperatures in the summer, the lack of outdoor space, the unfavourable microclimate in the neighbourhoods, and the ill-suitedness of the small standardised apartments to the house of big families that were typical for Central Asia.

---

91 van der Straeten, and Petrova, "Mud Bricks in a Concrete State."

92 See, for example, Philipp Meuser, *Die Ästhetik der Platte: Wohnungsbau in der Sowjetunion zwischen Stalin und Glasnost* (Berlin: Dom Publishers, 2015); Chukhovich, "Building the 'living East'"; Igor Demchenko, "Critical post-functionalism in the architecture of late soviet Central Asia." *ABE Journal* 13 (2018): 1–17.

This chapter unpacks the changing doctrines that architects and urban planners followed, and the strategies they adapted to overcome these tensions, which themselves followed political and economic dynamics of the Soviet Union. In the beginning of the 1960s – in line with the reckless modernistic optimism of the Khrushchev period – the idea of eliminating the "backward" old structures dominated. The gradual interest, acknowledgement and engagement with traditional architecture that followed in the subsequent years corresponds with a more pragmatic attitude and more freedom and scope for local action and initiative in the republics during the Brezhnev era.

Under the remaining imperative of "national in form, socialist in content" architects attempted to extract the "progressive elements" of traditional architecture, translate them into metrics used by Soviet architects and incorporate them into the standardised designs; the ideological appropriation of the *mahalla* as an inherently socialist form of neighbourhood community and its conceptual reconciliation with the micro-district as the basic unit of urban planning; studies on the demography of the respective city centres and the local peculiarities of every-day life. In the late 1960s and early 1970s, these efforts culminated in pilot projects in Tashkent consisting of standardised elements that emulated the traditional courtyard house. The pilot projects, however, remained singular and were not followed up. By the end of the 1960s and throughout the 1970s, the debate on adequate housing for big families in the city centre was soon overlaid with a discussion of how to preserve the aesthetics of the architectural ensemble around the central monuments, a discussion which was strikingly ignorant of the needs of the local population.

Beyond the ornamentation of the prefabricated multistorey apartment buildings, the ideas of a specific Central Asian form of socialist urban housing did not materialise beyond singular experimental projects. As far as residential areas were concerned, the redevelopment of city centres remained an all-or-nothing approach, that played out very differently in the respective cities. While Tashkent's city centre underwent an all-out transformation that accelerated after the earthquake, Samarkand's core was much less affected. Despite the increasing interest in local architectural traditions and the requirements for housing arising from the local climate, demography and social structures, most of the architects were unwilling or unable to fully engage with the daily realities of residents in the old *mahallas*, or their ideas and ethics of family and household organisation – not least because few architects were of Central Asian origin themselves. The encounter with the hybrid configuration of supposedly "old" and "new" technology in the Uzbek *mahalla*, provoked ideological (and, at times orientalist and colonial) reactions that made it impossible to embrace the local architectural legacy in its materiality. Beyond the dense private housing structure and practical issues of relocation, new ideas on housing had to overcome many other hurdles – the planning bureaucracy, the doctrine of prefabrication and mass-production, cost-reduction and the discrepancy between the desired technological possibilities and what was available.

II Networks: Comecon, GDR and the "Global South"

Monika Motylińska

A Cuban Nickel Plant made in the GDR? The Architecture of a Comecon Joint Venture

Introduction

In 2010, the economic press journals reported that a failed former investment of the Soviets, a nickel plant in Las Camariocas in Cuba, was to be concluded as a joint venture with Venezuela after China resigned from consigning three years earlier.[1] Yet the media coverage was imprecise in describing it as a Soviet project. In fact, it was initially a joint venture of the Council for Mutual Economic Assistance (Comecon) countries having different actors from the German Democratic Republic as decisive forces behind the project. Las Camariocas was by no means an exception; the investigation of international activities of the East German architects and planners proves that the vast majority of projects were executed in other Comecon countries or countries with an observer or associated status in this organisation. In addition, and more importantly for this chapter, the whole construction was implemented within a network of multi-facetted entanglements between different stakeholders such as central institutions, companies and local bodies from the regions where projects were implemented.[2]

In this chapter, I will scrutinise this joint Comecon effort, looking at several layers of the entanglements between Cuba and the European socialist states. This is an attempt to provide a suitable framework to address issues like the characteristic policies of the Comecon in the building industry towards the 'Third World Comecon countries' and to pick up actors playing a crucial role in the knowledge production and transfer across the Comecon in the context of architecture and

1 www.reuters.com/article/metals-cuba-nickel-idAFN2218739720100222 (accessed on 1 October 2017). http://havanajournal.com/business/entry/cuba-to-build-fourth-nickel-processing-plant-in-las-camariocas-holguin/ (accessed on 1 October 2017). Carmelo Mesa-Lago, "The Cuban Economy in 2006–2007." *The Association for the Study of the Cuban Economy* (2007): 4, //ascecuba.org//c/wp-content/uploads/2014/09/v17-mesalago.pdf (accessed on 25 March 2018).

2 Discussed results were obtained in the course of the research project *GDR-Architecture Abroad. Projects, Actors and Cultural Transfer Processes* at the Department for Historical Research of the Leibniz Institute for Research on Society and Space, funded by the Gerda Henkel Foundation from October 2016 till September 2018, principal investigators: Christoph Bernhardt, Andreas Butter; a preliminary draft on this topic was presented at the conference "Spaces of Interaction between the Socialist Camp and the Global South: Knowledge Production, Trade, and Scientific-Technical Cooperation in the Cold War Era" in Leipzig on 26 October 2017.

https://doi.org/10.1515/9783110658491-005

Fig. 1: One of the nickel plants in Holguín.
(source: https://www.prensa-latina.cu/2021/11/05/evalua-viceprimer-ministro-de-cuba-produccion-de-niquel; author: Foto Granma, accessed on: 1.07.2022).

urban planning. In addition, working on joint projects like the Las Camariocas nickel plant in Cuba also produced contentions between the interested parties. A closer look at this platform of exchange thus also allows us to shed some light on the rarely explored issues like the diverging visions of the actors in the decision-making and implementation procedures of these projects in the building industry, not only on the level of state policy but also on the meso level by analysing the institutes and construction companies involved. In other words, I aim to showcase how have the non-European members of Comecon interacted with their Eastern European comrades by not just focusing on the bones of contention between the recipient (i.e., Cuba) and the donors (i.e., European members of the Comecon) that decelerated the initial momentum,[3] but even more notably by looking at the materialised results of the joint venture.

In the following pages, however, I shall begin the story of the East-South relations in the building industry with a broader picture and introduce it in a somewhat exploratory way. Starting with a brief introduction to the international activities of East German architects and planners, the focus will be shifted to an overview of the involvement of the non-European actors in the building industry and architectural projects within the framework of the Comecon. Eventually, these two sections converge in a case study on the nickel processing plant, Las Camariocas in Cuba, an

3 Not surprisingly, the Comecon summit declaration of 1985 lambasted the European members for being too slow and even reluctant in joint technical assistance projects in Cuba, Mongolia and Vietnam.

exemplary Comecon joint venture in the building industry. Presented results are based on an extensive survey of German archives, with a particular focus on the German Federal Archive in Berlin (Bundesarchiv), the Archive of the Federal Foreign Office (Politisches Archiv) in Berlin, the State Archive Saxony-Anhalt in Dessau (Landesarchiv Sachsen-Anhalt), where the files of the VEB Zementanlagenbau Dessau, one of the companies involved in the construction, are stored, the Saxonian State Archive in Leipzig (Sächsisches Staatsarchiv in Leipzig), where the documentation of other construction companies that were deeply involved in the Comecon joint ventures is accessible, and the archive of the Leibniz Institute for Research on Society and Space (Leibniz-Institut für Raumbezogene Sozialforschung IRS), Erkner, with its archival documentation of the Institute for Urban Planning and Architecture of the German Building Academy (Institut für Städtebau und Architektur der Deutschen Bauakademie).[4] This should provide a starting point for further investigations, as the existing scholarly discourse has focused either on the central policy-making or particular international projects by the Soviet planners and architects.

GDR architecture abroad

Breaking away from the bipolar Cold War narrative within which most of the stories of this era had previously been embedded and which underlines the isolationist character of the socialist bloc, the various activities of the "Second World" in the countries of the "Third World" have been recently rediscovered and investigated by a host of scholars chiefly focusing on diplomatic and economic entanglements.[5] Moreover, experts with backgrounds in architectural history, urban

4 Founded in January 1951, it was the leading scientific institution of the GDR, focusing on architecture and construction, supervised by the Ministry for Construction. Its departments combined theoretical reflection with application-oriented approaches.

5 E.g. David Engerman, "The Second World's Third World." *Kritika* 12, no. 1 (2011): 183–211; Oscar Sanchez-Sibony, *Red Globalisation. The political economy of the Soviet Cold War from Stalin to Khrushchev* (New York: Cambridge University Press, 2014); James Mark, Tobias Rupprecht, "The Socialist Camp in Global History: From Absentee to Victim to Co-Producer," in *The Practice of Global History*, edited by Matthias Middell, 81–113 (Bloomington: Indiana University Press, 2019); James Mark, Artemy Kalinovsky, and Steffi Marung, eds., *Alternative Encounters. Eastern Europe and the Postcolonial World* (Bloomington: Indiana University Press, 2020); Sara Lorenzini, "Comecon and the South in the years of détente: a study on East–South economic relations." *Review of History: Revue européenne d'histoire* 21 (2014): 183–199. James Mark, and Quinn Slobodian, "Eastern Europe in the History of Decolonization," in *The Oxford Handbook of the Ends of Empire*, edited by Martin Thomas, and Andrew Thompson, 350–372 (Oxford: Oxford University Press, 2018).

history and cultural anthropology have contributed significantly to these efforts, mainly through case studies. Seminal analyses have been conducted recently by Łukasz Stanek regarding the knowledge circulation in architecture between Eastern Europe, the Middle East and West Africa, demonstrating the complexity of the relationship between ideology, economic needs and professional ambitions.[6] Christina Schwenkel has conducted extensive research on the appropriation of the GDR housing and town planning in Vietnam.[7] Coincidently, economic and cultural historians have been investigating knowledge circulations between the Global South and the Eastern Bloc.[8] The recent research project *GDR-Architecture Abroad. Projects, Actors and Cultural Transfer Processes* at the Leibniz Institute for Research on Society and Space (IRS), Erkner tied in with this line of discourse while choosing a more panoramic approach.[9] Its results confirm the suspicion that industrial buildings and sites were the most popular export product of the GDR in terms of architectural typology. Often, they were a part of a complex export package including heavy equipment and other technologies, experts' consultation and skilled workforce, as well as training of the local workforce and even further maintenance.

6 E.g. Łukasz Stanek, "Introduction: The 'Second World' architecture and planning in the 'Third World.'" *Journal of Architecture* 17, no. 3 (2012): 299–307. Łukasz Stanek, "Architects from Socialist Countries in Ghana (1957–67): Modern Architecture and Mondialisation." *Journal for Architectural Historians* 74, no. 4 (2015): 416–442. Łukasz Stanek: *Architecture in Global Socialism. Eastern Europe, West Africa, and the Middle East in the Cold War* (Princeton and Oxford: Princeton University Press, 2020). Ákos Moravánszky, "Peripheral modernism: Charles Polónyi and the lessons of the village." *The Journal of Architecture* 17, no. 3 (2012): 333–359. Andreas Butter, "Showcase and window to the world: East German architecture abroad 1949–1990." *Planning Perspectives* 33 (2018): 249–269.

7 E.g. Christina Schwenkel, *Building socialism: the afterlife of East German architecture in urban Vietnam* (Durham, London: Duke University Press 2020); Christina Schwenkel, "Affective Solidarities and East German Reconstruction of Postwar Vietnam," in *Comrades of Color: East Germany in the Cold War World*, edited by Quinn Slobodian, 267–292 (New York: Berghahn Books, 2015); Christina Schwenkel, "Traveling architecture: East German Urban Designs in Vietnam." *International Journal for History, Culture and Modernity* 2, no. 2 (2014): 155–174.

8 E.g. Uwe Müller, Dagmara Jajeśniak-Quast, *COMECON revisited. Integration in the Eastern Bloc and entanglements with the Global Economy* (Leipzig: Leipziger Universitätsverlag, 2017).

9 Aiming to produce a comprehensive compilation and being situated between architectural history, global history as well as heritage protection, a broad survey of international activities of East German architects and planners was undertaken. Over 500 realised and unrealised projects were identified through extensive archival research, interviews with contemporary witnesses and analysis of architectural journals. These are collected in a database which is considered a valuable tool for statistical evaluation – for example, to estimate which building types occurred more often than others, in which regions and periods.

The regional focus of East German interests lies in Eastern Europe, the Middle East, Tanzania, Vietnam and China. The activities abroad increased dramatically after the political turn of the early 1970s. Until then, most of the projects were realised within the Eastern Bloc. This development resulted from a diplomatic and economic struggle in the post-war period, as the state of the German Democratic Republic, founded in 1949 and itself a product of Cold War politics, strove desperately for international recognition.[10] This was quickly achieved within the Eastern Bloc – as the Soviet Union, as well as Soviet satellite states, tied diplomatic relations with the GDR immediately. However, due to the so-called "Hallstein doctrine" which was introduced by West Germany, establishing diplomatic relations with the Soviet occupation zone in Germany and thus recognising it as an independent state would be considered an unfriendly act towards the Federal German Republic – which could lead to breaking off diplomatic relations.[11] Until this policy was overturned by the social-democratic government of Chancellor Willy Brandt and his new "Eastern policy" (Ostpolitik) that led to the wide recognition of the GDR and its admission to the United Nations in 1973, the East German state sought indirect means and solutions to be present on the international arena, such as erecting trade missions in Western countries.[12]

The notion of the "architectural export" – the term "export" often appears in sources concerning foreign construction projects – corresponds with the GDR reality. Projects were often created in the abstract, as many architects were not allowed or could not travel to meet the constructors. Moreover, the Ministry of Foreign Trade supervised many vital realisations.

In the investigation conducted by the IRS team, it became clear that specific international organisations played a crucial role in the international transfer of knowledge and forging economic ties in the construction industry. The Comecon offered different platforms for official contacts on the state level – for instance, concerning the questions of public housing – and less formal connections between the experts. A comparison between the map of the architectural activities with the map of the member states of the Comecon shows that they overlap across the decades. This is confirmed by the results of the archival survey, thus proving that an intense exchange occurred. Summing up the quantitative evaluation of our database, it can be observed that at least 300 of the approximately 500 GDR projects abroad were executed or planned in other Comecon countries. As

10 William Glenn Gray, *Germany's Cold War: The Global Campaign to Isolate East Germany, 1949–1969* (Chapel Hill: The University of North Carolina Press, 2003), 196–198.

11 Gray, *Germany's Cold War*, 196–198.

12 Monika Motylińska, "Striving for recognition – GDR embassies from the 1950s and 1960s," unpublished paper presented at *71. International Conference of the Society of Architectural Historians* (2018).

for the full members, there were three non-European countries: Mongolia (since 1962), Cuba (since 1972) and Vietnam (since 1978) – there the GDR planned six, 14 and 41 projects, respectively; as for the typology, the majority of the investments were industrial sites such as cement factories. However, the East German planners also designed elements of social infrastructure (such as hospitals).[13]

The Comecon and non-European actors in the building industry

Yet were all the realised and unrealised architectural projects and other initiatives in the building industry merely 'exported' to the non-European Comecon countries? How did the non-European members of Comecon interact with their Eastern European partners working on collective projects at all?

The Comecon policy for the building industry aimed at intensifying productivity and output through standardisation and typification (Typisierung).[14] The Permanent Commission supervised the cooperation between the Comecon members within this branch of industry for Building Industry with its seat in Berlin. It was established in 1958; its first chairman was Gerhard Kosel, the former president of the German Building Academy (Deutsche Bauakademie).[15] Although the Permanent Commission edited many volumes on standardised building policies and their implementation and multilingual building lexicons and organised several conferences, its actual influence on building practice was rather low-powered. Even if some of its policies precipitated the activities of the Publicly Owned Operations (VEB, Volkseigener Betrieb[16]) in the field of construction, their impact

13 Evaluation of the database of the research project *GDR-Architecture Abroad. Projects, Actors and Cultural Transfer Processes.*

14 Manfred Engert, and Heinz Stephan, eds., *RGW-Lexikon* (Leipzig: Bibliographisches Institut, 1981), 27, 42–44.

15 Christine Hannemann, *Die Platte. Industrialisierter Wohnungsbau in der DDR* (Wiesbaden: Vieweg Verlag, 1996), 148. Gerhard Kosel (1909–2003) was an architect with professional experience in the Soviet Union (e.g. he designed the Opera in Ulaanbaatar, completed in 1948), who came to the GDR in 1954 and became active in the structures of the SED. Apart from his function in the Permanent Commission, between 1967 and 1972, he was the Vice-Minister for Construction and 1977 to 1984, the GDR deputy of the UN-Habitat.

16 Publicly Owned Enterprise – formed during mass nationalisation – was the East German industrial enterprise's main legal form.

was mostly restricted to general inquiries about cooperation with other companies within the Comecon[17] or conferences such as the one on the problems of planning and managing of a socialist construction company in October 1968 in Leipzig.[18]

Should we consider joint investments of the Comecon – most of them carried out in the Soviet Union – as both showcases of this involvement and testing grounds for applying new planning methods and building technologies, the activities of the non-European Comecon members were minimal. As it seems, they did not participate in any large-scale projects outside their territories. From the vantage point of the official publications of the Comecon, they mainly had the status of receivers of foreign investments such as industrial sites (e.g., an abattoir in Ulaanbaatar) or elements of social infrastructure, for instance, hospitals built according to the imported know-how and technologies. Often this was also the case with the building materials. How such complex collaborations were facilitated in Mongolia has been discussed in another chapter of this volume by Nikolay Erofeev and Łukasz Stanek.[19] One of the examples of the joint Comecon investments was also the nickel processing plant Las Camariocas in the eastern province of Holguín in Cuba, which will be discussed in the following part of this chapter.

The role of the non-European Comecon members as the addressees of external aid and investments contrasts with other forms of cooperation. For instance, scientific collaboration within the so-called Coordination Centers – Mongolia and Cuba actively established these institutions. Still, none of them was located beyond Eastern Europe (most of them had their seats in the Russian Soviet Federative Socialist Republic – in two cities only: Moscow or Leningrad).[20]

Usual forums of knowledge production and circulation were the conferences and cooperation within different working groups of the Permanent Commission for Building Industry.[21] Yet, compared to the Soviet Union and other countries of the Eastern Bloc, Mongolia, Cuba, and Vietnam were less active in this aspect.[22] In the GDR, the Institute for Urban Planning and Architecture (ISA, Institut für

17 In many cases these were just briefly declined by the VEBs and their departments, stating that no such cooperation took place (e.g., Partnerbeziehungen mit den RGW-Ländern, 17.10.1972, VEB Baukombinat Leipzig, Nr. 1068, Staatsarchiv Leipzig 20733).

18 Symposium zum Thema ‘Probleme der Planung und Leitung eines sozialistischen Baubetriebes’, vom 14.-18.10.1968 in Leipzig, VE Wohnungs- und Gesellschaftsbaukombinat Leipzig, Nr. 77, Staatsarchiv Leipzig 22348.

19 See chapter: 1–2.

20 Engert, and Stephan, eds., *RGW-Lexikon*, 128–131.

21 Sari Autio-Sarasmo, and Katalin Miklóssy, eds., *Reassessing Cold War Europe* (New York: Routledge, 2011), 1–15.

22 E.g. Bundesarchiv (in the following BArch) DE 1/49799. BArch DH 2/9892. BArch DH 2/9986.

Architektur und Städtebau), a department of the above-mentioned German Building Academy, was the central institution working on the guidelines and resolutions for the Permanent Commission for Building Industry. Therefore, many publications from the ISA series appeared with the logo of the Permanent Commission. Not until the 1980s did the international activities of the non-European Comecon members increase – they travelled frequently and organised colloquia such as the '16. Tagung des Rates des Internationalen Systems der w/t Information' in Cuba (20–23 September 1988).[23] Coincidently, an increase in courses and seminars offered to the Cuban, Vietnamese and Mongolian architects, engineers, and town planners occurred – for example, after a visit by a Cuban delegation in the summer of 1987, the ISA prepared a proposition for a course on physical and climatic issues of housing architecture under tropical circumstances.[24]

In 1974, on the occasion of the twenty-fifth anniversary of the Comecon, a significant conference of the Permanent Commission for Building Industry was held in Berlin, and its proceedings were published the following year. Probably because Cuba did not become a Comecon member until 1972, the only non-European voice in the conference volume came from G. Tleichan, the Mongolian minister of construction and housing. According to his report, the Comecon members, with the leading role of the Soviet Union, enabled and realised diverse significant projects in his country. These were not only examples of industrial architecture: for example, a carpet factory and a printing plant in Ulaan Baatar (Ulan Bator), both erected with the aid of East Germany, but also representative structures such as the state circus in the capital, its realisation supported by Romania. Contrary to the authors from Eastern Europe, Tleichan does not mention any international involvement of the Mongolian engineers or architects. The only actors mentioned are the skilled construction workers in the Soviet Union, Bulgaria and Poland.[25]

Far less is known about the working conditions abroad on the GDR construction sites.[26] But when written sources on the actual exchange between the actors seem scarce, the architectural analysis proves to be especially helpful. It shows

23 Terminplan für die Tagungen und Beratungen der mehrseitigen internationalen Zusammenarbeit im RGW im Jahr 1988 (Auszug) – unverbindlich. IRS Erkner, A 2.2.8 (1).

24 A letter to the Head of Department for Housing, branch office in Dresden, Dr.-Ing. H. Petzold from 2.09.1987. IRS Erkner, A 2.2.8 (1).

25 *Zusammenarbeit der Mitgliedsländer des RGW auf dem Gebiet des Bauwesens: Zum 25. Jahrestag des Rates für Gegenseitige Wirtschaftshilfe* (Berlin 1975: Bauakademie der DDR), 29–33.

26 Apart from the case of the cement factories erected by the Zementanlagenbau Dessau (Monika Motylińska, "A success story? The industrial architecture of the GDR in Asia," paper presented at the conference "Exporting Socialism, Making Business? Intercultural Transfer, Circulation and Appropriation of Architecture in the Cold War Period," 21.-22.06.2018, Leibniz Institute for Research on Society and Space (IRS), Erkner).

that the adaptation to local climatic or cultural circumstances occurred during the realisation of the imported (from the Cuban, Mongolian or Vietnamese perspective) projects. However, some planning mistakes could not be avoided. For instance, in the housing project in Vinh (North Vietnam), the architects had to adjust their concepts to the need for suitable ventilation, which led to the revitalisation of the housing typology.[27] There were also reasons to reduce apartment sizes to local conditions, making it impossible to implement the German standards.

Despite the publicised principles of mutuality and voluntariness, the GDR projects abroad, at least in some documented cases, were received by the local actors with apprehension or a high degree of suspicion concerning the ulterior motives of the East Germans. Supposedly, they were interested in selling their "backward technology", only to be paid once more for repairing it.[28]

Tracing projects means also tracing the people that were involved. This part of the research results is based on the evaluation of the archival sources of the East German Architectural Association.[29] Unsurprisingly, most of the GDR architects with international experience went to other Comecon countries – either as a part of jointly coordinated investments like the nickel plant in Cuba or, in some rare cases, thanks to an individual invitation (e.g., Peter and Ute Baumbach were invited to develop a masterplan for Addis Ababa in the late 1980s by the city mayor[30]). One of the popular non-European destinations was Cuba, the duration of stay varying between two weeks – if the experts went there for a conference such as the congress of the Union Internationale des Architectes (UIA) in 1963 – and a much more extended period if they supervised a large project such as the cement factories in Cienfuegos or Nuevitas. The personal freedom of choice was minimal. Who could go abroad, for how long and where mainly was a political decision.

Interestingly, the Permanent Commission for Building Industry was dissolved during its last meeting on 26 January 1988, even before the fall of the Comecon.[31] This step was one of the attempts at an institutional reform of this supranational association. It was resolved that instead of coordinating complicated joint investments, the focus should be shifted to bilateral projects – which might suggest that the Permanent Commission for Building was an inefficient institution, lacking a tangible impact

---

27 Butter, *Showcase and window to the world*, 18.

28 Haile Gabriel Dagne, *Das entwicklungspolitische Engagement der DDR in Äthiopien. Eine Studie auf der Basis äthiopischer Quellen* (Münster: LIT Verlag 2004), 48.

29 Digiporta, www.digiporta.net/index.php (accessed on 1 October 2017).

30 Telephone interview with Peter and Ute Baumbach, 16 September 2018.

31 Information über die 64. (abschließende) Tagung der Ständigen Kommission des RGW für die Zusammenarbeit auf dem Gebiet des Bauwesens. IRS Erkner, A 2.2.8 (1).

on the construction industry. Moreover, the GDR, Bulgaria, Hungary, Cuba, Mongolia, Poland and Czechoslovakia agreed on further voluntary cooperation concerning the significant directions in economic and scientific-technical development.[32]

Las Camariocas – A case study of a joint venture

One prominently mentioned project in the *Comecon Lexicon* is the Las Camariocas nickel processing plant in Cuba. On 26 June 1975, Bulgaria, Hungary, the GDR, Cuba, Poland, Romania, Czechoslovakia and the USSR signed a general agreement to build the plant and send metal constructions, machinery, materials and equipment as well as experts against the share in the Cuban nickel export.[33] The official sources present it as a typical joint venture in one of the non-European Comecon countries. Although not explicitly described as such, it appeared successful merely due to its inclusion in the lexicon. Yet the history of this project is far more complicated and elusive. It can be reconstructed through different lenses: one through the official governmental documents, one through correspondence by construction companies, one through local history and one through the visual data provided by satellite and conventional photography. The East German archival documents shed more light on this case and prove that it was far less successful than officially presented.

The starting date of the project was repeatedly postponed, initially until 1982.[34] The reasons for this delay can be identified in the analysis of the documentation by the GDR construction companies. However, tracing these actors proves to be challenging because the agreements between the Comecon states remain mostly vague, naming no parties commissioned with implementation. Therefore, it was crucial to conduct parallel archival research focusing on leading state-owned enterprises and not only on political bodies officially involved in the project.

The negotiations concerning the East German share in the Las Camariocas project were being prepared from 1976 on the level of companies – which remained open concerning the commercial aspects of the deal.[35] This early phase

32 Information über die 64. (abschließende) Tagung der Ständigen Kommission des RGW für die Zusammenarbeit auf dem Gebiet des Bauwesens. IRS Erkner, A 2.2.8 (1).

33 Protokoll zum Generalabkommen über die Zusammenarbeit beim Bau neuer Produktionskapazitäten für nickel- und kobalthaltige Erzeugnisse in der Republik Kuba. BArch DY 30/J IV 2/2/2083. Engert, and Stephan, eds., *RGW-Lexikon*, 22.

34 Anlage Nr. 9 zum Protokoll Nr. 42 vom 23.10.1984, BArch DY 30/J IV 2/2/2083.

35 Niederschrift: Ausrüstungslieferungen für die Nickelhütte Las Camariocas in Kuba durch den VEB Zementanlagenbau Dessau', 26.05.1977, Landesarchiv Sachsen-Anhalt, I 420 VEB Zementanlagenbau Dessau, Nr. 1068.

involved an official trip to Leningrad in September 1976, led by a civil engineer from the ZAB Dessau, Hans Sehm (1931–2020), who was an experienced negotiator. The official round of negotiations began in November/December 1978 in Havana; the second round occurred in September 1979 following the 4th Comecon Coordination Conference in Moscow.[36]

The archival sources do not explain why particular companies were commissioned. However, it can be assumed that international renown played a vital role in the decision, as they had the capacity and knowhow to work under various local circumstances. Besides, some of them were active in highly specialised branches of the construction market, as was the case with the VEB Zementanlagenbau Dessau (ZAB Dessau), the leading GDR company designing cement factories. In March and April 1980, experts from the ZAB Dessau and their colleagues from the company specialised in designing industrial sites, VEB Mansfeld-Industrieanlagenbau Dresden, went to Cuba to take part in a further stage of negotiations. Although the general contract was accepted, with the exception of prices and deadlines, it became clear that the parties' expectations diverged. A further round of trilateral negotiations (Cuba, Soviet Union, GDR) was scheduled for May/June in Leningrad; however, the location was changed in favour of Berlin for logistical reasons. The central point of contention was the scope of the investment. According to the interpretation of the GDR engineers, the Cubans demanded delivery of the complete equipment for the facility, being especially critical of the supposed lack of involvement of another East German party, the SKET (Schwermaschinenbaukombinat "Ernst Thälmann"), a heavy equipment producer from Magdeburg, regarding an ore drying plant (Trocknerei) and a vertical roller mill (Rohmahlanlage). The German site opted for submitting technical documentation only, whereas the Soviets supported the Cuban perspective. Another awkward issue posed the question of an expected guarantee – and a proposed solution that the GDR companies could construct the facilities based on the Soviet plans to avoid any responsibility for potential failures.[37] The East Germans also held on to this strategy in a later round of negotiations in July 1981.[38]

At this point, the narrative of the official archival documents stops but can be complemented by informal Cuban writing on local history – such sources prove

36 Technisch-kommerzielle Verhandlungen zu Ausrüstungen aus Ihrem Bereich für das Vorhaben 'Nickelhütte Las Camariocas/Kuba', Landesarchiv Sachsen-Anhalt, I 420 VEB Zementanlagenbau Dessau, Nr. 1068.

37 Reisebericht, 8.05.1980, Landesarchiv Sachsen-Anhalt, I 420 VEB Zementanlagenbau Dessau, Nr. 1068.

38 Briefentwurf [undated], Landesarchiv Sachsen-Anhalt, I 420 VEB Zementanlagenbau Dessau, Nr. 1067.

especially valuable in cases where the official documentation is fragmentary, offering no visual material.[39] While the 39th Comecon conference took place in Cuba, a momentous event was staged in Moa. On 1 November 1984, the Cuban president, Fidel Castro Ruz and the prime minister of the Soviet Union, Nikolai Ryzhkov, with the assistance of a worker, Miguel Angel Leyva, inaugurated the construction work.[40] A memorial square for Ernesto Che Guevara was also ceremonially opened.

In late 1988, the plans and the budget had to be adjusted.[41] In 1989, the GDR undertook the role of a significant investor, with 121.6 million ruble credit and extensive technical and planning support.[42] Afterwards, there is no more mention of the nickel plant in the German archival documents.

Rather strikingly, it is not easy to establish the exact location of Las Camariocas. Still, the analysis of satellite photographs accessible on Google Earth, as well as a short piece of information on the EcuRed website, suggest that the plant was built 10 kilometres to the east of Moa – and that would mean it is located in the proximity of the "Comandante Ernesto Che Guevara" plant.[43] Only (salt?) basins separate the industrial plant from the seashore. To the south, a road delimits the site. Two central smokestacks are visible, outlines of 21 tanks in the northern part of the area, many fragments of open processing plants and at least eight halls canopied with span or flat roofs. As of 2013, the plant seemed to be at least partially in use.[44] Besides, the plant could have played a marginal role as a cultural institution, as some local painters such as Hermenegildo Fernández Jiménez exhibited their works there.[45] Some sources prefer to describe Las Camariocas under its changed

---

39 Compare, Madalena Cunha Matos, Johan Lagae, and Rachel Lee, "Digital lieux de mémoire: Connecting history and remembrance through the Internet." *ABE Journal* 3 (2013), https://journals.openedition.org/abe/568 (accessed on 10 March 2018).

40 A blog by a local historian and journalist, Camilo Velazco Petittón, offers detailed information on the history of Moa and rich photographical documentation. Camilo Velazco Petittón, *La enseñanza universitaria en #Moa. #TenemosMemoria*, (17 June 2016), https://moaenimagenesytextos.wordpress.com/2016/06/17/la-ensenanza-universitaria-en-moa-tenemosmemoria/ (accessed on 20 March 2018).

41 Protokoll Nr. 20/82, Sitzung des Politbüros am 18. Mai 1982, BArch DY 30/J IV 2/2/1946-1947; BArch DC 20-I/4/6429.

42 Protokoll Nr. 8/89, Sitzung des Politbüros am 21. Februar 1989, BArch DY 30/J IV 2/2/2316.

43 The exact coordinates are 20.613457" _ N, 74.832804 "W. https://goo.gl/maps/FkS72qJHdAs (accessed on 27.03.2018).

44 https://mapsights.com/moa/moa-cuba/85961161 (accessed on 27 March 2018).

45 https://www.ecured.cu/Hermenegildo_Fern%252525C3%252525A1ndez_Jim%252525C3%252525A9nez (accessed on 27 March 2018), Some information from the Cuban websites could not be verified and is to be treated with caution.

Fig. 2: Nickel production sites in Moa (source: https://www.cubanet.org/noticias/industria-cubana-del-niquel-mira-con-esperanzas-el-acercamiento-a-eeuu/attachment/industria-niquel-moa/, author: culturewillcarryyoutocuba.blogspot.com, accessed: 1.07.2022).

name "CAME-I", identifying it clearly as a Comecon project (CAME – the Spanish name of the Comecon: Consejo de Ayuda Mutua Económica).[46]

Yet, the Las Camariocas investment is just a chapter in a much longer history of nickel production in eastern Cuba, concentered in and around the municipality of Moa, the second centre of nickel processing alongside Nicaro, located in the western part of the same province, Holguín. The story of nickel mining and processing began with the investments of companies from the United States dating back to the 1940s. Since the late 1950s, Cuba has been one of the world's largest producers and exporters of nickel – an essential ingredient in stainless steel production.[47] A significant investor had been the US enterprise Fredrick Snare Co, but all the plants were nationalised after the Cuban revolution. Afterwards, amid the Cold War struggle, *The New York Times* stated – not without satisfaction –

46 Sergio Díaz-Briquets, and Jorge Pérez-López, "Environmental Implications of Cuba´s Development Strategy during the Special Period." *Environmental Issues in Latin America and the Caribbean* (2005): 284–286. Compare also: www.ecured.cu/Moa_(Holgu%C3%ADn); http://flobaina.blogspot.com/2016/01/el-comandante-en-jefe-fidel-castro-en.html (accessed on 27 March 2018).

47 Rex A. Hudson, ed., *Cuba: A Country Study (Area Handbook Series)* (Washington: Government Printing Office, 2002), 186.

that "[t]he fact that nickel production is 'appreciably' below the levels maintained under American operation is admitted by officials at Nicaro. Well-informed sources in Havana say that a serious situation has developed due to Cuba's inability after nearly four years of Government operation to keep Nicaro's American-made mining machinery and trucks in good operating order".[48]

During the Comecon period, the supply chain functioned as follows: Cuba received oil from the Soviet Union and exported raw nickel in the course of barter exchange to the Soviet Union, where it was refined and distributed to the Comecon market and re-exported on the international market.[49] Other goods such as sugar and citrus were also included in the Cuban exchange deals to obtain industrial equipment and consumer products according to the principles of "international specialization" within the Comecon.[50] The process of extracting nickel ore proved a challenge for Comecon technologies and reduced output during the 1980s. Besides, from the viewpoint of US- experts "the most crucial reason for Cuba's inability to profit from the higher price of nickel on the world market is that a substantial portion of the output is committed to the Soviet Union and Comecon countries under agreement. This seriously prohibits Cuba from increasing hard currency earning by selling nickel on the world market".[51] The author of a study on the Cuban nickel industry from the late 1980s went even further, stating that the Cubans were not only in dire need of Western technology only multinational mining companies were able to supply (contrary to the Soviets) but also related to the emotional narrative of the binary perspective with a contrasting depiction of a backward socialist technology versus a progressive and highly desirable Western one:

> The hesitancy, uncertainty, and anxiety frequently accompany host-country representatives to the negotiating table in the Third World appear notably absent in Havana. Indeed, the theme of being weak and dependent pervades discussions elsewhere in Latin America and is not common in Cuban analyses of possible relations with transnational corporations. In sum, there is a clear interest and desire on the part of the Cubans to incorporate Western technology into their nickel industry, and remarkable confidence that they could do so quickly and successfully without damaging themselves socially or economically.[52]

---

48 Thomas J. Hamilton, "Nickel Smelting Lagging in Cuba." *Special to The New York Times* (3 August 1964).

49 Carmelo Mesa-Lago, "Economic Policies and Growth." *Revolutionary Change in Cuba* (1971): 315.

50 Irving Louis Horowitz, ed., *Cuban Communism (6th edition)* (Cambridge: Cambridge University Press, 1988), 219.

51 Office of Research & Policy, Radio Martí Program, Voice of America, eds., *Cuba Annual Report: 1988* (Washington D.C.: United States Information Agency, 1991), 173–174.

52 Irving Louis Horowitz, ed., *Cuban Communism (6th edition)* (Cambridge: Cambridge University Press, 1988), 263.

The collapse of the socialist economic system shook the Cuban nickel industry – Las Camariocas plant could not be completed, and the Punta Gorda plant had to be closed in 1992. Immediately after the political turn of 1989/1990, Western actors endeavoured to replace Comecon companies and achieve their share of the Cuban nickel supply. One of the major players was Sherritt International Corporation from Canada, which defied the US embargo and signed an import deal for nickel sulphides and, since 1994, has been a part of a 50–50 joint venture with the Cuban Government's Nickel Company in the Pedro Soto Alba plant in Moa. In contrast, the other completed plant "Ernesto Che Guevara" remains owned by the Cuban government.[53]

As mentioned at the beginning of this chapter, the Las Camariocas story's aftermath was rocky. The plant, which was only partially executed, was the subject of a joint venture contract in 2010 between Cuba and Venezuela to complete the construction after China had resigned from the deal – that was negotiated in 2003.[54]

Though, as more recent press reports suggest, some aspects of the Comecon economic policy might have survived in the agenda of Russian actors. In 2011, OAO Nickel Norilsk demonstrated interest in investing in Moa. In 2017, as suggested by Costa Rican newspaper *El País* a Russian company, Ruselprom, was about to invest in nickel mining in the region in question. The statements of stakeholders involved in negotiations make it seem like the period of 26 years after the fall of the Soviet Union in 1991 was just a brief interruption and now a continuity of economic ties could be reestablished: "After 1991, there was a temporary rupture, but at the moment, we are revitalising all those Russian pieces of equipment with spare parts, and as for those that need to be replaced, we are in the disposition and the capacity to do it.".[55] The story of Russian involvement in the

53 Simon Clow, *The International Nickel Trade* (Sawston: Woodhead Publishing, 1992), 65; U.S. International Trade Commission, ed., *The Economic Impact of U.S. Sanctions in Respect to Cuba* (Washington: U.S. International Trade Commission, 2001), 6–16; Clifford L. Staten, *The History of Cuba (The Greenwood Histories of the Modern Nations) 2nd edition* (Santa Barbara: Greenwood, 2015), 163.

54 www.reuters.com/article/metals-cuba-nickel-idAFN2218739720100222 (accessed on 1 October 2017). http://havanajournal.com/business/entry/cuba-to-build-fourth-nickel-processing-plant-in-las-camariocas-holguin/ (accessed on 1 October 2017). www.cubaheadlines.com/es/venezuela_trumps_china_in_cuba_feronickel_deal.html (accessed on 01.10.2017). "Nickel, but no dimes." *The Economist* (18 September 2003), www.economist.com/node/2076774 (accessed on 1 October 2017).

55 "Después de 1991 hubo una ruptura temporal, pero en estos momentos estamos revalorizando todos esos equipos rusos con piezas de repuesto, y los que requieran ser sustituidos estamos en la disposición y la capacidad de hacerlo" "Empresa rusa quiere colaborar con Cuba en industria del níquel." *El País* (2 November 2017), www.elpais.cr/2017/11/02/empresa-rusa-quiere-colaborar-con-cuba-en-industria-del-niquel/ (accessed on 27 March 2018).

Cuban nickel mining is presented as a natural consequence of the Comecon planning. Besides, a company from Bratislava (Slovakia), PPA Control, delivered and upgraded the heating system and the control system for the electrical parts in one of the nickel plants in Moa; unfortunately, it does not state in which of the three plants mentioned above, but judging by the orientation of the buildings, tank and smokestacks it can be assumed that it was the "Comandante Ernesto Che Guevara" plant.[56]

Fig. 3: Moa – view of the city with nickel plants in the background, state 2012.
(source: https://commons.wikimedia.org/wiki/File:Moa_Holguin.jpg#metadata, author: Ramon. rovirosa, CC BY-SA 3.0).

It remains yet to be verified if the involvement of the Eastern European actors also took place in the town planning and architecture of Moa: (Fig. 3). At least the planning of the western part of the city core, in contrast with the rest of the urbanised area, which is covered with low detached houses, might have been affected by the influences of the Eastern Bloc. This assumption is based on a comparison of the spatial arrangement of the four-storey slabs with similar plans from Vietnam (Vinh) and Tanzania (Michenzani) – in all the cases the slabs'

56 www.ppa.sk/referencie-item/elektraren-v-niklovej-huti-moa-kuba/?lang=en (accessed on 23 March 2018).

urban layout alternates between wide-angles and paralles, the rhythmic compositions of the façades is also typical, if not for the GDR specifically, than at least for standardised housing designs from the Eastern bloc (Fig. 4).

Fig. 4: Moa – apartment buildings in Las Coloradas quarter, state 2008.
(source: https://commons.wikimedia.org/wiki/File:Moa_-_Las_Coloradas_-_%D0%94%D0%BE%D0%BC_17_-_2008_-_panoramio.jpg, author: Maxim Nedashkovskiy, CC BY-SA 3.0).

Another – regional – source of inspiration should be though taken into consideration, namely the housing estates of the 1970s in Havana and other Cuban cities built as self-construction by microbrigades (Spanish: microbrigadas) that have recently become of interest for international, anthropologically oriented documentaries[57] and

57 Florian Zeyfang, Lisa Schmidt-Colinet, Alexander Schmoeger, '*Microbrigades – Variations of a Story*', film, HD, 31 min (2013), "http://schcsch.com/filter/Cuba/Microbrigades-Variations-of-a-Story" (accessed on 23 March 2018); "Havana Vignettes", part of the project *Alamar: An Archaeology of Socialist Domestic Infrastructure in Havana*, http://projectalamar.com/ (accessed on 23 March 2018); 'DOBLE FORZA', Re: centering Periphery 01. Alamar. Cuba (Digital Video, color, 30', 2008). Interestingly, the original footage of Alamar included in the last of the films was

spatial planning research.[58] Estates erected by state or social microbrigades attempted to overcome the housing shortage. Different building techniques and materials were applied. Apart from the use of cement bricks, prefabricated concrete panels were well-known; their production technology was supposedly based on "IMS technologies from Yugoslavia, a Sliding Scaffolding, and the Great Panel 70"; however, the authors of the investigation offer neither sources nor explanation for their line of argumentation leading to this assumption.[59] Further research on the circulation of licences and adaptation of the socialist mass-housing design seems necessary, as loose remarks on the transformation of Canadian, French, Yugoslav and Finnish building types need verification. Besides, some façades of the most well-known mass housing estate in Cuba, Alamar, are suspiciously reminiscent of the GDR designs of P2 and, Aisle House (Mittelganghaus).

Analysing photographs of housing estates in Moa,[60] including those showing the scale of devastation of hurricane Ike in 2008,[61] the dominance of prefabricated materials becomes clear. This would suggest that production of precast concrete slabs might have taken place in a plant on-site, especially when taking the distance to other urbanised areas and the high demand for concrete for the nickel plants into consideration.

Yet, Moa became more than an industrial site with a large population of miners and other workers housed in slabs and smaller settlements, as it aspired to become a hub in knowledge transfer in the nickel industry. In 1974, an Instituto Superior, a field department of the Universidad de Oriente from Santiago de Cuba, was established, including a Chair for Mining and a Chair for Geology. Only two years later, an Instituto Superior Minero-Metalúrgico de Moa (ISMMM) was

---

recorded on a North Korean film reel, www.recentering-periphery.org/films/doble-forza/ (accessed on 23 March 2018).

58 A detailed bibliography on this topic is to be found in a paper by Benedikt Brester, "Housing Policy, Neighbourhood Development, and Civic Participation in Cuba: The Social Microbrigade of Santa Clara." *Berkeley Planning Journal* 25 (2012): 79–80.

59 Roger Diener, *Public Housing in Havana: History of ideas* (Basel: ETH Studio, 200) 69, 75, 82. This observation was taken word-for-word from Joseph L. Scarpaci, Roberto Segre, and Mario Coyula, *Havana: Two Faces of the Antillean Metropolis (revised edition)* (Chapel Hill: The University of North Carolina Press, 2002), 142. Unfortunately, these authors also do not explain the circulation of ideas and implementation of foreign building licences.

60 www.flickriver.com/places/Cuba/Holguin/Moa/recent/. https://mapsights.com/moa/moa-las-coloradas-dom-12-2008/11245212 (accessed on 28 March 2018).

61 http://mauroflash.blogspot.com/2008/09/moa-tras-paso-del-huracn-ike.html (accessed on 28 March 2018).

created, and its seat was erected. Among its 11,101 graduates (as of 2016) were 504 foreigners from Latin American and African countries.[62]

The spatial context analysis cannot be completed without referencing landscape transformations caused by the mining and processing of nickel and ferronickel. The coastal area in the eastern part of the province Holguín has been changed irrevocably. As satellite photographs of this area demonstrate, opencast pits and processing plants are expanding like an infiltrating metastasis in their surroundings, advancing to the tropical rainforest of Alejandro de Humboldt National Park, declared as a UNESCO World Natural Heritage site in 2001, being "the most extensive and best-conserved remnant of forested mountain ecosystems in the Caribbean".[63] The environmental consequences did not seem to be of any concern to the commissioners of Las Camariocas and other industrial projects back in the Cold War period and this remains the case today.[64] This threat is reflected in the analysis of the integrity of this heritage site:

> Mining near La Melba led to the development of small farms for local food production in the surroundings of the small town. While logging and farming started in the 1940s and 1950s on the banks of the Toa and Jaguani Rivers, the affected areas have since been left to recover. More recently, beginning in the 1960s, logging of pines took place until the area was declared a protected area in the 1980s. While there have been past disturbances, and there continues to be a need to strike a balance between conservation objectives and the livelihood needs of adjacent communities, the overall integrity of AHNP has been maintained, with many previously disturbed areas being in the process of natural regeneration. In the long run, the most critical threat may be the pressure to exploit the rich mineral resources within the property, which would doubtlessly have severe direct and indirect impacts on the property.[65]

Scepticism concerning current and potential conflicts between expanding industrial sites and rainforest preservation cannot be attenuated with statements about the renouncement of the usage of cooling agents R-12 and R-22 to protect the ozone layer.[66] The documentation of massive air, water and soil pollution un-

---

62 Camilo Velazco Petittón, *La enseñanza universitaria en #Moa. #TenemosMemoria*, (17 June 2016), https://moaenimagenesytextos.wordpress.com/2016/06/17/la-ensenanza-universitaria-en-moa-tenemosmemoria/ (accessed on 20 March 2018).

63 https://whc.unesco.org/en/list/839 (accessed on 27 March 2018).

64 http://cubaindependiente.blogspot.com/search/label/Niquel (accessed on 27 March 2018).

65 https://whc.unesco.org/en/list/839 (accessed on 27 March 2018).

66 "Cuba-Empresas mineras protegen el medio ambiente en Moa", in *Area Minera* (8 October 2017), www.aminera.com/2017/10/08/cuba-empresas-mineras-protegen-medio-ambiente-moa/ (accessed on 27 March 2018).

derline the long-term costs and environmental and social impact of the nickel mining projects in the Moa region.[67]

5 Conclusion

Even if the majority of the GDR's architectural projects abroad were planned and executed in other Comecon countries, it would be too simplified to draw a causal connection between this fact and the actual involvement of the Comecon. As the Cuban case clearly shows, building practice differed strongly from the theory expressed in the official statements because the construction process proved to be more complicated and multi-layered than initially envisioned. Therefore, each case of the joint investments should be carefully analysed, as some of them were labelled as Comecon investments even if they were bilateral projects and the essential role of the Comecon was marginal. Furthermore, as demonstrated with the Las Camariocas example, tension between different goals of involved actors and expectations arose, leading to substantial delays in the implementation of projects.

Concerning the involvement of the non-European members of Comecon in the building industry, an imbalance of power can be observed, at least viewed through the lens of the East German sources. Mongolia, Cuba and Vietnam were mainly considered addressees or receivers of the international "fraternal" aid. Yet, according to analysed sources, at least in the late 1970s and 1980s, actors from these countries became more active in the international arena, participating in the circulation of ideas and construction methods.

Therefore, it is crucial not only to reconstruct the history of such joint ventures, contextualising the issues of knowledge circulation and economic pressure but also to embed them in their local topography, as realised industrial sites have had a lasting impact on the socio-environmental level. Thus, the tangibility of these processes cannot be unearthed if the investigation confines itself to written documents, especially in cases where the imbalance in the state of the research and the accessibility of archival sources lead to a somewhat biased perspective marginalising local voices. This should be regarded as a call for complimentary research focusing on the "receivers" of the Comecon joint ventures.

---

67 Sergio Díaz-Briquets, and Jorge Pérez-López, "Environmental Implications of Cuba's Development Strategy during the Special Period." *Environmental Issues in Latin America and the Caribbean* (2005): 284–286.

Anne-Kristin Hartmetz

Between Factory and Fiction – Planning and Implementation of Agro-Industrial Development Projects in Ghana in Cooperation with CMEA Countries, 1960–1966

Introduction

In December 1961, shortly before Christmas, the Ghanaian Committee on Economic Cooperation with Eastern European countries (CECEC) held its first meeting in Accra. The committee was responsible for coordinating economic cooperation with the socialist countries.[1] Krobo Edusei, Minister of Industry and the chairman of the committee, gave an opening speech:

> On the whole, over 120 development projects are to be implemented by Eastern countries in association with us on this fair land of ours in the next few years. Indeed, gentlemen, if the development program as envisaged by Osagyefo [Kwame Nkrumah][2] will be implemented, quite soon unemployment, poverty, want, disease and exploitation of man by man will be things of the past. This is the paradise our Osagyefo has promised us, and we have to speed up its realization.[3]

Edusei's statement shows the distinct development paradigm that permeated Ghana's domestic and foreign policy. Development was understood here as a

1 The full name of the committee was "Committee on economic cooperation with Eastern European countries, Soviet Union, China and Israel."

2 Kwame Nkrumah, since 1952 leader of Government Business of the Gold Coast under the colonial administration, Prime Minister from independence in 1957 and, from 1960 until his overthrow in 1966, President of the Republic of Ghana, is an important personality in Ghanaian contemporary history. However, in this chapter I will not focus on him. The growing personality cult around Nkrumah in Ghana in the 1960s was partly propaganda that was intended to serve the centralisation and preservation of power under difficult domestic political conditions. The honorary title "Osagyefo" for Nkrumah has been officially used in Ghana since 1960. In Twi, osagyefo roughly means "hero" or "strong, energetic man," which cannot be translated using the English "redeemer" as is often done. Honorary titles are widespread in West Africa. In this respect, the notion that Nkrumah acquired this title for himself out of a kind of messianic megalomania is a misunderstanding.

3 "Opening speech," Krobo Edusei (18 December 1961), Ghana National Archives (PRAAD) RG 7/1/2178, 260.

https://doi.org/10.1515/9783110658491-006

catch-up development in the sense that Frederick Cooper describes as a "down-to-earth aspiration", in which the aim was to provide the population with the resources like clean water, education, and housing that were part of normal life elsewhere in the world.[4] At the same time, Edusei's speech marked the shift to the East, which had shaped Ghana's economic policy since 1960. Both, postcolonial enthusiasm and close relations with the socialist countries, as well as ambitious development goals, economic problems and internal political tensions developed a remarkable dynamic in Ghana in the first half of the 1960s.

Southern agency is often neglected or marginalised in a rather Eurocentric research approach to international relations. Nevertheless, it did play an important role in defining and shaping spaces of exchange, competition, and cooperation in economic relations between East and South. Especially in these early stages of cooperation, neither CMEA countries like the post-Stalinist Soviet Union and Czechoslovakia nor independent Ghana had a ready-made agenda for establishing and maintaining mutual relations. This led to a dynamism that cannot be fully understood in the context of Cold War bipolar logics. It has to be examined against the background of old and new entanglements, overlapping ideologies, and newly emerging transnational networks. In Ghana in the 1960s, concepts of Pan-Africanism and Non-alignment dominated external politics, although economic ties bound Ghana to East and West.[5]

In this chapter, I will discuss how idealised notions of a socialist modernity were implemented in rural development projects with cooperation partners from the Eastern European socialist countries. This rural space was imagined as a complement to the urban modernity in Accra or Kumasi, which Lukasz Stanek has convincingly depicted.[6] The agro-industrial complex with Soviet-style state farms and a local processing industry (factory) was to be an important part of the process that would transform Ghana in the shortest possible time into a modern, African, socialist country where "work and happiness"[7] would be there

---

4 Frederick Cooper, *Africa since 1940: the past of the present* (New York: Cambridge University Press, 2002), 91.

5 Frank Gerits, "'When the bull elephants fight': Kwame Nkrumah, Non-alignment, and Pan-Africanism as an interventionist ideology in the Global Cold War, 1957–66." *The International History Review* 37 (2015): 952–953.

6 Lukasz Stanek, "Architects from socialist countries in Ghana (1957–67): Modern architecture and mondialisation." *Journal of the Society of Architectural Historians* 74 (2015): 416–442; see also Janet Bery Hess, "Imagining architecture: the structure of nationalism in Accra, Ghana." *Africa Today* 47 (2000): 35–58.

7 Convention People's Party, "Program for the Convention People's Party for work and happiness" (Accra: Ministry of Broadcasting and Information, 1962). "Work and happiness" was a program of the CPP, which, like the introduction of the seven-year plan two years later, was

for everyone. This remained largely wishful thinking (and a fiction). The construction of a sugar factory in cooperation with the Czechoslovakian foreign trade corporation Technoexport is an example of this kind of project. As the chapter will show, the negotiating and planning processes were complex and did not always lead to the intended results. It should be noted, however, that the time from planning to implementation was relatively short, as most projects were interrupted by the increasing economic crisis in Ghana and the political upheaval following the overthrow of Nkrumah in 1966.

I will begin by briefly outlining the development of relations between Ghana and the socialist states after Ghana's independence, with a focus on economic relations. In the second part the institutionalisation of these relations on the Ghanaian side will be presented and the negotiations in the Ghanaian Economic Committee CECEC will be examined in more detail. The third part deals with the renegotiation and implementation of one of the projects, the Komenda Sugar Scheme, as an example. The chapter thus zooms from the macro level of international relations, via the specific negotiations in Ghana, to the local (micro) level of a development project on the spot.

The chapter is based on materials from the Ghana National Archives (PRAAD) in Accra. Jeffrey Ahlman has aptly described the current state of the postcolonial files at PRAAD: "Increasingly, as one advances through the 1960s, any semblance of stable documentary records begins to evaporate. Files and narratives often lack context. Some are missing. Others may be dispersed or intermingled with unrelated material. Still others have found their way into catch-all collections [. . .]".[8] Nevertheless, the numerous fragmented files, which I was able to examine thanks to the support of the staff in the National Archives' reading room during several stays in Accra, allow a unique insight into the decision-making processes in Ghana after independence.

intended to promote the industrialisation and economic modernisation of the country. See also Jeffrey Ahlman, *Living with Nkrumaism: nation, state, and Pan-Africanism in Ghana* (Athens, Ohio: Ohio University Press 2017), 143; Kery Lambert, "It´s all work and happiness on the farms: agricultural development between the blocs in Nkrumah´s Ghana." *Journal of African History* 60 (2019): 25–44.

8 Jeffrey Ahlman, *Living with Nkrumaism*, 23; see also Jean Allman, "Phantoms of the archive: Kwame Nkrumah, a Nazi pilot named Hanna, and the contingencies of postcolonial historical writing." *American Historical Review* 118, (2013): 127–129.

A socialist honeymoon? Economic relations between Ghana and socialist states in the early 1960s

In 1957, Ghana gained full political independence from Great Britain. Independent Ghana found itself at the crossroads of two main axes of world affairs where Cold War East-West confrontation and the economic North-South inequality of a decolonising world met.[9] The policy of Non-alignment determined the foreign relations of the Ghanaian government under Kwame Nkrumah and the Convention Peoples Party (CPP). In terms of economic policy, the Ghanaian government chose the "socialist path" of development from around 1960 until the overthrow of the CPP government in 1966.

Attempts to implement state socialism in Ghana are often seen to be rooted in the close relations between Ghana and the Soviet Union from 1960 onwards. From this perspective, the Soviet Union functions both as a development partner and a role model.[10] However, this view could be questioned. First of all, ideas of socialism were not new in Ghana. They had existed within the CPP before independence. But in the early 1960s there was a new quality, as well as a new quantity, in using the concept of socialism.[11] The "socialist path" was a complex decision in Ghana with domestic conflicts and struggles within the ruling party. It was understood as a part of a bigger modernisation endeavor that included industrialisation and was closely connected to Pan-Africanism.[12]

---

9 Some of the more general observations on socialism in Ghana and Ghana's relations with the socialist countries in the 1960s presented here have been published in my contribution to a working paper at Leipzig University: "African Socialism under Construction: Economic Relations and Scientific-technical Cooperation between Ghana and Eastern European Socialist Countries", 1957–1972, in *East South relations during the Global Cold War: economic activities and area studies interests of East Central European CMEA countries in Africa*, edited by Anne-Kristin Hartmetz, Bence Kocsev, Jan Zofka, 16–21 (Leipzig: Leipzig Working Paper Series 11 SFB 1199, 2018).

10 Alessandro Iandolo, "The rise and fall of the 'Soviet model of development' in West Africa, 1957–64." *Cold War History* 12 (2012): 694–695; Sergey Mazov, *A distant front in the Cold War: The USSR in West Africa and the Congo, 1956–1964* (Stanford: Stanford University Press, 2010), 204–205; W. Scott Thompson, *Ghana's Foreign Policy, 1957–1966*, (Princeton: Princeton University Press, 1969), 292–293.

11 For concepts and aspects of socialism in the Global South, see Christopher Clapham, "The collapse of socialist development in the Third World." *Third World Quarterly*, 13 (1992): 13–25.

12 Gerardo Serra, "From scattered data to Ideological education: Economics, statistics and the state in Ghana, 1948–1966" (Dissertation, London School of Economics and Political Science, 2015), 22–23.

URL etheses.lse.ac.uk/3188/ (accessed 2 June 2022).

It is true that the Soviet Union was the largest partner for socialist development projects in Ghana during the 1960s. But it was not the only partner and certainly not the only role model. Ghana and Guinea were the first countries in Africa South of the Sahara were the Soviet policy towards African countries was tested as a showcase to win the hearts ad minds of politicians in other African countries. There was a shift from this Khrushchevian Africa policy which "[. . .] combined hardcore pragmatism with the most boisterous and ill-informed optimism"[13] to Brezhnev's Africa policy based on "[. . .] a sober assessment of the geopolitical value of individual countries".[14] This certainly affected relations between Ghana and the Soviet Union and other socialist countries from 1964 onwards.

But while sources from Ghanaian archives confirm that close contacts to the Soviet Union played an important role for ideas of a modern socialist society and economy, the story might be more complex. It should be noted that Ghana also established intensive contacts with other socialist countries besides the Soviet Union. Other states also had an impact. Israel, for instance, was around 1960 an important role model and cooperation partner. The Ghana National Construction Company (GNCC) was a joint venture between the Ghanaian government and the Israeli firm Solel Boneh. Farmer's cooperatives, the Ghana Young Pioneers and the Builders Brigade were formed after the Israeli rather than the Soviet example.[15]

As an economic system, a socialist planned economy seemed to be a path to rapid development in order to catch up with the advanced economies. Centralised planning was by no means a pure socialist idea. Planners and consultants from East and West were invited to take part in the ambitious planning of modern industrialised Ghana. Private companies and state agencies from the West were involved, and one can hardly examine postcolonial development plans in Ghana without mentioning the famous Volta River Project which was mainly financed by the World Bank and the US government.[16]

In a cartoon in the Ghanaian newspaper the *Evening News*, we see the "tree of development" which is watered by Nkrumah with "socialism". In the branches and

---

13 Maxim Matusevich, *No easy row for a Russian hoe: Ideology and pragmatism in Nigerian-Soviet relations*, 1960–1991 (Asmara: African World Press, 2003), 43.

14 Mazov, *A Distant Front*, 258.

15 Jeffrey Ahlman, *Living with Nkrumaism*, 96–101; Zach Levey, "The rise and decline of a special relationship: Israel and Ghana 1957–1966." *African Studies Review* 46 (2003): 159–160. For the Ghana National Construction Company, see Stanek, *Architects in Ghana*, 418.

16 The Volta River Project has been the subject of numerous studies. For a more recent paper on the Volta River Project as the core of Ghana's development policy in the 1960s, see Stephan F. Miescher, "'Nkrumah's baby': The Akosombo Dam and the dream of development in Ghana, 1952–1966." *Water History* 6 (2014): 341–366.

fruits of this remarkable tree we find all the ideas of development and institutions of socialist transformation that shaped the socialist experiment in Ghana (Fig. 1).

Apart from the Volta River Project there was a clear shift in Ghanaian development policy in the early 1960s and especially after Kwame Nkrumah's lengthy tour to all Eastern European countries and China in the summer of 1961. Now contracts for development projects were signed mainly with Eastern European countries and China. This tour has been described as a "pilgrimage",[17] but it resembled more of a shopping tour. Nkrumah brought proposals from all visited countries back home. By the end of 1961, the economic focus had clearly shifted to Eastern Europe:

> The Minister of Finance and trade explained that in order to maintain our balance of payments, the policy now is to direct most of Ghana's trade to the Eastern European countries. [. . .] purchases from Eastern bloc countries will be given priority in order to make the best use of the swing credit that Ghana has obtained from these countries.[18]

This shift to the East was not an ideological one, at least not in the first place. Despite socialist rhetoric it was primarily pragmatic. Ghanaian politicians hoped to get "aid without strings attached",[19] and aid on the base of equality. Rapid state-controlled industrialisation seemed to be the only way to achieve this. For the CPP government under Kwame Nkrumah the assumption that "industrialization equals development" was the basis of the whole economic strategy of the CPP government.[20] By this logic, fast industrialisation had to be achieved at all costs. Processing factories as part of an integrated agricultural-industrial complex seemed to be the perfect solution for industrialising the country, modernising agriculture and developing rural areas at the same time.

---

17 Matteo Landricina, *Nkrumah and the West: The "Ghana experiment" in British, American, German and Ghanaian Archives* (Zürich: LIT, 2018), 48.

18 "Minutes of the second meeting of the Committee for economic co-operation with Eastern countries," 21 December 1961, PRAAD RG 7/1/1672, 6.

19 Scott Thompson, *Ghana's Foreign Policy*, 164.

20 Tony Killick, *Development Economics in Action: A Study of Economic Policies in Ghana* (New York: Routledge, 2010), 202.

Fig. 1: Cartoon “Tree of Development”, *Evening News*, 8 January 1966, 7.

A closer look at the gifts: Re-negotiation, regulation and institutionalisation of East-South cooperation in Ghana

The contracts with Eastern European countries included trade agreements with a focus on barter trade and generous swing credits, technical and economic cooperation agreements and cultural cooperation agreements. The latter do not seem to belong to economics. But here the exchange of experts and the scholarship programs for the training of Ghanaians in the socialist countries were negotiated. In this early phase of mutual relations most of the socialist countries seemed all to ready to sign each and every contract, and often it was not clear who negotiated with whom. Some agreements and contracts were negotiated by officials from the Ghanaian delegations, some by ministries but some were just negotiated by enterprises like fishing corporations or collective farms.[21] After Nkrumah's return from Eastern Europe in September 1961, the government decided that contracts were supposed to be concluded only on a bilateral intergovernmental level.

In order to conclude these state contracts, the Ghanaian Minister of Industry, Krobo Edusei, travelled in October 1961 with a delegation and a suitcase full of aide memoirs to all the socialist countries Nkrumah had visited. In Edusei's eyes this tour was a great success.[22] However, the shopping lists that Edusei took on this trip were rather long. Many schemes overlapped and some agreements, such as an aviation agreement with Albania, which at that time had no air fleet at all, were of little use.[23]

In addition, ministries and government agencies continued to be very generous in independently concluding supply contracts for equipment and goods and charging the government for these supplies. The visibly overburdened Ghanaian State Control Commission tried to stop this practice in November 1961. It asked all authorities to involve the State Planning Secretariat and the State Control Commission

21 For example, in December 1961, a Ghanaian co-operative delegation was in Poland and concluded contracts there. The National Cooperative Council distance itself from this and informed the ministry of industries that the Ghanaians in Poland were probably members of fishing cooperatives, but that the council had no idea what they wanted in Poland. "Disassociation of agreement" (no date), National Co-operative Council to Ministry of Industries, PRAAD RG 7/1/2183, 122.

22 "Cabinet memorandum by the Minister of Light and Heavy Industries, subject: trade and economic agreements with Eastern countries and China" (no date [1961]), PRAAD RG 7/1/2178, 244–245.

23 "Aide memoire from Osagyefo Dr Kwame Nkrumah, president and head of the government of Ghana to His Excellency Mr. Mehmet Shehu, chairman of the council of ministers of the People´s Republic of Albania" (no date), PRAAD RG12/3/18, 136.

before ordering from Eastern Europe, signing contracts or inviting delegations and experts.[24] The accommodation of these visitors was a serious problem. "The shortage of hotel accommodation is one of the factors militating against speedy conclusion of contracts [. . .], and the position has recently got so bad that complaints have been received of members of foreign delegations being turned out of their rooms.", as the secretary of the Ghanaian development secretariate stated at a meeting with Nkrumah in the end of April 1961. Nkrumah decided at this meeting that "[. . .] a West German consortium should be assigned the job" to build a hotel to accommodate the Eastern European delegations.[25]

Overall, the responsibilities were not clearly defined. Neither the minister of industry nor anybody else had an overview over the projects planned. There were overlaps between contracts and projects and often it was not at all clear who was in charge on the Ghanaian side. Counting and collecting of data started in the ministries. To get an overview of the numerous contracts and projects and to coordinate the increasingly intensive cooperation with the socialist countries the Committee for economic cooperation with the socialist countries and China (CECEC) was established in December 1961. A Committee of the same name had been in place since 1960 under the chairmanship of Kwame Nkrumah as a subcommittee of the Standing Planning Committee. There were plans for an equivalent committee on relations with the West but I found no evidence in the Ghanaian National Archives that this body was ever established.[26] Instead, in addition to the CECEC, a Committee for Economic Cooperation with Israel (CECI), chaired by Nkrumah, was established in May 1961. This shows the shifting focus to the East even before Nkrumah's tour to Eastern Europe in July 1961 and the importance that was given to cooperation with Israel in the early 1960s.[27] However, both committees met only two or three times during the spring of 1961. They could therefore also be seen as an example for the constant change of the still little institutionalized economic policy in Ghana. In December 1961, after Nkrumah's tour to the East, the CECEC was formally re-established and considerably

24 "Bills of exchange and promissory notes drawn under contracts," State Control Commission (13 November 1961), PRAAD RG 7/1/2178, 222.

25 "Minutes of a meeting" (29 April 1961), PRAAD RG 7/1/1690, 36.

26 "Extracts from the minutes of a meeting of the cabinet held on the 23rd August 1960," PRAAD RG7/1/1690, 12a-13. The Standing Planning Committees name was originally Special Socialist Development Committee.

27 "Minutes of the first meeting of the Committee for Economic Co-operation with Israel, held at the Flagstaff House on Saturday" (13 May 1961), PRAAD RG 7/1/1685, 2–3; "Sub-Committees for economic cooperation with the Eastern countries and with Israel (CECEC and CECI)" (24 May 1961), PRAAD RG 6/2/7, 6. For the intense cooperation with Israel around 1960, see Levey, *Israel and Ghana*, 46–51.

expanded, merged with the CECI and placed under the authority of the Ministry of Industry. Nkrumah himself was not a member of this reorganized committee. Initially, it consisted of representatives of the Ministries of Industry, Trade, Agriculture and Finance and the Deputy Director of the Bank of Ghana, Kwesi Amoako-Atta.[28] This circle was constantly expanded over the next few months. In summer 1962, the attendance lists (or sometimes rather absence lists) included representatives of fifteen ministries and authorities.

The CECEC was "[. . .] meant to be [. . .] the central clearing house for all economic cooperation matters with the countries concerned", in order to organize the "centralization of executive action".[29] It developed a number of sub committees and was quite influential for some years. Its founding was an important step in institutionalizing international economic relations. In the beginning the committee met weekly, and delegations from all socialist countries were invited to the chairman's office to discuss projects and contracts. One point of renegotiations were the terms of payment. Shortly after Minister Edusei's return from Eastern Europe it became clear that most of the negotiated agreements were not as advantageous for Ghana as the officials had assumed. Interest rates and repayment conditions were more or less moderate compared to western offers. But the agreements included a lot of more or less hidden payments in pound sterling. Earning convertible currency surely was in the interest of the Eastern partners. But it was certainly not in Ghana's interest to pay in pound sterling, as Ghana also needed to save convertible currency. While some governments agreed to extend the general terms of repayment, the repayment in Ghana pounds instead of pound sterling was a different issue. The Polish government for instance simply refused to renegotiate this.[30]

Another point of permanent discussion was the role of experts in the planned projects. There was, for instance, a long-lasting discussion because the Ghanaian side wanted Soviet state farm experts not as consultants but as managers of the

---

28 Until September 1962, the Bank of Ghana was headed by Hubert Kessels, a German financial expert, but he rarely appears in Ghanaian documents and was not present at CECEC meetings. Amoako-Atta was formally his deputy, but he had far-reaching influence. He became Minister of Finance in 1964 and, among other things, had the difficult task of renegotiating the agreements with the socialist countries during the increasingly severe financial and economic crisis in Ghana in 1965. On Amoako-Ata's rise and the politicisation of the Bank of Ghana, see Robert L. Tignor, *W. Arthur Lewis and the birth of Development Economics*, (Princeton: Princeton University Press, 2006), 180–185.

29 "Memo," Principal Secretary Development Secretariat Millar-Craig (26 October 1961), PRAAD RG7/1/1278, 215a.

30 "Minutes of the 11th Meeting of the CECEC" (8 March 1962), PRAAD RG 7/1/1672, 65–66.

farms. This was vehemently rejected by the Soviet side for they saw this as interference in Ghanaian internal affairs.[31] A third point was the attempt to get all planned projects on a turnkey base. After lengthy discussions in the CECEC and other agencies Nkrumah informed the Cabinet in July 1962 that

> it was revealed that in almost all the cases in question the undertaking of the Eastern European Governments concerned was limited only to the provision of plant and machines. [. . .] as a result of this Osagyefo had called for a re-examination of all these arrangements to provide not only for the supply of machinery but also for the complete establishment of the factory on a turn-key base.[32]

This order, of course, meant profound changes in some of the contracts and not all partners were willing to renegotiate this.[33]

Moving a factory back and forth: The Komenda sugar scheme

Rural development played an important role in an agricultural dominated economy like the Ghanaian. Kwame Nkrumah wanted a "total break with primitive methods".[34] In socialist countries, Ghanaian delegations were introduced to the achievements of large-scale mechanized agricultural production. They were impressed by what was shown to them on tours in Soviet Tadzhikistan, Poland or Bulgaria, although it should be noted that this was not always the case. The Ghanaian ambassador to Bulgaria, for instance, warned his government: "I only recommend buildings from Bulgaria and not machines or agricultural tools. Most of the agricultural machines are manipulated by the use of horses. This to my mind is old fashioned and outmoded".[35]

But most Ghanaian delegates were enthusiastic about what they saw in the East. This enthusiasm together with the general guideline to plan development

31 Scott Thompson, *Ghana's Foreign Policy*, 274. See also, Anna Calori, Anne-Kristin Hartmetz, Bence Koczev, and Jan Zofka, "Alternative globalization? Spaces of economic interaction between the 'socialist camp' and the 'global south,'" in *Between East and South: Spaces of interaction in the globalizing economy of the Cold War*, edited by Anna Calori, Anne-Kristin Hartmetz, Bence Koczev, James Mark, and Jan Zofka, 1–32 (Berlin, Boston: De Gruyter, 2019), 1.

32 "Extract from the minutes of a meeting of the cabinet" (17 July 1962), PRAAD RG7/1/1674, 685.

33 "Information paper by the Minister of Industries and Chairman of the CECEC: review of contracts on turn-key basis" (no date), PRAAD RG 7/1/1672, 150–151; "Minutes of the 13th meeting of the committee for economic cooperation with Eastern countries and Israel" (19 December 1962), PRAAD RG 7/1/78, no page; see also: W. Scott Thompson, *Ghana's Foreign Policy*, 275–276.

34 Nkrumah quoted in Tony Killick, *Development Economics*, 51.

35 J.L. Appah-Sampong, "Report of a trip around Bulgaria" (11 July 1962), PRAAD RG7/1/1665, 214.

projects mainly with Eastern European partners, taking advantage of the supposedly generous conditions, resulted in the planning of predominantly large projects and state farms in the agricultural sector from 1961/1962 onwards with the help of the Eastern European socialist countries.[36] The Ghanaian government attempted to create a socialist modernity in rural areas and to establish a mechanised agriculture with processing plants in all parts of the country. "Factories spring up like mushrooms all over the country" is only one of numerous enthusiastic headlines in the Ghanaian newspapers that spread publicity for the CPP's rural modernisation program (Fig. 2).[37] The plan was to have a state farm and factories in every constituency.[38]

The Czechoslovakian sugar factory, which was to serve as part of an integrated local sugar industry, is an example of this endeavour. There had been a longstanding plan to supply the Ghanaian population with sugar from domestic cultivation instead of importing it. These schemes dated back to the early 1950s but they were delayed like many development projects from the late colonial period. Prior to Nkrumah's trip to Eastern Europe, the Ghanaian Industrial Development Corporation (IDC) had already signed contracts for the construction of two sugar factories. One contract about a sugar project in Atsutsuare was signed with the Polish state company CEKOP.[39] A second contract was signed with the Czechoslovakian state company Technoexport in June 1961.[40] While the Polish sugar project went quite well at the beginning, negotiations and renegotiations for the construction of the Czechoslovakian factory are worth a closer look. They contradict the sometimes expressed assumption that in the projects with Eastern European countries it was the Eastern side that had failed to fulfil the contracts or had delivered insufficiently.

The factory was originally to be located in Awudome. However, the area proved to be unsuitable for sugar cane cultivation, and it was therefore decided to offer the Czechs another area. This decision was taken at the first meeting of the CECEC in December 1961. Here, in addition to the sugar project, several projects already planned with other, mostly Western, partners were examined to see whether it would be possible to cancel the contracts and carry them out with

---

36 Lambert, "Work and happiness," 32–36.

37 *Evening News* (2 March 1963), 5.

38 Killick, *Development economics*, 253.

39 In Akuse, the construction design was drawn by Polish architects and feasibility studies were conducted partly by the Food and Agriculture Organization of the UN. So, in the beginning the implementation went relatively smoothly. In the end this did not mean that the project was more successful than the Czechoslovakian scheme. PRAAD RG 7/1/1916, 17–21, 154–156.

40 "Komenda sugar scheme" (24 December 1963), PRAAD RG 7/1/631, no page number.

Fig. 2: "Factories like Mushrooms", *Evening News*, 2 January 1963, 5.

partners from Eastern Europe.[41] It was decided to move the Czech sugar project to Komenda, where a Dutch consortium had been working for some time on preliminary investigations for a sugar scheme.[42] At the time of the decision, the Dutch sugar cane experts were just about to finish a study to plan the necessary irrigation in Komenda and had started a series of tests for industrial sugar cane cultivation. The Dutch contractors had to retreat to give way to the Czechoslovakian project.[43]

Shortly afterwards it became apparent that a major problem had been overlooked on the Ghanaian side. Agro-industrial complexes require expertise in the industrial and in the agricultural parts of the business. The expertise of the Czechoslovakians in building sugar refineries did not mean that they had experts in growing sugar cane. Since the Ghanaians were lacking experts as well and had cancelled the contract with the Dutch experts, they expected the Czechoslovakian side to cover the agricultural part of the project. But for obvious reasons negotiations about nonexistent Czech sugar cane experts turned out to be fruitless. Moreover, nobody on the Ghanaian side seemed to feel responsible for solving the problem by hiring experts from Cuba or India. That was a suggestion, the Czechoslovakian side made during re-negotiations of the project in 1963.[44]

At least the ministries involved in Ghana tried to solve the irrigation problem, because growing sugar cane requires a sufficient supply of water. Here expertise was sought from different partners in the East and West. These were companies who already had offices in Accra, for instance the West German Stahlunion which was involved in many projects. There were also consultants from a Pakistani company as well as from the Yugoslav Energoprojekt. Finally, an Israeli company tried to take over the irrigation part of the planned sugar cane project.[45]

---

41 "Review of agreements" (18 December 1961), PRAAD RG 7/1/1672, 4. Other projects with Western partners under review were, for instance, a cement project with Portland Cement, a brick and tile factory planned with Taylor Woodrow and a factory for plastic shoes with the British Utrilon Industries.

42 Het Raatgevend Ingenieursbureau Bish&Partners N.V., Den Haag.

43 "Minutes of the meeting held in the Ministry of Industries on 18th October 1962" (24 October 1962), PRAAD RG 7/1/1919, 1–3.

44 J. Janda, First Secretary (Commercial) Embassy of the Czechoslovak Socialist Republic in Ghana to K.K. Apeadu, Principal Secretary, Ghana Ministry of Industries (28 January 1963), PRAAD RG 7/1/1701, 429. In September 1962, the US government offered to train three Ghanaians in the techniques of industrial sugar cane cultivation; PRAAD RG7/1/634, 25.

45 "Komenda sugar project irrigation and water supply scheme" (11 March 1964), PRAAD RG 7/1/631, no page number. Energoprojekt was involved in many development projects and is still active in Ghana. Today, Energoprojekt Ghana is one of the companies shaping the new skyline of Accra that has changed remarkably during the last few years.

In the meantime, the machines and plants that had been produced within the agreed time were rotting back in Europe. The Czechoslovakian side was almost begging to get the permission necessary to ship them to Ghana. They suggested starting with building the factory, adding some machinery and using it temporarily as a refinery to process imported raw sugar. It was also requested that the Ghanaian side should take care of the Czech experts who had been in Ghana for months but had no contracts and found themselves in a difficult situation.[46]

But while the equipment was ready the factory was not. There was no plan for a building to house the equipment. Not even temporary warehouses were available. Again, the Ghanaian files give the impression that the factory buildings were simply assumed to be included in the price. In the controversial renegotiations at the beginning of 1963, the Ghanaian Minister of Industry correctly stated, "that machinery and equipment alone would not make a factory".[47] However, the contract of June 1961 actually mentioned "complete machinery equipment of a cane sugar mill". It was pointed out in the contract that there would only be sketches and measurements of the machinery and equipment and that the Ghanaian contract partners would erect buildings at their own expense.[48] During the tenacious negotiations on this issue, the Ghanaians repeatedly tried to convince their contract partners to convert their offer into a turnkey project. The Czechs made concessions regarding the supply of building materials, but refused to build the factory. The contract was awarded to the Ghanaian architect Kwame Frimpong. Frimpong, a freelance architect, was hired directly by the ministry of industries.[49]

The construction of the factory was further delayed. The new Ghanaian Minister of Industry, Imoru Egala, as chairman of the CECEC, informed the Czech ambassador in February 1963 that Ghana wanted to build Komenda with the Dutch again.[50] It was now planned to have the Czech factory built at the original location at Adidome, which was not suitable for sugar production. After all, minister Egala stated, the Czechs were not prepared to realise the entire project and the Dutch had made a better offer in the meantime. He asked that this proposal be accepted,

46 Janda to Apeadu (28 January 1963), PRAAD RG 7/1/1701, 429.

47 Sackeyfio to Janda (27 February 1963), PRAAD RG 7/1/1701, 449.

48 "Supply contract concluded in the framework of the agreement on economic co-operation between the government of the Czechoslovak Socialist Republic and the government of the Republic of Ghana" (22 May 1961), PRAAD RG 7/1/631, no page number.

49 "Notes concerning appointment of architectural and engineering consultants" (2 April 1962), PRAAD RG 7/1/1969, 123–125; "Assignment K. Frimpong" (6 June 1962), PRAAD RG7/1/634, 7–11.

50 Other documents show that this decision was based on an order from Kwame Nkrumah himself: "Minutes of the 29th meeting of the Committee for Economic Cooperation with Eastern Countries and Israel" (27 February 1963), PRAAD RG 7/1/78, no page number.

"in the same friendly spirit in which it has been made".[51] The Czechoslovakian side took the change in a slightly less friendly spirit. The Czech ambassador informed the Ghanaian Foreign Ministry that he would forward the request to his government but could not imagine that the Czechoslovak side would accept this change and further delay.[52] In the subsequent dispute between the Ministry of Industry and the Czechoslovak embassy the fronts hardened. This was probably because Egala had to implement instructions from Kwame Nkrumah and did not have much leeway himself. The Czech government, however, could not agree, because building the sugar factory at the proposed site of Awudome would have been practically useless.

The Czech embassy secretary J. Janda, who was in charge of the negotiations, suggested that there should be cooperation with the Poles who were building the sugar factory and distillery in Atsutsuare on the Volta. A joint Ghanaian state-owned enterprise could then produce sugar in both factories and alcohol at the distillery planned by the Polish partners.[53] This idea did not receive approval on the Ghanaian side, "for many reasons", as C. Sackeyfio, the responsible and quite influential secretary in the Ministry of Industry vaguely put it.[54] The negotiations continued to drag on. The minutes of a meeting between the responsible Secretary of State in the Ghanaian ministry of industry H.R. Amonoo and the deputy director of Technoexport F. Samek at the beginning of May 1963 state: "As far as he [Amonoo] was concerned the Ghana Minister of Industries had informed the Czechoslovak Ambassador in Accra that this factory will be built. Mr. Samek asked: 'But when?'"[55]

Nevertheless, the Ghanaian side started to reexamine the unsuitable area around Awudome.[56] The files are not preserved in their complete form, therefore it is not possible to say exactly when and how often this decision was reversed. Finally, the Czech factory site was "moved" again back to Komenda and in September 1962 there was a Czech expert in Komenda. At the same time, in a rather defensive tone, the minister Egala asked the Czech side for a little more patience until the factories and infrastructure for Komenda and other joint projects had been built.[57] At that

51 Egala to Sobotka (20 February 1963), PRAAD RG 1/7/1701, 432.
52 Sobotka to Egala (21 February 1963), PRAAD RG 7/1/1701, 437.
53 Janda to Egala (11 March 1963), PRAAD RG7/1/1701, 452–453.
54 Sackeyfio to Janda (18 March 1963), PRAAD RG7/1/1701, 455.
55 "Note of a meeting between Mr. H.R. Amonoo and Mr. Frantisek Samek, vice-president of Technoexport" (25 April 1963), PRAAD RG7/1/1701, 463.
56 "Awudome sugar project" (16 March 1963), PRAAD RG7/1/1701, 468.
57 "Mr. Z. Hejhalek" (17 September 1963), PRAAD RG7/1/1701, 499; "Review of industrial projects" (25 September 1963), PRAAD RG7/1/1701, 500.

time the Ghanaian economy was already in serious trouble and Ghana could not afford to raise her own contribution for the ambitious development and industrialisation programme.

In the end, however, the Polish state-owned company CEKOP built the factory in Atsutsuare as originally planned, and Czechoslovakian Technoexport built the factory in Komenda (Fig. 3). Sugar production at both locations began in 1967, after the fall of Nkrumah and the CPP.[58] The Komenda sugar factory and the Polish sugar scheme in Atsutsuare never operated on a commercial level. In 1972, both factories still needed massive support from the Ghanaian development budget. Even a new state operator, Ghana Sugar Estate Limited, was unable to make a profit.[59] Although the factories were working, there was never enough supply of sugar cane and import substitution was never reached. Only the state-owned distillery made some profit.

Fig. 3: "Komenda Sugar Factory", Ghana Sugar Estate ltd., *Annual Report 1973/74*, 16.

58 Leslie E. Grayson, "A Conglomerate in Africa: Public-sector manufacturing enterprises in Ghana, 1962–1971." *African Studies Review* 16 (1973): 315–345, 317; Killick, *Development Economics*, 254. Paul van der Wel, *The Sugar Industry 1960–70: An Exercise in Ex-post Evaluation* (The Hague: Working Paper 26, Social Studies Institute, 1973), 1.

59 At the beginning of the 1970s, for example, they reached only about 10 percent of their full capacity. Grayson, "Conglomerate in Africa," 336; Killick, *Development Economics*, 276–277; van der Wel, *Ghana Sugar Industry*, 1–3.

Conclusion

The implementation of the Komenda sugar project with Czechoslovakian aid is not a success story of 1960s' East-South cooperation. We do not know what a longer period of intense cooperation between Ghana and socialist countries would have meant for the Ghanaian economy. Yet examining the processes of negotiation and institutionalisation of this cooperation allows us to gain insight into an early Cold War economic East-South encounter in Africa on the spot.

For the Ghanaian side the aim of all efforts to negotiate with the East (as well as with the West) was development. It should be reached by modernisation through industrialisation. Centralised planning, the establishment of state-owned farms and enterprises, and the organisation of commissions and committees followed these development logics. Ghana was primarily concerned with building a manufacturing industry in order to supply the population and produce for the African market, but also to reduce dependence on the world market price for raw materials and on imported consumer's goods.

At the same time, the objective of development in the ideas of many Ghanaian protagonists was an industrialised modernity. These ideas of modernisation and modernity were expressed not only in large-scale projects such as the Akosombo Dam or in urban architecture. In rural areas, too, progress and modernity were to be visible in the topography of large mechanised state farms and in the construction of local manufacturing industries. The symbolic dimension of this planning of a decentralised socialist modernity in Ghana is evident in Ghanaian press reports of the time. Work and happiness, prosperity and modernity should be for everyone, including the rural population. This dream of postcolonial rural modernity should be realised through favourable contracts with partners from socialist countries.

Although the plan remained largely a fiction, it continues to shape the ideas of rural development in Ghana. With the "one district – one factory" programme, which has been in operation since 2016, the Ghanaian government is attempting to implement the idea of decentralised rural modernisation and industrialisation once again. In each of the 254 administrative subdistricts, a factory is to ensure rural development (Fig. 4). To achieve this, either new complexes are to be built or old plants are to be renovated with the help of private investors and state funds. This programme is intensively debated in Ghana and shows very moderate success so far.[60] The refurbishment of the sugar factory in Komenda, which has not produced sugar for a long time, is also part of this programme.[61]

Fig. 4: "One District One Factory", iwatchafrica.org/2017/11/09/1d1f-govt-set-miss-target-establish-50-factories-50-districts-close-2017/ (10 June 2022).

60 The government programme website counts 76 reconstructed or newly built factories. However, there are only three showcase projects on the website. Links to the project overview are empty. Research in the Ghanaian media also suggests that the figure of 76 factories is implausible. See 1d1f.gov.gh (12 June 2022).

See also, Frank John Eshun, "A critical look at the Ghanaian one district one factory industrial policy in relation to climate change." *African Journal of Environmental Science and Technology* 13, no. 4 (2019): 155–161.

61 I visited the area in the summer of 2019. There seemed to be an Indian investor, but the facilities were in poor condition and no one could provide information about when the factory would start working. The reopening of the sugar factory has been delayed since. Still, there is not enough locally grown sugar for the factory. It also appears that the plant is not operational.

Rachel Lee

Of Mobility and Earth: Hannah Schreckenbach's Engagements with Indigenous Architectures in Ghana

From 1960 to 1982 Hannah Schreckenbach, a woman architect and town planner from Germany, worked in Ghana. She spent 15 years with the Public Works Department in Accra, seven teaching at the University of Science and Technology in Kumasi, and the final two writing the book *Construction Technology for a Tropical Developing Country* for the GTZ (German Technical Cooperation Agency, now GIZ). Her work impacted the architecture and town planning realms in post-colonial Ghana through the numerous projects that she designed and realised, as well as through her teaching and activism, particularly in relation to local building cultures. Throughout her career in Ghana, Schreckenbach regularly visited rural settlements, documenting the communities' building practices and analysing their use of space and materials through interviews, photographs and drawings. What began as an interest soon became a constitutive part of her practice as, motivated by hostile government housing policies and a perceived lack of awareness in professional circles, she increasingly devoted time to developing a consciousness and understanding of the country's indigenous architectures. Her extensive networks, built through social and professional activities, enabled her to work in different regions in Ghana and in a variety of positions. They also granted her access to a wide range of social spheres, finally allowing her to leave Ghana and continue her career in Germany.

Schreckenbach's unusual biography, which cross-cuts five German political systems as well as 22 years of post-independence Ghana, provides a generative lens for studying shifts in architecture and planning practices during the Cold War and creating a more nuanced understanding of how international politics and individual agency impacted local situations, in this case in Ghana. Strongly independent and highly mobile, Schreckenbach's practice was transnational, defying the standard Cold War binary categories of East and West. Indeed, this essay responds to the editors' call to move beyond binary Cold War narratives of confrontation to study different *modi operandi* that contributed to the construction of the built environment during that era, particularly in post-colonial and decolonising nations.[1]

1 See the introduction of Christoph Bernhardt, Andreas Butter, and Monika Motylińska in this book, 2.

https://doi.org/10.1515/9783110658491-007

In her home in Magdeburg, Schreckenbach holds a substantial collection of material relating to her work in Ghana. This material remained unavailable because Schreckenbach did not permit visits. Due to a lack of mobility funding, it was not possible to travel to Ghana to visit her built works or archives there or connect with former colleagues and friends.[2] The following essay thus draws on a rather limited range of sources and undoubtedly presents an uneven and unbalanced picture. Hopefully future researchers will be able to access more varied material and construct more complete arguments. Schreckenbach's writings, as well as interviews and email correspondence with her undertaken by the author in 2014 and 2015, formed the main sources for this essay.

Schreckenbach's written works encompass a variety of genres: praxis-oriented technical publications on aspects of building and construction (with a particular focus on earth or clay as a construction material), written with architects, students of architecture, and builders in mind; essays that explore Ghana's indigenous architecture using ethnographic and visual methods; and personal memoirs describing her time in Ghana. The latter include the unpublished manuscript "Ein Haus für die Ziegen des Präsidenten" and *Herzensheimat Ghana: Erinnerungen an ein Land im Aufbruch*, which was published in 2018.

These memoirs provide the most varied and detailed information about Schreckenbach's life and career and are drawn upon substantially in the following essay. In addition to Schreckenbach's memories and secondary literature, both books are based on letters and cards that she sent her mother from Ghana. Schreckenbach discovered these, neatly bound together, after her mother's death in 1992.[3] For the most part, her memoirs document her daily life, describing the people and places that she encountered, and giving insights into the activities she undertook, sometimes in surprising detail, for example: "I also bought some groceries that are no longer available in Ghana such as custard powder, vanilla sugar, lentils, raisins and a bottle of French red wine".[4]

In addition to everyday events, she reflects on Ghanaian politics and, more briefly, on world events, including the assassination of John F. Kennedy or the terrorist attacks at the Olympic Games in Munich. She does not take a critical

---

2 The research for this essay was conducted with funding from the German-Israeli Foundation through the research grant: Architecture, Planning and Foreign Policy: Israeli and GDR Development Cooperation in sub-Saharan Africa 1950–1990.

3 Hannah Schreckenbach, "Ein Haus Für Die Ziegen Des Präsidenten" (unpublished manuscript, 2014), 3.

4 Schreckenbach, 249. Original: "Ich kaufte außerdem ein paar Lebensmittel ein, die es in Ghana gar nicht mehr gibt wie Puddingpulver, Vanillezucker, Linsen, Rosinen und auch eine Flasche französischen Rotwein."

approach to recounting her life in Ghana. It is presented as a work in progress, as plans and actions, as pragmatic doing. She does not dwell on failures, problems or sorrows, but does recount achievements, joys and banalities.

In places, the language she uses is offensive, as the following quotation evidences: "Kofi [Schreckenbach's long-term domestic worker] got us a garden boy from his 'extended family' who diligently plants flowers everywhere".[5] Here, perhaps unwittingly, she describes an unnamed, black person (he remains unnamed in the rest of the book) in transactional terms as an object that is "got". Occasionally she makes generalisations that verge on the absurd, as when, according to Schreckenbach, "there was no racism" during her time in Ghana.[6] She neither reflects on her positionality, nor on the privilege that she, as a white, educated European woman, clearly possessed.

The intention of this essay is not to include Schreckenbach in an existing architectural historical canon, or to associate her work with a particular architectural movement. Rather, this study of her biography helps shed light on architectural practices during the Cold War, at a time when the world was divided along political lines into East, West and Non-Aligned, and categorised as First, Second and Third. As her biography traverses all of these groupings, it makes an unusual case study that has the potential to unsettle established historical narratives and provide new insights into the workings of the Cold War era, with particular focus paid to a decolonising sub-Saharan nation state. At a more personal level, as a woman architect, Schreckenbach's independence and mobility are also noteworthy, as are the professional choices she made and the projects she chose to invest her energies and resources in. As architectural history continues to be dominated by the biographies of male practitioners, exploring and documenting the work of women architects remains an important historiographical practice, both to recuperate overlooked histories and to expand the boundaries of the discipline.[7]

---

5 Schreckenbach, 120. Original: "Kofi hat uns aus seiner "Großfamilie" einen Gartenjungen besorgt, der überall fleißig Blumen pflanzt."

6 Hannah Schreckenbach, *Herzensheimat Ghana: Erinnerungen an ein Land im Aufbruch* (Hamburg: Palmato Publishing, 2018), 862. Original: "Es gab zwar auch schon zu meiner Zeit einige ethnische Auseinandersetzungen, bei denen es meistens um Partei- oder Religionszugehörigkeiten oder um Landfragen ging. Aber es gab keinen Rassismus."

7 Much important work has been done in this regard in recent years. For an overview, please consult the introduction and footnotes to the open access publication Anooradha Iyer Siddiqi, and Rachel Lee, eds., "On Margins: Feminist Architectural Histories of Migration." *ABE Journal. Architecture beyond Europe* 16 (2020), DOI: https://doi.org/10.4000/abe.7126.

Becoming an architect and planner in Dresden, Karlsruhe and London

Hannah Schreckenbach's early years were marked by profound shifts in the German political climate – from the Weimar Republic, through the National Socialist period, to the founding of the German Democratic Republic (GDR) – as well as by personal relocations. She was born in Osnabruck, Germany, in 1932, in the final year of the Weimar Republic. Her father, an engineer in the civil service, had been posted to Osnabruck after stints working in Magdeburg and Tilsit. Following another such reposting, she grew up in Magdeburg, starting school in 1938 after the Nazi Party had seized power and Germany was on the brink of war. After the bombing of Magdeburg, she was moved to the relative safety of Uslar, near Gottingen, to stay with her aunt. Following World War Two, when Schreckenbach was a young teenager, she returned to Magdeburg, which soon became part of the German Democratic Republic.

Barred from studying architecture immediately after graduating from high school due to her father's white-collar occupation, as part of the GDR's socialisation policy she was advised to "get closer to the proletariat" before entering the higher education system.[8] To achieve this, she successfully apprenticed as a bricklayer. A rather untypical choice for a woman, her training provided valuable experiences both in working in a male-dominated environment and in the basics of construction.

Significantly for her later work in Ghana, during this period Schreckenbach began to work with earth as a building material. Earth was used in villages, and occasionally in urban areas, during post-war reconstruction. Its appropriateness as a construction material was documented in the *Lehmbaufibel* (Earth building primer), which was published in 1947 by the University of Weimar in a series edited by Hermann Henselmann, one of the most prominent architects in the early years of the GDR. A practical guide to building with earth, the publication opens with images illustrating earth-built buildings in different contexts (Mesopotamia, Turkey, Yugoslavia, Austria, Hungary, East Prussia and Weimar), in an attempt to show its diverse, sophisticated usage and to present an argument against it being a 'primitive' material. Despite the significant contributions women were making to rebuilding cities and villages in the GDR following World War Two, the book's illustrations show men constructing earth buildings. One woman is pictured emptying a pail of water – perhaps the least skilled job on the building site.

8 Schreckenbach, "Ein Haus Für Die Ziegen Des Präsidenten," 5.

From 1952 to 1955, Schreckenbach studied architecture at the Technical University Dresden (TU Dresden), where despite, or perhaps due to the devastation the city had suffered during the war, she and her colleagues initially experienced a spirit of optimism. In addition to her studies, she spent time sketching the ruins of the Baroque cityscape and, eager to gain more practical building experiences, interned as a carpenter during her semester breaks. As Mary Pepchinski and Mariann Simon point out in *Ideological Equals*, choosing a career as an architect was not uncommon in the GDR, indeed it was encouraged by the state's ideology. Women who studied architecture could expect to establish careers as architects, at least theoretically: "In principle, the new generation of women architects entering the profession in the 1950s and early 1960s were offered the same opportunities as their male colleagues."[9]

During this time, however, the Cold War politics of the GDR were becoming increasingly oppressive. The TU Dresden was not exempt from this. Schreckenbach was unimpressed by the architecture school's focus on socialist realism and "*Zuckerbäckerarchitektur*" (confectioner's architecture), as she calls it – the state-sanctioned approaches to architectural design.[10] Following the violent and brutal suppression of the 17 June 1953 uprising, professors at the Technical University of Dresden began to leave the country.[11]+[12] After it became clear that the Staatssicherheit had begun monitoring students, Schreckenbach left Dresden in 1955, taking a train to Berlin and seeking asylum in Berlin-Charlottenburg before flying to Frankfurt am Main.[13] With her move to West Germany (BRD), at the age of 23, Schreckenbach closed the chapter on socialisation and education in a socialist state. She and some of her closest friends from Dresden who had also fled the GDR completed their architecture studies in Karlsruhe in BRD. As a political refugee, she did not visit the GDR for over a decade, keeping in contact with her friends and family through letters.[14] Despite the relatively short separation of the two Germanies, Schreckenbach felt like an outsider in the BRD. Her views on the sovereignty of the GDR led her to be branded a "leftist" and she was shocked at

---

9 Mary Pepchinski and Mariann Simon, *Ideological Equals: Women Architects in Socialist Europe 1945–1989* (London: Routledge, 2016).

10 Schreckenbach, "Ein Haus Für Die Ziegen Des Präsidenten," 9.

11 Schreckenbach, "Ein Haus Für Die Ziegen Des Präsidenten," 9–10.

12 Prominent architects also left the GDR during this period. See, for example, Annika Levels, "Across the Border. Ties of Architects and Urban Planners between East and West Germany: The Case of Egon Hartmann, 1954–1976." *Planning Perspectives* 32, no. 4 (2 October 2017): 557–576, https://doi.org/10.1080/02665433.2017.1317015.

13 Schreckenbach, "Ein Haus Für Die Ziegen Des Präsidenten."

14 Schreckenbach, 10.

the continued prevalence of former Nazi Party members in the contemporary BRD government.[15]

With a German Academic Exchange Service (DAAD) scholarship she left for London in 1958 to take a postgraduate course in town planning at University College London, and later worked at the London County Council as a planning assistant, overcoming significant language barriers through her determination to master English, which she had not been taught in school. In London she became integrated into a community of international students (often from British colonies or Commonwealth countries) who took part in university courses as well as weekend excursions organised by the British Council. Through discussions with these students, she began to consider Ghana, alongside Tanganyika, Nigeria, Kenya, Canada, New Zealand and Venezuela, as an option for continuing her architectural and planning practice.[16] A Ghanaian student informed her that the Public Works Department (PWD) in Accra was interested in recruiting innovative foreign experts to replace the old guard of colonial figures who had dominated the country's architecture and planning scene for decades. After confirming with him that female experts were also welcome, she applied and was accepted for the position of Architect for Development in the Public Works Department of the Ministry of Works and Housing in Accra.[17]

Thus, Schreckenbach did not rely on existing professional networks to secure her professional mobility and independence, nor did she achieve it through familial privilege. Indeed, her father's position proved to be a hindrance to her studies. She did not draw on links with the colonial past. Instead, she constructed her own networks and became increasingly independent by virtue of her own educational achievements. As her experiences in Dresden and London illustrate, she actively built friendships that opened her professional horizons. Rather than academic institutions, cultural organisations such as the British Council played a crucial role in facilitating the development of her professional and personal relationships through their programmes. By the time she left London for Ghana in 1960, Schreckenbach had lived in a variety of cultures and political systems and built up an international portfolio of professional experiences. Socialised and educated in the GDR, Schreckenbach rejected the socialist German state before quickly becoming disillusioned with what capitalist West Germany had to offer. It was in the non-aligned Republic of Ghana, beyond the cursory division of east and west, that she was able to find professional and personal fulfilment.

15 Schreckenbach, 10.
16 Schreckenbach, 13.
17 Schreckenbach, 14.

PWD architect for development in Accra

Schreckenbach worked at evolving iterations of the PWD in Accra and Tamale for 15 years following her arrival in September 1960 (Fig.1)

A mid-nineteenth-century invention of the British colonial regime in India, the PWD was later instated across the territories of the British empire.[18] It was the technical arm of the colonial administration with responsibilities including the construction of infrastructure and buildings, such as post offices, prisons, hospitals and civil-servant housing. The form of these buildings was systematised into adaptable standard plans and type designs.[19] Following Ghana's independence in 1958, the PWD became part of the Ministry of Works and Housing. In 1961 it was renamed the Division of Public Construction, and in 1962 merged with the Ghana National Construction Company (GNCC), which had been founded by the state-owned Industrial Development Corporation and the Israel Construction Company before

Fig. 1: Hannah Schreckenbach at her drawing board in the PWD, 1963. Credit: Hannah Schreckenbach, *Herzensheimat Ghana: Erinnerungen an ein Land im Aufbruch*. Hamburg: Palmato Publishing, 2018, unnumbered photo insert.

18 For more on the PWD, see Peter Scriver, "Empire-Building and Thinking in the Public Works Department of British India," in *Colonial Modernities: Building, Dwelling and Architecture in British India and Ceylon*, edited by Peter Scriver, and Vikramaditya Prakash, 69–92 (Taylor & Francis, 2007); Iain Jackson, "The Architecture of the British Mandate in Iraq: Nation-Building and State Creation." *The Journal of Architecture* 21, no. 3 (17 May 2016): 345–417.
19 Scriver, "Empire-Building and Thinking in the Public Works Department of British India," 82.

being fully nationalised. Through the continued use and development of type designs and handbooks, as well as guidelines and regulations, aspects of the colonial era PWD persisted in the PWD/GNCC of the early post-colonial period. As Schreckenbach noted, "[t]he regulations all came from the colonial era and were totally out of date, a state of affairs that was untenable in the long run for an independent developing country."[20] The PWD was also housed in a colonial building.[21+22] In 1966 the GNCC was restructured and renamed PWD, before becoming the Architectural and Engineering Service Corporation (AESC) in 1973. As the institution was called the PWD for the majority of the time that Schreckenbach worked within it, that is how I refer to it here.

As a woman architect and planner, Schreckenbach felt that she was afforded many more opportunities for professional development at the PWD in Accra than she would have been in commercial practices or government agencies in Eastern or Western Europe. Indeed, part of the appeal of working abroad was the freedom to design. The post-independence Ghanaian PWD welcomed foreign experts, teaming them from the first working day onwards with Ghanaian counterparts. As well as designing and supervising the construction of buildings, the task of the foreign experts was to transfer professional know-how, especially when the first professionally accredited Ghanaian architects returned from their studies abroad. They had trained in different socialist countries as well as the UK, USA, Canada, Australia, etc. The post-independence PWD in Accra was initially led by a Ghanaian civil engineer who had studied in England, while the post of Chief Architect was held by an Englishman before being taken over by Victor Adegbite, a Ghanaian who had studied at Howard University in Washington DC, in the early 1960s.[23+24]

Schreckenbach's non-Ghanaian colleagues stemmed from a wide variety of nations including Venezuela, India (especially civil engineers), Germany, Hungary, UK, USA, Yugoslavia, Bulgaria and Poland: from both hemispheres and from both sides of the Iron Curtain. As a founding member of the Non-Aligned Movement committed to forging an independent path without affiliating itself to the politics of either the USSR or USA, Ghana was able to cooperate with the Eastern

20 Schreckenbach, "Ein Haus Für Die Ziegen Des Präsidenten," 38. Original: "Das ganze Regelwerk stammte noch aus der Kolonialzeit und war total veraltet, ein auf die Dauer für ein unabhängiges Entwicklungsland unhaltbarer Zustand."

21 Łukasz Stanek, *Architecture in Global Socialism: Eastern Europe, West Africa, and the Middle East in the Cold War* (Princeton University Press, 2020), 39.

22 Schreckenbach, "Ein Haus Für Die Ziegen Des Präsidenten," 38.

23 Schreckenbach, "Ein Haus Für Die Ziegen Des Präsidenten," 84.

24 Stanek, *Architecture in Global Socialism*, 41.

and Western Blocs.[25] Over the course of a few years, the PWD ceased to be dominated by British planners with roots in the colonial regime, and became, as Schreckenbach described it, a "mini architectural UN."[26] While working in such a richly intercultural environment would not have been possible in Britain or in Germany, there may have been similar situations in other recently independent African countries in the 1960s and 1970s. Public Works Departments and their subsequent decolonising incarnations could prove to be significant sites of international cooperation during the post-colonial period – transnational locations where knowledge was shared and ideas exchanged.

The degree of professional freedom that her work with the PWD afforded her was new to Schreckenbach, who developed projects from sketch designs to completed buildings, supervising the construction work on site. In her work, Schreckenbach asserted that she rarely experienced particular challenges or limitations based on her gender, and she was not the only single foreign woman to work at the PWD: she had unmarried female colleagues from Poland and Venezuela. According to my correspondence with her, by following the conventions of Ghanaian society and positioning herself as a guest, she was able to conduct her work without any difficulties resulting from her gender. To further mitigate possible gender-based issues, she developed protocols for potentially conflictive situations – for example, she never spoke directly to the construction workers on the building sites but delegated the task to one of the draughtsmen she had trained and who accompanied her on site visits.[27]

Schreckenbach worked on a vast range of building projects for the PWD, from developing standard housing types, to designing a nautical college and an office building for the Forestry Department, to renovating and extending the Parliament House in Accra, a task that was originally intended for a Ghanaian architect but was, according to Schreckenbach, assigned to her due to the extremely tight schedule and diverse workload it entailed.[28] (Fig. 2)

---

25 As a founder of the Non-Aligned Movement, Ghana was vehemently non-aligned and pan-African in its ambitions. However, Ghana's first president, Kwame Nkrumah, had socialist leanings. See Thomas Botchway, and Akwasi Amoako-Gyampah. "The Non-Aligned Movement, Ghana and the Early Days of African Diplomacy: Reflections on a Developing Country's Foreign Policy," in *The 60th Anniversary of the Non-Aligned Movement*, edited by Duško Dimitrijević, and Jovan Čavoški, 289–303 (Belgrade: Institute of International Politics, 2021).

26 Hannah Schreckenbach to Rachel Lee, 'Career in Ghana,' April 2015.

27 Schreckenbach to Lee.

28 Schreckenbach, "Ein Haus Für Die Ziegen Des Präsidenten," 223.

Fig. 2: The extension to the parliament building in Accra, designed by Hannah Schreckenbach, 1972. Credit: Hannah Schreckenbach, *Herzensheimat Ghana: Erinnerungen an ein Land im Aufbruch*. Hamburg: Palmato Publishing, 2018, unnumbered photo insert.

A 'senior architect' from 1964, her design work drew on the principles of 'tropical architecture,' employing narrow floor plans, sun shading devices and features such as verandahs to maximise the performance of the buildings in the tropical climate, while focusing on the human scale. Some of these design approaches had been developed by the PWD.[29]

29 For more on 'tropical architecture' see, for example, Jiat-Hwee Chang, *A Genealogy of Tropical Architecture: Colonial Networks, Nature and Technoscience* (Routledge, 2016); Hannah le Roux, "The Networks of Tropical Architecture." *The Journal of Architecture* 8, no. 3 (2003): 337–354, https://doi.org/10.1080/1360236032000134835; Rachel Lee, "Otto Koenigsberger, Transcultural Practice and the Tropical Third Space." *OASE*, no. 95 (December 2015): 60–72; Iain Jackson, "Tropical Architecture and the West Indies: From Military Advances and Tropical Medicine, to Robert Gardner-Medwin and the Networks of Tropical Modernism." *The Journal of Architecture* 22, no. 4 (2017): 1–29, https://doi.org/10.1080/13602365.2013.781202; Iain Jackson and Jessica Holland, *The Architecture of Edwin Maxwell Fry and Jane Drew: Twentieth Century Architecture, Pioneer Modernism and the Tropics* (Farnham: Ashgate Publishing, Ltd., 2014).

Building international networks in Ghana

Like many foreign architects who practised in colonised or newly independent contexts in the mid-twentieth century, Schreckenbach was involved in international networks. She represented Ghana at a UIA meeting in Hungary in 1964, for example, and collaborated with locally based, expatriate colleagues such as Kenneth Scott (UK) and Max Bond (USA). She also worked and maintained contact with Bernard Trevallion, Maxwell Fry's successor at the Planning Department in the Ministry for Works and Housing.[30]

Perhaps among these international networks, it was connections to West German architects and institutions that proved to have the most sustained traction in her professional life and in the development of her career. At the international trade fair in Accra in 1967, she was delighted to meet the German architect Georg Lippsmeier, whose office Lippsmeier+Partner had designed the German pavilion there. She knew Lippsmeier from her childhood in Magdeburg, where they had lived on the same street.[31] At the time of their meeting in Ghana, Lippsmeier was beginning to focus more on projects in Africa and Asia, soon becoming an important node in the networks of tropical architecture through his 1969 publication *Tropenbau / Building in the Tropics* and his Institut für Tropenbau (Institute for Building in the Tropics), which was established in the same year.[32] When Schreckenbach left Ghana in 1982, returning to West Germany to work with the GTZ, her connections to Lippsmeier's practice became more significant. Another important West German acquaintance was Lutz Christians, who was based in Kumasi, where he taught architecture at the University of Science and Technology (UST). In 1972, Christians invited Schreckenbach to take part in a research trip to the north of Ghana to investigate the indigenous architecture there. It was her first collaboration with the university at which she would later teach.

As the political situation in Ghana became increasingly unstable through the 1970s and early 1980s, Schreckenbach's contact with West German institutions, including the embassy in Accra and the GTZ became more important. She became financially dependent on the BRD in 1968 when her PWD salary was augmented by the West German Federal Ministry for Economic Cooperation and Development (BMZ) following the devaluation of the Ghanaian *cedi* in 1967. The BMZ used

---

30 Schreckenbach to Lee, 'Career in Ghana,' April 2015.

31 Schreckenbach, "Ein Haus Für Die Ziegen Des Präsidenten," 164.

32 The author of this article, Rachel Lee and the co-editor of this volume, Monika Motylińska, are currently conducting research into the impact of the Institute for Building in the Tropics within the framework of the Canadian Centre for Architecture's 'Centring Africa' project. See https://www.cca.qc.ca/en/61282/centring-africa-postcolonial-perspectives-on-architecture.

the model of 'integrierte Fachkraft' [integrated expert] in a developing country to support her work in Ghana. While living in Kumasi, she used a fixed-frequency radio, whose antenna was mounted high among the trees in her garden, in order to maintain contact with the GTZ and West German embassy in Accra. As her career in Ghana progressed and the political situation shifted, the radio installation illustrates that having reliable access to West German institutions was clearly a priority.[33] Indeed, she credits the West German ambassador, Dr. Gottfried Fischer, with convincing her that she should return to West Germany before it was too late for her to set up a career and home for herself there.[34] After leaving Ghana in 1982, she became a full-time consultant for the GTZ. Among other projects, she collaborated with Kiran Mukerji, the long-time director of Lippsmeier's Institut für Tropenbau, on GATE (German Appropriate Technology Exchange) and BASIN (Building and Advisory Service and Information Network) projects and publications.[35] In contrast to these meaningful cooperations with West German figures and institutions, Schreckenbach seems to have associated little with actors from the GDR.

While international and West German networks were important in stabilising and furthering her career in Ghana, Schreckenbach has stated that her most important allies and supporters were her Ghanaian colleagues and friends.[36] These included her draughtsmen, superiors, and contacts in governmental offices, as well as the students and lecturers at UST, where she worked from 1975 to 1982. Particularly significant was her long-term partner, Christian A. Lokko. He was a lawyer whom she met during her work on the parliament extension – at that time he was the director of the parliament administration. Nelson Yaw Agbesi, regional commissioner for the Volta Region and later minister of agriculture, supported her work with students in the Volta Region and became a close friend. Both Lokko and Agbesi were negatively affected by the government coup in 1981: Lokko went into exile in Nigeria and Agbesi was imprisoned.[37]

Schreckenbach built her networks through her work and by actively taking part in local social and cultural events. Among these, sporting activities, notably polo, were particularly significant. For over a decade she was a member of the Accra Polo Club, first as a player and later as a referee. Club members included diplomats,

---

33 Schreckenbach, *Herzensheimat Ghana*, 242.

34 Dieter Mai, "'Meine Alte Maurerkelle Habe Ich Noch' – Eine Begegnung Mit Hannah Schreckenbach," in *Clayblog* (blog), 18 July 2012, http://www.clayblog.de/2012/07/meine-alte-maurerkelle-habe-ich-noch-eine-begegnung-mit-hannah-schreckenbach/.

35 For example: Kiran Mukerji and Hannah Schreckenbach, *Self-Help Housing Options for Eritrea* (Eschborn: GTZ / gate, 1994).

36 Hannah Schreckenbach, telephone interview by Rachel Lee (2014).

37 Schreckenbach, *Herzensheimat Ghana*, 256.

businesspeople, lawyers, and members of the military. They stemmed from Ghana and other parts of the world including the UK, USA, Canada, Lebanon, India, Switzerland and the Netherlands. According to Schreckenbach, she was the only German member.[38] In addition to polo and horse-riding, she also played tennis, went swimming and enjoyed water sports, among them surfing, fishing and water-skiing.

These sporting activities suggest that Schreckenbach was integrated into the local social elite, which her expatriate status and BMZ-augmented salary granted her access to. The Accra Polo Club, a colonial institution dating from 1902, was undoubtedly a place of privilege. Indeed, in post-colonial societies, sporting clubs often maintained their exclusivity, remaining significant sites for the social, cultural and economic reproduction of the elite classes.[39] Schreckenbach appreciated the exclusivity that membership fees guaranteed. Of a Lebanese-owned club with a sea-water swimming pool which she regularly used, she noted that the membership fee, "kept the number of users within an acceptable range".[40] In addition to financial liquidity, these activities also required motorised mobility. For her regular water-skiing, surfing and fishing trips she would drive with non-Ghanaian, expatriate friends over 100km to Ada or around 20km to another "paradise" where "the children regularly clean the small area and provide refreshing coconuts, and their mothers sell us oranges and bananas."[41] The inequality inherent to the scene she describes is palpable.

As well as sports, Schreckenbach also engaged in local cultural activities, including weekend 'Highlife' parties. Highlife is a form of neo-folk music that originated in Ghana during the early twentieth century and became popular in other parts of West Africa. It is associated with Ghana's decolonisation and Africanisation.[42] At the Star Hotel in Accra, Schreckenbach regularly attended the 'Afternoon Jump' sessions in the company of two PWD draughtsmen who were determined to teach her to dance to the Highlife beats.[43] Part of the local cultural scene, Highlife was not elitist or exclusionary. Gaining access to it through her Ghanaian colleagues, Schreckenbach clearly benefitted from a wide range of social mobility.

38 Schreckenbach, "Ein Haus Für Die Ziegen Des Präsidenten," 96.

39 Niko Besnier, Susan Brownell, and Thomas F. Carter, *The Anthropology of Sport: Bodies, Borders, Biopolitics* (Berkley: University of California Press, 2018), 51.

40 Schreckenbach, "Ein Haus Für Die Ziegen Des Präsidenten," 187. Original: "die wegen ihrer Beitragshöhe die Anzahl der Benutzer in einem akzeptablen Rahmen hält."

41 Schreckenbach, 178. Original: "Die Kinder säubern den kleinen Platz regelmäßig und sorgen auch für erfrischende Kokosnüsse, und ihre Mütter verkaufen uns Orangen und Bananen."

42 Dele Adeyemo, "The Modernizing Beat." *Canadian Centre for Architecture*, Centring Africa, 2021. https://www.cca.qc.ca/en/articles/80058/the-modernizing-beat.

43 Schreckenbach, 108.

Aside from sports and dancing, Schreckenbach engaged with the local community in more actively constructive ways. Shortly after taking on her work as an architect at the PWD, Schreckenbach, who was much admired for her drawing skills, began teaching in her free time. On a weekly basis she offered lessons to improve the PWD employees' drawing techniques. Sitting on stools in a school courtyard with small drawing boards balanced on their knees, the class also became a weekly fixture for local inhabitants who enjoyed watching the process. The graduates were given the title of 'draughtsman' and many worked with Schreckenbach on her projects at the PWD. After gaining some professional experience, some of the draughtsmen went on to study architecture in Kumasi. Schreckenbach's ad-hoc drawing lessons soon became formalised into an official training course. (Fig.3)

Fig. 3: Hannah Schreckenbach (seated, centre) with unnamed participants of the draughtsman's course, 1962. Credit: Hannah Schreckenbach, *Herzensheimat Ghana: Erinnerungen an ein Land im Aufbruch*. Hamburg: Palmato Publishing, 2018, unnumbered photo insert.

Beyond architecture, she collaborated with Kojo Gyinaye Kyei on the book *No Time to Die* – an illustrated collection of Kyei's poetry inspired by slogans painted on 'mammy lorries.'[44] Schreckenbach contributed the photographs and drawings. With its fascination for the aesthetics and semiotics of the local environment, and its commitment to documenting these, this project could be seen as related to Schreckenbach's deep-rooted interest in indigenous architecture, to which I will now turn.

Documenting indigenous architecture in northern Ghana

Having worked on designs for apartment complexes for development aid organisations and a regional centre for crafts and small industries (neither of which were realised) Schreckenbach's first major design and construction task was a motel in the Mole Game Reserve, a new national park in a wet savannah region west of Tamale. In May 1961 she undertook the 3,000 km journey to visit the building site in her white VW Beetle alone, staying at PWD guesthouses along the way. This was Schreckenbach's first encounter with rural Ghana and with the indigenous architecture and spatial practices of the country's different ethnic groups. The compounds of circular earth buildings sparked a profound fascination for employing earth as a construction material that she maintained for the rest of her career. Writing to her mother she explained: "For me the earth houses of the Lobi were particularly interesting because the wall construction was similar to the old cob earth walls in Saxony. The earth is built up in layers and the exterior wall has a scale-like finish so that the rainwater can run off".[45] She later recounted that "[i]n German villages earth was a rebuilding material after the war, but when urban rebuilding started earth was exchanged with cement. For me as a learned bricklayer earth has always been a suitable and cheap building material."[46]

She immediately started recording the earth buildings through photographs, sketches and analytical drawings. As well as documenting the construction methods she paid particular attention to the decorations that were applied or inscribed into the exterior walls, as a way of archiving a building culture that

44 Kojo Gyinaye Kyei and Hannah Schreckenbach, *No Time to Die* (Accra: Kojo Gyinaye Kyei and Hannah Schreckenbach, 1976).
45 Schreckenbach, "Ein Haus Für Die Ziegen Des Präsidenten," 54. Original: Für mich waren besonders die Lehmhäuser der Lobi interessant, deren Wandkonstruktion unseren alten Wellerlehmwänden in Sachsen ähnelt. Der Lehm wird schichtweise aufgebracht und an der Außenwand schuppenartig verstrichen, sodas Regenwasser ablaufen und abtropfen kann.
46 Schreckenbach to Lee, 'Career in Ghana,' April 2015.

she perceived as threatened, not just by development, but by the national government's housing policies.

Back in the PWD offices in Accra, Schreckenbach's enthusiasm for the indigenous earth architecture found little resonance with her colleagues, who met her suggestion of experimenting with earth construction techniques in urban areas with hostility. Earth was regarded by some Ghanaians at that time as being a part of a primitive past that had no place in the country's modern, independent future.[47+48] She became known as the "earth aunty," a moniker that was meant disparagingly, but that she became proud of.[49+50] Although her passion for what she terms "the oldest and healthiest building material" almost cost her job at the PWD, her commitment to documenting the structures continued unabated. She even planned her architectural projects around trips to the northern region, convincing her colleagues and superiors that she should be based in Tamale during the construction of the motel and an office complex project she was working on, while pursuing her agenda of documenting the local architecture.[51]

By the end of the 1960s, Schreckenbach had published two articles in the German journal *Baumeister* on earth architecture in Ghana: "Ghana: Alte und Neue Wohnbauformen" (1966) and "Volksarchitektur in Nordghana: Wohnzellen + Arbeitszellen = Biotektur?" (1969). The first article addresses traditional forms of living in Ghana, focusing on the "compounds" that are arranged around interlinked courtyards and feature individual buildings with circular floor plans. She notes that in many compounds the chief's traditionally single-story round house had been replaced by a two-story house on a rectangular floor plan, clearly showing the influence of external building forms. In the second part of the article, Schreckenbach discusses the influence of the compound typology on contemporary housing projects in Ghana's urban areas including Accra, and the new town of Tema. While these residential projects, designed by the Tema-Accra-Development-Corporation sometimes in collaboration with consulting architects, such as Doxiadis Associates, address the housing needs of diverse income groups, Schreckenbach devotes most of the article to projects for low and low-middle income workers, and to those that attempt to meet the needs of new urban dwellers, such as the resettled fishermen of Tema, through the incorporation of external cooking areas and toilets. She concludes her brief survey of what she regards as the successful urban translation of the compound typology

47 Schreckenbach to Lee.
48 Stanek, *Architecture in Global Socialism*, 134.
49 Schreckenbach, *Herzensheimat Ghana*, 146.
50 Original: Lehmtante.
51 Schreckenbach, "Ein Haus Für Die Ziegen Des Präsidenten," 63.

by stating that in addition to developing the forms of indigenous settlements and architectures there was also a pressing need to experiment with local materials that could potentially be used in place of the expensive, imported materials employed in many of the "tropical architecture" projects.

The second article focuses on what Schreckenbach terms the "anonymous architecture" of northern Ghana. Rather than conceiving of the indigenous building practices as timeless or fixed, she understands them to be evolving and in a state of transformation. Analyses of recent developments in the architecture, such as the introduction of rectangular forms into compounds dominated by buildings with circular plans, as well as verandahs, stairs, windows and doors, illustrate the influence of external building practices and the flexibility of the indigenous architecture to absorb and reproduce them. She concludes: "We must hope that the responsible national government authorities support this positive development and do not destroy the anonymous architecture in this part of the country through a narrow-minded commitment to 'progress'."[52]

In the 1960s, neither East nor West German architecture magazines devoted many pages to articles about architecture in Africa.[53+54] Schreckenbach's contributions are all the more noteworthy because the few articles that were published tended to focus on the work of German architects – East German housing on Zanzibar, a hospital in Lomé, Senegal, by Lippsmeier + Partner, or a school in Yaoundé, Cameroon, by Olaf Jacobsen, for example. Schreckenbach's articles, which take an ethnographic approach to discuss local building practices, are outliers. It is likely that Schreckenbach's contact with *Baumeister* came through Georg Lippsmeier. Lippsmeier was a close friend of Paulhans Peters, the editor of *Baumeister* from 1960 to 1991, and the magazine had published articles on Lippsmeier's projects in the global South since 1963. *Baumeister* was published by the Munich-based Callwey Verlag, which also published the majority of Peters' books and Lippsmeier's *Tropenbau / Building in the Tropics*. Schreckenbach intended to consolidate her research through writing a doctoral dissertation, making contact with Professor Josef Wiedemann at the

52 Original: "Man muss hoffen, dass die verantwortlichen Regierungsstellen des Landes diese erfreuliche Entwicklung unterstützen und nicht mit engstirnigem Fortschrittlichseinwollen die anonyme Architektur in diesem Landesteil vernichten."

53 According to calculations based on research conducted in 2014 at the Habitat Unit, TU Berlin, for the project "Beyond East-West: Development Cooperation in sub-Saharan Africa in Divided Germany (1949–1990)," Bauwelt (BRD) published 12 articles on architecture in Africa, Baumeister (BRD) published 14, and Deutsche Architektur (GDR) published eight.

54 Rachel Lee, Philipp Misselwitz, and Sam Lanckriet, "Beyond East-West: Development Cooperation in Sub-Saharan Africa in Divided Germany (1949–1990)," Habitat Unit (2014), http://habitat-unit.de/en/research/beyond-east-west/.

Technische Universität München in this regard in 1972.[55] Although this intention remained unfulfilled, she did leave active architectural practice to work in higher education.

Teaching construction: Senior lecturer at UST

In 1975, Schreckenbach left the PWD in Accra to teach at the UST in Kumasi. After 15 years of work as an architect, she felt that she was ready for a new challenge.[56] As a senior lecturer at the Faculty of Architecture she taught courses in "Construction Technology", "Building Services for Architects" and "Introduction into Structures." The position had been created for her by Lutz Christians, a West German architect and head of the architecture department, who had been collaborating with Schreckenbach on research projects for several years. Schreckenbach and Christians shared an interest in indigenous architecture and had made trips to the Bolgatanga region in the north of Ghana to document buildings in the early 1970s.

Lutz Christians left Ghana in 1974 to take up a newly created professorship at the Technische Universität Berlin: the Chair for Planning and Building in Developing Countries. According to Hannah Le Roux, by the time Schreckenbach began teaching in Kumasi, the school had undergone major changes.[57] Following the Architectural Association's (AA) overhaul of the curriculum under John Lloyd from 1963 – which included introducing projects based on actual situations, such as the resettlement of communities that had been displaced by the damming of the Volta River – the school had become something of a cosmopolitan hub, attracting guests such as Buckminster Fuller, teaching staff from the AA, the Polish architectural historian Zbigniew R. Dmochowski, as well as the African American architect Max Bond, who had previously worked with Schreckenbach at the PWD.

Following the coup and Nkrumah's exile in 1966, the atmosphere and conditions at the school changed again. Many of the more progressive figures, including John Lloyd and Max Bond, left Ghana and under new leadership the school became more conservative. Despite this shift, for Schreckenbach the Faculty of Architecture proved to be a very fruitful environment for studying, developing and expanding her work on indigenous architecture, and the students and staff were open and committed to

55 Schreckenbach, "Ein Haus Für Die Ziegen Des Präsidenten," 250.
56 Schreckenbach, *Herzensheimat Ghana*, 190.
57 Hannah le Roux, "Modern Architecture in Post-Colonial Ghana and Nigeria." *Architectural History* 47 (1 January 2004): 361–392.

her ideas. This was a stark contrast to the PWD, where her passion for trying to introduce earth as a construction material had threatened her career.[58]

It is important to point out that in relation to her commitment to earth architecture Schreckenbach was not working in a vacuum. Max Bond had also produced designs that were based on indigenous architectural forms, notably the Bolgatanga Library from 1967[59] while Labelle Prussin, an architectural historian from the USA, published *Architecture in Northern Ghana* in 1969, the first of many publications she made on indigenous architecture in Africa. In Nigeria, Zbigniew R. Dmochowski was also researching and analysing building practices, the results of which were published posthumously in *Introduction to Traditional Nigerian Architecture*.[60]

At the conclusion of her teaching career, Schreckenbach spent two years working on a book – *Construction Technology for a Tropical Developing Country* that was funded and published by the GTZ in 1984. The book opens with a full-page colour image of an earth building in northern Ghana and an entire chapter is devoted to traditional building methods (Fig. 4).

Schreckenbach was convinced that the book's documentation of indigenous building methods was necessary to illustrate the wealth of indigenous building knowledge in the country. Moreover, the richly illustrated book provided guidelines as to how this know-how could appropriately be adopted in modern and climate-oriented building construction with locally available building materials. Similar to the *Lehmbaufiebel*, this book is illustrated with line drawings that show construction methods and processes as well as plans and sections of buildings, and external views of parts of the settlements. The drawings in the book were all made by Schreckenbach and her assistant and co-author Jackson G.K. Abwanka, better known as Kojo. Here the gendered division of labour is described in the text and represented in the drawings (Fig. 5 and 6).

Among her most important achievements in Ghana, Schreckenbach lists the inclusion of earth as a building material in the General Building Regulations and Standards of Ghana.[61] The inclusion process took more than a decade. Combined with her teaching and publication work, Schreckenbach's labour with indigenous architecture and her focus on local building practices began to impact the

---

58 She was awarded a Federal Cross of Merit '*Bundesverdienstkreuz*' by the BRD for her work at UST in 1981.

59 Ola Uduku, "Bolgatanga Library Adaptive Modernism in Ghana 40 Years On," in *The Challenge of Change: Dealing with the Legacy of the Modern Movement: Proceedings of the 10th International DOCOMOMO Conference*, edited by Dirk van den Heuvel, Maarten Mesman, W Quist and Bert Lemmens (IOS Press, 2008).

60 Stanek, *Architecture in Global Socialism*, 134.

61 Schreckenbach to Lee, 'Career in Ghana,' April 2015.

Fig. 4: Opening illustration of *Construction Technology for a Tropical Developing Country* showing an earth building in the chief's compound at Sandema, Northern Ghana, 1968. Credit: Hannah Schreckenbach and Jackson G.K. Abankwa. *Construction Technology for a Tropical Developing Country*. Eschborn: GTZ, 1984, 2.

Fig. 5: "Men are the builders. They build the walls and roofs of the buildings," write Schreckenbach and Abanka about the construction of buildings in northeastern Ghana. Credit: Hannah Schreckenbach and Jackson G.K. Abankwa. *Construction Technology for a Tropical Developing Country*. Eschborn: GTZ, 1984, 22.

Fig. 6: "[. . .] the women plaster the in- and outside of the buildings, lay and beat the floor and apply decorative finishes to the walls" (p. 22). Women pounding a floor in north Ghana. Credit: Hannah Schreckenbach and Jackson G.K. Abankwa. *Construction Technology for a Tropical Developing Country*. Eschborn: GTZ, 1984, 30.

production of architecture in Ghana and elsewhere, particularly through the work of her former students.

Through her sustained engagement with architecture in Ghana, Schreckenbach, as an individual woman architect, whose professional activities were not directed by the policies of a foreign nation state (although she was financially supported by the BRD) or an international organisation such as UNESCO, and who did not rely on colonial or institutional networks to attain her professional mobility or capacity to practice abroad, succeeded in creating an awareness of the significance of indigenous building practices from the ground up. Her commitment to the subject resulted in a gradual shift in government policy and contributed to the development of a form of regionalism in Ghanaian architecture. When Schreckenbach left Ghana for the BRD in 1982, she took her passion for earth architecture with her. Working as a consultant for the GTZ and related projects including GATE, she was able to share her enthusiasm and knowledge about the construction material with communities in Germany and around the world, widening the impact of the knowledge she had gained in Ghana and contributing to a growing acceptance of earth as a viable, sustainable building material.

While Schreckenbach's career is unusual, there are instances of other migrant women architects and planners working with local communities and documenting indigenous building practices. Erica Mann, a Jewish refugee who worked in Kenya from the 1940s,[62] and with whom Schreckenbach collaborated on Mann's "Women of

62 Rachel Lee, "Erica Mann and an Intimate Source." *ABE Journal. Architecture beyond Europe* 4 (1 July 2013), https://abe.revues.org/772; Benjamin Tiven, "The Delight of the Yearner: Ernst May and Erica Mann in Nairobi, 1933–1953." *Nka Journal of Contemporary African Art* 32 (1 March 2013): 80–89, https://doi.org/10.1215/10757163-2142278.

Kibwezi" project in the late 1980s,[63] is an example of such a figure, as are Sybil Moholy-Nagy, Lina Bo Bardi, Minnette de Silva, Jaqueline Tyrwhitt and Denise Scott Brown. More, particularly comparative, research into these figures and their practices could help us sharpen our understanding on the production of architectural knowledge in the twentieth century and complicate established narratives.

Beyond gender, Schreckenbach's career forces us to rethink the significance of individual agency within Cold War narratives. Brought up and educated in a socialist country, Schreckenbach worked for 22 years in a newly independent, sub-Saharan nation that, at least in the early post-independence period, harboured socialist inclinations within a wider commitment to non-alignment. However, as a political refugee who fled the socialist system and was dedicated to improving the built environment through promoting local solutions rather than blanket ideologies, Schreckenbach cannot be considered a socialist architect. Undoubtedly, her practice was shaped by the GDR's socialist doctrine, both through ingestion and rejection, while formative experiences in the BDR and UK familiarised her with Western approaches. Beholden to neither, Schreckenbach was able to navigate these two dominant ideologies, finding fertile ground to grow her architectural practice in a third space of non-alignment. To some extent, her biography subverts polarising Cold War narratives, illustrating that beyond the frontiers of East and West there were possibilities for different ways of creating and understanding architecture.

63 Hannah Schreckenbach, "Eigene Kleinprojekte," undated.

Franziska Klemstein

Stralsund – More than Exchange of Experiences

Introduction

During the 1970s, efforts to preserve the old city centres intensified in the GDR. For this purpose, the know-how of foreign, in particular Polish, specialised companies was often used. The lack of native specialists in this field was also caused by the Khrushchev era, when the serial production of buildings and standardisation of construction processes was imposed. As a result of these developments, traditional craftsmanship in construction received less attention, creating a shortage of skilled professionals in this field.

The following chapter examines the exchange between the Polish People's Republic (Polish: Polska Rzeczpospolita Ludowa, in short: PRL) and the German Democratic Republic (GDR) in the field of historic preservation practice and construction work. As a case study, the activities of the Polish special factory PKZ Szczecin (Polskie Pracownie Konserwacji Zabytków, in short: PKZ) in the Hanseatic city of Stralsund are examined, which in the 1970s was involved, for example, in construction work on Knieperwall, Mühlenstraße, Ossenreyerstraße and Fährstraße. (Fig. 1)

The Polish experts' support was not limited to carrying out the construction work. Rather, they planned the entire process, conducted architectural-historical investigations, and provided the tools and labor for the entire project.

The aim of this essay is, on the one hand, to present the diverse activities of the PKZ Szczecin as a sign of the German-Polish exchange of experience. On the other hand, on the basis of an selected cases used as examples, the concrete procedure is analysed and evaluated against the background of developments in the building industry and regarding monument preservation concerns in the GDR.

Urban planning and reconstruction efforts

In the following, urban planning and reconstruction efforts in relation to Stralsund will be examined. Based on this, the handling of the city's heterogeneous inventory of historical buildings and structures in the field of tension between construction, historical preservation and political objectives will be shown in order to be able to characterise the working and operational field of the PKZ. Subsequently, the activities of the PKZ are examined in more detail and evaluated on

https://doi.org/10.1515/9783110658491-008

Fig. 1: Map representation of the places where the PKZs were active. Compiled by Franziska Klemstein.

the basis of a practical case. Finally, the German-Polish exchange on the political level is considered in order to embed the activities of the PKZ in Stralsund in the context of general intergovernmental efforts.

> The sea travellers of our time, the skippers, but also the numerous holidaymakers who make the return journey from Hiddensee to Stralsund, are faced with a changed and yet also the same picture as five or six centuries ago. Added to this are the large warehouses of the harbour, the Rügendamm bridge, the Volkswerft shipyard and, more recently, the northern town, near the coast, the Knieper-Nord and Knieper-West districts – striking signs of our time. However, the old Stralsund with its mighty parish churches, the town hall with its magnificent facade and the numerous gabled houses crouching beneath the churches has remained unchanged in the distance.[1]

The quotation by the preservationist Heinrich Trost from the *Kunstgeschichtliche Städtebücher* published by the Leipzig VEB Seemann Verlag describes the Hanseatic city of Stralsund as a conglomerate of old and new. At the same time, it is a statement about the interplay of urban development, town planning and historical preservation in the historic Hanseatic city.

In his book *Stralsund. Eine Stadt im Systemwandel vom Ende des Kaiserreiches bis in die 1960er Jahre* Detlev Brunner describes how the urban characterisation of the city, which Trost carried out in 1973, was by no means a matter of course. While the mayor of the city, Bruno Motczinski, stated in the 1958 publication *Die Altstadt von Stralsund* that "the urban planning demands of the socialist society had to be coordinated with the structural conditions of the old city and the city had to be designed as an organic unit",[2] the SED district leadership pursued other goals. In a submission for the reconstruction of the city passed on 8 May 1959, the district administration rejected a reconstruction plan for the inner city passed by the city council, as it did not meet the requirements of socialist reconstruction and the "findings of socialist urban planning".[3] The conceptual draft came from

1 In the original: "Den Seereisenden unserer Zeit, den Schiffern, aber auch den zahlreichen Urlaubern, die von Hiddensee die Rückreise nach Stralsund antreten, bietet sich ein verändertes und doch wiederum gleiches Bild wie vor fünf oder sechs Jahrhunderten. Hinzugekommen sind die großen Speicher des Hafens, die Rügendammbrücke, die Volkswerft und in jüngster Zeit die nördliche Stadt, in Küstennähe, errichteten Stadtviertel Knieper-Nord und Knieper-West – markante Zeichen unserer Zeit. Geblieben und in der Fernsicht unverändert aber ist auch heute noch das alte Stralsund mit den mächtigen Pfarrkirchen, dem Rathaus mit seiner prachtvollen Fassade und den zahlreichen unter den Kirchen sich duckenden Giebelhäusern." Heinrich Trost, *Stralsund*, (Leipzig: Seemann, 1973), 7–8.

2 Deutsche Bauakademie, *Die Altstadt von Stralsund Untersuchungen zum Baubestand und zur städtebaulichen Denkmalpflege*, (Berlin: Verl. Technik, 1958), 7–8; Detlev Brunner, *Eine Stadt im Systemwandel vom Ende des Kaiserreiches bis in die 1960er Jahre*, (München: Oldenburg Wissenschaftsverlag, 2010), 87.

3 Brunner, *Eine Stadt im Systemwandel*, 88.

Stralsund's urban planning director Karl-Heinz Loui, who had based the reconstruction plan for the city centre on the "Sechzehn Grundsätze" (transl.: "Sixteen Principles").[4] At a time when the socialist reconstruction of towns and villages was called for, it is hardly surprising that Loui's ideas were not picked up. However, even the socialist reconstruction, which the SED district leadership had made a maxim, was not implemented.

Preservation, reactivation and socialist urban planning

Heinrich Trost emphasised in 1973 that the old city centre held a different range of tasks for the building industry than the new development areas in Knieper-Nord and Knieper-West. Nevertheless, he underlined, with a reference to the building of the Water Management Directorate (Badenstraße 18/19), that "modern buildings were also constructed there".[5] "But the main task in the old town is the care, preservation and above all the utilization of the numerous historical buildings [. . .]"[6] continued Trost.

The "reactivation" or "utilization" was of importance in order to secure that preservation – not only for Trost. At the same time, the term "utilization" implies that in some cases extensive adaptations and modifications were possible or at least conceivable under the guiding mantle of (new) utilisation. At the same time, the economic constraints that strongly influenced institutional monument conservation in the GDR become clear. The preservation of the historical inventory was less concerned with the significance of the monument, but rather with its state of preservation – i.e. the necessary cost of restoration – in order to be able to guarantee future use.

At the beginning of the 1970s, the *Deutsche Bauakademie*[7] (in short, DBA) dealt with the development of socialist urban planning and socialist architecture in the GDR, which took a completely different path than the socialist reconstruction a few years earlier. A working paper states:

> A decisive prerequisite for a cohesive and interesting architectural design of the city is the inclusion of the old in the developing new shape of the socialist city. That which is also

4 Brunner, *Eine Stadt im Systemwandel*, 88.

5 Trost, *Stralsund*, 151.

6 Trost, *Stralsund*, 151–152.

7 The Bauakademie was the central scientific institution for architecture and Civil Engineering in the GDR.

> useful in the future enters into a specific unity with the new. From the organic connection between the old and the new grows the continuity of the urban design, which has a significant influence on the historical and cultural consciousness. At the same time, it is possible to preserve and further develop the typical features of the image of a city.[8]

The preservation, care and integration of the "old" had thus not only gained in importance but had also become one of the guiding principles in urban design. This also meant an upgrade of the preservation of historical monuments in the GDR, as it now had to be more strongly integrated into urban planning processes. Accordingly, the working material of the *Bauakademie* and the *Bund der Architekten der DDR*[9] (in short, BdA) stated that an "urbanistically oriented preservation of monuments [. . .] has to preserve not only individual buildings and groups of buildings, but also streets, larger urban ensembles as well as urban structures and connections".[10] As positive examples of such a development and successful preservation of historic buildings and monuments, the working material referred to the "inner cities of Stralsund, Potsdam, Görlitz and Erfurt"[11] in addition to the Berlin Forum and the street Unter den Linden in Berlin, thus elevating Stralsund to an example of best practice in 1971.

Exchange of experiences – GDR and PRL

Over the years of the existence of the GDR, not only changes in urban development and architectural concepts can be observed, but also shifts in the principles of historical preservation practice. While in the immediate post-war period, not only the extent of reconstructions and restorations of various monuments, but also the fundamental question of their feasibility (technical, financial and ideological) were

---

8 In the original: *"Eine entscheidende Voraussetzung für eine geschlossene und interessante architektonische Gestaltung der Stadt ist die Einbeziehung des Alten in die sich entwickelnde neue Gestalt der sozialistischen Stadt. Das auch künftig Brauchbare geht eine spezifische Einheit mit dem Neuen ein. Aus der organischen Verbindung zwischen Altem und Neuem wächst die Kontinuität der städtebaulichen Gestaltung, die ganz wesentlich das Geschichts- und Kulturbewußtsein beeinflußt. Gleichzeitig ist es dadurch möglich, das Typische einer Stadtgestalt zu bewahren und weiter zu entwickeln."* Anon., *Entwicklung des sozialistischen Städtebaus und der sozialistischen Architektur in der Deutschen Demokratischen Republik*, Arbeitsmaterial, Deutsche Bauakademie zu Berlin/ Bund der Architekten der DDR (Berlin, Mai 1971), 20.

9 The BdA was a professional organisation of the architects of the GDR and co-editor of the journals *Architektur in der DDR*, *Landschaftsarchitektur* and *Farbe und Raum*.

10 Anon., *Entwicklung des sozialistischen Städtebaus*, 20.

11 Anon., *Entwicklung des sozialistischen Städtebaus*, 20.

discussed. At the same time, as early as 1950, attempts were made in Görlitz "to develop a methodology for the planned care and preservation of particularly valuable old town quarters."[12]

The conservators of the monument authority in the GDR met with their Polish colleagues consulting them in professional matters and matters of institutional structure. The first director of the central office of the Institute for Historical Preservation, Kurt Lade, had already undertaken such a study trip from 27 April to around 14 May 1956. He recorded his impressions in a kind of travel diary, in which not only talks with various representatives in the field of urban planning and monument preservation were noted, but also visits to the Polish Factories for Historical Preservation Practice (*Pracownie Konserwacji Zabytków*, or PKZ). According to Lade's notes, the conversations were primarily about the organization of the Polish Monument Authority and about the developments in architecture, whereby Lade noted "agreement" in brackets, presumably referring to the development of Polish architecture, which – just as in the GDR – relied primarily on historical formal elements. Conclusions about Lade's thoughts on historical preservation practice are also possible through his notes. For the Warsaw Historical Museum, for example, he not only noted the way in which the buildings at the Old Market Square had been reconstructed, gutted and connected for their intended purpose, but also evaluated this procedure as "a good example of modern use in the outer form of reconstructed medieval houses".[13] For him, at least in relation to Warsaw, the reconstruction of a uniform and most historically authentic cityscape was decisive. The completely free design of the interior, allowing for a creative use in the sense of an appropriate use of the building or building complex was crucial to him and thus the legitimation of the reconstruction.

In terms of urban planning, however, the GDR initially continued to pursue the goal of creating spacious city centres by means of new development, abandoning the historic city structures. Developments in the building industry, which demanded and attempted to implement not only more efficient industrialisation and typification, but also the socialist redesign of towns and villages, led to pressure for change in monument conservation, too.

It was not until the second half of the 1960s that "efforts were stepped up to preserve historical buildings through restoration and, above all, through new use in accordance with the needs of society, and to open them up for the development of socialist culture".[14] In the 1970s, this development was reinforced by "new

12 Deutsche Bauakademie (Autorenkollektiv), *Städtebau und Architektur in der DDR: Eine historische Übersicht, Teil 1*, Bauinformation (Berlin: Bauinformation, 1989), 98.

13 AdK-Archiv, Kurt-Lade-Archive 38, Reisetagebuch.

14 Anon., *Städtebau und Architektur in der DDR*, 101.

tendencies in architectural development [. . .], the urge for more historical relevance in the further design of cities, which at the same time went hand in hand with discussions about a deeper exploration of progressive traditions from the whole of German history".[15]

At the same time, topics and issues regarding to the preservation of historical buildings were more present in public and were discussed more frequently. This can be attributed to developments in foreign policy, especially in the Honecker era. For the actors in the field of preservation and conservation, the GDR's admission to UNESCO and ICOMOS meant the opportunity to participate in international discussions, but also international recognition and an increase in importance in national politics within the GDR. At the same time, international relations were not meant to weaken the relationship with the community of socialist states, so attention was paid to the adherence to common themes and demarcations as well as to a constant exchange.

Behind gothic facades – The image of an old town

Stralsund's historical building stock was extremely heterogeneous, as shown by a compilation of objects that had been supervised by the honorary conservator, Käthe Rieck[16] during the 1950s. She was involved in the reconstruction of heavily destroyed churches, town houses and movable art objects and took part in consultations on the development of reconstruction plans for Stralsund's inner city. In addition, Rieck always sought to exchange ideas with the public. In numerous articles and essays, she explained the value of various objects and historical preservation practice, provided information on the work currently being carried out, and occasionally commented critically on the previous procedures of state institutions as well as architectural and construction measures on Stralsund's historical buildings.

In the course of the 1970s and 1980s, the focus increasingly shifted to the preservation of the historic fabric in connection or interplay with the socialist transformation of the city centres. In the daily newspaper *Neues Deutschland*, Stralsund was already characterised in 1962 with the words: "Where once rich patricians

15 Anon., *Städtebau und Architektur in der DDR*, 101.

16 Käthe Rieck (7 February1902–23 August 2004): Art historian, voluntary conservator and Director of the Cultural History Museum Stralsund (1950–1962).

lived, today the working people are building a new life".[17] The new identification mark was to be the harbour, which was to develop from a "city of civil servants" into a "modern industrial city" on the basis of socialism. Although the history of the city was not negated, it was limited to the old town centre around the "famous town hall, which is one of the most magnificent secular buildings of Dutch brick Gothic".[18]

In a city like Stralsund, which "had long since grown far beyond the medieval city walls",[19] as the newspaper *Neues Deutschland* put it in 1978, preserving the historical substance while at the same time calling for adjustments to "contemporary" conditions was a great challenge – also for honorary conservators like Käthe Rieck.

The former city fortifications and gates were particularly suitable for cultural purposes.[20] As early as 1956, Rieck had already made efforts to restore and extensively recondition the Kütertor and the city wall. But for further preservation, the historical buildings had to be assigned a sensible use. While the city archive moved into the former Johanneskloster in 1964, the Kütertor and part of the extended city wall were converted into a youth hostel in 1963, thus ensuring their continued preservation throughout the GDR era.

Architects, monument conservators and urban planners faced great challenges in improving the housing conditions in the city while at the same time preserving the fabric of the buildings. In 1978, the newspaper *Neues Deutschland* commented on the building activities in the Hanseatic city, whose "old town centre [belonged to] the two dozen historic city centres that were included in the central list of monuments in the GDR"[21] under the heading "Behind Gothic facades in Stralsund".[22] According to the article, the preservation and conservation of the old town on the one hand and the creation of modern living space on the other hand were not contradictory. Quite the reverse, the decision of the city council to establish a programme for the care and preservation of the old town was one of

---

17 Anon., "*Stralsund Stadt an der Ostsee. Wo einst reiche Patrizier praßten, bauen die Werktätigen heute an einem neuen Leben.*" *Neues Deutschland* (14 July 1962): 9.
18 Anon., "*Stralsund Stadt an der Ostsee,*" 9.
19 Christa Lier, "*Sehenswertes in alten Stadttoren. Mittelalterliche Wehranlagen werden als Museen, Galerien, Klubs und Jugendherbergen genutzt.*" *Neues Deutschland* (31 October 1978): 2.
20 Cf. Lier, "*Sehenswertes in alten Stadttoren,*" 2 and Gudrun Hartmann, "*Klubhaus, Atelier und Museum in altem Gemäuer. Historische Gebäude in Ostseestädten sinnvoll genutzt.*" *Neues Deutschland* (11 August 1981): 4.
21 Frank Starke, "*Hinter gotischen Fassaden in Stralsund. Rekonstruktion der Altstadt wurde begonnen. Historisch wertvolle Bauten vielfältig genutzt.*" *Neues Deutschland* (27 February 1978), 3.
22 Starke, "*Hinter gotischen Fassaden in Stralsund,*" 3.

the “first steps of a comprehensive reconstruction”.[23] This meant primarily the preservation of the facades, while at the same time (completely) redesigning the interior. Thus the Mayor of Stralsund, Horst Lehmann, described that “behind Gothic and Baroque facades [. . .] modern apartments for over 100 families were built in Knieperstrasse and Fährstrasse alone”.[24] Above all, the difficulty in implementing this “comprehensive reconstruction” lay in the necessary combination of industrial (housing) construction methods and traditional craftsmanship. In Stralsund, this meant that the construction companies VEB Stadtbauhof and VEB Hochbau had to work towards the most efficient realisation of the construction project. In contrast, the Stralsund craftsmen within the PGH [*Produktionsgenossenschaft des Handwerks*] were committed to measures to preserve the economic value of the historical building to the highest extent possible. In this way, PGH and VEB had opposing objectives to fulfill and had to mutually agree on the works to be carried out.

At the latest, by the 8th Party Congress of the SED (1971), efforts to combine the development of new housing with the reconstruction or socialist redesign of old towns and cities intensified, which strongly influenced the topics and working methods of historical preservation practice. Just in time for Stralsund’s 750th anniversary celebration, the newspaper *Neue Zeit* reported under the title “Gables, Gothic and comfortable rooms. Modern apartments are being built in old Stralsund”[25] on the GDR’s claim of combining old with new and to balance the three areas of historical preservation practice, building and urban development:

> Since the 8th Party Congress of the SED in 1971, 400 apartments have been converted and extended in the city on the Sund, 220 of them in the old town by reconstructing 14 residential buildings. [. . .]. Most impressive, apart from the acquisition of modern apartments and social spaces, is time and again the affectionate treatment of the historical, in high gothic or renaissance style with its emphasis on the horizontal, its expressiveness on the floors. [. . .] The basic elements of the styles are worked out again everywhere, here the elevated ground floor, typical for Stralsund, which will be inhabited again, there a front with exposed monastery formats, these oversized bricks from the Middle Ages, which now make the original true and present again.[26]

23 Starke, “*Hinter gotischen Fassaden in Stralsund*,” 3.
24 Starke, “*Hinter gotischen Fassaden in Stralsund*,” 3.
25 Starke, “*Hinter gotischen Fassaden in Stralsund*,” 3.
26 In original: “Seit dem VIII. Parteitag der SED 1971 wurden in der Stadt am Sund 400 Wohnungen um- und ausgebaut, davon 220 in der Altstadt durch Rekonstruktion von 14 Wohngebäuden. [. . .] Am meisten beeindruckt neben der Gewinnung moderner Wohnungen und gesellschaftlicher Räume immer wieder der liebevolle Umgang mit den historischen, in hochweisender Gotik oder im Renaissancestil mit seiner Betonung der Horizontalen, seiner Ausdruckskraft in den Geschossen. [. . .] Es werden überall die Grundelemente der Stilarten wieder herausgearbeitet, hier

The question of adequate solutions for (new) construction in existing buildings had now also become an issue of historical preservation practice in the GDR. In the same article, for example, the rebuilding of the house at Alter Markt 12 is praised. It states that this would not be a "purely new building", but that "with services of this kind" one would nevertheless meet the demand for "modern living and the preservation of historical monuments".[27]

The work of the PKZ Szczecin

For this type of construction, which was intended to enable "modern" living in historic buildings, the construction companies in the GDR lacked the experience. For the implementation of such hybrid projects, which were a mixture of renovation and new construction, they therefore sought contact with the Polish specialist factories (PKZ) of the Polish Monument Authority, which already had many years of experience in the preservation of historic buildings.

The PKZ was established in 1951 as a result of a reorganisation of the state-owned restoration companies. They employed numerous people who had specialised in the fields of restoration and preservation of historical buildings and monuments. Among others, architects, conservators, art historians, archaeologists, ethnologists as well as craftsmen and skilled construction workers from various trades belonged to the PKZ. In 1975, 14 district offices with different specialisations in different Polish cities were under the central administration of the PKZ.[28] After its foundation, the PKZ was initially to carry out restoration work in the fields of architecture, sculpture, painting, graphics and jewelry art. From 1952 onwards, their activities also included documentations and construction services in field of historical preservation. Local branches were formed throughout the Polish People's Republic from 1955.[29]

The high degree of specialisation, the many years of practical experience in various rebuilding-, reconstruction- and restoration-projects, as well as the scientific-theoretical work within the PKZ led to commissions in socialist and non-socialist foreign countries. These foreign commissions gave PKZ employees the opportunity to exchange experiences and also created direct contact with foreign

---

das für Stralsund typische erhöhte Erdgeschoss, das wieder bewohnt werden wird, dort eine Front mit freigelegten Klosterformaten, diesen übergroßen Ziegeln aus dem Mittelalter, die nun Ursprüngliches wieder wahr und gegenwärtig machen." Starke, "*Hinter gotischen Fassaden in Stralsund*," 3.

27 Starke, "*Hinter gotischen Fassaden in Stralsund*," 3.

28 Anon., *Die Staatlichen Werkstätten für Denkmalpflege* (Warszawa: PKZ, 1975), 8.

29 Józef Pilch, *Die Werkstätten für Denkmalpflege PKZ* (Warszawa: Wydawnictwa PKZ, 1987), 7.

institutions for historical preservation. The foreign projects of the PKZ included among others projects in the Federal Republic of Germany (Munich, Isar Gate), in France (Paris, Hotel Sagan, Rue de Tallyrand 1 – seat of the embassy of the VRP as well as Paris, former Polish school, Rue de Lamande No. 15), in Egypt (Cairo, mortuary temple of Hatshepsut) as well as in the German Democratic Republic.[30]

The range of work that the PKZs offered abroad included the preparation of art historical documentation, including architectural, laboratory and other studies, archaeological research, the preparation of technical, laboratory, economic and other reports for individual objects as well as for historical building ensembles and art collections, execution of complex architectural designs for monuments including projects of all related fields, such as static constructions, irrigation and drainage, heating, lighting, ventilation, as well as execution of structural-conservation and installation works in the field of restoration, adaptation and reconstruction of objects of monumental, urban and vernacular architecture (including transfer of the latter to open-air museums).[31]

The outstanding importance of the PKZ for the PRL results from the broad range of its activity profile and the training and encouragement of highly specialised professionals for a wide variety of tasks in the field of restoration and historical preservation. At the same time, its work had an enormous political impact both at national and international level, acting as a prestigious flagship for Polish professionals in the field of restoration and preservation of buildings, which also acquired an official character with the admission of PKZ to ICOMOS and ICCROM at the turn of the year 1984/85.[32]

In Stralsund, the branch of the PKZ Szczecin had been commissioned with various projects. Among the objects were city fortifications, representative residential buildings (Olthofsches Palais, Wulflam House) and sacred buildings (*Heilgeistkloster*), which were located in the old town area of Stralsund [See Fig. 1]. The range of tasks included art-historical and architectural (preliminary) investigations, archive research, complex reconditioning and reconstruction works and their planning, structural-conservational works as well as the rebuilding of small historical-urbanistic districts.

30 Anon., *Die Staatlichen Werkstätten für Denkmalpflege*, 54.

31 Anon., *Die Staatlichen Werkstätten für Denkmalpflege*, 52.

32 Pilch, *Die Werkstätten für Denkmalpflege PKZ*, 9.

Press reviews and documentations – The case of Fährstrasse 26

The national daily press of the GDR occasionally reported on the work of the PKZ Szczecin in Stralsund. Under the headline "Convalescence cures for historical walls. Polish specialists help with reconstruction in Stralsund",[33] Hans Burmeister described the reconstruction project in the Berliner Zeitung in 1977 which the Polish specialists had already been involved in for several months. According to Burmeister, the aim was to reconstruct the defence wall and the gabled houses in Mühlenstraße, Fährstraße and Schillstraße as "in their old glory"[34] and to give them an appearance "as in the Middle Ages".[35] It is clear that it was not the preservation of historical monuments that was decisive, but the creation of a specific historical image, which probably never existed in this form. The concept of recovery in particular suggests that the architectural reconstruction of history was not intended to revive the lifestyle or living conditions of the Middle Ages, but only to evoke a specific emotion. By referring to the "more than 400 objects"[36] that were listed as historical buildings in Stralsund, the author also made clear that Stralsund was a special town with an extraordinary architectural heritage that required such a remarkable approach.

In another report from the daily press entitled "Beautiful Homeland GDR",[37] the reconstruction of the Knieper Wall by the Polish experts is assessed as a restoration of "its original beauty". The reference to the previous ruinous state also makes clear that this was an extensive reconstruction, which is also impressively demonstrated by a photograph of the new Knieper Wall.

The balancing act between the creation of a specific historical image and a serious approach to the historical preservation of the building inventory can be exemplified by the detailed report of the honorary conservator Käthe Rieck on the reconstruction of the building Fährstraße 26 [Fig. 2]. In an article[38] for the "Denkmalpflege in der DDR", Rieck described the construction project and also mentioned the steps required to realize the project. Thus Rieck explained that the Fährstraße had "always been one of the most important connecting routes between Stralsund's

---

33 Hans Burmeister, "*Genesungskuren für historische Gemäuer. Polnische Spezialisten helfen bei der Rekonstruktion in Stralsund.*" *Berliner Zeitung* (1 July 1977): 6.

34 Burmeister, "*Genesungskuren für historische Gemäuer,*" 6.

35 Burmeister, "*Genesungskuren für historische Gemäuer,*" 6.

36 Burmeister, "*Genesungskuren für historische Gemäuer,*" 6.

37 Anon., "*Schöne Heimat DDR.*" *Neue Zeit* (12 October 1979): 3. Photography: ZB/Busch.

38 Käthe Rieck, "*Rekonstruktion eines Barockhauses in Stralsund durch polnische Denkmalpfleger,*" in *Denkmalpflege in der DDR* (Berlin: Deutscher Kunstverlag, 1975), 38–44.

Fig. 2: Fährstraße 26, Stralsund. Photographie by Franziska Klemstein, August 2020.

city centre and the harbour", the appearance of which had been documented in the nineteenth century to the present day through photographs and lithographs.[39]

During the so-called Wilhelminian time, the street and town image changed enormously, among other things due to the partial demolition of the former town gates. Rieck went on to say that "in those years there had been many, mostly unpleasant changes to the historic buildings" and that "even the house at Fährstraße 26 lost its historic gable".[40] After the end of the Second World War and the removal of war damage at the beginning of the 1950s, it was the Monument Authority itself that suggested "to re-gable the aforementioned house no. 26 with a gable". The basis for the gable restoration at house no. 26 was to be a lithograph

39 Rieck, "*Rekonstruktion eines Barockhauses,*" 41.
40 Rieck, "*Rekonstruktion eines Barockhauses,*" 38.

from 1842, which was understood as "suggestion and model". However, the house was privately owned and the negotiations with the owner, which began in 1958, were initially unsuccessful.[41] According to Rieck, new possibilities arose from the new "Verordnung über die Pflege und den Schutz der Denkmale" of 1961, in the context of which the "Old Town of Stralsund was confirmed as a 'monument of urban architecture' of international importance".[42] It is quite conceivable that the adoption of the new regulation provided more effective means for the monument authority, since it was primarily an adaptation of the 1952 ordinance to the real conditions and structures. Apparently, the pressure on the house owner was increased to such an extent that he first "agreed to repair" the house, but then even sold it. The house became the property of the state VEB Gebäudewirtschaft which enabled the conclusion of a contract with the PKZ, which "provided not only the workers but also all the building materials".[43]

However, this did not yet mark the beginning of the construction work on house no. 26, but rather an "investigation of the building fabric and [the] necessary archival studies" by the people from the PKZ. These brought to light "a photograph from the period 1860–70", which in turn showed a different gable than the lithograph, that was initially intended to serve as a model. Finally, the planning of the repair and reconstruction measures was carried out on the basis of the photograph.[44]

Rieck summarised her report on the work that had been carried out by saying: "The value of this reconstruction lies less in the acquisition of living space than in its urban value for the Fährstraße with its numerous historical buildings from various stylistic eras". Ultimately it is "an essential enrichment of the street scene" and "a stimulating example of high-quality, modern interior design with an individual touch".[45]

Rieck's statement makes it clear that the tradition of a specific (historical) image was at the forefront of the repair of Fährstraße. The preservation of the facades was linked to the task of making city history experienceable in its diversity. Accordingly, the demands of historical preservation, especially in the preparation and monitoring of the measures, were extraordinarily high. Not only because they were committed to preserving as much of the historical substance as possible, but also because they brought in the Polish state-owned factories. Rieck, on the other hand, as an honorary conservator, was responsible – more or less officially – for communicating and disseminating knowledge about the historical inventory, preservation and

41 Rieck, "*Rekonstruktion eines Barockhauses*," 39.

42 Cf.: Liste der Denkmale von besonderer nationaler Bedeutung und internationalem Kunstwert vom 02.01.1962, II. Denkmale der Stadtbaukunst.

43 Rieck, "*Rekonstruktion eines Barockhauses*," 43.

44 Rieck, "*Rekonstruktion eines Barockhauses*," 41.

45 Rieck, "*Rekonstruktion eines Barockhauses*," 44.

restoration, in order to ultimately promote greater awareness for monument conservation in general.

Political claim of reconstruction and knowledge exchange

On 18 May 1971, the building at Fährstraße 26 was ceremonially handed over to the city. In the regional section of the *Ostsee-Zeitung* this event was extensively discussed, and titled "Symbol of Polish architecture".[46] The local report shows great appreciation for the work of the Polish experts. On the one hand, for the work done within only one year. On the other hand, for the provision and involvement of "about 30 experts from different fields"[47] who made this extremely complex reconstruction project possible by using and incorporating the existing building stock.

The political significance of the work of the *PKZ Szczecin* in Stralsund can be seen in another local report on the topping-out ceremony of the first construction phase of the reconstruction of the Knieperwall:

> Brass music, intoned by the orchestra of the voluntary fire brigade, initiated the topping-out ceremony on Monday afternoon on the construction site of PKZ 'Reconstruction of the city wall'. With a bouquet of red carnations each, the Polish construction manager Jerzy Gniot greeted the 1st secretary of the SED district leadership, comrade Günter Rosenfeld, the consul general of the Polish People's Republic for the three northern districts of the GDR Zdzislaw Kitlinski, the secretary of the SED district leadership, Günter Lüskow, the mayor Horst Lehmann and the director of PKZ, Frantizek Dzialak.[48]

Not only the publicity event and reporting of it, but above all the presence of the SED district leadership and the PKZ director testify to the political and economic dimension of the occasion, which culminated in a speech by the first secretary of the SED

---

46 Anon., *"Symbol polnischer Baukunst. Heute, 10.00 Uhr: Übergabe des Barockhauses durch PKZ." Ostsee-Zeitung* (18 May 1971): 8.

47 In original: *Blasmusik, intoniert durch das Orchester der Freiwilligen Feuerwehr, leitete am Montagnachmittag das Richtfest auf der Baustelle von PKZ 'Rekonstruktion der Stadtmauer' ein. Mit je einem roten Nelkenstrauß begrüßte der polnische Bauleiter, Jerzy Gniot, den 1. Sekretär der SED-Kreisleitung, Genossen Günter Rosenfeld, den Generalkonsul der VR Polen für die drei Nordbezirke der DDR Zdzislaw Kitlinski, den Sekretär der SED-Kreisleitung, Günter Lüskow, den Oberbürgermeister Horst Lehmann und den Direktor von PKZ, Frantizek Dzialak.* In Anon., *"Symbol polnischer Baukunst,"* 8.

48 Anon., *"Polnische Bauarbeiter vom PKZ übergaben 1. Abschnitt. Hübsche Richtkrone ziert die Mauer. Generalkonsul der VR Polen, Zdzislaw Kitlinski, begrüßt." Ostsee-Zeitung* (12 October 1977): 8.

district leadership, Günter Rosenfeld. Rosenfeld placed the event in the context of the 28th anniversary of the founding of the GDR and the 60th anniversary of the October Revolution, which – in his view – founded the German-Polish friendship.

In addition to individual reports on the reconstruction measures of the PKZ in Stralsund, in which the Polish specialists “drew their tracks into the city”,[49] numerous photographs have been preserved that document the work of the PKZ and the process of change in the city. They show the extensive spectrum of activities, which ranged from typical construction work to detailed restoration work. At the same time, the photographs, some of which also appeared in the regional and national daily press, advertised the building practice and practical urban preservation in the Hanseatic city. With the frequent reference to the PKZ Szczecin in the captions, the photos were also a sign of German-Polish exchange and of the cohesion of the community of socialist states.

Many of the pictures were taken by the photographer Edelgard Skop[50] and Harry Hardenberg.[51] Hardenberg’s photographs also include interior shots of the reconstruction of Ossenreyerstrasse 1–2 (Olthofsches Palais), which document the restoration work carried out by PKZ specialists [Figs. 3 & 4]. At the same time, the interior photographs form a contrast to the more frequent exterior photographs, which show exclusively male PKZ employees who were busy with demolition work or other construction activities or who posed together for the photo [Fig. 5]. In contrast, the interior photographs show the filigree and investigative work of the Polish restorer Hanna Smolinska of the PKZ Szczecin in Hackert’s Wallpaper Hall.[52] Another photograph by Hardenberg shows Smolinska with a colleague standing or sitting on scaffolding in front of the wallpaper while working. In this way Hardenberg not only documented the working methods of the PKZ and the architectural and urban changes in the city of Stralsund by the Polish specialists,

---

49 Anon., “*Polnische Bauarbeiter vom PKZ übergaben 1. Abschnitt*,” 8.

50 Edelgard Skop worked as a photographer from 1965 to 1974 in the Museum of Cultural History before she went on to work in a state combine for building and montage and in archaeological and historic conservation until 1990. See Miriam Weber, Stralsunderin zeigt Foto-Schätze von Ulbricht bis Krug. Ostsee-Zeitung website: https://www.ostsee-zeitung.de/Vorpommern/Stralsund/Stralsunderin-zeigt-Foto-Schaetze-von-Ulbricht-bis-Krug, (accessed 23 August 2020).

51 Harry Hardenberg first worked as a painter at the Volkswerft Stralsund before he decided to take up photography. In 1969, he began distance learning at the Academy of Visual Arts in Leipzig. From 1970 he worked as a photo journalist and has been a freelance artist since 1984. See Miriam Weber, Die Geschichte der Volkswerft in Bildern. Ostsee-Zeitung website: https://www.ostsee-zeitung.de/Vorpommern/Stralsund/Die-Geschichte-der-Volkswerft-in-Bildern, (accessed 23 August 2020).

52 Smolinska, for example, was also involved in making the copy of the bronze doors (Płock Gates) of the St. Sophia Cathedral in Novgorod. See Jakub Chojnacki, “Drzwi Płockie w dniu 23 listopada 1981 roku w Bazylice Katedralnej,” *Notatki Płockie* 26, no. 4–109: 59–64.

Fig. 3: Photograph by Harry Hardenberg, in: Stadtarchiv Hansestadt Stralsund, Signature: VIII-15-03-155.

Fig. 4: Photograph by Harry Hardenberg, in: Stadtarchiv Hansestadt Stralsund, Signature: VIII-16-03-117.

Fig. 5: Photograph by Harry Hardenberg, in: Stadtarchiv Hansestadt Stralsund, Signature: VIII-05-01-005.

but at the same time, also reflected – consciously or unconsciously – the gender ratio that prevailed in the field of construction and historical preservation and restoration.

German-Polish cooperation

In the European Architectural Heritage Year (1975), the newspaper *Neue Zeit* reported on the new types of usage of historical buildings.[53] In addition to Görlitz, Freiberg and Quedlinburg, the article in the daily newspaper mentioned the "systematic reconditioning work"[54] in Stralsund. It also reported, with reference to statements by the General Conservator Ludwig Deiters, on the "good cooperation between Polish and GDR restorers in the restoration of historical monuments in the Republic".[55] In this context, the Güstrow Castle and a half-timbered house in

53 Anon., "Im UNESCO-Jahr der Denkmalpflege. Historische Bauten neuartig nutzen. Rekonstruktion und Pflege von DDR-Kulturdenkmälern." *Neue Zeit* (26 June 1975): 4.
54 Anon., "Im UNESCO-Jahr der Denkmalpflege," 4.
55 Anon., "Im UNESCO-Jahr der Denkmalpflege," 4.

Quedlinburg are mentioned, which "upon completion will serve as a club and exhibition centre" as well as for residential purposes. The cooperation with restorers "also from other socialist countries in the coming years" should also be further intensified.[56]

The demand for specialists from the PKZ companies to work in the context of heritage conservation projects was enormous. Especially in the case of monuments of special national and international significance (e.g. the old towns of Stralsund and Quedlinburg as well as Güstrow Castle) the GDR's conservators did not seem to want to do without Polish expertise and aimed at strengthening the cooperation. However, Deiters emphasised that the cooperation would not only apply to Poland, but to the entire community of socialist states.

The socialist transformation efforts in particular posed an enormous challenge for the preservation and protection of historical monuments in the GDR. A suitable reasoning had to be repeatedly sought for this, i.e. one that corresponded to the location of the city or was suitable for the efforts of the building industry. For this reason, Ludwig Deiters, as General Conservator for the preservation of monuments and sites in the GDR, together with his staff, tried to be more closely involved in the planning processes of the building industry in order to be able to take timely action for the preservation of monuments and historical buildings, as early as the 1960s. Parallel to these developments, the members of the BdA came to the conclusion that "decisions qualified for the reconstruction [. . .] must be prepared, since the companies [. . .] had hitherto been oriented essentially only towards new buildings"[57] in 1973.

Ultimately, the conservators of the Institute for Preservation of Monuments and Sites were permanently caught between the conflicting priorities of advancing industrialisation, constant pressure to economise and the endeavour to preserve historic buildings, historic city layouts and traditional city skylines to the greatest possible extent. According to their self-image, they not only wanted to guarantee the preservation and protection of the most outstanding individual monuments, but also, in accordance with the Monument Protection Ordinance of 1961, wanted to include the "surroundings, insofar as they are important for the character and effect of the monument".[58]

The exchange and the relationship between the conservators and experts of the states had not been the decisive factor for the binational working relationship between the GDR conservators and the specialists of the PKZ. Rather, the cooperation was based on political and economic agreements and treaties within the

56 Anon., "Im UNESCO-Jahr der Denkmalpflege," 4.

57 BLDAM, L 6/2, Protokoll der Konservatorenbesprechung (14 February 1973), 2.

58 Verordnung über die Pflege und den Schutz der Denkmale (28 September 1961), in *Gesetzblatt der Deutschen Demokratischen Republik* Part II, no. 72 (23 October 1961): 475–477, 475, § 3.

framework of the Council for Mutual Economic Assistance (RGW) and protocols on the agreed mutual deliveries of goods and services between the two states. The long-term trade agreements were regularly renewed, for example, during a visit by Polish Foreign Minister Wojtaszek to the House of the Council of Ministers in 1977.[59]

The protocol on mutual deliveries of goods and services between the GDR and the PRL in 1977 was signed by the Ministers of Foreign Trade of both countries, Horst Solle and Jerzy Olszewski. Championing the advancement of socialism, they agreed on which cooperations and products should be exchanged and supplied in the future. Thus the GDR committed itself to send machine tools and products of electrical engineering and electronics as well as scientific equipment to the Polish People's Republic. In return, the VRP undertook to export raw materials such as hard coal and lignite to the GDR. In addition, the Poles agreed "to provide construction, assembly and reconstruction services for the implementation of investments in the GDR".[60]

The reconstruction projects of the PKZ Szczecin in Stralsund were thus part of the binational economic agreements within the community of socialist states. For the preservationists in the GDR, the support of the Polish specialist companies was indispensable, as the companies in the GDR were primarily oriented towards new construction. The fact that the PKZ Szczecin was used particularly and considerably in Stralsund was also due to the outstanding importance attributed to the old town of Stralsund in particular and the Hanseatic city in general.

Stralsund, like Greifswald, Rostock or Wismar, was among the cities that served as showcases for non-socialist foreign countries during the so-called Baltic Sea Week.[61] In 1959, Stralsund's 750th anniversary was to be celebrated at the same time as the Baltic Sea Week, so that Stralsund, in addition to the main venue Rostock, was to fulfil a prominent representative function across the entire Baltic Sea region.[62] In fact, during the Baltic Sea Week in 1959, Stralsund was visited by people from the Federal Republic of Germany, West Berlin, Sweden, the Netherlands, Poland, Latvia, Denmark and Norway. In the years that followed, the Baltic Sea Week remained an important international event, with international guests also turning their eyes to Stralsund. Thus, the Swedish daily newspaper "Svenska

59 Cf: Anon., "Freundschaftliche Begegnung im Hause des Ministerrates." *Neues Deutschland* (4 February 1977): 2.

60 Anon., "*Warenaustausch mit der VRP wird bedeutend erweitert Außenhandelsminister unterzeichneten das Protokoll für 1977.*" *Neues Deutschland* (26 February 1977): 2.

61 The Baltic Sea Week was an international festival held annually in the GDR from 1958 to 1975. It usually took place at the beginning of July in the district of Rostock and had the motto: "The Baltic Sea must be a sea of peace."

62 Brunner, *Eine Stadt im Systemwandel*, 169.

Dagbladet", in a travel report on the Baltic Sea Week, also paid tribute to the care of the cultural heritage in Stralsund, which also included preserving the "remnants from Swedish times".[63]

Conclusion

To sum up, it can be stated, that the PKZ for the preservation of historical monuments have inscribed themselves into the city and the cityscape through their many projects in the Hanseatic city. Through numerous reports and photographs in the local and national daily press as well as in publications on monument conservation and urban history, the various works on the city's heterogeneous heritage have been well handed down. They bear witness to the achievements that have resulted from the exchange between the People's Republic of Poland and the German Democratic Republic. At the same time, they contributed to the preservation of a historical townscape.

The activities of the PKZ in Stralsund must be seen against the background of the developments in the construction industry in the GDR. These demanded more efficient industrialisation and typification. Likewise, politics and the construction industry demanded the socialist transformation and reconstruction of the cities and villages and attempted to implement it.

As a result, the preservationists in the GDR were permanently caught between the conflicting priorities of advancing industrialisation, constant pressure to economise, and the desire to preserve the historical fabric of old buildings, historical city layouts, and traditional cityscape to the greatest possible degree. According to their professional self-perception, they not only wanted to guarantee the preservation and protection of the most outstanding individual monuments, but also, in accordance with the Monument Protection Ordinance of 1961, to include the surrounding area in as far as it was important for the character and effect of the monument.

However, the preservation of historic fabric or the documentary value of a site were not in the focus of many reconstructions. Instead, they were concerned with the protection and/or creation of an image of an historical town and thus with a certain effect that should be created in the urban space – not only in Stralsund.

The exchange between the PRL and the GDR was intended to strengthen the relations between the COMECON-countries and to be a symbol of the strength of socialism. The reports on the work of the PKZ Szczecin are characterised by recognition for the work done and testify to the exchange on an equal footing.

63 Anon., "*Vorbildliche Denkmalpflege.*" *Neues Deutschland* (30 July 1966): 8.

III Media, Perceptions and Afterlives of Socialist Architecture and Planning

Jasna Galjer

Architecture of International Zagreb Fair between the East and West

In the Cold War period, Yugoslavia held a specific position both between and outside the Eastern and Western block. Its model of "socialism with a human face" was reflected in particular in the political strategy of promoting social and cultural values which represented the new state on the international political scene in a modern shape. Such an orientation was a consequence of the turnabout in government policy in 1948: a parting of ways with the USSR and a rapprochement with the West, from which Yugoslavia received military and economic aid and where it found new political allies.

The concept of modernity is most often defined as a clash between repressive systems and real-utopianism, the typology of which is considered mostly at the level of the formal features of the representative samples of architecture, design or art, and a comparative analysis of these and of contemporary production in the West. At the same time, the universal politicisation of society and identity crises experienced in socialist Yugoslavia are additional obstacles to any overall comprehension of the continuity of modernity in essentially changed circumstances of social and ideological structure, where the national and the international still represent opposing trends.

The premise of this chapter is that a state which has yet to articulate its identity on the international scene can use exhibitions as a very efficient means of propaganda, ranging from ideology to cultural policy strategy. Using the case study of the Zagreb Fair, the purpose of this essay is to examine the characteristic manifestations of how the exhibition functioned in the context of the 1950s and 1960s was defined not only by the industrialisation and urbanisation of the "first wave of modernisation" but also by the unique model of socialism, worker self-management and the foreign policy of non-alignment. For this reason, apart from the propaganda value, another aspect of importance was the didactic aim of specialised exhibitions that were continuously organised at the Zagreb Fair at the end of the 1950s and in the early 1960s, conceived as a manifesto of modern architecture used to foster social prosperity.

Some of the segments of the series of *Family and Household* exhibitions,[1] such as the building standards and criteria for quality of life, industrial design,

---

1 Jasna Galjer, and Iva Ceraj, "The role of design in everyday life as presented at the Family and Household exhibitions (1957–1960)." *Radovi IPU* [Journal of the Institute of Art History] 35 (2011): 277–296.

https://doi.org/10.1515/9783110658491-009

social policy, urban culture, or perhaps of the promotion of these, constitute a key aspect of societal modernisation, from the point of view of both the cultural dominant and of the strategy of social development.[2] The aim is to present the development and specificity of the social and political system, culture and art, where the model of worker self-management was "the guiding red thread". Putting self-management up front at the level of a key concept shows how articulate the programme was in making the idiosyncrasy of the state clear, for which appearances at international trade fairs and exhibitions were considered opportunities for (self-)promotion.

Furthermore, this strategy envisaged an important place for the presentation of the Yugoslav foreign policy of "peaceful coexistence" neither in the East nor West, which at the beginning of the 1960s would turn into the Non-Aligned Movement.[3] The entire definition of the Yugoslav model of socialism had acquired additional importance because of the political context and the foreign policy of FPRY (Federal People's Republic of Yugoslavia), which, after it had opened up to the West in the mid-1950s, was also characterised by an increasing normalisation of relations with the USSR. The characteristic conceptual modes that contributed to this process of "translation"[4] are, among others, exhibitions.

Yugoslav political propaganda draws attention to the very early appearance of the awareness of the importance of international (self-)representation. The aim of this chapter is to shed light on exhibition architecture and its role in expressing the awareness of the need to promote cultural and political identity, economic and industrial production, as well as its codes and specific methods of working on constructing a modernist cultural paradigm. More specifically, the aim is to

---

2 Among the many recent contributions on the topic, Martino Stierli, and Vladimir Kulić, eds., *Toward a Concrete Utopia Architecture in Yugoslavia, 1948–1980* (New York: The Museum of Modern Art, 2018).

3 Important recent studies of the diplomatic history of this period of the Cold War include Nataša Mišković, Harald Fischer-Tiné, and Nada Boškovska Leimgruber, *The Non-Aligned Movement and the Cold War: Delhi, Bandung, Belgrade* (Abingdon: Routledge, 2014); Rinna Kullaa, *Non-Alignment and Its Origins in Cold War Europe: Yugoslavia, Finland and the Soviet Challenge* (London: I.B.Tauris 2012); Svetozar Rajak, "No bargaining chips, no spheres of interest: the Yugoslav origins of Cold War non-alignment." *Journal of Cold War Studies* 16, no. 1 (2014): 146–179. A still invaluable contribution to the case study of the Yugoslav contribution to the Non-Aligned Movement is the work by Dennison Rusinow, *The Yugoslav Experiment 1948–1974* (Berkeley and Los Angeles: University of California Press, 1978).

4 An analogous theoretical framework is applied in the study of migrations of modern architectural concepts by Esra Akcan, *Architecture in Translation: Germany, Turkey, and the Modern House* (Durham N.C.: Duke University Press, 2012).

document and contextualise the architecture of the Zagreb Fair as a response to the awakening of consumer society.

In the early 1950s, journals such as *Casabella, L'Architecture d'Aujourd'hui* and *The Architectural Review* began to publish numerous architectural designs and realisations from the other side of the so-called Iron Curtain, illustrating that the exchange between Eastern and Western European countries was quite intense during the Cold War, particularly with regard to promoting international modernism as a global phenomenon. *Concrete Quarterly,* a British journal renowned for promoting structural exhibitionism in the 1950s, published an article titled *Some post-war buildings in Hungary and Yugoslavia* (1956) including several exceptional examples of precast reinforced concrete structures. Yugoslav architecture was usually interpreted by architectural critics as a mediator of international modernism focused on the West as unexpectedly modern and democratic.[5] Mapping the discourse, George E. Kidder Smith concludes in the first survey of *The new architecture of Europe* (1961) that, "[i]f there is an architecture which stands in need of shrewd and deep interpretative study at present it is the Yugoslav example".[6] This statement is actually a quotation from an article published in *Architectural Review* in 1960, where the specificity of Yugoslavia is qualified by a "geographical and political intermediate position between East and West [which] appears to be resolved in a very full comprehension of the culture of each, so that its architecture has a tendency to resemble the crucial phases of both".[7] Coincidentally, in the same year a special issue of *Casabella continuità* devoted to Yugoslav architecture published a survey titled *Politics and architecture in Yugoslavia: Revisionism and orthodoxy,* which included an analysis of three case studies: Zagreb, Ljubljana and Belgrade, focusing on the implementation of modernist architecture in the contemporary political situation.[8]

In an ideological and technical sense, a decisive factor in the establishment of these new cities was the intention to build on a location without urban history – in other words, a place where no urban structure had been formed in the whole of history. Only in such a place, without an urban history of the city, could a directly and liberally supra-historical reality of the construction of a new capital of "people's democracy" (later socialism) be carried out. Nevertheless, the debates surrounding newly planned capital cities as interventions in a

5 Jérôme Bazin, "Some post-war buildings in Hungary and Yugoslavia." *Concrete Quarterly* 29 (April–June 1956): 27–34.

6 George Everard Kidder Smith, *The New Architecture of Europe* (Harmondsworth, Middlesex: Pelican/Penguin Books, 1962), 323.

7 "Usable forms . . . symbolic Value." *Architectural Review* 8 (1960): 21.

8 Aurelio Cortesi, "Politica e architettura in Jugoslavia: revisionismo e ortodossia." *Casabella continuità* 255 (1961): 4–23.

tabula rasa environment, like Abuja, the new capital city of Nigeria, reflect the ideological background of these concepts.

The period from 1956 to 1965 was one of stability and progress of the Yugoslav state in economic, social and cultural terms. The policy of non-alignment marked the epoch that began with Stalin's death in 1953 and consequent "reconciliation" with Soviet authorities. In international terms this meant an openness of the state borders both towards the West and the East, and especially the South, where the affiliation with the Non-Aligned Movement in 1961 – whose foundation was initiated by Yugoslav authorities among others – enabled the economic expansion of Yugoslavia to Asian and African countries. In this way, Yugoslavia succeeded in maintaining friendly relations with all states, regardless of their political and economic systems. This was particularly in evidence at the time of the Zagreb Fair, when the city served as a meeting point between the East and West, as well as an important backdrop for the propaganda and affirmation of the non-aligned countries of Asia and Africa, which rallied around Yugoslavia.

Trade fairs in Zagreb have had a long history, starting from the beginning of the twentieth century. The Zagreb Assembly was founded in 1909 with the aim of promoting trade, craft, industry, tourism and culture. The chronology of how (the originally called) *Zagrebački zbor* transformed into *Zagrebački velesajam* serves to illustrate how the original fairground eventually developed into a fully-fledged trade fair.[9] In under a century the fair was relocated five times: always to the city's outskirts, representing the strategies to generate urban development of newly planned environments.[10] The dislocations were also symptoms of the modernisation and metropolisation of the city, which redefined its measurements and its urban identity within this period.

After the new Kingdom of Yugoslavia was founded, the Zagreb Fair was revived as a trade fair with an international focus and experienced its greatest prosperity in the interwar period. Due to its expansion, it moved in 1936 to a newly built complex, dominated by the national pavilions of France, designed by architects Robert Camelot and Jacques Paul & Herb, along with constructor Bernard Lafaille; Italy (arch. Dante Petroni); Germany (arch. Otto Roemer); and Czechoslovakia (arch. Ferdinand Fencl). Its urban concept, designed by Croatian architect Marijan Haberle, implemented the

---

9 See Kruno Sabolić, *Od zbora do Velesajma 1909–1999: 90 godina Zagrebačkog velesajma* [From *zbor* to *velesajam* 1909–1999: 90 years of the Zagreb Fair] (Zagreb: Zagrebački velesajam/Ars media, 1999). The book was published on the occasion of the fair's 90th anniversary.

10 For the survey of the first phase of the Zagreb Fair, see Marina Bagarić, "Architecture of Zagrebački Zbor between 1910 and 1935." *Radovi IPU* [Journal of the Institute of Art History 34 (2010): 165–180. and Goran Arčabić, *Zagrebački zbor kao poveznica hrvatskog i europskog gospodarstva (1922–1940.)* (Zagreb: Srednja Europa/MGZ, 2013).

typology of international fairs and exhibitions, from Paris 1937 to the site of the Venice Biennale. Curiously, the pavilion of the Third Reich in Zagreb was designed as an elegant, atrial, skeletal structure in the Bauhaus style, contrary to the contemporary design of the German pavilion, executed by Albert Speer for Paris 1937 the same year. As the international affirmation of *Zagrebački zbor* reached its peak and a new "trade fair city" was built next to the arterial road of *Savska cesta*, other international fairs began to prosper in Yugoslavia. They soon grew to be important places of cultural transfer and their significance greatly superseded the confines of commerce-oriented exchange at specialised fairs. The Ljubljana Fair was established as early as 1921 and the Belgrade Fair in 1937. The latter had been strongly supported by state institutions since its very inception, in order to affirm the central position of the capital city.

The postwar history of the Zagreb Fair may be divided into the period from 1947, when the activities of *Zagrebački zbor* were reinitiated, and the move to its new location across the River Sava in 1956.[11] The political circumstances had experienced a complete transformation, which led to key changes in the organisational and programme-related structure of the Zagreb Fair.[12] In 1941, the last *Zagrebački zbor* exhibition took place, marking the end of the period which had seen this event transform into one of the most significant trade fairs of the region. The location was turned into a military barracks and eventually experienced complete devastation. Post-war social and political changes required that the Zagreb Fair be reorganised in a way that suited the policy of self-promotion and representation of the newly established Socialist Federal Republic of Yugoslavia. The political government at the time aimed to demonstrate the economic achievements of the newly formed state and founded a major international fair in Southeastern Europe to become a symbol of communist prosperity. But its image was deeply embedded in the continuity of modernity from the interwar period and the language of modern architecture rather than a "national identity".

A characteristic example of the complex inter-relationship between avant-garde tradition and contemporary international architectural culture of the 1950s is the activity of EXAT 51 (Experimental Atelier 51) focused on experimental and constructivist approach and promoting the idea of synthesis of art and architecture. Collaborative practices of the members included Yugoslavian pavilion designs for

11 Mira Kolar, "Projekt povijesti zagrebačkog velesajma iz 1967." *Časopis za suvremenu povijest* 2 (1999): 319–339.

12 Following a significant upturn, the 1980s saw a period of stagnation, and finally, following 1991, the demise of Zagreb's reputation as a trade fair city.

international trade fairs and exhibition designs.[13] The public was invited to "read" architecture as the evidence of complex interactions of social and economic forces, and images were created on different scales and media.

A culmination of these tendencies was the Yugoslav appearance at the Expo 58 in Brussels, proclaimed as one of the most successful at the World Fair, mostly due to the innovative architectural concept of the pavilion designed by Croatian architect Vjenceslav Richter.[14] As a consequence of Tito's split with Stalin, in 1948 an attempt was made to sabotage the Zagreb Fair:

> [T]he countries of the Cominform bloc wished to obstruct the fair by first hiring pavilions and then cancelling their participation at the last moment. Thanks to the resourcefulness of the Zagreb Fair management, this scheme was not only prevented – quickly filling the entire exhibition space previously hired by the USSR – but was also turned to the advantage, the western side of the fairgrounds being expanded by three new pavilions.[15]

The changes in Yugoslav foreign policy towards the East and West were reflected in a dramatic increase in the number of international exhibitors as well as an increased turnover beginning in the 1950s. Thus, in 1955, the Zagreb Fair (once again) hosted the USSR, the Czech Republic, Poland, Romania and East Germany, as well as the USA, Great Britain, Belgium, the Netherlands, Denmark, Sweden, France, Lichtenstein, Switzerland, Italy, Austria, Greece, Israel, Japan and West Germany.

Nevertheless, during the Cold War the Zagreb Fair was one of the rare international fairs that offered a common ground for exhibitors from both sides of the Iron Curtain, as well as non-aligned countries: everything – from fashionable clothing to industrial products – was displayed side by side, exceeding the fair's commercial function.[16] In Project Zagreb, Eve Blau and Ivan Rupnik claim that, "the relocation of the International Fair to the south side of the Sava has opened up new terrain for the development and expansion of the city. Furthermore, the prefabricated principle was later applied in the construction of New Zagreb

---

13 See Katia Baudin, and Tihomir Milovac, eds., *EXAT 51: Synthesis of the Arts in Post-War Yugoslavia* (Dortmund: Verlag Kettler, 2017).

14 The topic is examined in the monograph, Jasna Galjer, *Expo 58 and Yugoslav pavilion by Vjenceslav Richter* (Zagreb: Horetzky, 2009).

15 *Narodni list* (14 September 1952).

16 The Zagreb Fair in the context of exhibition architecture was the topic of the article: Mirna Meštrović, and Aleksander Laslo, "The fairground as a political playground: The Zagreb International Trade Fair and Cold War circumstances," in *Ephemeral Architecture in Central and Eastern Europe in the 19th and 21st Centuries*, edited by Miklós Székely, 265–280 (Paris/Budapest: L'Harmattan, 2015).

apartment blocks".[17] In the spring of 1953, experts gathered at the site where the Zagreb Fair was to be built in order to consider the possibilities afforded by the expansion of both the fair and the city across the river. The idea was initiated by Mayor Većeslav Holjevac, a man of great influence in the political circles of his time, and was a response to the growing tendency of the Belgrade Fair to take over the role of the country's premier fair. Leading government bodies were investing in the construction, and the new fair in the capital of Yugoslavia was meant to link the country along with its capital city to European trends, as well as to represent an icon of architectonic design and technological innovation. It is interesting to note that those involved in the design of the fair had gone on a study visit to Munich, Hannover, Paris and Milan in order to become acquainted with the contemporary trends in exhibition architecture.[18] Following its opening in 1957, the Belgrade Fair began to hold regular exhibition events and quickly acquired great popularity as a sort of symbol of the socialist version of the spectacle society: promoting the flamboyant architecture as a "spectacle" that embodied multilayered and conflicting political, ideological and performative meanings of public space and reality.

The general layout of the exhibition ground, the architectural concept and governing regulations of the Zagreb Fair in the new urban district were designed by architect Marijan Haberle, who had contributed to the design of *Zagrebački zbor* at the *Savska cesta* location. The lead contractor, a construction company called *Tehnika*, took a mere 114 days (a record) to set up the necessary municipal facilities and build the initial 41,000 sqm of exhibition space and accompanying infrastructure. It was thus as early as September 1956 that the first fair was held at the new site. As soon as the first construction phase had been completed, the Zagreb Fair invited bids for further construction.

The winning project was designed by Božidar Rašica, whose urbanistic plan envisaged the incorporation of the Zagreb Fair into the urban space across the river, as well as the possibility of using more pavilions and other facilities, not only while the fair was in progress. The urbanistic concept and the positions of the various pavilion sites intended for different countries fully reflected the criteria used to assign them: the appeal of the pavilion sites depended on the countries' political power. The struggle for prestige was reflected in the organisation of events marking particular occasions, for instance, national days with programmes planned specially for the occasion. An ambitious architectural-urbanistic project envisaged the

---

17 Eve Blau, and Ivan Rupnik, *Project Zagreb: Transition as Condition, Strategy, Practice* (Barcelona: Actar, 2007), 221.

18 Bratislav Ilić, "The structural systems of Belgrade fair exhibition halls." *Nauka + praksa* 12, no. 1 (2009): 39–42.

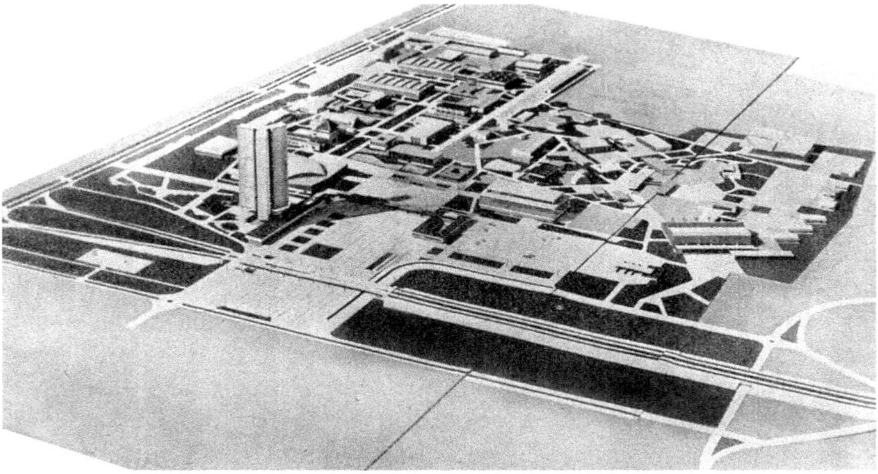

Fig. 1: Božidar Rašica: Urban planning concept of Zagreb Fair from 1957, scale model. Source: Čovjek i prostor [Man and Space] 67 (1957): 1.

transformation of the fairground into a multifunctional new city centre, complete with a nine-floor hotel, child-care facilities for visitors, and a sports centre and stadium. The whole complex would be dominated by a 180-metre tower topped by a restaurant and an observation deck, whose concept evokes the tradition of visual symbols ranging from the Eiffel Tower to the Skylon.

Most of the pavilions were built in the first phase (Fig. 1) of construction from 1956 to 1960, but intensive activity continued from 1961 to 1970. By the end of the second phase of construction, the requirements for the fairground had changed – for instance, modularity was required – because it was to be used all year round. In the first phase, 13 pavilions were built, seven of which were designed for foreign countries by selected national architects, most of them already experienced in exhibition architecture. The first USSR pavilion, designed in 1956 by Juri Abramov, one of the co-authors of the USSR pavilion at Expo 58, was 14.2 metres in height with a 27.5 metre arch span, constructed of prefabricated mounting elements on two reinforced-concrete frames. Romania (Ascanio Damian, 1956), Czechoslovakia (designed in 1956 by Josef Hrubý, also the author of the design for the pavilion at Expo 58, as the only major building at the Zagreb Fair whose load bearing structure was made of wood), the German Democratic Republic (Richard Paulick, 1956), China (Cheng Sung Mao, 1957), Hungary and Poland took the opportunity to build new structures, with a total exhibition area of 19,432 square metres.

The Zagreb Fair was much more than just a commercial event, which is reflected in the spatial disposition centred around the 'Avenue of Nations' *Aleja nacija*, along which 18 pavilions were located. It was the central communication axis as well as a symbolic link between the various pavilions. Božidar Rašica's project envisaged the Avenue of Nations as the central axis of the fairground city, its centrality further accentuated by the Palace of Nations, whose construction was planned as part of a design competition in 1956. An audacious structure of the central type covered with a paraboloid roof construction by Ivan Vitić won; however, it was never built. Similar to the entry he submitted for the Yugoslav pavilion competition at the Brussels Expo, Vitić designed a pavilion with a central layout, covered by a parabolic roof structure. Instead of his proposal, in 1957 another structure was built, equally attractive and a radical departure from the conventions of exhibition architecture followed at the Zagreb Fair (Fig. 2).

Fig. 2: International 'collective' pavilion (Pavilion No. 40), Zagreb Fair 1957. Design: Ivan Vitić. Source: Croatian State Archives, Zagreb. AG FOTO L-996-003.

This was a result of a political decision made by Zagreb mayor Holjevac, i.e., the struggle for prestige with the Belgrade Fair. Ivan Vitić, who designed the pavilion, and engineer Kruno Tonković produced a representative and expressive structure: Pavilion No. 40, intended for countries which did not have their own national pavilions.[19] The contrast between the suspended roof structure and the brutalist concrete gables clearly belongs to contemporary global trends of spectacular architectural

19 Pavilion No. 40 was also known as the Pavilion of Nations because of the purpose it served.

forms, such as, for instance the Kresge Auditorium at the MIT Campus in Cambridge, Massachusetts by Eero Saarinen (1950–1955) and the Dorton Arena in Raleigh, North Carolina by Maciej Nowicki (1952).[20]

For Yugoslav exhibitors, the Zagreb Fair authorities built five pavilions totalling 20,464 sqm in area. Due to an unexpectedly high interest on the part of the exhibitors and a lack of space, two other pavilions originally built for local exhibitors were used by India, Austria and West Germany. In September 1956, Marshal Tito opened the 51st International Fair in Zagreb, which was covered by Zagreb Television in their first live broadcast. During the opening it was pointed out that the Zagreb Fair "is becoming a manifestation of two permanent policy aspirations of Yugoslavia: economic progress and cooperation between Yugoslavia and other countries".[21]

As part of President Eisenhower's foreign economic policy, starting from 1954, the United States' participation at international trade fairs expanded rapidly, including participation at trade fairs in countries behind the Iron Curtain. US Secretary of Commerce, Sinclair Weeks, devised a special programme to present the American economy at international trade fairs: the campaign of "People's Capitalism". The idea of promoting consumer society as a strategy in the Cold War power struggle was heralded by sociologist David Riesman in his 1951 satirical essay *The Nylon War*, in which he described a fictional bombing of the USSR by American consumer goods (refrigerators, nylon stockings, cigarettes, and the like).[22]

The United States debuted at the Zagreb Trade Fair in September 1955 with the *Atoms-for-Peace* exhibition organised and designed by USIA (The United States Information Agency). The exhibit had the greatest success ever in any communist country and reached more than 150,000 visitors in 12 days.

While little was expected in terms of immediate trade, the United States' participation at the Zagreb Fair in 1956 offered a chance to counter Soviet propaganda and present an approach to American life and resources displayed to demonstrate the "soft power" of American self-promotion, as argued by Jean-Louis Cohen in a comprehensive analysis of the "Amerikanizm" in Russian architecture, determined by the USSR's fascination with American technology and culture.[23] The topic of the display was America at home, where the Yugoslav public were invited to compare their daily lives with those of their American

---

20 Ivo Podhorsky, "The Construction of Pavillion No. 40 at the Zagreb Fair." *Architecture* 1, no. 217 (2005): 117–136.

21 *Narodni list* (7 September 1956).

22 David Riesman, *The Nylon War in Abundance for What? And Other Essays* (New York: Doubleday, 1964), 71.

23 Exhibition curated by Jean-Louis Cohen, *Building a New New World: Amerikanizm in Russian Architecture* (Canadian Centre for Architecture, 13 November 2019–5 April 2020).

counterparts. Designers of Raymond Spilman's office developed the theme against the background of a photo-story of the average American industrial worker, shown at some previous fairs. The fairytale rendition of the American Dream was presented as an "Ed Barnes Story": a photo exhibition of the everyday lives of a happy "typical" American family.[24] On the occasion of the first US appearance at the Zagreb Fair, the US trade delegation representatives were taken to visit six cities and numerous factories in Yugoslavia. The visit was organised by the Yugoslav Chamber of Commerce and several trading agreements were struck, as well as invitations issued to Yugoslav business entities to visit the US. This was in line with the Eisenhower administration policy which did not resort to open political propaganda, but rather relied on psychological strategies which incorporated national security policies, propaganda, international public opinion and the needs and customs of local communities.[25] The purpose of cultural diplomacy was to use subtle methods to bring those who held political and economic power in communist countries to the US, so that they might experience for themselves the myth of abundance and democracy.[26] An overview of US propaganda at selected international trade fairs, titled Design as a political force and published in Industrial Design in 1957, includes Saloniki, Bari, Damascus, Vienna, Kabul, Izmir and Zagreb as pioneering achievements of the new policy.[27]

As Beatriz Colomina pointed out in her seminal essay "The Media House" (1995),[28] the question of the house is understood as a question of identity politics, pointing out that the way the house occupies the media is directly related to the way the media occupies the house. At one level, architecture is transformed by the media in which it is exhibited. At another level, the design of the house concerns the media itself. In the twentieth century exhibiting experimental houses at trade and world fairs was intended to depict the effects of science and technology on industry and everyday life. In 1956, Alison and Peter Smithson created another imaginary dwelling entitled *The House of the Future*, which was displayed at the *Daily Mail*'s Ideal Home Exhibition later that same year. In this high-tech capsule

---

24 "ZDA na zagrebškem velesajmu." *Slovenski poročevalec* (22 August 1956).

25 See, for example, Laura A. Belmonte, *Selling the American Way: U.S. Propaganda and the Cold War* (Philadelphia: University of Pennsylvania Press, 2008); Greg Castillo, *Cold War on the Home Front: The Soft Power of Midcentury Design* (Minneapolis/London: University of Minnestota Press 2010), 139–140; 116–117; Justin Rogers-Cooper, "Rethinking Cold War Culture: Gender, Domesticity, and Labor on the Global Home Front." *International Labor and Working Class History* 87 (Spring 2015): 235–249.

26 Kenneth Osgood, Total Cold War: Eisenhower's secret propaganda battle at home and abroad (Lawrence: University Press of Kansas, 2006).

27 Jane Fiske Mitarachi, "Design as a Political Force." *Industrial design* 4 (February 1957): 47.

28 Beatriz Colomina, "The Media House." *Assemblage* 27 (1995): 55–66.

projected into 1981, they attempted to reconcile architecture and everyday life by promoting the concept of mass production focused on design. In the context of the Cold War, this futurist house might be perceived as an isolated space, more a shelter than a spaceship.

In John M. Johansen's project, material plays an essential role as well. Although "gunite" or sprayed concrete was invented at the beginning of the twentieth century and was widely used for swimming pools, its more common use in architecture started after Le Corbusier implemented it as a structural and sculptural element at Ronchamp (1950–1955). Meanwhile, Frederick Kiesler had completed his long-term project *Endless House,* begun in the 1920s, featuring a biomorphic, sculpturally designed space of maximum flexibility. This was an experimental project commissioned by the American Concrete Association, just a year after the first version of Johansen's *Sprayed House #2,* which was meant to be the architect's family home but was never built. A comparison with the contemporary radical departures from modernist design and the notion of the house as a "box", points to the contemporary quality of attempts to redefine the habitation conventions of the 1950s, including not only a formal redefinition but a critical reflection on the psychosocial aspects of space and the environment.

It is significant that the Zagreb Fair was chosen to promote this project in Europe, as it was in a unique position to establish a dialogue between the East and West within the context of global politics. This is further supported by the fact that both USSR leader Nikita Khrushchev and Indonesian president Ahmed Sukarno visited the fair on that occasion. Even though Johansen had not been satisfied with the quality of the pavilion constructed in Zagreb, the project soon achieved considerable popularity among the European architectural avant-garde. For Michael Webb, a founding member of Archigram, he immediately became a "genuine American hero".

The display model was a "pumpkin": a pumpkin-shaped dwelling of sprayed concrete designed by the architect John MacLean Johansen especially for the Zagreb Fair (Fig. 3).

> It is the first building of its kind in the world [. . .]. The structure of the building is made of a concrete shell covering over the pipe framework. A concrete circular dome covers a floor of about 15 m in diameter. The frame, coated with concrete, is mounted on the edge of the circular foundation and connected at the top to a tubular joint. The most interesting thing is that the roof of this building does not require any central pillar, so the entire surface of the building is completely free for decoration.[29]

29 Mitarachi, "Design as a Political Force," 47.

Fig. 3: US pavilion at the Zagreb Fair 1956. Display model designed by John M. Johansen. Source: Industrial Design 4 (1957): p. 47.

Even though reviews of the US exhibit in the Yugoslav media were reserved, particular comments made it clear that the public saw the abundance of consumer goods as a sensation. This impression was further strengthened by the difference from the architecture of transparent cubes, which conformed as much as possible to the need to maximise the available exhibition space. The US pavilion introduced elements of popular taste to this structuralist design in a manner which Douglas Haskell compared to jazz, i.e., the play of free musical improvisation as opposed to the uniform and impersonal rhythm of modernist architecture.[30] This was confirmed by the organisers' claim that products displayed in the US pavilion should be understood as a wish to showcase tastes, needs and a way of life.[31] The products on display included the latest television models, solar powered radios, refrigerators, household appliances, ice-cream makers, children's toys and a four-room prefabricated house, complete with a garage inside which a car was parked.

30 Douglas Haskell, "Jazz in architecture. It makes more fun and better sense." *Architectural Forum* 3 (113) (September 1960): 110.

31 *"Paviljon SAD: Upoznavanje sa potrebama američkog potrošača,"* [The US pavilion: Meeting the needs of the American consumer] *Privredni pregled* (12 September 1956).

For the following year, 1957, the new fairground was complete for the rendezvous of the East and West, substantially enlarged in line with the design conceived by Božidar Rašica and comprising a total of 21 pavilions: nine for domestic exhibitors, designed by renowned Croatian architects, ten for other countries (the existing pavilions were joined by those for the USA, Austria, West Germany and German Democratic Republic, one for collective foreign shows and one for local representatives of foreign industries). The pavilions were a display of modern architecture, designed by the leading protagonists of modern architecture in Croatia: Marijan Haberle, Ivan Vitić, Božidar Rašica, Vjenceslav Richter, Drago Korbar and Aleksandar Dragomanović, while architects were hired directly for certain pavilions in the international section. The overall architectural display was the result of an interaction between organisers, comissioners and architects, as was pointed out by an overview of the newly built fairground in the architectural journal *Man and Space* in 1957.[32]

Among the highlights is the pavilion of *Đuro Đaković*, a leading representative of Yugoslav industry at the time, which "imported" the model of Buckminster Fuller's geodesic dome just three years after its world premiere at the Milan Triennial in 1954 where it had won the *Gran Premio* Award. By coincidence, the US also used Buckminster Fuller's geodesic dome at the Poznań Fair, where the mass-produced goods on display in the dome proved an irresistible magnet for visitors despite the negative propaganda originating from the local media.

In the context of the ideologisation of science and technology, architecture which was characterised as experimental obtained a special status, supported by the state. In taking on the role of researchers, architects' interests were focused on technical matters and the logic of the design process. Striking architectural designs of exhibition pavilions at the Zagreb Fair based on ostentatious structural forms[33] could be interpreted as a declaration of faith in a technologically determined conception of modernity.[34] Reminiscent of the Leipzig Trade Fair, which like the Zagreb Fair during the 1950s aimed to establish communication between East and West,[35] the only exception was the pavilion of the Republic of China, designed in

32 *"Novo urbanističko rješenje Zagrebačkog velesajma."* [A new urbanistic proposal for the Zagreb Fair]. An interview with the architect, Božidar Rašica. *Čovjek i prostor* [Man and Space] 67 (1957): 1, 4–5.

33 Most of the pavilions were based on modular display technologies.

34 A critical overview of selected examples at the Zagreb Fair was presented in the article "Zagrebački velesajam." *Čovjek i prostor* [Man and Space] 82 (1959): 2–3.

35 See Katherine Pence, "A World in Miniature: The Leipzig Trade Fairs in the 1950s and the East German Consumer Citizenship," in *Consuming Germany in the Cold War*, edited by David F. Crew (Oxford/New York: Berg, 2003), 21–50.

the shape of a hybrid traditional architecture. As David Crowley argues, horizontality and openness were claimed as new architectural values drawn from the modernist credo based both on the qualities of building materials (steel and glass) and the aim to express the rhetoric of transparency as a denominator of state politics.[36]

In the spring of 1957, experts at the American Consulate in Belgrade and Zagreb were first told about the concept of the US exhibit planned for Zagreb's forthcoming autumn fair. Their reactions were indicative: they thought that the slogan "Seeds of freedom bear the fruit of democracy" should not be prominently displayed, although the idea that "material progress depends on productivity which flourishes in a society that rewards significant progress with greater personal income" should permeate the entire exhibit. The US exhibit at the 1957 Zagreb Fair – "the most spectacular" that had ever been designed, according to experts[37]– was revealed to the global public in New York at the end of July.[38] Over 600 businesses contributed to the furnishing of the US pavilion – a supermarket installation which had been showcased at the Third International Congress of Food Distribution in Rome in 1956.

The first US pavilion at the new fairground was designed by the Walter Dorwin Teague Association and contained 4,250 sqm of exhibition area (Fig. 4). The local media had given considerable space to the construction and opening of the pavilion, emphasising that the Zagreb Fair was among the first international fairs where the US had its own pavilion. Paul Medalie, the director of the US pavilion, said the following on that occasion: "We are building it in the modern architectural style and I believe it will be an excellent fit, not only in terms of the Zagreb Fair but of the city itself, as it has moved ahead considerably in terms of modern architectural expression".[39] Most of the construction materials were made in Yugoslavia, including ten Y-shaped steel posts supporting the building, each stretching its arms 29 metres across the width of the building. Aluminum louvers covering the façade were fabricated in the US and shipped across the ocean with instructions on how they were to be assembled. Besides the supermarket, the visitors admired one of the latest models of an air-conditioned, US-manufactured and fully power-equipped Ford,[40] a fully

36 David Crowley, "Thaw Modern: Design in Eastern Europe after 1956", in *Cold War Modern: Design 1945–1970*, edited by David Crowley, and Jane Pawitt, 128–153 (London: V&A Publishing, 2008), 136.

37 Robert H. Haddow, *Pavilions of Plenty: Exhibiting American Culture Abroad in the 1950s* (Washington, D.C.: Smithsonian Institution Press, 1998), 64.

38 "U.S. supermarket soon will invade Tito's domain." *New York Times* (24 July 1957): 11.

39 "Showcase for America's Business and Industry Rises in Yugoslavia – U.S. Pavilion at Yugoslav Fair Built for Shoestring $ 240,000." *The New York Times*, 1957 (1 September): 4.

40 "Novi model automobila prvi put izložen na Velesajmu", [New car model first showcased at Zagreb Fair] *Vjesnik* (17 September 1957).

Fig. 4: US pavilion at Zagreb Fair 1957. Design: Walter Dorwin Teague Associates. Source: Croatian State Archives, Zagreb. AG FOTO L-996-024.

furnished American style five-room apartment, displays of agricultural equipment and household appliances, including a fully automated laundromat. Female students from Zagreb University were hired as "shoppers" and "cashiers", presenting a self-service system previously unknown to the Yugoslav audience. After the fair, the process of "Americanisation" achieved even greater success.

On America Day, 14 September 1957, Sinclair Weeks, the US Secretary of Commerce, posed for the camera while pushing a shopping cart.[41] At the exit of the pavilion the model apartment with a living room and dining area (Fig. 5), two bedrooms, a nursery, a modern kitchen and a bathroom was displayed to demonstrate that exhibiting a high standard of living was a reality of the American economic system. The United States sold the American supermarket model, including a host of attendant technologies, and in April 1958 the first supermarket opened in Belgrade.

41 Weeks made his official visit to the Zagreb Fair following visits to international fairs in Stockholm and Vienna. On the occasion of America Day he held a press conference and an official reception was given in his honour at the US pavilion. This marked an important change in official government policy in comparison with 1955, when the organisers of the US exhibit at the Zagreb Fair were not permitted to air propaganda clips nor organise a reception.

Fig. 5: Sinclair Weeks, the US Secretary of Commerce at the Zagreb Fair on America Day 14 September 1957.
Source: Croatian State Archives, Zagreb. AG FOTO AG FOTO L 0894-062.

The immediate impact of the "American Dream" presentation was evident at the 1958 Zagreb Fair, when the second part of the *Family and Household* exhibition was held. The exhibition, propagandistic and didactic in character, showcased a prototype of a department store and a supermarket. When the fair ended, the prototype was relocated to the centre of Zagreb and became the first department store in Croatia. This project by architects Aleksandar Dragomanović and Ninoslav Kučan launched the typology of a simple, glass-encased modular structure, which would result in a series of similar buildings in all larger towns in socialist Yugoslavia over the next several years.[42]

42 The opus of architect Aleksandar Dragomanović, a leading representative of late modernism in Yugoslav architecture, includes as many as 14 department stores and shopping centres which recognisably derive from the prototype of 1958. Source: Alen Žunić, and Zlatko Karač, "Robne kuće i opskrbni centri arhitekta Aleksandra Dragomanovića." [Department stores and shopping centres designed by the architect Aleksandar Dragomanović] *Prostor* [Space] 23 (2015): 276–303.

Therefore, the Zagreb Fair demonstrated the new concept of modern architecture and modes of self-service shopping, but also, by virtue of being implemented into the urban fabric of the city, presented Yugoslavia as a modern industrialised country with strong integrative forces, able to gather representatives of radically opposed ideologies in one place, and demonstrate its model as the optimum form of a political and economical system: communism with elements of consumer societies. This presentation of the fair was a symbolic declaration of belonging to the developed world, in whose added value the citizens of a communist country could participate. An indicative example is the exhibition of modern housing called *Family and Household*, held from 1957 to 1960 at the Zagreb Fair and conceived as a socialist counterpart to *America at Home.*

Coincidentally, the first *Family and Household* exhibition was held at the Zagreb Fair in 1957, together with the American supermarket, which demonstrated the US government strategy of promoting the high standards of living possible within the American economic system. The Yugoslav variant of a department store at the *Family and Household* exhibition was a display of what Greg Castillo defined as a style of "consuming Socialism" in contemporary East Germany and a socialist rehabilitation of modernism.[43] Thus the exhibition becomes a powerful medium of mass communication and an expression of the awareness of the need to promote one's own cultural identity. For socialist Yugoslavia as a new state on the international scene, the opportunity to participate at the *International Housing Exhibition* together with countries established in the field of design was an opportunity to demonstrate how the unique model of "socialism with a human face" fit into the modernist paradigm.

The US pavilion at the 1957 Zagreb Fair drew visitors with a series of appealling exhibits that were not yet customary in socialist Yugoslav society, while the pavilion of the USSR, dominated by huge machinery and special vehicles, presented a new model of the Volga passenger wagons, trucks, and a self-propelled combined harvester SK-3. Only the free sightseeing flight by an Aeroflot helicopter went some way toward matching the delights of American abundance.

The supermarket idea has caught on here since then – about 14 are said to have been built in Zagreb and Belgrade. Reporting from the fair, the Russian newspaper *Moskovskaia pravda* obviously criticised Tito's short visits to the pavilions of socialist countries (three to seven minutes), as opposed to the US pavilion, where he stayed for over 30 minutes. They concluded that Tito's attitude to the fair was just as questionable as his views on Marxist doctrine. Throughout the years "rival suitors – the United States and the Soviet Union – woo Yugoslavia with

43 Castillo, *Cold War on the Home Front*, 173–202.

technological triumphs" developing competition that was intended to maintain economic, military and political interests in this part of the globe. In 1959, for instance, the main Soviet exhibit was Sputnik 3, an automatic laboratory spacecraft promoted as one of the sensations a year earlier at the Brussels Expo. That same year the United States countered with a North American X-15 rocket-powered aircraft, along with the Transland Ag-2, and cars such as the Chevrolet Impala and Studebaker Lark VI. Thus the most significant achievements from the Space Race were exhibited at the Zagreb Fair shortly after their use. In comparison with the 1958 Brussels World Fair, faceting divergent international, regional, structural and popular tendencies in exhibition architecture, yet clearly divided world of superpowers and "others", the Zagreb Trade Fair assumed a specific diplomatic role. Instead of an idealised image of the world, mostly dismantled after the end of Expo, the politics of representation at Zagreb Fair manifested the dynamic of political and ideological power during several decades. Most of the pavilions built during the second half of the 1950s and early 1960s, saw international exhibitors participate in funding and use the building as a national pavilion. After certain period of time, buildings were put at disposal of the Fair, which led to several changes of its "identity". West European countries and superpowers USA and USSR commissioned several pavilions, each time becoming more ambitious.

Italy constructed three new national pavilions in 1956, 1959 and 1962, selling their previous ones to Poland, the Netherlands and Switzerland respectively. The original Hungarian pavilion of 1956, with a light and easy-to-dismantle metal structure, made way for the new West German pavilion and moved nearby, while Hungary shared a new pavilion with Spain.

Particularly visually expressive is the third Italian pavilion, designed and built in 1961 by Giuseppe Sambito and Raffaele Contigiani: a structure of inverted pyramids made of lightweight ribs clad in metal and glass. The impressive construction evokes the Palace of Labor designed by Pier Luigi Nervi and his son Antonio for the Turin exhibition of 1961, particularly Nervi's typical isostatic ribbed slabs, constructed using moveable ferroconcrete formwork (Fig. 6).

Božidar Rašica designed the Hypar pavilion of 1964 – a reinforced concrete shell for an information point – and the German Democratic Republic's (East German) pavilion based on a modular spatial system, where six major load-bearing concrete piers carry inverted pyramids. The mantle object is derived from what was at the time an entirely new building material: molded glass elements. The largest pavilion built for another country was the second USSR pavilion designed by Boris S. Vilenskiy in 1967. That same year, the second American pavilion was also built, designed by Fritz Bornemann using the innovative Mero system of nodes and beams, positioned closer to the main city axis.

Fig. 6: Third Italian pavilion, Zagreb Fair designed by Giuseppe Sambito and Raffaele Contigiani (1961). Source: Souvenir brochure International Zagreb Fair. Zagreb, 1966.

In the chronology of the Zagreb Fair, the 1950s and 1960s were the years of greatest success, with a fast-growing economy and particularly rapid industrial advances. This enabled the further strengthening of international trade and politics. The expansion of the fair in 1963 was mainly due to developing countries in Africa and Asia using international trade exhibitions to promote themselves as part of the world economy. Within the Non-Aligned Movement, the Africa-Yugoslavia-Asia (AYA) – exhibition centre played an important role in world relations. The *Round table of developing countries*, a permanent forum for stimulating cooperation among developing countries, used especially for the transfer of knowledge and technology, also took place at the Zagreb Fair, along with its pioneering role in presenting developing countries to the rest of the world. In the 1970s, the trend in fairs tended towards specialised events, while by the end of the 1980s, the history of the Zagreb Fair had reached another turning point with the break-up of socialist Yugoslavia.

As a signifier of radical urban, social and political transformations of the socialist Yugoslavia, the Zagreb Fair has had a strong impact on economic development of the newly founded state. From its urban and architectural conceptual framework coded by "Avenue of Nations" and content of display, to the spatial articulation of the pavilions, the Zagreb Fair is a manifestation of progress and prosperity of socialist modernisation. The ideological concept of "socialism with a human face" adopted various promotional forms for design in the social community from the outset. One has to bear in mind that the end of the 1940s and the early 1950s were a period of profound economic crisis, of great shortages and the purchase of ordinary items in exchange for "points", when the FPRY made extensive use of American aid in food and money just to survive. The fact that in such circumstances there was systematic participation in international events and that the architects and artists involved in these projects were among the privileged classes, shows the highly political and ideological character of this activity, common in the Second World during the 1950s.

Thus, the targeted local audience included not only professionals and politicians, but also organised groups and individual visitors: workers, youth, union representatives. Due to successfully coordinated actors of economic propaganda, education, culture, and leisure, the Fair became a symbol of communist prosperity of sorts. Furthermore, this concept shows how articulate the programme was in making clear the idiosyncrasy of Yugoslavia for which the Zagreb Fair was an extremely important opportunity for (self)representation and (self)promotion. Thus, the aim of the Fair far exceeded the local frame of carefully planned economic propaganda, since it was the only International Trade Fair to promote new strategies relating First and Second Worlds with Third World countries during the Cold War. As an integral part of political decision-maker's strategy of promoting foreign trade to serve the aims of political goals, it envisaged a place for the presentation of the Yugoslav foreign policy of "peaceful coexistence" in-between East and West, which would later turn into the Non-Aligned Movement.

Tracing an international network of people, ideas, encounters and cultural transfers such as the case study of the Zagreb Fair confirms that architecture was considered part of a general narrative on prosperity, proving that the traditional geopolitical concepts of East and West seem too simplistic to describe the complex movement of capital and its territorial repositioning in the last few decades. However, this does not mean that there has been a change in the prevailing thought or rhetoric about the centre and a periphery which constantly trails after it, through which post-communist countries are defined as cultural spaces in which modernism has been halted for decades. In the dominant discourse of cultural history, it blurs the boundaries between the East and West. What still needs to be done, however, is to deconstruct the hegemonic narratives of the East and West and point out the ways in which they continue to determine the relations of cultural production far beyond politics of representation.

Andreas Butter

Shell Sheds for China: Exported Industrial Architecture from the GDR – Intentions and Reception

This chapter deals with the application of the Zeiss-Dywidag concrete shell system and its derivatives by GDR project planning companies in the People's Republic of China in the 1950s. Extensive factory halls, which had already been roofed with semi-circular and quarter-circular shells in Germany before and during the war, were considered efficient in terms of their construction and access to daylight. They also proved to be vibration-resistant and thus suitable for the conditions of air warfare. But there is a longer history behind this: lighting via vertical or sloping skylights with rear roofing – "sheds" – had already emerged in England in the mid-nineteenth century. They enabled uniformly illuminated, glare-free work and avoided overheating. Over time, the characteristic sawtooth shape of the building's silhouette acquired the figurative semantics for "industry" par excellence, an association that was given an additional avant-garde aura with the shell construction.

After 1954, in the conflict-ridden transitional period from architectural traditionalism to modernism, factory halls made of prefabricated elements in particular were seen as the development path of progressive industrial architecture. They appeared both in factories within the GDR and in developing countries. Inspired by "internationalist" solidarity during the Cold War, but even more for economic reasons, communist China became the main recipient of East German industrial architecture in the course of the "Great Leap" policy of the decade. Varying in shape, size and construction, the shell-roofed halls were earthquake-resistant – important for the region – and gave a specific look to some of the most important Chinese industrial complexes of their time.

The buildings, often associated with the Bauhaus movement, were and still are highly regarded in China. This popularity may come as a surprise, as most of them have already disappeared or are threatened with demolition, a result of the rapid industrial transformation and the aggressive real estate market. In some cities, such as Beijing or Zhengzhou, the remaining buildings have now become visual attractions, a perception that encourages the reuse of older industrial ensembles and is integrated into overarching concepts of urban regeneration.

This essay traces a chapter of transnational architectural transfer that has been almost forgotten in Germany and analyses the functional, aesthetic and historical reasons for the unexpectedly positive reception of the *Schalenshed* halls in China.

https://doi.org/10.1515/9783110658491-010

Enthusiastic yet difficult relationships

The history of German-Chinese connections[1] in the field of architecture reaches back to the eighteenth century. Lacquer paintings and porcelain conveyed a picture about traditional Chinese buildings in Europe that became influential for aristocratic park architecture, such as teahouses. At the turn to the twentieth century, the pendulum swung back after Western powers had established their subsidiaries in coastal Chinese cities like Shanghai and Tianjing. Therefore, in the interwar period a fascinating variety of buildings emerged in China, being created not only by European, American, Japanese architects but also by young Chinese designers. Featuring Beaux Arts, expressionist and functionalist characteristics, they followed Western pathways but in many cases their work was also related to old-time Chinese inspirations.[2] The intertwining of an Asian and modernist understanding of good form was echoed in quite different approaches such as art deco ornaments in Paris and complex spatial patterns, created by Gropius' students in Harvard.[3] When Richard Paulick, former Gropius-assistant and till 1949 chief planner in Shanghai, after his homecoming in 1950 drafted housing blocks in East Berlin, he implied window grills inspired by Chinese hieroglyphs – unfortunately a too exotic or expensive element in the eyes of the planning authorities to being realised.[4] However, Chinese design and art was present 1950s in East German publications because of parallel socialist approaches. By balancing aspects of Eastern and Western architectural understandings this essay explores the impact of an advanced typology of factory buildings in the minds of Chinese people today.

In 1951, after a short bloom of modernism, the communist leaders of the GDR, like in the other "Peoples Democracies", at Moscow's request enforced the appropriation of a neoclassic yet regionally flavoured canon, the "National Traditions" aka "Socialist Realism". Industrial architecture was not exempt from that but remained to a certain degree a stronghold of technically constituted aesthetics. The dispute about appropriate style and technology in factory design continued during the modernist comeback in East Germany after Nikita Khrushchev in his speech in December of 1954 at the All Union Conference had demanded economisation by

---

1 The author wishes to thank for kind support Tanja Scheffler, Dresden; Prof. Tao Chen, Shanghai; Prof. Yaohui Shao, Nantong; Prof. Xin Yi, Nanjing; Prof. Jin Juo, Beijing; Horst Fuhrmann und Familie Albrecht, Dessau; Daniel Fischer, Dresden; Prof. Franz Kluge, Wiesbaden.

2 Eduard Kögel, "Emigration der Ideen. Das Bauhaus in China." *Ostasiatische Zeitschrift* 19, no. 37 (2019): 33–43.

3 Eduard Kögel, "Walter Gropius and Chinese Architecture." *Modern Vernacular – Articles – bauhaus imaginista*: 1–16. www.bauhaus-imaginista.org/articles/343/modern-vernacular (accessed 17 May 2022).

4 Andreas Butter, *Neues Leben, Neues Bauen. Die Moderne in der Architektur der SBZ/DDR 1945–1951* (Berlin: Hans Schiler, 2006), 206.

pre-fabrication in the building sector. The huge industrial projects realised by the East Germans in China turned out as a test field for modern building technologies. Factories in general were part of a complex export package including heavy equipment and other technologies, experts' consultation and skilled manpower as well as training of local workforce.[5]

During the first two decades of its existence, the socialist state's courtship for worldwide diplomatic recognition (hardened by the West German Hallstein-Doctrine) was a driving force for exportation, conflated with campaigns for "anti-imperialist solidarity" and – in particular towards Red China – for admiration. The People's Republic on the other hand mobilised, assisted by the URSS, for a rapid industrialisation: intensified from 1955 by the policy of the "Big Leap" with its focus on building heavy industry. East Germany established a means to bypass the Western embargo against China, imposed during the Korea war, via a Berlin based China-Import-Export-Company. In 1955, procured by the *Büro für komplette Anlagen* (Agency for complete plants) and realised by state owned GDR-companies, 11 factories were scheduled for construction, 14 more being expected for completion until 1960.[6] At the end of the decade the official count was 41.[7] When GDR newspapers then correctly mentioned trade contracts and deliveries of food – that helped to end post-war rationing – in return,[8] 30 years afterwards they spoke instead about "selfless help"[9] and "solidarity"[10] with China. It is true that one can assume that there was an impulse of solidarity on the East German side, as Tao Chen states,[11] but this was even more strongly linked to commercial aspirations than is evidenced in the GDR's reconstruction projects for North Korea.[12] Boosting the exchange of goods with

5 For an outline about the research project on East German architectural export, sponsored by the Gerda Henkel foundation, see Andreas Butter, "Showcase and window to the world: East German architecture abroad 1949–1990." *Planning Perspectives* 33, no. 33 (2018): 249–269. www.tandfonline.com/doi/full/10.1080/02665433.2017.1348969?needAccess=true; https://leibniz-irs.de/en/research/projects/project/gdr-architecture-abroad-projects-actors-and-cultural-transfer-processes (accessed 17 May 2022).

6 List from 15 November 1955, BArch (Bundesarchiv), DL 2/1935, 389–390.

7 Maschinen für 41 "Betriebe in China." *Berliner Zeitung* (23 January 1959).

8 Lutz Zempelburg, "Volkschina als Handelspartner." *Neues Deutschland* (4 March 1958).

9 Heinz Landmann, "Vor 30 Jahren wurde die VR China gegründet." *Neues Deutschland* (2 October 1979): 6.

10 Hermann Axen, "Eines der bedeutsamsten Ereignisse des Jahrhunderts." *Neues Deutschland* (30 September 1989): 3.

11 Letter to the author (12 April 2019).

12 Rüdiger Frank, "Lessons from the Past: The First Wave of Developmental Assistance to North Korea and the German Reconstruction of Hamhŭng." *Pacific Focus* 23, no. 1 (2008): 46–74. www.researchgate.net/publication/249499718_Lessons_from_the_Past_The_First_Wave_of_Developmental_Assistance_to_North_Korea_and_the_German_Reconstruction_of_Hamhung_East_German_Assistance_to_North_Korea (accessed 17 May 2022).

China was an imperative for Berlin. In 1954, three years after architect Selman Selmanagic, a former Bauhaus student and convinced modernist, was sent to Beijing to create blueprints for a prospective *Handelshaus* [commercial representation] for giving shelter to exhibition space, offices and apartments, another Bauhaus educated architect, Franz Ehrlich was assigned to the project. His design featured a mix of neoclassical, traditional Chinese and, on the social buildings to the rear, modern elements.[13] Due to the steel shortage, which had even led to a halt to construction at industrial plants, the realisation of the complex was scrapped.

The last of the facilities, the grinding wheel factory in Zhengzhou (Fig. 1), was completed in 1964 – delayed after Chinese complaints about numerous problems caused by immature technical solutions such as the ventilation system. Caused by the cooling of Soviet-Chinese relations in 1956 and followed by the Chinese Communist Party's unsuccessful attempt to woo the Soviets' closest vassal,[14] no further projects were commissioned. This, against a backdrop of a disastrous famine in China, came along with unaccomplished deliveries of soybeans and butter to Berlin,[15] and a massive reduction in the exchange of goods had already been indicated in 1957.[16] During the construction period, however, all conflicts, which were fed by political controversies, feelings of envy towards the highly paid engineers from the GDR and their – from the Chinese point of view – arrogant attitude towards Chinese workers, were resolved pragmatically. Despite the harsh criticism of the Germans expressed in internal minutes, the East German contribution is still appreciated by the Chinese public today.[17]

13 Zusammenfassender Bericht (18 October 1954), BArch, DL 2/4045.

14 Harald Möller, *DDR und VR China: Unterstützung der VRCH auf politischem, ökonomischem und militärischem Gebiet (1949–1964): eine Dokumentation (Beiträge zur Friedensforschung und Sicherheitspolitik, vol. 8)* (Berlin: Dr. Köster, 2003).

15 Tao Chen, "East German pragmatism, China's policy of differentiation, and Soviet miscalculation: Hermann Matern's 1961 trip to China revisited." *Cold War History* 19, no. 1 (2019): 1–18. https://doi.org/10.1080/14682745.2018.1483341 (accessed 17 May 2022).

16 Information für Minister Rau (29 July 1957), BArch, DL 2/1933.

17 Tao Chen, "Weathering the Storms: East German Engineers in Zhengzhou (1954–1964)." *China Review* 19, no. 3 (2019) Special issue: Personnel Exchanges Between China and the Socialist Countries During the Cold War: 39–64.

Fig. 1: Zhengzhou, grinding wheel factory, the big hall, 2017 (Andreas Butter).

Thin concrete shells – A German asset from pre-war times

From the totality of projects in China a certain typology stands out: manufactory halls, covered with semi- and quarter-circular roof elements in concrete. We have evidence for at least seven cases of projects featuring this structural shape, realised in different constructive approaches. In the following account, the spelling of the city names mentioned in German sources come first:

The Radio-, chemical and a glass factory in *Peking* (Beijing),
- a glassworks in *Dschi-Dschia-Tschuang* (Shijiazhuang),
- a plant for artificial silk in *Paoting* (Baoding),
- a factory for Measuring instruments in *Sian* (Xi'an)
- and the aforementioned grinding wheel factory in *Dschängdschou* (Zhengzhou).[18]

Similar forms have been achieved in different ways, the realisation developing from being handcrafted in-situ before moving towards assembled construction.

The technology of the thin concrete shell, reinforced with an iron meshwork, was invented in the early 1920s by Franz Dischinger, Walther Bauersfeld and Ulrich Finsterwalder and refined in consultation with leading concrete experts from France and Belgium.[19] Originally conceived for planetarium domes on behalf of the Carl Zeiss Jena optical company, it became widely used for workshops by the *Dyckerhoff und Widmann* (Dywidag) construction group. Even before this time, during World War One, the company had realised the first steel-concrete shed, but still in a conventional saw-tooth/zigzag shape.[20] The later semi-cylindrical solution could span 25 metres; it also helped to save steel and optimise natural lighting by eliminating interfering grids. More than three million square metres of production area were covered in this way by 1945,[21] with the system also exported as far as Turkey. Some authors at the time regarded the system as very much appropriate to wartime conditions due to issues of economy and air raid protection[22] and, in the

18 Anja Feege, *Die DDR und China 1949 bis 1990. Politik – Wirtschaft – Kultur; eine Quellensammlung (Quellen zur Geschichte der deutsch-chinesischen Beziehungen 1897 bis 1995*, edited by Werner Meissner. (Berlin: Akademie-Verlag, 1995), 260–261.

19 Roland May, "Schalenkrieg. Ein Bauingenieur-Drama in neun Akten (Franz Dischinger zum 125. Geburtstag gewidmet)." *Beton- und Stahlbetonbau* 107, no. 10 (2012): 700–710. For the international embedding, see Andrew Saint, *Some Thoughts about the Architectural use of Concrete. Case study II: The Concrete Arch Tradition.* www.jstor.org/stable/29543748?origin=JSTOR-pdf&seq=1#page_scan_tab_contents (accessed 17 May 2022).

20 Knut Stegmann, *Das Bauunternehmen Dyckerhoff & Widmann. Zu den Anfängen des Betonbaus in Deutschland 1865–1918.* Diss. ETH Zürich. (Tübingen: Wasmuth, 2014), 229–230.

21 Olaf Bartels, "Der Krieg und die Zweckform. Godber Nissen und der Industriebau während des Nationalsozialismus." In *Godber Nissen. Ein Meister der Nachriegsmoderne (Schriftenreihe des Hamburgischen Architekturarchivs)*, edited by Hartmut Frank, and Ullrich Schwarz, 20–33 (Hamburg: Dölling und Galitz Verlag, 1995), 21.

22 "Der Krieg und die Baukunst – neue Formen im Industriebau." *Bauwelt* 35, no. 21/22 (1944): 207–210, 208.

course of its simplified forms, an aesthetic improvement compared to older alternatives.[23] We find examples of this outstanding modern feature at places like the Avia airplane factory in occupied Prague, at the Volkswagen factory in Wolfsburg and for an ammunition-box factory in Berlin Rummelsburg.[24] However, in the last two cases the distinctive sheds are rather hidden from the exterior view by walls and higher front wings that indicate some aesthetic reservations by the Nazi authorities.[25] In some cases the step towards pre-fabricated shell components was successfully undertaken before the war ended.[26]

After 1945, East and West German architects applied the shell shed for many projects, by using both of the ways: formed in situ, and – preferred because of cost and flexibility against weather conditions – precast modular sheds. In 1953, Ernst Balser published drafts for shell sheds, consisting of grid segments on curved trusses.[27] In East Germany, shell sheds became appreciated due of their being lightweight that faciliated the foundation-construction and their characteristic of providing unrestricted interior space,[28] but not without those advantages being played down by some critics.[29] Most research was provided by the Technical University (TH) Dresden, by absorbing the latest findings from abroad.[30] In particular, Reinhold Rabich, a former Dyckerhoff & Widmann staff member, and the young engineer Hermann Rühle, co-founder in 1957 of the International Association for Shell and Spatial Structures (IASS) laid the foundation for an innovative and diverse East German shell production, from which the hyperbolic paraboloids of Herbert Müller and those

23 Hermann Seeger, "Einfluss der durch den Luftschutz erzwungenen Senkrechtstellung der Oberlichtglasflächen auf die Gestaltung industrieller Hallen." *Deutsche Bauzeitung* 76, no. 1 (1942): 52–54.

24 Construction in 1943 is documented by Google Earth. After 1951, the complex was remodeled as a GDR broadcasting studio complex by Franz Ehrlich.

25 For a critical assessment of the significance of modernist tendencies in Nazi-period industrial architecture, see Ernst Mittig, "Industriearchitektur des NS-Regimes: das Volkswagenwerk," in *Städtebau und Staatsbau im 20. Jahrhundert*, edited by Gabi Dolff-Bonekämper, and Hiltrud Kier, 77–112 (München/Berlin: Deutscher Kunstverlag, 1996).

26 Walter Schulze, "Stahlbetonschalen." *Bauwelt* 35, nos. 23/24 (1944): 220–221.

27 Gustav Lampmann, *Ernst Balser. Ein Baumeister unserer Zeit* (München: Bruckmann, 1953), 150.

28 H. Luks, "Montagehallen aus Stahlbetonfertigteilen." *Bauplanung und Bautechnik* 7, no. 1 (1953): 11–14.

29 G. Richter, "Stalbetonshedhallen und Industrialisierung." *Deutsche Architektur* 7, no. 10 (1958): 563.

30 Gerhard Bienert, "Schalen- und Faltwerkdächer aus Stahlbetonfertigteilen." *Wissenschaftliche Zeitschrift der Hochschule Dresden* 4, no. 2 (1954/1955): 253–270.

of Ulrich Müther emerged.[31] In the mid-1950s, Rühle, together with Walter Henn (who moved to the Federal Republic of Germany in 1954 and led the shell roof construction to be applied to further applications there),[32] explored ways to make advances towards standardised "types" of shells that were solely designed to make pre-fabrication profitable.[33] The range of use was not restricted to factory halls and there were modifications to span much wider distances than before. Notwithstanding of all utilitarian demands for standardised mass solutions, those swinging sheds emerged in customised, exalted forms, such as the roofs of the *Großmarkthalle* Hamburg (Bernhard Hermkes 1958–1964) or the predator house in East Berlin's *Tierpark* (Heinz Graffunder, 1963).

Approaches to outstanding "organic" aesthetics in the late 1950s, a transitional period in East German architecture, could provoke conflicts. When a team of young architects in 1957 presented a competition entry for a cigarette plant in Lebanon,[34] featuring shell roofs and a curved layout that followed the topography, they earned harsh criticism. Richard Paulick, by then professor at the Building Academy in East Berlin, uttered two conflicting demands: More respect for the 'national traditions'[35] and, for economic reasons, the use of a building set of highly standardised concrete skeleton elements, as his long time fellow Rudolf Hamburger demonstrated for a weed-cellulose-factory in Romania.[36] In contrast, architect Otto Dziadek and engineer Stefan Hartung emphasised the shell roofs' potential for gaining architectural appeal from fulfiling technological needs.[37] Besides issues of efficiency and functionality, the question becomes evident, how were East German shell sheds, an example of Western modernist architecture, received in China and how could they be sustained despite the purposes for which they were built being discontinued today.

31 Wolfgang Mosch, "Professor Dr.-Ing. Herrmann Rühle 60 Jahre." *Bauplanung und Bautechnik* 28, no. 7 (1984): 315; Tanja Scheffler, "Development and application of precast hyperboloid shells in East and West Germany from the 1950s to the 1980s," in *Proceedings of the IASS Annual Symposium 2017 "Interfaces: architecture. engineering. science", 25–28th September*, edited by Annette Bögle, and Manfred Grohmann, 1–10 (Hamburg: HafenCity University Hamburg and IASS, 2017).

32 Walter Henn, *Bauten der Industrie*, vol. 1. (München: Callwey, 1955), 183.

33 Walter Henn, and Hermann Rühle, "Typung der Schalenbauweise im Industriebau." *Bauplanung und Bautechnik* 7, no. 10 (1953): 442–445; Hermann Rühle, "Die Rationalisierung des Entwurfs und der Ausführung von Schalenbauten." *Bauplanung und Bautechnik* 10, no. 3 (1956): 111–119.

34 Horst P Schoebel, Ernst Schneider, and Bernhard Altenkirch, "Eine Wettbewerbsarbeit für den Libanon." *Deutsche Architektur* 6, no. 5 (1957): 373–376.

35 Richard Paulick, "Einige Bemerkungen zur Architekturdiskussion." Deutsche Architektur 6, no. 9 (1957): 479–481; Richard Paulick, "Einige weitere Bemerkungen zur Architekturdiskussion." *Deutsche Architektur* 7, no. 4 (1958): 224–225.

36 "Entwurfsbüro für Industriebau II. Schilfzellstoffwerk Rumänien, Anwendung des industriellen Bauens in der Export-Projektierung." *Deutsche Architektur* 7, no. 1 (1958): 12–13.

37 Otto Dziadek, and Stefan Hartung, "Das Schalendach als Architekturelement im Industriebau." *Deutsche Architektur* 5, no. 3 (1956): 147.

Factory 718: Functional design but handcrafted structure

The most prominent project was industrial complex 718 in Chaoyang on Beijing's north-eastern outskirts. This "718 North China Wireless Electronic Equipment Joint Factory," German codename DOC ("Dokumente Chinas"),[38] included several plants related to the defence industry and therefore was handled confidentially. In addition, 718 was considered by the Chinese leaders as a "principal establishment in the campaign for 'the fight against the Right and for the improvement of the style of working'",[39] an internal political 'cleansing' measure. On the other hand, in her essay US-journalist Lee Ambrozy emphasised the utopian aspects that she found: "[I]t exemplified factory living as social progress with amenities, extra curriculars, and even a tropical fish-tank".[40] However, the sources tell us that intended social and cultural facilities had been excluded for cost reasons, with only a canteen, polyclinic and a breastfeeding room remaining in the schedule.[41] On 30 September 1959, SED leader Walter Ulbricht visited the factory, emphasising how important it was for the goal of industrialisation experiences to be shared from the GDR and to learn how to respond to the specific conditions of a country in order to assist other nations in the future.[42]

Planning started with the support of the Soviets who continuously asserted their leadership after they suggested that the East Germans be recruited in 1952. The heart of the compound, the "Radio-component" plant (beside radar devices,[43] radios and speakers were also produced) no. 157, was built between 1954 and October 1957, covering 640,000 sqm, the erection involving a variety of firms with about 230 foreign specialists, among them 49 from the GDR.[44] The masterplan was conceived by VEB

---

38 *Geschichte des Staatlichen Kombinats 718. Staatliches Kombinat für Funktechnik Nordchina 1952–1964*. Beijing Sevenstar (Science & Technology Company Limited) Stefanie Thiedig, ed. (Beijing: 2015/Berlin: 2017), 171.

39 "Niederschrift über die Unterredung beim Ministerpräsidenten Tschou En-Lai" (21 September 1957), BArch, DL 2/1692, 87.

40 Lee Ambrozy, "A Brief Early History of 798," in *The Best of Beijing 798 Guide 2010–2011*, 8–15 (Beijing, 2009), 9.

41 *Geschichte des Staatlichen Kombinats 718*, 532 (Bericht über die Reise in die Volksrepublick China, Adolf Hegemann, [31 May 1954]).

42 "Bericht über den Besuch des Genossen Walter Ulbricht im DOC," BArch, DL 2/1489, 8–13.

43 Möller, *DDR und VR China*, 24.

44 "Factory 798: History," in *Beijing 798: Reflections on a 'Factory' of Art*, edited by Huang Rui, 164–172 (Chengdu: Sichuan Fine Arts Publishing House, 2008), 164.

Zentrales Projektierungsbüro für Schwermaschinenbau Berlin Köpenick.[45] Chief of the preparatory group and since 1953 Chinese Head Engineer was Peilin Luo (Chinese: Luo Peiling), who held a US doctoral-degree; the German Head Engineer for construction (supposedly not an architect but a technologist) was a Dr. Pfeiffer,[46] in charge of realising the buildings, while an at least 60 year-old engineer, Schnauer, is also mentioned,[47] with another influencial expert being Hans Beck.[48]

Before planning started, Luo, guided by a German engineer named Nagler, inspected 20 factories in the GDR. Refusing Soviet inspired first drafts that featured Chinese palace decorations, Luo urged the laying aside of references to any "National Shapes" and to instead provide a simplistic functional design – for administrative buildings also.[49] The layout of the German preliminary project dates from 10 January 1953 (Fig. 2) and shows many modernist details, but the buildings have been arranged in a strict symmetry including extended green areas. The shell-shed-covered workshops are hidden behind facades as in Wolfsburg. When the planning progressed, the production halls became more connected and the open spaces, still huge, were reduced. Lots of additional structures in the following years filled the gaps.

For the sheds, the proven on-site-concrete-technology was applied (Fig. 3a); they thus had nothing truly avant-garde about them, nor were they created in a particularly effective way. The attached windows were oriented to the north in order to catch scattered light. Half a century later, Pailin stated that he had seen "those kinds of saw-tooth style factory" before, in Tianjin's machine plant 712, built by the Japanese during their occupation.[50] This statement could suggest that Japanese "colonial" architecture, supposedly complying with a patent from the German Empire, could have inspired the application of an East-German model in Red China. However, older Google Earth pictures (since 712 was demolished between 2010 and 2016) indicate that the halls in Tianjin only comprised old-style triangular zigzag sheds and not rounded Zeiss-Dywidag shells. Moreover, in a more recent record Luo stated that the buildings were made from wood, which would exclude shell sheds.[51]

---

45 *Geschichte des Staatlichen Kombinats 718*, 147.

46 "Handelsrat Neuber to Minsterium für Außenhandel" (26 October 1957), BArch, DL 2/1692. Often he is also referred to as "Pfeifer."

47 *Geschichte des Staatlichen Kombinats 718*, 40.

48 Peilin Luo, "Recollections of the history of 718," in *Beijing 798: Reflections on a 'Factory' of Art*, edited by Huang Rui, 58–61 (Chengdu: Sichuan Fine arts Publishing House, 2008), 59.

49 Luo, "Recollections of the history of 718," 59. On China's self-conscious and selective approach to Soviet concepts, see Susanne Stein's essay in this volume.

50 Luo, "Recollections of the history of 718," 59.

51 *Geschichte des Staatlichen Kombinats 718*, 39.

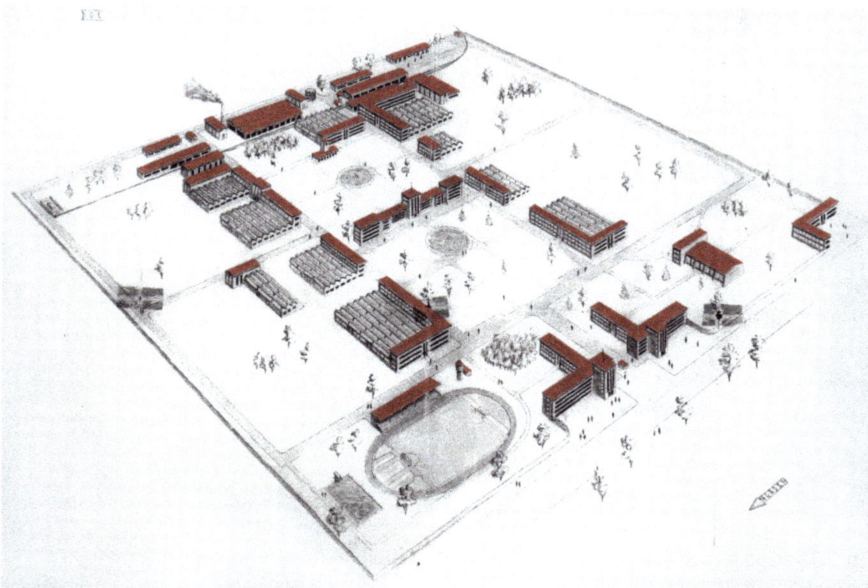

Fig. 2: Beijing, Joint factory 718/DOC, preliminary plan, January 1953 (Beijing Sevenstar Science @Technology Co. Ltd.).

The designers of DOC's buildings left few traces in the archival records, but the member files of the East German builders guild, BdA (*Bund der Architekten der DDR*), mention two architects in connection with the project, Horst Fuhrmann and Wilhelm Schulze, with the latter stating that he had drafted the carpentry shop of DOC.[52] Both worked for the planning bureau *Entwurfsbüro für Industriebau*, later renamed *Industrieprojektierung*, Ipro Dessau. Fuhrmann explained in an interview that he had to calculate the construction of the shell sheds and shell-building veteran Reinhold Rabich was responsible for the overall statics.[53] Asked about a connection to the Weimar school of architecture (today's Bauhaus-Universität) as mentioned by Ambrozy,[54] Fuhrmann assumed that this was derived from the fact that Rabich's assistant and concrete construction specialist Günter Ackermann had worked for the Weimar school.

52 At the IRS Erkner, scientific collections.

53 Conducted by the author on 12 September 2012 in Dessau.

54 Ambrozy, "A Brief Early History of 798," 11. I would like to thank Prof. Thilo Hilpert, who drew my attention to this text and thus to the factory itself in 2010.

Fig. 3: Building technologies. 3a Beijing, in-situ construction in 718 (Beijing 798: Reflections on a 'Factory' of Art). 3b Zhengzhou, assembling of prefabricated shed elements (Deutsche Architektur 7 (1958), no. 1).

Erhard Hampe, who, like Rabich had worked for the building college in Cottbus, also conducted research on shell construction in Weimar.[55]

However, there is no evidence of the school's direct involvement. In calculating the reinforcements, Fuhrmann mentioned it was a collaboration with the "Arbeitsgemeinschaft für Bau" in the Bautzen prison, which was notorious for imprisoning political opponents. The overall role of this hitherto unknown group and its participation, ironically in a secret export project, requires further research. But the involvement of Ipro Dessau was proven during research by a remark in a file stating that the "Chinese friends", becoming annoyed had already started with construction work, while lacking important documents and despite German specialists not having arrived yet. Therefore, "special measures" with regard to the Dessau-based corporation had to be taken.[56] Late in our research it turned out that the construction manager in Beijing was Joseph Larisch, a specialist for shell shed realisation, working for Ipro Dessau.[57] He had started his career for Dyckerhoff und Widmann

55 Information given by Günter Zumpe (19 April 2019).

56 "Handel mit der Volksrepublik China" (28 September 1954), BArch, DL 2/1935, 442.

57 Thanks to Prof. Franz Kluge, Wiesbaden, for establishing contact with Larisch's family in Dessau in January 2020.

in 1927, and was in charge of the implementation of the wind channel for the Junkers aircraft factory in Dessau from 1934 to 1936.[58]

An essential precondition for realising this huge amount of factory buildings was access to cement. The Dessau company Polysius, which was renamed Zementanlagenbau (ZAB) in 1957, had an international reputation for the construction of cement factories; after the Second World War, these were usually realised in co-operation with Ipro Dessau. In the 1950s alone, ZAB supplied seven cement plants to the People's Republic of China.[59] Both companies realised an enormous number of joint projects. This may have led to the Dessau partner company being commissioned with the first of these concrete shell buildings in Beijing, as the thin shells placed the highest quality demands on the cement.

The shed factory buildings in Beijing had to withstand severe earthquakes. Such a high level of safety was rejected by the Soviet general contractors for cost reasons. Supported by the Chinese Ministry of Defence, however, the Germans refused to agree to lower earthquake protection standards. They stipulated that the construction should withstand a magnitude of eight, based on previous seismic events in the region. In the face of many problems, the Chinese managed to produce a special type of stable brick, which enabled the structure to actually prove resistant to severe earthquakes a few years later.[60]

From the armaments to the art industry

In 1964, the "718 Joint Factory" was divided into six sections: 706, 707, 761, 797, including the radio component plant as "798" and the chemical complex, section 50, as "751". In the early 2000s, the entire site was abandoned and its demolition planned, which unfortunately also applied to the impressive administration building with its frontal staircase designed by the Chinese themselves. Soon the site of 798 was occupied by young artists who set up their informal studios here and organised festivals for independent culture. After seven years, the "Dashanzi 798 Art Zone" had developed into a professionally managed gallery district of international repute and one of Beijing's top attractions. Today, both areas, 798 and neighbouring

---

58 His first work location became Gräfenhainichen in the 1920s, but a local shell-shed covered factory hall, similar to that found in Beijing, was, according to the municipal archivist Peter Petz, built 15 years later in 1943. Larisch's employment file and a detailed site journal are being kept by Mr. and Mrs. Albrecht, Dessau.

59 "Abschlussbericht" (28 November 1958), BArch, DL 2/1935, 297.

60 Luo, "Recollections of the history of 718," 60.

751, are characterised by a dazzling mix of rusting technical equipment, repurposed manufacturing buildings and business chic. New buildings in many cases show design allusions to the shell roofs (Fig. 4). Modifications have been made to the original buildings: A glass façade fronted by a water basin replaced the north front of the great shed hall of 798 (Fig. 5).

Fig. 4: Beijing, references to sheds at art district 798, 2014 (Andreas Butter).

Fig. 5 a/b: Beijing, Art district 798, 2014 (Andreas Butter).

With trans-regional impact in China, 798 unfolded as a centre for the workings of a new "symbolic importance of the arts within the financial system and urban image construction", triggering gentrification in the surrounding neighbourhoods and contributing to the competition between cities for investors.[61]

But incorporated as "one of the government's 'development zones' of the new cultural variety", the price for the success is seen by critics as a loss of authentic bottom-up-charm. In the words of Lee Ambrozy, the danger arose, it could serve as "ammunition to counterattack international criticism of Chinese censorship" and therefore draw attention from the real avant-garde that had moved away to new locations.[62]

Other players introducing new constructions

When experts from the GDR visited Beijing in 1956 to sound out the field for the construction of a Zeiss-Jena planetarium dome, they complained about the Chinese workers' lack of experience in working the metal for concrete shells. But at the same time exactly that skill was applied not far away at the DOC construction site at a large scale. On this occasion, Dr. Karl, from EFI (*Entwurfsbüro für Industriebau Dresden*, renamed *Entwurfsbüro des Ipro Dresden I* in 1957) in front of 600 Chinese engineers gave a presentation about prefabricated shells.[63] The construction expert then discussed the project of a glass factory in Beijing with foreign trade managers from both sides. In fact, Ipro Dresden realised four projects in the Beijing region with circular segment shells over the next three years. However, these were modules prefabricated under cover close to the construction site and assembled with cranes. The termination of building blocks of different heights by these "barrel vaults" in rows contributed to a somewhat more differentiated overall composition than the large-scale shed roof zone was able to achieve. As early as 1950, East Germany's most prominent architect, Hermann Henselmann had even proposed those serial shells for pavilions of a cultural centre in Germany showing their aesthetic

61 See Jennifer Currier, "Art and Power in the New China: An Exploration of Beijing's 798 District and its Implications for Contemporary Urbanism." The Town Planning Review 79, no. 2/3 (2008): 237–265.

62 Lee Ambrozy, *An Elegy for 798* (14 July 2008), www.artforum.com.cn/words/870# (accessed 31 Mar 2019; deleted in 2022, copy privately saved).

63 "Abschlussbericht" (21 May 1956), BArch, DL 2/1935, 455–457. The document "Anlagen für die VR China," (15 November 1955), same file, 389, counts two domes.

potential.[64] But more important for the customers, it appeared they could be produced continuously throughout the year.

Since the documents did not contain precise information about locations in China, the address of one of the listed objects remains uncertain: Thus, references were found to a small test factory for synthetic fibres made of polyamide, "Perlon", and the associated caprolactam distillery, which was under construction between 1956 and 1959.[65] Proposed for faraway *Chintang* (Jintang)[66] in the Sichuan region, it was allegedly realised in Beijing at an unknown location possibly as part of the chemical plants of "718".[67] However, there is an object the authorship of which is still unclear. Furthermore, within Complex 718 there is an industrial ensemble planned by the GDR, the exact origin of which is still unclear, namely "Department 50". It was used for gas extraction from hard coal, hydrogen and oxygen production. Its most striking building, the power plant's boiler house (Fig. 6), is covered with concrete circular segment shells. The construction corresponds to the Dresden system, but here too the architects Fuhrmann from Dessau and Schreinert (probably Johannes Schreinert of Ipro Berlin) are named as being involved.[68] This indicates a collaboration between the companies. Following a renovation concept from Germany, Kesselhaus 751 was to be put to a new use as an exhibition space, party and wellness area, with plans to transition its rough charm into retro-futuristic elegance.[69] However, none of this has yet been realised in 2022.

As another object in the capital area, featuring prefabricated shell-modules, we need to mention the artificial silk factory in Baoding (Fig. 7), built between 1957 and 1960. It is located next to other GDR-objects, paper factory 103, a power plant and a sugar refinery that was completed two years before. The spinning mill has since been converted into an industrial park project, managed by the local administration as a cultural monument with reference to the achievements of GDR build-up aid.[70]

---

64 Hermann Henselmann, "Gedanken und Erläuterungen zu dem Entwurf eines Kulturzentrums in Buna." *Planen und Bauen* 4, no. 6 (1950): 182–190.

65 "Liste der 37 Objekte für 1958," BArch, DL 2/1934, 10.

66 "Betr. Viskosekunstseide and Perlonanlage" (14. March 1958), BArch, DL 2/1935, 146. Here the location is only characterised with "30 degrees latitude".

67 "Ergebnis der Überprüfung von Liefermöglichkeiten" (29 July 1958), BArch, DL 2/1935, 311.

68 *Geschichte des Staatlichen Kombinats 718*, 362.

69 www.triad.de/de/projekte/751-d-park/ (accessed 31 Mar 2019; deleted in 2022, copy privately saved).

70 www.htfiber.com/s/1084-3843-1053.html; the whole industrial area shown at http://ddr-planungsgeschichte.de/auslandsprojekte/ (accessed 17 May 2022). Thanks to Daniel Fischer who provided the photo from the construction site.

Fig. 6: Beijing, boiler house in factory 751. 6a Situation in 2014 (Andreas Butter). 6b Redevelopment study, 2019 (Fabian Schludi, Triad Berlin).

Fig. 7: Baoding, artificial silk factory, covered with circular segment shells, end of 1950s (10 Jahre Ipro Dresden, collection Daniel Fischer).

Furthermore, there were two projects for glass factories, using the prefab shell roof design from Dresden, the statistics for which were calculated by Rabich: A "chemical-technical" glass plant in Beijing (Fig. 8) and a "pharmaceutical" one in Shijiazhuang (Fig. 9). The expert for the arrangement of the production processes was Günther Fleischer. Both were realised by 1958 but demolished in 2004 (Beijing) and 2013 (Shijiazhuang). The Beijing project also included five much larger, rounded roofs, the construction of which is unknown, but which were probably prefabricated as well. Surprisingly, after having abandoned the building, the project's GDR-background is not forgotten on the company's website which presents a model of the vanished plant.[71] The Shijiazhuang- (likely also for Beijing too) architectural project-drawing initially was conceived by Joachim Zeh[72] who also, at the same time, was in charge of designing the wind tunnel building for the Aerodynamics Institute of the TH Dresden.[73] There, he had also used shell roofs and façade structures of the same type and received harsh criticism by the conservative GDR-*Architekturkontrolle*.[74] Although this had no practical effect in the transitional period of moving away from "national traditions", the repressive climate caused Zeh to leave Dresden at the end of 1955. After his departure for West Germany, Andreas Welser and Peter Albrecht Kluge took over.[75] Welser's name is also associated with both of the projects for artificial fabrics.[76] Otto Auerswald, who gave a detailed report about the building workflow in the press, guided the assembling.[77]

In the implementation of the designs in Shijiazhuang, the shell roof at the head of the building was dispensed with. Among other minor simplifications, only one half of two planned identical production areas was realised. In terms of concept and style, the project remained unchanged.

A short time later, the boom of this construction method came to an end, as the high upfront investment only paid off with very high quantities. When the same department of Ipro Dresden, worked between 1959 and 1963 with another team of architects around Erich Sobe as consultants for a glass factory in Haiphong, North Vietnam, the concept of serial shell roofs was abandoned for more

---

71 Bomex online catalogue: //bqvg.com.cn/BOMEX2010catalog/page5-8.pdf (accessed 17 May 2022).

72 Photos of the model, authorised by stamp by Zeh, in the Scientific Collections, IRS Erkner, D1_19_8.

73 See Günther Ackermann, "Der Bau von Schalen für Dachtragwerke aus Stahlbeton im Osten Deutschlands (1945–1985)." *Bautechnik* 78, no. 1 (2001): 18–35, 21.

74 Interview with Joachim Zeh, September 1999.

75 Andreas Welser, and Peter Albrecht Kluge, "Planung und Anwendung von Kreiszylinderschalen bei Industrieanlagen." *Deutsche Architektur* 8, no. 11 (1960): 595–598.

76 "Protokoll" (4 May 1956), BArch, DL 2/1935, 128 and "Protokoll" ([day and month unreadable] 1956), 154.

77 Otto Auerswald, "Herstellung und Montage großer Dachschalen." *Bauplanung und Bautechnik* 12, no. 6 (1958): 259–263, 373.

Fig. 8: Beijing, chemical-technical glass plant. 8a Model of the built factory (Bomex online catalogue). 8b During completion, ca. 1959 (*Deutsche Architektur* 8 (1960), no. 11).

conventional solutions,[78] not least because the GDR was not prepared to get practically involved here.[79]

78 Erich Sobe, "Volksrepublik Vietnam. Glaswerk Hai-Phong." *Deutsche Architektur* 13, no. 9 (1964): 539. The model still showed some bigger round-shaped roofs, but the realised plant does not.
79 "Liste kompletter Alagen" (27 November 1961), BArch, DE 4/23088.

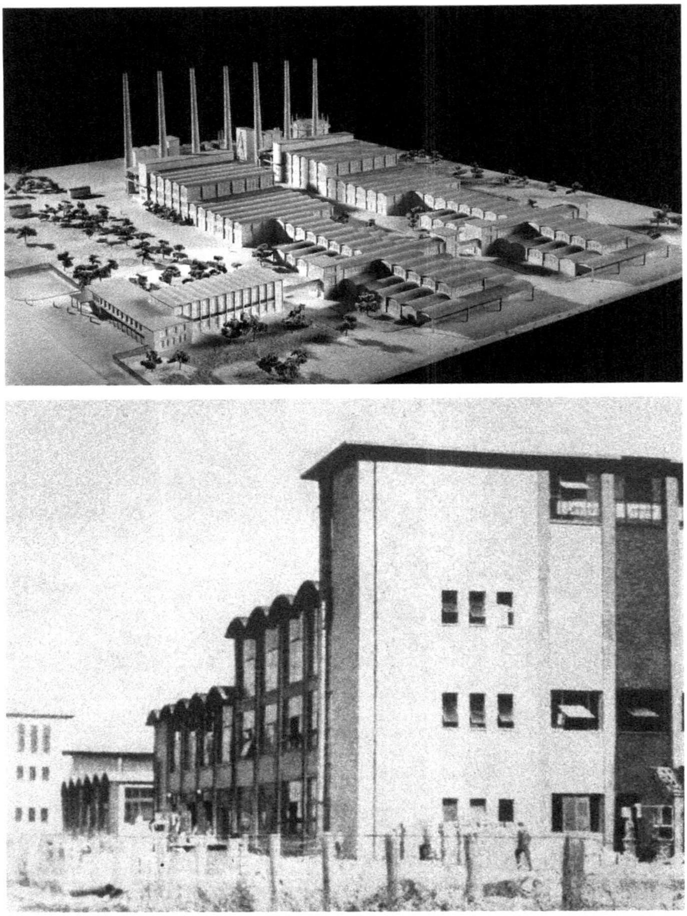

Fig. 9: Shijiazhuang, pharmaceutical glass plant. 9a Model of the planned factory, 1955 (IRS Erkner, D1_19_8.). 9b During completion, ca. 1959 (*Deutsche Architektur* 8 (1960), no. 11).

Xi'an and Zhengzhou – Monuments of the economic awakening in the heartland

During the first Five-Year-Plan, the Chinese Communist Party attached particular importance to the industrialisation of the centrally located and fertile but underdeveloped Huáng Hé (Yellow River) basin. Here with Soviet support, 156 large scale projects were conducted.[80] We have knowledge of two East German built industrial complexes with shell sheds in the region.

In 2017, the Mesuring Instruments Factory, codename "Mena" was still operating in Xi'an (Fig. 10). It was planned in 1956 for a location 1.4 km west from the walled inner city. However, it was located at an archaeological site of the old imperial capital of China, Chang An, and excavations took place on the site until the factory was built between 1957 and 1959.

Among 32 Germans from different companies who worked in Xi'an, as supervisors for the production design, the names Worm[81] and Haas[82] are documented. Eight experts came from Ipro Magdeburg (which was the superior organisational unit for Ipro Dessau until January 1952), managing the construction carried out by local workers.[83]

The shed halls became, like in Beijing, realised with in-situ concrete. However, in contrast to the sheds on the DOC, they have continuous trusses up the outer face, which gives the design a dynamic, constructivist facet. They are surmounted by the brightly tiled main production building on an H-shaped plan. Its symmetrical façade opens onto a leafy main street, which widens out here like a square. It was attributed to Soviet partners by factory employees; sources indicate that GDR project designers were at least involved here as well and during construction they reduced the intended height for cost reasons by two floors and translocated their functions to an additional shed-covered hall.[84] The hot and dusty climate, the lack of skilled labour and the Chinese practice of already starting production on unfinished buildings led to problems especially in the early days. However, despite partial abandonment and plans for demolition today, the author received a friendly and cooperative reception when visiting the plant. Nicknamed by the Chinese, according to an East German newspaper, as "Cristal of friendship", the buildings still seem to be valued today; hence the party secretary expressed his desire for the preservation of this "architectural heritage of the heroic beginnings of the People's Republic". In addition to the harsh working conditions in the early years – photos of the construction site show no cranes, only wooden scaffolding – one aspect of social modernisation completes the pic-

80 Lutz Zempelburg, "In chinesischen Betrieben." *Neues Deutschland* (30 January 1958): 5.

81 Karl-Heinz Cikursch, "Ein Kristall der Freundschaft." *Berliner Zeitung* (16 October 1959).

82 "Bericht über den Kontrollbesuch" (15–23 July 1959), BArch, DE 4/23088.

83 *Festschrift zum zehnjährigen Bestehen des VEB Industrieprojektierung Magdeburg 1950–1960.* (Magdeburg 1960), 11.

84 "Bericht über den Kontrollbesuch" (15–23 July 1959).

Fig. 10: Xi'an, factory for mesuring instruments. 10a Model of the planned factory, ca. 1956 Festschrift zum zehnjährigen Bestehen des VEB Industrieprojektierung Magdeburg. 10b Under construction, 1959 (Bundesarchiv DE 4/23088).

ture: The management of the factory, including the construction process, was in the hands of a woman, Mrs. *Tschau Di-zi*.[85]

In Zhengzhou, which is located 400 km east from Xi'an, the state-owned contractor from *Entwurfsbüro für Industriebau Karl-Marx-Stadt* Stadt (today Chemnitz) working under the supervision of Karlheinz Möckel realised the Abrasive Wheel Factory 402, listed in Chinese sources as "Two Sands" and "Er-Sha" and in German

85 See Cikursch, "Ein Kristall der Freundschaft."

documents as “Schach” (Fig. 11). Planned originally for a stepwise realisation (initially for an output of 5,040 tons) plans changed for production in one go (12,000 tons),[86] which dramatically increased the pressure on those responsible. To meet these obligations some design principles were set up: Following a strict grid system, depending on a basic dimension of 2.5 metres, prefabrication and restriction to – few as possible – basic prefab elements and the customer’s obligation to provide cranes.[87] The halls in Zhengzhou therefore sprang from the Fordist approach of a modular system that saves steel and construction time, while being easier to handle than the difficult-to-move half-shells from Dresden. It consisted of closely spaced, curved concrete rafters covered with strips of the same material (see Fig. 3b). The 300 m long and 65,000 sqm large main hall impresses with its powerful silhouette and soft slopes, which reminded a GDR reporter of “ocean waves”.[88] Due to its leaps in height, it conveys a monumental sense of space inside (see. Figure 1); the extremely long window fields draw the eye far into the depths. A later Chinese publication did not emphasise the aesthetic quality of the “curved serrated roof” but the efficiency of the construction and claimed a mixture of German and Chinese construction methods, support for which there is no evidence so far, but which can be taken as proof of identification with the building.[89]

Cross-connections exist between the individual GDR projects: The buildings with their interplay of concrete and brick walls showed typical East German features of the time, evident in the fire station tower. The typology of the gallery house for accommodating the staff was unusual in East German industrial architecture, but present in Beijing’s 751 too. However, the building system for the sheds was also applied at a textile plant in Chemnitz, built by the same contractor,[90] a dairy factory in Berlin Pankow[91] and the cellulose plant in Magdeburg-Rothensee.[92] Here, it was adapted by the same planning bureau that, considering the handcrafted in-situ technology more appropriate, built the factory “Mena” in Xi’an.

---

86 “Aide memoire” (25 October 1955), BArch, DL 2/1935.

87 Karlheinz Möckel, “Eine Industrieanlage – industruiell projektiert und gebaut.” *Deutsche Architektur* 7, no. 1 (1958): 14–16.

88 Zempelburg, “In chinesischen Betrieben.”

89 Editorial Office of the History of Ersha, ed., *Ersha changzhi 1953–1985 (History of Ersha 1953–1985)* (Hefei: Anhui Xinhua yinshuachang, 1986), 49–62.

90 “Forschungsinstitut für Textiltechnologie in Karl-Marx-Stadt.” *Deutsche Architektur* 8, no. 9 (1959): 509.

91 Andreas Butter, and Ulrich Hartung, *Ostmoderne. Architektur in Berlin 1945–1965* (Berlin: Jovis 2004), 82.

92 Gustav Hartwig, Asbestbetonwerk Rothensee. *Deutsche Architektur* 9 (1960), no. 11: 599–603.

Fig. 11: Zhengzhou, grindig wheel factory. 11a Model of the planned factory, 1955 (Deutsche Architektur 7 (1958), no. 1). 11b/c Situation in 2014 (Andreas Butter).

Factory 402 in Zhengzhou, during the author's visit in December 2017, was, in its bigger part, still producing, while the smaller appeared derelict and had no restriction of access. Following the example of 798 in Beijing, in 2013 urban creative people had tried to establish clubs and art studios here, calling it "798 Zhengzhou".[93] Some coloured windows, graffiti and a hanging Che Guevara stencil (Fig. 12), advertising a "Bolshevik Creative Workshop", indicated an alternative appropriation, but there was no such activity going on in the daytime. Websites refer to broader approaches for an integration into urban renewal concepts. The developers of the renamed "Factory 1953" complex use the motif of the 'wavy landscape' of the sheds to put the visual appeal of the existing

93 news.zyloushi.com/201705/568090/568090-1.html (accessed 17 May 2022).

building on the map.[94] The project for conversion into a shopping centre with mixed functions – shopping, office, culture – enlivens the shed halls planned for redevelopment with green courtyards cut out of the building block; glass fronts

Fig. 12: Zhengzhou, grindig wheel factory, reuse. 12a Situation in 2017 (Andreas Butter). 12b Conversion project, 2018 (logon.design).

94 www.zztzkg.com.cn/item/detail?id=326 (accessed 17 May 2022).

are to be inserted.[95] However, the efforts seem to have been frozen. After all, a hanging ring sculpture 40 metres in diameter was still inaugurated on the site on 5 December 2020 in memory of the German experts and the Chinese workers.[96]

Modernism and Chinese spirit

Industrial heritage has become a fertile field for planners in modern China. Faced with the dystopian monotony of speculatively built high-rise residential areas, and their pace of growth, the need for local identity combined with the narrative of long-lasting economic progress became a powerful impulse. Often, converted industrial sites combine recreational, commercial and cultural functions to enhance the quality of life.[97] In a more symbolic way, we also find this already implemented in Zhengzhou, two kilometres northwest of the grinding wheel factory, on the site of the former textile combine. As a whole five times bigger than factory 402 but structurally similar, the vast complex was built between 1949 and 1954 without GDR involvement, featuring old-style saw tooth sheds. It became almost completely replaced by apartment towers between 2009 and 2014.[98] Just a "Soviet style"[99] – neoclassic with some traditional Chinese ornaments – administration building and three shed-units, a contrasting form amid many verticals, it was left over as a small landmark district in the centre of the new neighbourhood.

It is obvious that the clear geometric shape of the shed roof – whether round or angular – in its iconographic association with the *topos* of "industry" has the potential to create an identifying feature.[100] Consequently it helps to create brandings and was applied in the old saw-tooth style for the "Finder Art District" in Nanjing (Fig. 13), accordingly the rounded shell shape with "798 Zhengzhou", and, as shown above, repeatedly quoted in Beijing "798" (see Fig. 5). The same intention to create a bond with this history and visual significance is documented

95 www.logon-architecture.com/portfolio-item/factory-1953-creative-park/ (accessed 31 March 2019; deleted in 2022, copy privately saved).

96 https://www.imago-images.com/st/0107723797 (accessed 17 May 2022).

97 The author was given the fruitful opportunity to attend one of the biannual conferences on the subject, "Industrial Heritage, Cultural Industries and Innovative Urban Development" at the School of Architecture, Southeast University Nanjing in 2017.

98 According to Google Earth.

99 hn.leju.com/zhuanti/zzssl/ (accessed 17 May 2022).

100 This recent and popular connotation was confirmed by Jin Luo, son of Peilin Luo in a meeting, 12 March 2020.

in Berlin, where after the aforementioned 1960s dairy factory had been torn down in the late 1990s, on the new supermarket's roof decorative allusions to the vanished shell sheds were added.[101]

Fig. 13: The shed as a branding element. 13a Nanjing, Finder Art District, 2017 (Andreas Butter). 13b Zhengzhou, 2017 (Andreas Butter).

Often factory 798, the only example broadly known outside China, due to the location of the project office in Dessau is linked in the sources with "Bauhaus style", which contributes to its high regard, and was even noticed with "dramatic"[102] surprise by the current owners. The shell sheds' functionalist approach may display a basic conceptual connection, but by construction and form it stands for a self-reliant route of development. Neither was the shell shed a Bauhaus product nor had the involved

101 vimudeap.info/de/atlas/milchhof-berlin-pankow/images/ (accessed 31 Mar 2019).
102 *Geschichte des Staatlichen Kombinats 718*, 129.

architects attended the legendary art school in Dessau, even if, by accident, architects from that city were involved in Beijing (none of the few Bauhaus trained architects, who had stayed in Dessau, worked for Ipro). However, the sheds and other building forms used in 798, such as horizontal window bands, represent the new turn towards Bauhaus-inspired modernism in the second half of the 1950s. Developments after a traditionalist-Stalinist period were moving in the same direction in the Soviet Union, China and the GDR at this time.

Apart from that, there are actually two direct references to the concrete shells to the Bauhaus: But there are more concerning the shell sheds: When Bauhaus master László Moholy-Nagy admired the shell construction in the 1920s, his fascination was not based on the outer form but stimulated by the structural idea of the network and the spatial expansion it provides for the interior.[103] Walter Gropius thought the other way: When he designed the building for the Bauhaus Archive in 1964 (realised between 1976 and 1979 in West Berlin), the curvy shed skyline found its way into the canonised imagery of the Bauhaus, but just as a backdrop, not as a real concrete shell construction.

Beside the fascination with functional form, associated with the Western avant-garde and the People's Republic's rebirth as an industrial power, there could be a further explanation for the shell shed's popularity in China – a resonance with traditional aesthetic preferences. The striking horizontality, loosened by swinging elements – more specifically a change of weakening to strengthening, a dialectic of "balance and equilibrium" – permeates classic Chinese architecture and provides points of contact to modernist design philosophies.[104] This was achieved here without a deliberate allusion, such as the wave cornice, conceived by Franz Ehrlich in his *Handelshaus* draft for Beijing. Ehrlich's ornament came as a quotation from a plaster cornice at Beijing's old Zhengyangmen city gate, but this element here was, ironically, itself an adapted addition by the German architect Curt Rothkegel from 1915.[105]

In the case of the shell roof, the functional structure may be sufficient to convey a kind of aesthetic appeal that could well be appreciated in another culture.[106]

103 László Moholy-Nagy, *Von Material zur Architektur, Neue Bauhausbücher.* (Facsimile of the first edition from 1929), ed. Hans M. Wingler (Mainz: Florian Kupferberg, 1968), 235.

104 Amos Ih Tiao Chang, *The Tao of Architecture* (Princeton: Princeton University Press 1956 [2017]), 41–58.

105 Wolfgang Thöner, *Bauhausmoderne und Chinesische Tradition. Franz Ehrlichs Entwurf für ein Haus des Handels in Peking (1954–1956).* bauhaus imaginista Journal, Edition 3, Moving Away. http://www.bauhaus-imaginista.org/articles/1086/bauhausmoderne-und-chinesische-tradition?0bbf55ceffc3073699d40c945ada9faf=901k2htvhoc2u5rcbqqc67hab6. See also, www.tsingtau.org/rothkegel-curt-1876-1945-architekt/ (both accessed 17 May 2022).

106 The author's hypothesis was taken into consideration and viewed as likely by Prof. Xin Yi, expert in architectural history, Southeastern University Nanjing, in a discussion on 10 January 2020.

For the understanding of a form that follows function, a traditional Chinese building typology can be taken as a parallel: When architectural historians analyse the "sweeping curvature that rises at the corners of the roof (flying eaves)",[107] invented in China during the Han dynasty 2,000 years ago and applied for temples and palaces, they mostly focus on functional reasons, like rain protection and maximisation of light.[108] Older theories about warding off evil spirits are widely rejected. But regarding the point of a sensual reception of the form, we encounter – and this may also apply to the shell sheds – the experience of a vibrant rhythm, related to the fluent brushstrokes of calligraphy.[109] Or, in the words of Chinese author Gustavo Zheng, "[c]urving the roof upwards, the building began to 'smile'."[110]

Conclusion

Concrete shell roofs proved to be the preferred type of construction for factory buildings in the People's Republic of China in the 1950s for contractors from the GDR and their clients because they met the economic and functional requirements. A frequently mentioned Bauhaus connection was rather indirect. But, and this is an unintended side effect that is all the more important today, they corresponded with certain cultural patterns. The wave form of the sheds corresponds to a traditional Chinese architectural aesthetic, represents a positively connoted industrial history associated with successful German-Chinese cooperation, and acts as a motif for branding in transformation projects of industrial sites. It proved significant for GDR architectural history that the architects achieved a synthesis of the competing concepts of industrial architecture with the use of prefabricated shell elements in Zhengzhou to save time and steel: Here, the "organic" approach with shell roof halls and the prefabrication of a limited range of concrete elements were reconciled. The practical effects are ambivalent: It can be seen that many of these buildings, although receiving public recognition, have been demolished and others are under threat. However, because of its qualities, factory 798 became a model for many conversion projects in historic industrial areas in what is now the People's Republic of China. It is to be hoped that the halting of some of these projects, which probably occurred for economic reasons and became entrenched under the pressure of the COVID-19 pandemic, will not lead to a permanent loss of the structural evidence.

107 buffaloah.com/a/DCTNRY/c/chinaroof.html (accessed 17 May 2022).
108 Thomas Thilo, *Klassische chinesische Baukunst* (Leipzig: Koehler und Amelang, 1977), 150.
109 www.chinalink.de/kultur/kunst/architektur.html (accessed 17 May 2022).
110 www.quora.com/Why-are-most-ancient-Chinese-roofs-curved-upward (accessed 17 May 2022).

Paul Sprute

Settlements of Post-Socialist Development? Reconstructing East German Solidarity through Housing Projects in the Global South after 1990

Introduction

After the opening of the Berlin wall and German reunification, international solidarity in the East German form ceased to be a German state interest.[1] Nevertheless, reunification did not necessarily mean the end of international solidarity altogether as it was continued by East German civil society within reunified Germany. So far, this history of post-socialist international solidarity has hardly been acknowledged despite the intense scholarly interest in Cold War solidarity relations and the "Second World's Third World" to which this volume testifies as well.[2] The standard bearer of post-socialist solidarity was the *Solidaritätsdienst International* (SODI) which emerged out of the formerly official *Solidaritätskomitee* of the GDR. SODI's activities were still deeply influenced by socialist practices and ideas of solidarity. However, in its daily business, it had to balance them with the demands and constraints of development cooperation facilitated by the reunified German state.[3] Through these influences, something new and decidedly different emerged which should be termed a compromise, or settlement of post-socialist development.

---

1 For an overview of the GDR's international solidarity, see Detlev Brunner, "DDR 'transnational'. Die 'internationale Solidarität' der DDR," in *Deutsche Zeitgeschichte – transnational*, edited by Alexander Gallus, Axel Schildt, and Detlef Siegfried, 64–80 (Göttingen: Wallstein, 2016). Parallel to the GDR, the political left and religious actors in West (and East) Germany pursued their own solidarity, see *Internationale Solidarität. Globales Engagement in der Bundesrepublik und der DDR*, Frank Bösch, Caroline Moine, and Stefanie Senger, eds. (Göttingen: Wallstein, 2018). For politically marginalised, religiously inspired international solidarity in the GDR, see Maria Magdalena Verburg, *Ostdeutsche Dritte-Welt-Gruppen vor und nach 1989/90* (Göttingen: V&R unipress, 2012).
2 David C. Engerman, "The Second World's Third World." *Kritika: Explorations in Russian and Eurasian History* 12, no. 1 (2011): 183–211.
3 For an overview of development cooperation of the West German kind, see Michael Bohnet, *Geschichte der deutschen Entwicklungspolitik: Strategien, Innenansichten, Zeitzeugen, Herausforderungen* (Stuttgart: UTB, 2015).

https://doi.org/10.1515/9783110658491-011

This contribution examines SODI's history through some of its major projects in resettlement and housing from the 1990s onwards.[4] Thereby, it goes beyond the Cold War period, but still underlines how the Cold War "made our times".[5] Complementary to Christina Schwenkel's contribution, I am offering another epilogue to the study of global entanglements in architecture and planning in the Cold War period, namely a view as seen from the former 'Global East'. Specifically, this chapter explores in how far SODI's construction of housing in Vietnam and Namibia represents one of these entanglements and, foremostly, a medium connecting SODI's development cooperation to the GDR's international solidarity. My research mostly relies on SODI's own publication, most notably its newsletters with project reports, as well as interviews with SODI employees. This set of sources makes it possible to examine how SODI's projects were presented to its supporters as well as to closely follow the different stages in the implementation of the project. The interview partners provided more details on the conception, practical organisation, and realisation of these projects seen from the perspective of the organisation.

In this study, I depart from the late GDR's projects of material solidarity and attempts to export planning and housing.[6] Eventually, this makes it possible to discuss how far SODI's projects were rooted in the Cold War. As concrete cases, I focus most notably on village resettlement projects in Vietnam to overcome the consequences of the US war, but also present a housing project in Namibia after the country's independence from South Africa in 1990 and refer to further examples in Sri Lanka and India following the 2004 tsunami. I discuss how these projects situated themselves in SODI's structure overall, as well as which kinds of planning ideas they represented, and through which means they were implemented.

SODI's persistent interest in construction projects as well as its regional focus were important continuities from the GDR's international solidarity. As it seems, SODI's donors remained attached to these causes, while the development aid of

---

4 The basis for this article is my M.A. thesis at the Freie Universität and Humboldt-Universität in Berlin on "The Afterlives of Solidarity: The Solidaritätsdienst International and its re-interpretation of the German Democratic Republic's programmes of global development in re-unified Germany." However, the housing projects only play a marginal role in the thesis, in which I instead focus on the broader institutional development of SODI from the year of reunification to the mid-2000s.

5 Odd Arne Westad, *The Global Cold War: Third World Intervention and the Making of our Times* (Cambridge: Cambridge University Press, 2005).

6 "Architekturprojekte der DDR im Ausland: Bauten, Akteure und kulturelle Transferprozesse: Online-Datenbank zum Architekturexport der DDR," Leibniz-Institut für Raumbezogene Sozialforschung, Erkner 2018, www.ddr-planungsgeschichte.de/auslandsprojekte (accessed 12 June 2022); Hubertus Büschel, *Hilfe zur Selbsthilfe: Deutsche Entwicklungsarbeit in Afrika, 1960–1975* (Frankfurt: Campus, 2014), 452–481.

reunified Germany initially avoided places like Vietnam or was late to Namibia. Especially in SODI's donation campaigns within Germany, there were strong echoes of the GDR's international solidarity: To the donors of SODI, the reconstruction projects were especially attractive as they were very concrete, visible and tangible, as if they were continuing such sort of projects from GDR times.

However, while it is important to investigate such continuities, most importantly through donations as a central social practice of solidarity in East German society, pointing out that the call to build global socialism still reverberated, it is equally crucial to account for the many ways in which these projects represented a meaningful departure from GDR times. SODI had to adjust its projects to the logics and workings of development cooperation, with its different framings, modes of funding, or set goals. As I will demonstrate in this contribution, SODI and its partners in the Global South interacted by co-shaping the set-up of these settlements according to different models than the ones of the GDR's material solidarity or architectural export. Especially in Vietnam, the facilitation of the village projects was reversed, they were led by local political agendas and based on self-built housing. The project in Namibia had a focus on the return to the presumably local material and technology of clay building through knowledge transfer and a default building model. In these interactions, ambiguities and compromises between different influences and interests, another post-socialist settlement of solidarity relations emerges. It is striking that the examined projects nonetheless were among SODI's most successful ever.

From solidarity to development: The *Solidaritätskomitee* becomes *Solidaritätsdienst*

The *Solidaritätskomitee* and the GDR's international solidarity

In a scattered institutional landscape, the GDR's *Solidaritätskomitee* was the only organisation exclusively charged with coordinating the East German state's efforts of international solidarity. Its main duties lay in coordinating donation campaigns, but it also organised the delivery of material solidarity in cooperation with other East German institutions.[7] While regular donations to international solidarity were

7 Lothar Brock, and Hans-Joachim Spanger, *Die beiden deutschen Staaten in der Dritten Welt. Die Entwicklungspolitik der DDR – eine Herausforderung für die Bundesrepublik Deutschland?* (Wiesbaden: VS Verlag für Sozialwissenschaften, 1987), 215–218.

quasi-obligatory at East German workplaces, certain campaigns were driven by large parts of the East German population, around a third of which took part in solidarity with Vietnam, for example.[8] The *Solidaritätskomitee* and the East German press routinely praised themselves for the great quantities of donations, such as 120 tons of furry toys collected,[9] or the number of train wagons and special flights needed for the transport of donated items to their far destinations. This shows that the idea of making a material impact played an important role for the GDR's solidarity efforts. In a country marked by material scarcity and a synchronous obsession with the achievement of great numbers in the fulfilment of plans,[10] this might seem contradictory at first, but ultimately logical.

Beyond such donation campaigns, the GDR was active in some humanitarian, development, or training projects in the 'newly independent states' (to use GDR jargon) of the Global South. The *Solidaritätskomitee* usually did not take a leading role in this context but was still charged with their coordination or partial projects, especially in the 1980s. One example is the development centre of the South African ANC in Dakawa,[11] Tanzania, which had been established by the UN Commission for Human Settlements. From 1987, the *Solidaritätskomitee* funded the training of 12 experts of the ANC in a combinate in Bautzen, who acquired the skills necessary to operate a prefabrication system of units for around 100 flats, school buildings, and other facilities. The committee also delivered building materials and tools as well as all kinds of other goods to the ANC. Apart from the *Solidaritätskomitee*, a collective of members of the official East German youth organisation FDJ, a so-called *Freundschaftsbrigade*,[12] was sent to Dakawa for support and students in Weimar participated in an architectural competition organised by the *Solidaritätskomitee*.[13] Beyond Dakawa, the committee also erected a so-called 'children's village' for the Namibian liberation organisation SWAPO in a refugee camp in Angola's Kwanza Zul province. Among

8 Frank Bösch, "Internationale Solidarität im geteilten Deutschland: Konzepte und Praktiken." *Internationale Solidarität*: 15, 24, 32.

9 Achim Reichardt, *Nie vergessen! Solidarität üben* (Berlin: Kai Homilius, 2006), 89.

10 E.g. Stefan Wolle, *Der große Plan: Alltag und Herrschaft in der DDR* (Berlin: Ch. Links, 2013).

11 For the case of Dakawa, please refer to Jakob Marcks, "Self-help Architecture in the Global Cold War: The Case of Dakawa (Tanzania), 1982–1992," Paper presented at Between Trade and Aid: Theories, Practices, and Results of Attempts of Exporting State-Socialist Development Models for the Third World, Leipzig, July 1, 2022. Also see "Doors of Learning: Microcosms of a Future South Africa" Bauhaus Lab 2022, Bauhaus Dessau, https://www.bauhaus-dessau.de/en/bauhaus-lab-2022/doors-of-learning.html (accessed 6 September 2022).

12 Eric Burton, "Solidarität und ihre Grenzen: Die Brigaden der Freundschaft der DDR." *Internationale Solidarität*.

13 Reichardt, *Nie vergessen!*, 80.

others, the GDR's *Solidaritätskomitee* was furthermore involved in the construction of hospitals in Ho Chi Minh City and in Managua, Nicaragua.[14]

Among the East German public, officially condoned solidarity was legitimised and popularised from state-coordinated media to education. International solidarity was present(ed) as an ideological argument for the continued benefits of the East German political order despite the GDR's lethargic state.[15] The 'omnipresence' of this 'mission' instilled it as an integral part of the political consciousness of GDR citizens.

With regards to the discursive functions of international solidarity within the GDR, Gregory Witkowski argues that the campaigns for solidarity were supposed to mobilise East Germans into action by stressing the dependency of its recipients but also calling for a change of consciousness among GDR citizens. The predominant narrative was to position the GDR society "on the side of moral righteousness",[16] and perpetuated a hierarchized worldview.[17] Toni Weis equally stresses the importance of the anti-colonial imaginary of solidarity and describes it as a vague ethic at the same time.[18] Exploring the causes of the perpetual stability of the discourse, Weis introduces the picture of a "working misunderstanding" in the political relations of East German and African actors: The "rhetoric of solidarity remained abstract enough to be filled with different contents by the two partners and used for their own respective agendas".[19] With regards to the discourse within the GDR, Weis assesses how "[t]he image of the 'other' was confined to the framework of solidarity, which in turn reflected back – ideally in a positive way – on the GDR itself".[20]

Becoming the *Solidaritätsdienst* in re-unified Germany

The last major humanitarian project of the GDR was the relief for the victims of the Armenian earthquake in 1988. Impressed by a striking reversal of relations

14 Reichardt, *Nie vergessen!*, 72–73.

15 Ulrich Mählert, and Gerd-Rüdiger Stephan, *Blaue Hemden – Rote Fahnen: Die Geschichte der Freien Deutschen Jugend* (Opladen: Leske und Budrich, 1996), 187–188.

16 Gregory Witkowski, "Between Fighters and Beggars: Socialist Philanthropy and the Imagery of Solidarity in East Germany," in *Comrades of Color: East Germany in the Cold War World*, edited by Quinn Slobodian (New York: Berghahn, 2014), 76.

17 Witkowski "Between Fighters and Beggars," 88–89.

18 Toni Weis, "The Politics Machine: On the Concept of 'Solidarity' in East German Support for SWAPO." *Journal of Southern African Studies* 37, no. 2 (June 2011): 352.

19 Weis "The Politics Machine," 352.

20 Ibid., 363–364.

between the GDR and the Soviet Union that asked for international aid for the first time since the Second World War, East Germans donated over DDM 55 million to the *Solidaritätskomitee*, showing how much social engagement could still be mobilised by quests for solidarity in the waning GDR. The committee organised the railway transport of 'spontaneously collected' clothing in 33 container wagons. Part of this effort was the delivery of 50 prefabricated houses from Bauelementewerk Stralsund and their construction by November 1989 (Fig. 1).[21] Consisting of a wooden framework, a filling of mineral wool, covered by asbestos cement and gypsum boards, this kind of house in Germany in the long run often caused problems with its energy balance, wetness damage and algae formation. Another reconstruction project co-organised by the *Solidaritätskomitee* and reaching beyond the end of the GDR was conducted in El Rama, Nicaragua from 1988. The GDR had initially agreed to build 400 houses after the destruction caused by a hurricane and the *Solidaritätskomitee* saw itself obligated to take over the state's commitments reduced to 150 houses in the political turbulences of the GDR's last months. Peter Stobinski, deputy head of the committee and later head of SODI asked: "Which impression would have been produced among suffering families [. . .] whose entire hope for a humane home rested on the completion of the German planned houses?"[22] In the second half of 1990, SODI, as the committee's successor, constructed 86 houses before problems arose with the new government of Nicaragua, whom SODI suspected of acting with animosity to former notions of socialist solidarity.[23] Eventually, the project was entirely taken over by the German government after SODI and the German Ministry for Development failed to reach an agreement on its joint finalisation.

A similar case in Nicaragua was the above-mentioned hospital "Carlos Marx" in Managua, which had been a prestige project of East German solidarity and under construction since 1985. The further construction and operation of the hospital was also taken over by the West German Gesellschaft für Technische Zusammenarbeit, GTZ in 1990, although it did not fit into their frameworks of development aid: An external expertise had found "high operation costs and insufficient integration

21 "Über 55 Millionen Mark Spenden für die Erdbebenopfer Armeniens." *Solidarität* no. 3 (1989): 1; "Gemeinsam wurde die solidarische Hilfe für die Erdbebenopfer in Armenien realisiert." *Solidarität* no. 12 (1989): 3.

22 Peter Stobinski, "SODI beendet Einsatz in El Rama oder der Umgang mit einer 'Altlast,'" *SODI-Rundbrief* nos. 8–9 (1991): 10.

23 Sandinista Nicaragua had been a central locale for East (as well as West) German solidarity throughout the 1980s. However, the revolutionary government unexpectedly lost power to a broad opposition coalition in the internationally overseen election of February 1990. See Stefanie Senger, "Getrennte Solidarität?, West- und ostdeutsches Engagement für Nicaragua Sandinista in den 1980er-Jahren." *Internationale Solidarität.*

Fig. 1: The "GDR village" in Armenia, house type FH E 108 (*SODI-Report* no. 1 1990, 3).

into the domestic Nicaraguan health system".[24] But by abandoning the project the Bonn government saw the danger of a highly visible German 'developmental ruin' in Managua which would stand for the unreliability of German commitments. Unified Germany's government's special attention to construction projects in this regard showed that it understood their symbolic value, in a manner not much different from the GDR government which had initially set them up.

While the Nicaragua projects were ongoing, the *Solidaritätskomitee* had lost its institutional basis and the stable flow of donations from the GDR's mass organisations had run dry with the rapid dissolution of official GDR society following the fall of the wall.[25] Answering to common calls for a more participatory and

24 See Iris Borowy, "East German Medical Aid to Nicaragua: The Politics of Solidarity between Biomedicine and Primary Health Care." *História, Ciências, Saúde – Manguinhos* 24, no. 2 (April 2017): 411–428.

25 For detailed background on the course of the committee and later SODI across these ruptures, please see Reichardt, *Nie vergessen!*. For the course of East German international solidarity through reunification more broadly, see *Noch die internationale Solidarität? Ansichten und Informationen zur Vereinigung der deutsch- deutschen Entwicklungspolitik*, ed. Bundesministerium für

transparent approach, the *Solidaritätskomitee* re-established itself as SODI[26] which took over the committee's networks, resources, and personnel, but could also recruit representatives of more religiously inspired international solidarity for its cause.

The establishment of SODI was the first step in a long transformation process to a development NGO. This process was initially determined by conflict with the German government about SODI's claim to solidarity donations from the GDR period. The dispute was only resolved in a judicial deal in 1992 according to which SODI agreed to the transfer of most funds to an independent foundation.[27] In consequence, SODI had to work with greatly diminished financial capacities. Furthermore, it could not rely on the logistical support or direct funding of the German state anymore.

SODI retained core orientations of GDR times and its predominantly East German supporters continued to identify the association with East German solidarity *pars pro toto*. SODI also was a place for its supporters to reaffirm and adapt their political opposition against the global economic order of neo-liberalism and wars suspected of being imperialist.[28] SODI remained committed to humanitarian missions as a traditional preference, albeit on a much smaller scale, for example in Eastern Europe.[29] Furthermore, its supporters continued to be invested in participating in the world through the social practice of donations. Donation campaigns were often organised in cooperation with other organisations of the former official GDR, e.g. the PDS (the Socialist Unity Party's successor), or its erstwhile press organ *Neues Deutschland*, but cooperation also extended to chapters of the Social Democrats of the SPD or municipalities, such as Berlin's Lichtenberg district. Construction projects became, if anything, more important to SODI following reunification than they had been to the *Solidaritätskomitee*. Thus, they signify a pronounced continuity between "real socialist" and post-socialist times.

wirtschaftliche Zusammenarbeit und Entwicklung (Bonn: Deutsche Stiftung für internationale Entwicklung, 2000).

26 "Solidaritätsdienst-international e.V., Nur ein neuer Name für eine alten Einrichtung? Nein! – Eine richtige Idee für eine gute Sache? Ja!." *Solidarität* no. 8–9 (1990): 1.

27 "Ausfertigung des Vergleichs vor dem Verwaltungsgericht Berlin. Anlage zum Protokoll vom 21. Februar 1992 – VG 26 A: Vergleich," in Reichardt, *Nie vergessen!*, 318–322.

28 Paul Sprute, "Die Nachleben der Solidarität: Ideen und Praktiken des Solidaritätsdienst International im wiedervereinigten Deutschland." *Archiv für Sozialgeschichte* 60 (2020): 261–280.

29 E.g. "Mit Optimismus ins fünfte Jahr: Bilanz und Ausblick auf SODI-Mitgliederversammlung." *SODI-Rundbrief* no. 1 (1995): 5.

"Peace Villages" in Vietnam along the 17th degree of latitude

The outlook of the villages

SODI made its first inroads into the German public consciousness from 1992 onwards thanks to its active participation in the "International Campaign to Ban Landmines," which was awarded the Nobel Peace Prize in 1997.[30] This campaign was of extraordinary importance for SODI as it helped to further integrate the organisation among development NGOs and made SODI's causes visible to its supporters.[31] SODI's activities in the campaign were complemented by specific projects, first in Mozambique, where SODI had a core of its activity, and the clearing of landmines.[32]

Vietnam was another central locale of the former GDR's solidarity, which had been aimed against the US war. From the mid-1970s, it found one of its major expressions in the planning and reconstruction of the city of Vinh, the capital of the Nghe An province.[33] The GDR's *Solidaritätskomitee* itself had supported a vocational school for construction work in Vinh, which was renovated with the help of SODI's donations in the early 1990s. SODI contrasted its continued commitment there to the German government's assumed foot-dragging in establishing development cooperation. When German-Vietnamese relations were finally normalised in 1995, SODI had an opportunity to claim vindication.[34] SODI also contributed to a village development programme, followed by construction projects of schools and childcare centres in the region. Nghe An remained a regional focus of SODI's activity, where the population and state representatives continued to positively associate SODI with previous GDR solidarity.[35]

---

30 Peter Stobinski, "Wieder eine wichtige Etappe geschafft – und noch immer nicht am Ziel angelangt." *SODI- Report* no. 1 (1999): 6.

31 Hans-Jürgen Ebert, "Solidarität heißt Widerstand organisieren." *SODI-Report* no. 3 (2000): 7.

32 Monika van der Meer, "Gehen Kriege nie zu Ende?." *SODI-Report* no. 4 (1997): 4; "Aufbruch am 17. Breitengrad: Hilfe für Opfer eines vergessenen Krieges." *SODI-Report* nos. 1–2 (1998): 1.

33 Christina Schwenkel, "Den globalen Sozialismus aufbauen: Zur Geschichte der DDR-Stadtplanung in Vinh." *Arch+* no. 226 (2016): 30–41. Also see the contributions by Schwenkel in "Affective Solidarities and East German Reconstruction of Postwar Vietnam" and by Bernd Schäfer in "Socialist Modernization in Vietnam: the East German Approach" both in Slobodian, ed., *Comrades of Color*.

34 "Entwicklungshilfe als politisches Druckmittel?." *SODI-Report* no. 5 (1994): 3; Horst van der Meer, "Jetzt können Gräben zugeschüttet werden." *SODI-Report* no. 1 (1995): 2–3.

35 Ilona Schleicher, "Die Solidarität geht weiter . . .: SODI und Vietnam," in *Die DDR und Vietnam. Berichte – Erinnerungen – Fakten* (Berlin: Verband für internationale Politik und Völkerrecht, 2010).

SODI eventually committed to another reconstruction project elsewhere, echoing the case of the reconstruction of Vinh, but also representing a major departure: In a programme based on SODI's clearing of landmines, the organisation established a project that would be crucial for its overall success. SODI presented this project as an "integrated concept" including practical components of reconstruction and resettlement, economic opportunities, as well as peace work and took pride in its pioneering role implementing a programme "so far unique in its complexity"[36] and very much going beyond the collection of donations. With funding from the German Foreign Office, SODI signed up former GDR soldiers in a company from Brandenburg to clear land of mines in Vietnam. From their beginning, in 1998, the projects were located in different provinces.[37]

The first three villages in the Quang Tri province with 219 houses were reconstructed between 1998 and 2006, and a village in the former Southern Vietnamese province of Thua Tien Hue with 60 houses followed between 2009 and 2011.[38] (Figs. 2 and 3) Apart from housing, the reconstruction project included childcare centres, primary schools, community centres and village roads, as well as access to water and electricity. Each family to be resettled received a contribution to the building costs for a house. Microcredits and initial funding for the growth of gum and pepper were to give the families an economic basis. Between 1999 and 2011, the project cost €9.8 million, of which SODI collected around €500,000 in donations, while German state institutions funded the vast majority. Beyond these villages, SODI also realised a project together with the Vietnamese Fatherland's Front to subsidize the construction of houses and give microcredits for livestock to 322 families affected by mines and use of Agent Orange.[39]

When the project was initially set up, it was conceptualised together with the Vietnamese authorities of the local and district government, who also suggested the sites of the villages to be resettled. The first villages were chosen for their location along the former demarcation line at the 17th degree of latitude. As a consequence of the war, the inhabitants had moved from their destroyed home villages into the river valley where they faced annual flooding. SODI's close cooperation with Vietnamese state institutions had the decided advantage that the choice of villages fit into the provincial development plan maximising the benefit to the

36 Ilona Schleicher, "Betrogene Hoffnungen auf Frieden und Sicherheit: 50 Jahre Indochina-Abkommen." *SODI-Report* no. 3 (2004): 11.

37 Schleicher, *Die Solidarität geht weiter* . . . .

38 "Das neue Jahr des Tigers in Lim." *SODI-Report* no. 4 (2009): 3.

39 Ilona Schleicher, "15 Jahre Integriertes Programm – Ein Rückblick." *SODI-Report* no. 3 (2013): 4–5.

Fig. 2: The third village of SODI in Vietnam and some of its inhabitants on a photo for SODI's newsletter (*SODI-Report* no. 3 2006, 1).

Fig. 3: A house with its owner in the fourth resettled village in Vietnam (*SODI-Report* no. 4 2009, 1).

local population, as Ilona Schleicher, the later project manager, recalls.[40] While the reconstruction of Vinh by the East German state had been characterised by its elaborate planning, SODI did not engage in comprehensive attempts at rural and architectural planning in its own resettlement project thereby limiting its risks of failing to implement them. The designs of the family homes were instead decided by their future residents, who also went on to construct the homes independently, while SODI contributed two thirds of the material costs. "They were the typical homes to be found everywhere in Vietnam":[41] The facades were rather narrow; the houses were built to broaden backwards with a pointy roof and a veranda. Some of the families planned for bigger houses, others were smaller, reflecting different needs but also financial means. Generally, the houses initially had one story on a concrete foundation. The corner poles of reinforced concrete were installed in such a way that it would be convenient to later add a second floor. The building material varied between hollow cement blocks or clay bricks. SODI limited itself to setting few minimum requirements, for example by making sure that each house had a toilet.[42]

The public facilities – a communal building, a school, and a childcare centre – for the villages, on the other hand, were built according to the common type of buildings in Vietnam, if possible next to each other. (Fig. 4) In their fundamental structure, the villages had a square in their centre and one or two main roads. The different stages of planning represented a learning process as the Vietnamese side began to construct the roads first in order to guarantee access for the construction vehicles and further realised the importance of a big village square where cows could be kept overnight.[43]

Overall, the villages were envisioned in distinct demarcation from examples of more rigid planning and, by consequence, a more homogenous outlook. In preparing the initial project, a village financed by the British organisation Mines Activities Council, with a symmetrical set-up and uniform houses, became a bad example. Ilona Schleicher points out that such a design was rejected by the Vietnamese, who sought more individualised solutions to later extend their houses beyond the first room.[44] Such extensions, which seemed problematic in the urban context of Vinh,[45] were turned into an integral part of the process in this example

40 Interview with Ilona Schleicher (24 July 2020). The interview was conducted over the phone by the author.
41 Interview with Ilona Schleicher (24 July 2020).
42 Ibid.
43 Ibid.
44 Ibid.
45 Schwenkel, "Den globalen Sozialismus aufbauen," 39.

Fig. 4: A type-building kindergarten in Vietnam (*SODI-Report* no. 2 2010, 6).

of rural reconstruction. Naturally, SODI praised this "lively and diverse" character of the village(s): "[I]t will develop itself. The people here will paint the very own picture of their village".[46]

In conclusion, the village projects of SODI in Vietnam seem unassuming. SODI mostly constrained itself to offering a vital part of the funding after having cleared the future village sites of mines, as well as having organised political support. However, these projects still resonate beyond their immediate case. Not least, it is striking how far these reconstruction projects had moved on from the example in Vinh, a case of sophisticated planning and architectural design, for which the GDR mobilised substantial resources. In contrast, in SODI's rural reconstruction project, the organisation left the field to the irregular pattern of Vietnamese settlement which shows that SODI had developed a firm grasp on the extent of its own capabilities.[47]

46 Ilona Schleicher, "Drittes SODI-Friedensdorf." *SODI-Report* no. 2 2004, 1.
47 Schwenkel, "Den globalen Sozialismus aufbauen," 39.

Looking at the villages

Broader continuities between the socialist project of Vinh and the post-socialist villages exist at the same time, especially regarding their communication within Germany. Through its village projects, SODI continued to relate its reconstruction efforts to the highly symbolic event of the Vietnam war. The mine clearing and village reconstruction programme was, in fact, presented as an active effort to undo the American "dirty war against the Vietnamese people".[48] Reflecting upon ten years of SODI's existence, the organisation stressed the importance of these projects for its overall approach encompassing a political and pacifist position:[49] "SODI has never hidden itself politically and used many occasions to take position for the poorest of the poor in this world against the causers of exploitation, hardship and poverty. To that counts our consequent stance against war [. . .] and the noted project in Vietnam." The (in)direct historical connotations to (the Vietnam) war made it comparatively easy for SODI to collect money in its campaigns among its East German base of supporters.[50] Through donations, SODI suggested the opportunity to potential donors to formally enter this pacifistic moral community.

Strikingly, SODI's most successful donation campaign ever was to the benefit of the Vietnam housing project. However, it was, in fact, executed independently of SODI by the actress Käthe Reichel, who had excelled in Brecht plays in the GDR period and was known for her political activism.[51] Stressing a practical obligation to help, Reichel sought to fund 100 buildings with a contribution of DM 1,000 per house and eventually managed to collect DM 140,000. Reichel spoke at demonstrations, to the PDS party, but also to trade unions and in churches. Often, she presented Brecht's *Die Heilige Johanna der Schlachthöfe* on an evening when she collected donations. For Käthe Reichel, who had grown up in poverty during the Weimar Republic, her donations were deeply entangled with her own experiences of being evicted as a child and her anti-capitalist beliefs: "In the democracy, it's not enough for everyone, if it is capitalist".[52] According to Reichel, the gift of 'the poorer to the even poorer' was the paramount proof of solidarity. In 2002,

48 Ilona Schleicher, "Drittes SODI-Friedensdorf." *SODI-Report* no. 2 (2004): 1.
49 "SODI vor neuen Herausforderungen." *SODI-Report* no. 1 (2000): 3–4.
50 Interview with Ilona Schleicher (24 July 2020).
51 *Wer war Wer in der DDR*, s.v. "Käthe Reichel," (Berlin: Ch. Links-Verlag, 2009), www.bundesstiftung-aufarbeitung.de/de/recherche/kataloge-datenbanken/biographische-datenbanken/kaethe-reichel. Also see, Eckart Spoo, "Käthe Reichels Dorf Ai Tu." *Ossietzky* no. 4 (2002), www.sopos.org/aufsaetze/3c7d4777a6b06/1.phtml.html.
52 See the documentary movie by Richard Engel, Petra Kelling, and Christine Boyde, *Aus den Träumen eines Küchenmädchens: Annäherung an Käthe Reichel* (2014), min. 110.

she accordingly told the residents of the second reconstructed village in Vietnam that "there were many poorer people in Germany who wanted to help the even poorer. And when the ones, who are poor themselves, gave me money, the little money was very big money".[53]

Käthe Reichel's humanitarian activism and practical ethics clearly echoed the GDR's hierarchising public solidarity discourse, analysed by Witkowski, with its focus on the dependency of the recipients and the call to a change in consciousness among East Germans to position themselves on the side of moral righteousness.[54] Importantly, this call was directed primarily at East Germans who were often challenged by post-socialist economic transformation but found a possibility to stabilise their position here. This impact was at odds with SODI's attempts to integrate the reconstruction projects into larger schemes of development cooperation. These were aimed at enabling the Vietnamese side. Ilona Schleicher's position represents this view of the organisation:[55]

> Not we have built the villages, but the Vietnamese. There, one has to watch out. It has been the achievement of the Vietnamese and we have supported it. They have really done it out of their own strength, conceptually and in their own execution [. . .] and we have accompanied them and obtained political and especially financial support.

SODI's development project in distinction from Käthe Reichel's donation campaign had a complex agenda of also strengthening communes and women's causes as well as tackling environmental issues, which SODI saw as unique compared to the work of other organisations. At the same time, SODI was in dire need of donations in order to be eligible for additional public funding. SODI's focus therefore had to be on the question of which kinds of campaigns worked, accepting problematic emphases.[56] Speaking with Weis, SODI (as a development NGO) and donation campaigners therefore established their own "working misunderstanding" as the "rhetoric of solidarity remained abstract enough to be filled with different contents [. . .] and used for their own respective agendas"[57] and which could be endorsed "to different degrees and for a variety of reasons" – encompassing the desire to help of its supporters and the development agenda of a professionalizing NGO.[58] This project is therefore a key to understanding SODI's post-socialist settlement overall.

---

53 Engel, Kelling, and Boyde, *Aus den Träumen eines Küchenmädchens,* min. 112.

54 Witkowski "Between Fighters and Beggars," 76, 88–89.

55 Interview with Ilona Schleicher (24 July 2020).

56 Ibid.

57 Weis, "The Politics Machine," 352.

58 Ibid., 359.

Shunned by public donors following its conflict with the German government in the early 1990s, donation campaigns had been an (even more) important lifeline to SODI, before the anti-mining and village programme unexpectedly played a central role in opening possibilities of cooperation with the German state. On the one hand, the many different components of the project worked to SODI's benefit, making it easy for German state institutions to fund it as an exemplary development project. On the other hand, SODI took advantage of the new political interest by the German Foreign Office in the relations with Vietnam and the diplomatic cause against landmines. The presence of SODI and its connections in Vietnam thereby turned into an asset for SODI as the Foreign Office funded the mine clearing programme in full. The support by the Foreign Ministry as well as a change of federal government in 1998 eventually also opened the door to funding by the most important Federal Ministry for Development for the first time: "Reservations and Objections could quickly be brushed aside, SODI could prove itself as a solid partner".[59]

By no means was it therefore coincidental that SODI made these inroads into the German state's development complex with this project, and still it is noteworthy that such a decidedly East German project with a strong focus on reconstruction paved the way. Unsurprisingly, this project became of the highest importance to the organisation and served as a unique feature. Within SODI, there was considerable "pride of having succeeded together"[60] despite little experience and capacities.

It has also become clear that planning and architecture in the strict sense did not play a prominent role in these village projects for SODI. However, the calls to fund houses as a reconstruction effort after the Vietnam war clearly captured the imagination of SODI's donors. For this symbolic power of 'providing shelter' to work, it was not necessary that the villages and their houses represented a specific architecture. What is more, it is exactly the variety of types of houses built by the Vietnamese which shows that the reconstruction effort also captured their imagination.

Clay Houses, "a Namibian stone's throw away from the Waterberg"

SODI's commitment to housing projects extended well beyond the ones in Vietnam, most notably to Namibia, but also to Sri Lanka and India. Taken together, they make clear that construction projects were an important focus of

59 Interview with Ilona Schleicher (24 July 2020).
60 Ibid.

the organisation overall. In this chapter, the projects in Vietnam will therefore be contrasted with others involving SODI. Thereby, certain parallels between them will appear clearly, as well as differences, reflecting changes in the demands to the organisation.

SODI's second central resettlement project, starting in 2002, was based in the Namibian city of Otjiwarongo. Over previous years, SODI had conducted a number of "self-help projects" in Namibia that were aimed at the integration of displaced people into Namibian society.[61] The projects supported agrarian cooperatives or the establishment of social care centres, as well as six childcare centres.[62] Generally, SODI benefitted from the history of the GDR's solidarity with the SWAPO liberation organisation, now leading the Namibian government.

In Otjiwarongo, SODI cooperated with the Namibian-based NGO "Clay House Project" in the construction of altogether 260 such buildings between 2002 and 2009 to improve the living environment of around 1,500 slum dwellers.[63] This was a highly visible and prestige project for SODI in Namibia over the long term, as well as the most complex project for SODI in Southern Africa. It was therefore important for the organisation overall and there were practical similarities to the project in Vietnam: SODI supported the future inhabitants of the clay houses themselves with the building costs and stressed how they co-constructed their houses, and the project also pursued the construction of childcare facilities.

The cooperation with the partners in Namibia was of paramount importance as SODI lacked the capacities to manage such a project on its own. Decisively, SODI had been approached for cooperation by the partner organisation in Namibia, which had also conceptualised the project.[64] This external impetus shows that the projects in Vietnam and Namibia were not immediately linked to each other, neither in the genesis of the Namibian project, nor through their forms of organisation. Having moved on from the times of confrontation with the state, SODI successfully applied for funding with the European Union and the Federal Ministry for Development.

The project relied on the technology of earth constructions offered by the Clay House Project and its German founder, Peter Arndt.[65] At the same time, it was dependent on the cooperation with the city administration of Otjiwarongo, which

---

61 "SODI-Projekte vorgestellt: . . . jetzt sorgen wir selbst für uns!." *SODI-Report* no. 4 (1998): 10.

62 Ilona Schleicher, "SODI in Namibia – eine besondere Geschichte." *SODI-Report* no. 2 (2005): 10.

63 "Ein Vorzeigeprojekt: Lehmhaus-Projekt in Otjiwarongo." *SODI-Report* no. 2 (2003): 9.

64 Interview with Andreas Bohne (3 August 2020). The interview was conducted over the phone by the author.

65 "Clay House Project." Ecosur (13 June 2005), www.english.ecosur.org/index.php/past-editions-e-magazine-285/63-edition-13-june-2005/255-clay-house-project-overview (accessed 12 June 2022).

was provided readily. This was important because the administration had to accept and legally register the new tenants' rights to their land. Furthermore, the city also offered cheap credit for the individual house builders. Yet, the new houses were not linked to the electricity (or water) supply, although the administration generally supported the integration of the formerly segregated township. While the state institutions were gatekeepers to public facilities, the Clay House Project itself organised the lists of future inhabitants (on a first-come-first-serve basis) and the city administration actually refrained from attempts to intervene.[66]

Curiously, the comparatively great independence of the Otjiwarongo project from the state went along with a great uniformity of housing. This was because of the focus on one specific technological solution, the principle of the clay house, while the project in Vietnam, organised in closer alignment with authorities, had been characterised by its technological openness and the diversity of independent solutions of the house builders. The Namibian houses had a uniform design, and size of 35 sqm. The impression was only softened by the many different colors in which the walls were painted. The constructions were based on a steel frame, which the workers employed by the Clay House Project initially set up. The Project was equally responsible for the production and assembly of the roof tiles out of lightweight concrete, the window and door frames were also supplied by the NGO.[67] The Namibian partner NGO developed a waterless toilet as a sanitary solution which would become the basis for a consecutive third development project in cooperation with SODI.[68] (Fig. 5)

In the Vietnamese case, the focus had been on materially enabling the Vietnamese population to build a new life according to their own construction ideas and means, but not on the transfer of a particular set of skills. This was altogether different in Namibia. The future inhabitants of the houses participated in the building process, specifically the brick laying, as they were supposed to learn how to maintain clay structures. Apart from financial considerations, the Project thereby sought to spread the gospel of clay building as a cheap, local, and long-lasting alternative to unaffordable and imported solutions based on concrete and (more) steel. In this mission, wider discourses concerning so-called "appropriate building technologies" were reflected.[69] More specifically, the transfer of clay (or earth) and

66 Interview with Andreas Bohne (3 August 2020).

67 Ibid.

68 Alfred Hensel, "Wohin selbst der Kaiser zu Fuß geht." *SODI-Report* no. 3 (2008): 5.

69 This discourse was institutionalised in the unit "German Appropriate Technology Exchange" of the West German public development organisation GTZ. While the GDR had its own discourse on the use of local technology, it did not provide the point of reference in this case. See Bauakademie der DDR, Muster- und Experimentalprojekt, BArch DH2/10121, "Die Lehmbauweise als eine traditionelle und zukünftige Bauweise," and BArch DH2/10119, "Eigenheim in Lehmbauweise".

Fig. 5: The Otjiwarongo Clay House Project in Namibia. (*SODI-Report* no. 1 2008, 3).

other low-cost building technologies as a means of development aid had been popular among (West) German architects and development workers, most notably Kiran Mukerji of the Institut für Tropenbau or Hannah Schreckenbach.[70]

All in all, the mission was still conceived as "help to help oneself", German *Hilfe zur Selbsthilfe*,[71] or capacity building. This was echoed by the inhabitant Selma Petrus who was quoted thanking SODI's donors for the "house building giving hope and strength to many slum dwellers to take their fate into their own hands".[72] This published statement glosses over the fact that it was not necessarily easy to promote clay building within Namibia, as the material was deemed to be short-lived and unclean, as well as connected to a lower social standing. The same connotation with poverty was common for the waterless toilet. While the

70 Both had professional links to German Appropriate Technology Exchange. For Hannah Schreckenbach, please refer to Rachel Lee's contribution in this volume. Kiran Mukerji published extensively on the topic, for example see Kiran Mukerji, Paulhans Peters, and Georg Lippsmeier, *Tropenbau / Building in the Tropics* (Munich: Callwey, 1980); or Kiran Mukerji, and Roland Stulz, *Appropriate Building Materials* (Rugby: Practical Action Publishing, 1981). The Canadian Centre for Architecture holds an archival collection on Mukerji. "Kiran Mukerji Collection," Canadian Centre for Architecture, www.cca.qc.ca/en/archives/486850/kiran-mukerji-collection (accessed 12 June 2022).

71 For the inception of this discourse, see Hubertus Büschel, *Hilfe zur Selbsthilfe: Deutsche Entwicklungsarbeit in Afrika, 1960–1975* (Frankfurt: Campus, 2014).

72 Klaus-Dieter Peters, "Eine glückliche Selma Petrus träumt weiter." *SODI-Report* no. 1 (2005): 8.

Clay House Project worked well as a funded development effort, its ambitions to set up a successful commercial operation accordingly failed.[73]

To SODI, the Otjiwarongo project was of major importance as it catered to the relevant contemporary themes in development, of localised and ecological sustainability. It was widely known in Namibia and its success confirmed by as different actors as the United Nations' HABITAT programme and the German conservative Konrad-Adenauer-Stiftung.[74] It was also the main interest of a student initiative within SODI which discussed it theoretically with regards to the contemporary UN Millenium Development Goals.[75] The student group, of whom several members would later become SODI employees, found great support within SODI's structures, dominated by elderly learned citizens of the GDR.

The Otjiawarongo project also became an important site for SODI's public relations and donation campaigns as SODI again had to provide partial funding itself. The campaign for donations echoed the Vietnamese in some respects, as it used historical references and was, in some ways, decidedly East German. Hans-Georg Schleicher, the last and only GDR ambassador to Namibia, for example penned a letter of support and SODI addressed its common base of supporters by running a joint campaign with the newspaper *Neues Deutschland*.[76]

As in Vietnam, SODI emphasised the surrounding historical space in its donation campaign: Located close, or rather 70 kilometres away from a central site of the German genocide of the Herero people, SODI stressed a connection.[77] In this campaign, SODI linked a so far unaddressed German responsibility for colonial rule with Apartheid as the more common antipode of East German solidarity, the organisation's grown expertise in Namibia, and its implementation of development projects – notably housing constructions representing the future:[78]

> For SODI, solidarity with Namibia remains a [. . .] political commitment and practical help to self-help for people who are still suffering from the consequences of colonialism and racism. Through cooperation in partnership, we help to reduce poverty in this far, yet close country. The creation of the foundations for a life in dignity for all Namibians is, to us, the best way towards historical reconciliation between our peoples. In our clay house project in

73 Interview with Andreas Bohne (3 August 2020).

74 Ibid.

75 "Die Entwickler," 20 November 2005, www.ht-elektronik.onlinehome.de/index.htm (accessed 12 June 2022).

76 E.g. Irmtraud Gutschke, "Lehmhäuser am Potsdamer Platz: Solibasar der Berliner Journalisten sammelte für Projekt in Namibia." *Neues Deutschland* (29 August 2005), www.neues- deutschland.de/artikel/77169.lehmhaeuser-am-potsdamer-platz.html?sstr=otjiwarongo.

77 E.g. Susanne Laudahn, "Festes Haus – ein großes Glück." *SODI-Report* no. 1 (2004): 1.

78 "Ohne bewusste Erinnerung kann es keine Versöhnung geben." *SODI-Report* no. 3 (2004): 1.

> Otjiwarongo, only a Namibian stone's throw away from the Waterberg, the results of our solidarity are feasible. With each new building here, a piece of shared future grows.

The above statement reflects SODI's acknowledgement of a shared responsibility in the national atonement for colonial guilt, a notable departure from the GDR's emphasis on its character as an anti-colonial state. Taken together, SODI found different angles through which it could politically mobilise donors and also benefitted in its donation campaigns from being one of only very few German development organisations in Namibia at the time, with very good relations to the SWAPO government. While the reference to overcoming Apartheid worked especially well among SODI's East German core of supporters, to whom Namibian independence had been an extremely hopeful political moment, West Germans were especially taken by the reference to colonialism. Thereby, SODI was successful in collecting donations beyond its common clientele.[79]

All in all, the Otjiwarongo project was of major importance to SODI and represented a departure for the organisation. In terms of the development framework, it was more visible, comprehensive and of clearer rationale than the house building in Vietnam, not least due to its technological focus. Moreover, SODI succeeded in raising interest and mobilising donations for the Otjiwarongo project by balancing handed down, more strictly East German concerns with a greater openness.

Following the tsunami in the Indian Ocean of late 2004, SODI also became involved in reconstruction projects in the region. In Sri Lanka, where SODI had not been active before, the organisation constructed an "eco village" which, again, followed some of the practices of the former projects, but also was notably different in other regards. This time the project was funded by a 'big tent' donation platform of German NGOs, Aktion Deutschland Hilft. In positioning itself within this NGO network, SODI could point to its previous housing projects. The "eco village" of Weligama included the construction of multi-apartment buildings of ten two-story houses with five flats each,[80] again representing a different model of settlement but certainly not an 'appropriate building technique' of common development cooperation. (Fig. 6) In contrast to Vietnam and Namibia, where the local authorities had been important partners, SODI got into conflict with the ones in Sri Lanka over land distribution to future dwellers and the question according to which criteria people would be allowed to move into SODI's houses.[81] However, the project was

79 Interview with Andreas Bohne (3 August 2020).

80 Hans-Jürgen Ebert, "Die ersten Reihenhäuser stehen im Rohbau." SODI-*Report* no. 2 (2006): 13.

81 The Sri Lankan authorities wanted to distribute the flats according to criteria such as political reliability, against the politically tense background of the ongoing civil war. Hans-Jürgen Ebert, "Die ersten Reihenhäuser stehen im Rohbau." *SODI-Report* no. 2 (2006): 13.

eventually completed, together with a production facility for dried fruits to offer employment opportunities.[82] SODI's construction of two villages in the Krishna delta in India to resettle Dalit equally was part of tsunami relief.[83] This project of around 220 houses, offering flooding refuge on the roof, resulted in a uniform housing solution, as a model building could be designed to withstand all kinds of weather conditions. (Fig. 7)

Fig. 6: The "Eco Village" Weligama, Sri Lanka (*SODI-Report* no. 4 2006, 12).

Conclusion

Construction projects, whether in Vietnam or Namibia, but also South Asia, remained important for SODI and were among its largest and most visible, but also most complex operations overall. For SODI, the activities in Vietnam and Namibia came to unsatisfying ends when the funding ministry of the German government decided that they had completed their purpose in development cooperation. By contrast, their purpose would remain unfulfilled according to the humanitarian

82 Klaus-Dieter Peters, "Endlich Bio-Früchte aus Weligama." *SODI-Report* no. 1 (2009): 4.
83 Jochen Reinert, "Häuser für indische Dalits." *SODI-Report* no. 2 (2008): 11.

Fig. 7: An ecclesiastical delegation inspects SODI's villages for the Dalit in India (*SODI-Report* no. 1 2009, 3).

perspective of SODI's donors, as long as 'dignified' housing had not been achieved for everyone. For the German government, the lack of knowledge transfer in Vietnam was a problem, while it doubted the feasibility of the Otjiwarongo project's next stage which would have introduced the delayed construction of clay houses in different steps, so-called quick shelters, from an initially set-up metal frame.[84] While the reconstruction efforts in Sri Lanka and India had played to SODI's preferences, they had been due to the special circumstances of disaster relief as well and were never meant as a more long-term programme. The centrality of the resettlement and housing projects overall is underlined by the crisis in which SODI was plunged with their end in 2014, also marking one ending point of SODI's post-socialist history, but not its existence altogether.[85]

Acknowledging the long-term importance of the examined reconstruction and housing in Vietnam and Namibia for SODI and recognising continuities with projects of the GDR's *Solidaritätskomitee*, it is necessary to assess the reasons for

84 This concept has certain parallels to the expandable housing in Vietnam. However, it might have raised concerns of developmental ruins again. See "Wie weiter in Namibia?." *SODI- Report* no. 1 (2011): 7. On Vietnam, see "SODI beendet nach 15 Jahren Projekte humanitärer Kampfmittelräumung." *SODI-Report* no. 1 (2014): 3. On the equally ending projects of material donations, see Detlev Lezim, "Ein Projekt ist beendet." *SODI-Report* no. 1 (2014): 7.

85 Sylvia Werther, "Außerordentliche Mitgliederversammlung ermöglicht Neuorientierung von SODI." *SODI-Report* no. 1 (2014): 12.

their centrality. This is especially pertinent as such projects were in no way normal in the environment of mainstream German development aid at the time.[86] Ilona Schleicher, the project manager in Vietnam, pointed out that construction projects reflected the mentality of the donors. The villages were palpable, "they were something to work with".[87] A dimension of this preference for the tangible was to claim a certain construction by naming it after oneself, as the prominent donor Käthe Reichel demanded. On the one hand, such preferences might simply reflect a once common way to execute development aid, and therefore generational preferences. On the other hand, they appear specifically strong in SODI's activities, which is why it is necessary to root them in SODI's specific history as the successor of a state socialist organisation. After all, the *Solidaritätskomitee* had played a paramount role in conceptualising, and constantly confirming solidarity as a connection to materially reshape Africa and Asia by measuring solidarity in tons and train wagons. The desire for continued material solidarity and its slogans therefore clearly had one of its roots in the socialisation of SODI's donors in this spirit.

The reconstruction efforts represented an especially pronounced example of the persisting orientations of the GDR's material solidarity. The history of Vinh, activities in Southern African refugee camps and the "GDR village" in Armenia found their instalment in the Vietnamese and Namibian projects covered in this chapter. Andreas Bohne, a former project manager in Southern Africa, underlines that their focus on infrastructural measures, improvements to everyday life, and basic services were exactly what was known from GDR times. While Ilona Schleicher referred to the centrality of the "tangible," Bohne related to the "visible".[88]

Beyond observing this continuity, it would be worthwhile to examine in more detail in how far the idea of building socialism and a rhetoric connecting construction efforts to the broader development of the society might still have reverberated in the examined projects just as well. Ultimately, the focus on the reconstruction and housing in East German solidarity is reminiscent of the reconstruction propaganda of the post-war era in the GDR.[89] All considered, it therefore seems clear that

86 See Bohnet, *Geschichte der deutschen Entwicklungspolitik*, Uwe Andersen, "Entwicklungspolitik seit den 1990er-Jahren," and "Deutschlands Entwicklungspolitik im Internationalen Vergleich," *Informationen zur Politischen Bildung. Entwicklung und Entwicklungspolitik.* 9 June 2005 (Bonn: Bundeszentrale für Politische Bildung, 2005).

87 Interview with Ilona Schleicher (24 July 2020).

88 Interview with Andreas Bohne (3 August 2020).

89 Markus Hinz-Wessels, and Annette Würz, "Bauen im Sozialismus," Stiftung Haus der Geschichte der Bundesrepublik Deutschland, "Lebendiges Museum Online," www.hdg.de/lemo/kapitel/geteiltes-deutschland-gruenderjahre/wirtschaft-und-gesellschaft-im-osten/bauen-im-sozialismus.html (accessed 12 June 2022).

a long-term preference for the material in connection to the constructed, amplified by the common modes of GDR solidarity, also expressed itself in the examined projects.

At first, it might therefore seem a paradox that they could become so successful within the new 'development' framework of SODI's activities. This was because SODI unexpectedly found itself politically well-placed in both locales, but also because both were more complex development projects, just that the different, less tangible dimensions moved into the background compared to the donation calls for €800 or €1,000 to fund an entire house (which, of course, concealed the majority contributions by the public donors). Yet, these donations still provided the material basis that enabled SODI to set up such development projects, so that both dimensions depended on each other.

For the success of both projects to SODI, architectural planning in the strict sense or stringency between the projects was hardly important. Indeed, the flexibility in the shape of the village planning is striking. Here, the different demands by funding parties and internal logics of the projects played a paramount role. In this context, it is noteworthy that the "vernacular architecture"[90] of choice would have been based on concrete in both Namibia and Vietnam while the presumably "authentic"[91] local building material of clay had to be externally promoted after its technological upgrading. SODI stressed the pragmatic benefits of the use of clay, yet the presumably vernacular building technology was still romanticised on the pages of SODI's newsletter – underlining recurring ambiguities between the set-up of projects and their communication.

Indeed, development cooperation was SODI's proclaimed business model and its approaches to solidarity had to change with the demands and economic constraints of this framework. Furthermore, in a shift between Vietnam and Namibia, the latter represented a more clear-cut example of common development aid, while the Vietnamese building subsidies lacked direction seen from a development perspective. This shift towards the more common in development cooperation extended to the slogans. The villages in Vietnam were still presented as "villages of peace", alluding to the broader political context of their construction. The effort in

90 For a discussion of underlying perspectives on (contemporary) "vernacular architecture," see Juan A. García- Esparza, "Epistemological paradigms in the perception and assessment of vernacular architecture." *International Journal of Heritage Studies* 21 (2015): 869–888.

91 For a discussion on the shifting meanings of authenticity in the built heritage and problems in its conceptualisation, see Christoph Bernhardt, Martin Sabrow, and Achim Saupe, "Authentizität und Bauerbe: Transdisziplinäre Perspektiven," in *Gebaute Geschichte: Historische Authentizität im Stadtraum*, edited by Christoph Bernhardt, Martin Sabrow, and Achim Saupe, 9–22 (Göttingen: Wallstein 2017).

Namibia was instead known as the "clay house project," centralising the material and technology, despite the still strongly reverberating, but more open historical connections to the colonial past. In the story of these two reconstruction and housing projects of SODI we therefore find a shifting post-socialist compromise between the timely demands of development, humanitarian concern, and the reminders of the GDR's international solidarity. This compromise, which should not be misunderstood as mere nostalgia, reflects how Cold War impressions could be actively reconfigured by comparatively weak and constrained actors, such as SODI in East Germany's 'transformation society.' Examining to what effects such actors used their post-socialist room for manoeuvre can complicate common narratives of West German domination in re-unified Germany without denying it and brings unexpected results underlining their promise for further research. In the examined cases, they appear in their clearest in the contrast between them: Strikingly, the project in Vietnam, with its stronger connections to the GDR's solidarity was the more open, or liberal, in its form, leaving living arrangements to the choice of the future inhabitants. The project in Namibia, which instead stressed the transfer of technological skills and better fit into the contemporary development framework was also the more controlled and authoritative, resulting in more uniform living superficially covered by wall paint in many different colours.

Christina Schwenkel

The Afterlife of Architectural Aid to Vietnam: A View from the Global South

Recent years have seen an expansion of interest in the unique modernist architecture produced in the "Socialist East" during the Cold War. This trend, exemplified in a growing number of conferences, exhibitions, publications, blogs, TV shows, and other mass media representations, is a testament to the re-valuation of socialist architectural forms – and socialist urbanisms more broadly – that now seems to captivate rather than repulse European publics. Once-maligned buildings are now deemed worthy of display, exploration, and commercialisation, as evident in the number of coffee-table books that have been released over the past decade with rich colour photographs of the period's surprising "stunning diversity" and its curious "cosmic creativity".[1] Socialist architecture in the global North has seemingly become the unlikely object of nostalgic ruin-gazing, though such broad interest has done little to challenge Cold War ideological frameworks that continue to portray "the East" as fundamentally Other to "the West".[2]

At the same time, scholars have shifted the horizon of analysis beyond socialist Europe to the perhaps less spectacular but no less fascinating socialist architectures built in the global South.[3] That is, they have become more aware of the Cold War-era circulations of architectural models between socialist countries in the industrialised North and the postcolonial South – what used to be called the "Second" and "Third" Worlds – often as a form of assistance or "aid." From the perspective of an anthropologist, one limitation to this growing body of literature is that it tends to privilege these oft-orientalist productions as static built forms – that is, as part of an already built environment – rather than as inhabited, lived spaces subjected to remaking and repurposing across time, as I propose here.

This chapter focuses on East German (GDR) architectural aid to Vinh City, Vietnam framed as a humanitarian gesture of solidarity to help rebuild a war-torn society – what I have referred to elsewhere as "traveling architectures" that are mobile

1 See, for example, Frederic Chaubin, *Cosmic Communist Constructions Photographed* (Berlin: Taschen Books, 2011).
2 Vladimir Kulić, "Orientalizing Socialism: Architecture, Media, and the Representations of Eastern Europe." *Architectural Histories* 6 (2018), doi: http://doi.org/10.5334/ah.273.
3 See, for example, Łukasz Stanek, *Architecture in Global Socialism: Eastern Europe, West Africa, and the Middle East in the Cold War* (Princeton: Princeton University Press, 2020).

https://doi.org/10.1515/9783110658491-012

across time and space.[4] I do so from the perspective of the receiving country, rather than that of the donor country, however, to offer a postcolonial perspective that provincialises the North. This shift in standpoint to Vietnamese planners, officials and inhabitants of GDR-designed buildings calls into question the use of passive terms to describe "transfers" of knowledge and building technologies "exported" to Third World countries, which are easily reduced to submissive (and grateful) beneficiaries of Northern "progress". Inspired by the architectural historian Esra Akcan's proposal to adopt the more dynamic term "translation" to describe how such forms and practices undergo change as they travel,[5] I emphasise the agency and countervisions of aid recipients, who possessed their own ideas about social organisation and the future of development through built forms, especially housing. A view from the global South – from contemporary Vietnam – thus reveals shortcomings in modernist planning practices presumed to be universal by highlighting the contested and culturally-embedded notions of socialist modernity transmitted through architectural mobilities.

In this chapter I build on Akcan's idea of translation in architectural encounters by expanding the analysis beyond elite actors – the professional class of architects and planners – to also include the users of modernist built forms who are equally innovative "translators" and interpreters of traveling technologies – if not ad hoc designers of built forms.[6] In so doing, I make several spatial and temporal observations about socialist aid through architecture and its afterlife. First, the "import" of urban prototypical designs circulating at the time that were associated with socialist modernisation, and especially mass housing, did not simply mimic the standardised architectural forms found across cities in socialist countries, despite belief – on all sides – in the universality of their application. Rather, there was significant redrafting, redesigning, and – much later – repurposing that took place across time, which vernacularised and diversified buildings, giving them their own unique characteristics while making for more culturally appropriate living environments. Local planners, for instance, redrew urban blueprints and residents modified their allotted apartments that were designed in collaboration with the "children of Marx in the land of Hồ Chí Minh," as the East German specialists

4 Christina Schwenkel, "Traveling Architecture: East German Urban Designs Abroad." *International Journal for History, Culture and Modernity* 2 (2014): 155–174. Several of the ideas in that article appear here in modified form.

5 Esra Akcan, *Architecture in Translation: Germany, Turkey, and the Modern House* (Durham, NC: Duke University Press, 2012).

6 Christina Schwenkel, *Building Socialism: The Afterlife of East German Architecture in Urban Vietnam*. Durham (NC: Duke University Press, 2020), 261.

on the project were called.[7] I highlight two primary reasons why such "translations" occurred despite sustained attention to, and social scientific study of everyday urban life: first, to overcome the disconnect between utopian aspirations tied to what was technologically possible in East Germany at the time and the infrastructural realities encountered on the ground in Vietnamese cities devastated from the war; and second, to remedy the cultural incommensurabilities that stemmed from different visions of urban futurity as manifested in concrete material forms and ways of organising society.

Pointing to innovation and translation does not, however, imply failure, a common trope used to dismiss socialist world-making projects, rather than take them seriously by asking: what did these projects do and in which ways do they endure, that is, how do they continue to inform urban life? Or, as Tania Murray Li asked of development schemes in Indonesia: "What are their messy, contradictory, multilayered, and conjunctural effects?"[8] Peter Van der Veer's observation about radical religious encounters under colonialism resonates with transformative architectural encounters under socialism: "The immense creativity in [such] encounters [. . .] is often done little justice in accounts that rather stress failure than innovative practice", which made "new imaginations of community" and forms of social organization possible.[9] Cultural gaps between design and implementation in GDR architectural aid to Vietnam, in other words, should not be taken as yet another dismissive account of a failed socialist agenda. Rather, my goal is to highlight the creative forms of agency that transpired at different scales and among different groups of people who came together under catastrophic conditions to collectively imagine, plan, and build a better world in the aftermath of urbicide or place annihilation. Through formal and informal architectural interventions across time, we see how those translated built forms continued to undergo change as they aged and decayed and were subsequently remade when confronted with their premature or unplanned obsolescence.

In what follows, I examine how GDR architectural models and building technologies were applied transnationally to design socialist cities in non-European geographies. I argue that the dissemination of ideas about socialist modernity through the circulation of planning practices, couched as "assistance" (*Hilfe*), was as much about the architectural engineering of urban space as it was about providing aid. Historically, the construction of urban infrastructure, including housing, was central to

7 Schwenkel, *Building Socialism*, 112.

8 Tania Murray Li, "Beyond 'the State' and Failed Schemes." *American Anthropologist* 107.3 (2005): 383–394, 384.

9 Peter van der Veer, "Introduction," in *Conversion to Modernities: The Globalization of Christianity*, edited by Peter van der Veer, 1–21 (London: Routledge, 1996), 7.

biopolitical strategies for regulating populations in socialist cities.[10] This was also the case in Vietnam after its independence from French colonialism with the support of both influential allies, including China and the Soviet Union, and less powerful "friends" in the East Bloc, like the GDR. I examine how this bilateral (GDR-Vietnam) project and its logics transpired transnationally across national and cultural boundaries, arguing against the assumption that the application of modernist architecture as a solution to "deliberate demodernization"[11] reflects the imposition of a "foreign" ideology, or is even a form of indirect colonisation. This is not a case of socialist imperialism, where liberation struggles were subjected to foreign rule and control over the morphology of cities, and to suggest so risks historical reductionism. Despite new dependencies on socialist technical and material aid, I agree with Stephen V. Ward's observation that the geopolitical situation was quite unlike colonialism, where there was never any doubt where power lay and which authorities were in charge.[12] In contrast, relationships on the ground between Vietnamese officials and East German experts were ambivalent – marked by affective solidarities, but also distrust – and urban plans were subject to negotiation, with Vietnamese authorities having the final word on formal planning decisions, which users of buildings would then alter according to their own ideas about livability. Without losing sight of power inequalities that informed such collaborations and directed the flow of resources from the socialist North to the postcolonial South, I show how users of modernist architecture, in particular, contested European spatial practices by reconfiguring housing typologies, including those already redesigned by Vietnamese planners. My approach thus challenges assumptions about socialist architectural uniformity and top-down understandings of power and planning by showing the messiness of architectural development schemes that were productive of new forms of design knowledge and practice among users – the inhabitants of mass housing – to mitigate the gap between project aspirations and outcomes.[13]

---

10 Stephen J. Collier, *Post-Soviet Social: Neoliberalism, Social Modernity, Biopolitics* (Princeton: Princeton University Press, 2011).
11 Which, Stephen Graham argues, was the "hallmark of US air power." Stephen Graham, "Switching Cities Off: Urban Infrastructure and US Air Power" *City* 9 (2005): 169–193.
12 Stephen V. Ward, "Transnational Planners in a Postcolonial World," in *Crossing Borders: International Exchange and Planning Practices*, edited by Patsy Healey, and Robert Upton, 48–72 (London: Routledge, 2010), 63.
13 Li, "Beyond 'the State'," 391.

Architectural modernisms

Cities have long been a focus of high-modernist improvement projects.[14] Irrespective of geography or political economy, "the urban" has long been a yardstick against which the "non-modern" has been measured. Of course, claims to essential rural-urban differences are themselves cultural and historical constructs that deny critical webs of interconnection between the country and the city. It is precisely this condition of ambiguity and the threat of blurred boundaries that has been the object of state-led planning interventions to improve the human life. Socialist urban planners, for example, pointed to the chaos and disorder of "capitalist cities" arguing that unchecked growth and planning lowered the standard of living for all but the wealthiest residents.[15] On the other hand, critics of socialist urbanisms have pointed to the lack of innovation and agency in urban development strategies, resulting in the drab and monotonous landscapes of a prefabricated modernity, in contrast to the presumed creativity of capitalist cities.[16] In response, scholars have argued that socialist modernist architecture was far more heterogeneous and experimental than is commonly recognised.[17] Even communal dormitories in Russia were designed as "futuristic experimental prototypes",[18] as "cosmic enthusiasts" steeped in social discourses of utopian futurism shaped the material and technological landscapes of socialist societies.[19]

Despite attention to such innovations in form, the idea that modernism produced bland uniformity remains surprisingly commonplace. Indeed, Svetlana Boym's observation that "we are surrounded by the anonymous buildings of our common modernity" neglects the rich diversity of lived experience of modernism and modernity on the ground as those buildings become embedded in distinct social and cultural worlds.[20] A closer look at Vietnam's architecture of this period likewise reveals a range in form, meaning, and practice of socialist modernism

---

14 James Scott, *Seeing Like the State: How Certain Schemes to Improve the Human Condition Have Failed* (New Haven, CT: Yale University Press, 1998).

15 Deutsche Bauakademie, "Thesen zur 1. Theoretischen Konferenz der Deutschen Bauakademie," *Deutsche Architektur* 9.10 (1960). Supplement.

16 Krisztina Fehérváry, *Politics in Color and Concrete: Socialist Materialities and the Middle Class in Hungary* (Bloomington: Indiana University Press, 2013).

17 See, for example, Vladimir Kulić, ed., *Second World Postmodernisms: Architecture and Society under Late Socialism* (London: Bloomsbury Academic, 2019).

18 Caroline Humphrey, "Ideology in Infrastructure: Architecture in Soviet Imagination." *Journal of the Royal Anthropological Institute* 11 (2005): 39–58, 44.

19 See Eva Maurer, Julia Richers, Monica Rüthers, and Carmen Scheide, eds., *Soviet Space Culture: Cosmic Enthusiasm in Socialist Societies* (London: Palgrave, 2011).

20 Svetlana Boym, *Architecture of the Off-Modern* (New York: Architectural Press, 2008), 76.

that counters Boym's "anonymous buildings". By decentring Europe, it also becomes easier to identify overlap in architectural design between the Cold War adversaries: as modernist buildings in northern and southern Vietnam show surprising similarities that offer entry points into wider discussions about urban housing.[21] Kenny Cupers's work on France's "social project" of post-war housing estates makes this point abundantly clear for Europe as well.[22] In fact, a 2015 exhibit on Cold War modernism in East and West Berlin at the Berlinische Galerie showed more continuities in form across the Wall than difference. Indeed, Susan Buck-Morss has suggested that urban developments in East and West Europe were but "variations of a common theme, the utopian dream [of] industrial modernity".[23] In Vietnam, a target of recurrent international intervention, a duality has long existed between national and foreign technologies, urban forms, and styles of living: from colonial French villas to socialist block housing. Assuming a perspective outside of Europe from the postcolonial South thus allows for a rethinking of the relationship between socialist modernity, urbanisation, and architectural design in more globally interconnected and less Eurocentric ways.

Shifting the conversation away from Europe also enables us to move beyond the problematic evaluation of socialism as backwards and un-modern – which posits capitalism as the pinnacle of modernity – and to see the lived experience of socialist modernism as a transformative project of rebuilding society and improving the welfare of the population. Under socialism, cities were important sites for the "full-scale makeover of the state, society, material culture, and citizens alike".[24] Architects and planners saw the built environment as a biopolitical tool to shape the values and conduct of urban residents in their quest to build worker-oriented cities. Moreover, imaginaries of the socialist "good life" could be conveyed to the urban masses through the built environment, especially through mass housing.

As cities were the ideal spaces in which socialist modernism could take concrete material form, the devastated urban landscapes of postwar Europe provided fertile ground for architectural experiments to design optimal living and working spaces. With rapid reconstruction underway, urban planners turned their attention

---

21 Phạm Phú Vinh, *Poetic Significance: Sài Gòn Mid-Century Modernist Architecture* (Helena, MO: Architecture Vietnam Books, 2021).

22 Kenny Cupers, *The Social Project: Housing Postwar France* (Minneapolis: University of Minnesota Press, 2014).

23 Susan Buck-Morss, *Dreamworld and Catastrophe: The Passing of Mass Utopia in East and West* (Boston: MIT Press, 2002), xiii–xiv.

24 Katherine Pence, and Paul Betts, "Introduction" in *Socialist Modern: East German Everyday Culture and Politics*, edited by Katherine Pence, and Paul Betts, 1–34 (Ann Arbor: University of Michigan Press, 2008), 8.

to building dwellings that prioritised people rather than capital in order to solve the dire problem of housing. France, for example, had an estimated unhoused population of three million people due to extensive war damage to its already outdated housing stock.[25] In the socialist East, the science of urban planning had a utilitarian imperative: to deliver the maximum number of modern accommodations to the greatest number of workers quickly and efficiently. This imperative resulted in a number of experimental housing typologies and construction technologies, such as prefabricated and standardised mass housing.[26] A new utopian vision found its form in the housing estate, a centralised system of living with services and amenities in close proximity to serve the physical, spiritual, and social needs of the work force.

Yet architecture was not only central to the production of a European socialist modernity; it was also exported to other places in need of "development" after warfare and anti-colonial revolutions. Traveling architectural forms would disseminate persuasive ideas about socialist modernization through industry transnationally. Across Africa and Asia – from Tanzania[27] to North Korea[28] and Vietnam – postcolonial cities provided the "laboratories" for East German architectural experiments framed as "assistance", "solidarity", and "mutual cooperation" to emphasise collaboration based on a common set of interests and values.[29]

Travelling architectures: Rebuilding post-war Vietnam

In the United States, air power has long been considered the instrument for achieving swift victory. Strategic bombing, it has been assumed, involves both material and affective impacts: it can destroy capability as well as resolve.[30] During the war in Vietnam, US leaders believed that strategic bombing could definitively defeat

25 Cupers, *The Social Project*, 3.
26 Steven Harris, *Communism on Tomorrow Street: Mass Housing and Everyday Life Under Stalin* (Baltimore: Johns Hopkins University Press, 2013), 277–278.
27 Ludger Wimmelbücker, "Architecture and City Planning Projects of the German Democratic Republic in Zanzibar." *Journal of Architecture* 17 (2012): 407–432.
28 Frank Rüdiger, *Die DDR und Nordkorea: Der Wiederaufbau der Stadt Hamhùng von 1954–1962* (Aachen: Shaker Verlag, 1996).
29 Andreas Butter, "Showcase and Window to the World: East German Architecture Abroad 1949–1990." *Planning Perspectives* 33 (2017): 249–269.
30 Mark Clodfelter, *The Limits of Air Power: The American Bombing of North Vietnam* (Lincoln: University of Nebraska Press, 2006), 2.

Hanoi and "win the war", as it had in World War Two. Between 1964 and 1973, the United States carried out fierce and sustained air attacks across the Democratic Republic of Vietnam (DRV, or "North Vietnam"), called America's "War of Destruction" (*Chiến tranh Phá hoại*) in Vietnamese national memory. The primary objective of the air attacks was to destroy infrastructure that enabled lines of communication and transportation, and thus the ability of northern troops to carry out prolonged military operations in the south of the country. The port city of Vinh, an industrial centre located in Nghệ An province, midway between Hanoi and the dividing line at the seventeenth parallel,[31] occupied a strategic node in the DRV's complex transportation network, facilitating the movement of troops and supplies to southern battlefields. Located on a major branch of the "Hồ Chí Minh Trail" – a series of small roads that wound through the jungles of Laos into southern Vietnam – Vinh became a major target of protracted bombing to destroy its infrastructure. Between August 1964 and January 1973, the city and its environs were decimated by more than 5,000 air strikes, during which an estimated 250,000 tons of ordnance were dropped, leaving the region uninhabited and uninhabitable.[32]

The US military's assertion that precision-guided bombs would reduce civilian casualties and damage to non-targeted property proved a fallacy in the case of Vinh (and elsewhere in the country). When the bombing finally ended in 1973, hundreds of people had been killed and few structures were left standing on a cratered landscape.[33] Although the US did not officially target cultural heritage in its air campaigns, as Robert Bevan has argued, deliberate attacks on architecture and historical monuments have long been a strategy of urban warfare, or urbicide.[34] As in Europe, air attacks demolished Vinh's cultural heritage – including pagodas, churches, temples, and the ancient citadel – as well as public buildings, such as markets, hospitals, schools, and worker housing, as well as private civilian dwellings. Older residents describe their leveled city as "completely ravaged", with streets reduced to "piles of rubble and ash". They remember the thunderous explosions and thick, blinding smoke as they attempted to evacuate the city. "The Americans dropped bombs until

---

31 The provisional border between the Democratic Republic of Vietnam and the Republic of Vietnam ("South Vietnam") at the seventeenth parallel was unrecognised by the DRV.

32 Phạm Xuân Cần, and Bùi Đình Sâm, *Lịch sử thành phố Vinh, 1945–1975* [*History of Vinh City, 1945–1975*] (Vinh: Nghệ An, 2003), 217.

33 The municipal People's Committee reported 586 civilian deaths and 964 injured within the city proper, a death rate of just over 1 percent of the entire pre-war urban population. For details, see Chapter 2 in Schwenkel, *Building Socialism*.

34 Robert Bevan, *The Destruction of Memory: Architecture at War* (London: Reaktion Books, 2006).

no home was left intact", one elderly woman recollected in an interview I conducted in 2011 during my fieldwork in Vinh.

The socialist world had supported Vietnam in what was considered a revolutionary struggle against the malevolent forces of imperialism, so it was perhaps no surprise that after the signing of the Paris Peace Accords in January 1973 (which ended the bombing and US involvement in the war), Soviet Bloc nations pledged to assist Vietnam in its national reconstruction and economic recovery. Under the banner of "international socialist solidarity", much of this assistance focused on public works and the rebuilding of urban industry and infrastructure. Importantly, agreements between Vietnam and "fraternal" or allied socialist countries were considered not as foreign imposition but as pacts of mutual cooperation propelled by sovereign requests from the leadership in Hanoi. They were therefore distinct from colonial civilisation projects that mainly served French interests and French inhabitants of Vietnamese cities. However, there is no denying the political gains to socialist countries that practised solidarity based on their anti-colonial politics. A critical objective of Cold War aid from either the "West Bloc" or the "East Bloc" was to strengthen international alliances through the production of living environments that exemplified particular visions of development, aligned with either capitalism or socialism. The United States, for example, exported its ideas of democracy through housing aid and notions of home ownership as "progress" to the Philippines.[35] Destroyed cities thus emerged as the architectural battlegrounds of Cold War politics that gave material form to geopolitical alignments and their shapeshifting over time. Still, urban rehabilitation schemes were intended to benefit local populations (a strategy of winning hearts and minds) and undo colonial racialisation policies by bringing vital infrastructure to the masses.

The GDR's experience with mass urban destruction and rapid industrial reconstruction was well known in the DRV. Indeed, the discourse at the time emphasised historical similarities between Vietnam and East Germany: both countries had been divided and destroyed by American imperialists. Though the idea of "shared suffering" obfuscated major differences between these national histories (like the Holocaust), it was a powerful political force that fueled "solidarity" and architectural aid as part of its socialist "gift diplomacy".[36] On 19 May 1973, Prime Minister Phạm Văn Đồng sent a letter to the Chairman of the Council of Ministers in the GDR requesting assistance with rebuilding Vinh, Vietnam's "red city" and cradle of the revolution.

35 Nancy Kwak, *A World of Homeowners: American Power and the Politics of Housing Aid* (Chicago: University of Chicago Press, 2015).

36 Łukasz Stanek, Gift, Credit, Barter: Architectural Mobilities in Global Socialism, *E-flux Architecture* (July 2020), https://www.e-flux.com/architecture/housing/337850/gift-credit-barter-architectural-mobilities-in-global-socialism/.

The East German government readily agreed to take on what would become the largest and most successful urban reconstruction projects in Vietnam, despite facing significant impediments on account of its scale and complexity.

During the Cold War, architectural models and planning practises that circulated among allied or "fraternal" socialist countries, particularly between the socialist North and South, conveyed an aspirational, forward-looking vision of state-led modernisation. This persuasive vision of a socialist good life promised industrial productivity and a modern standard of living for vulnerable populations struggling with postcolonial precarity. As material resources, technologies, and expertise traveled from East Germany to Vietnam, international assistance, or *Hilfe*, also promoted an ethos of horizontal solidarity, that is, of non-hierarchical cooperation that would enable self-reliance rather than new forms of dependency. Kinship terminology – such as fraternal aid (*brüderliche Hilfe*) – suggested a level playing field and mutual benefits. *Hilfe* was thus thought to be distinct from the paternalist and neocolonial politics of pity that informed aid from the capitalist West.[37]

As in North Korea two decades earlier, East Germany's paramount project in Vietnam was to rebuild an industrial city that had been demolished by US air strikes at an even greater scale of industry. In Vietnam, the immense seven-year effort (1974–1980) referred to as "Assistance in the Construction and Design of Vinh City" (*Hilfe beim Aufbau und bei der Projektierung der Stadt Vinh*) aimed to transform the devastated provincial capital into a model city at the forefront of socialist modernity – even surpassing Hanoi in its infrastructure. Not unlike industrial towns across the Soviet Union and Eastern Europe, Vinh was to become a municipal centre for "civilising" its population, transforming rural migrants into a productive urban workforce through mechanisation and training – as well as through living environments to enable social reproduction.[38] This would be accomplished through the construction and allocation of mass housing with modern amenities and on-site public services, in conjunction with expanding the building materials industry and founding a new training infrastructure (Fig. 1).[39]

---

37 On solidarity as distinct from a politics of pity, see Hannah Arendt, *On Revolution* (New York: Penguin, 2006), 78–79. On the GDR's differentiation between capitalist aid and socialist assistance, see Jude Howell, "The End of an Era: The Rise and Fall of GDR Aid." *The Journal of Modern African Studies* 32 (1994): 305–328.

38 For a detailed account of how this took place through urban design and architecture, see Katherine Lebow, *Unfinished Utopia: Nowa Huta, Stalinism, and Polish Society, 1949–56* (Ithaca, NY: Cornell University Press, 2013).

39 This included the founding of a technical school to train workers in new building technologies like prefabrication, as well as construction of a concrete factory, among other industrial workplaces, in addition to new urban infrastructure, including a wastewater system.

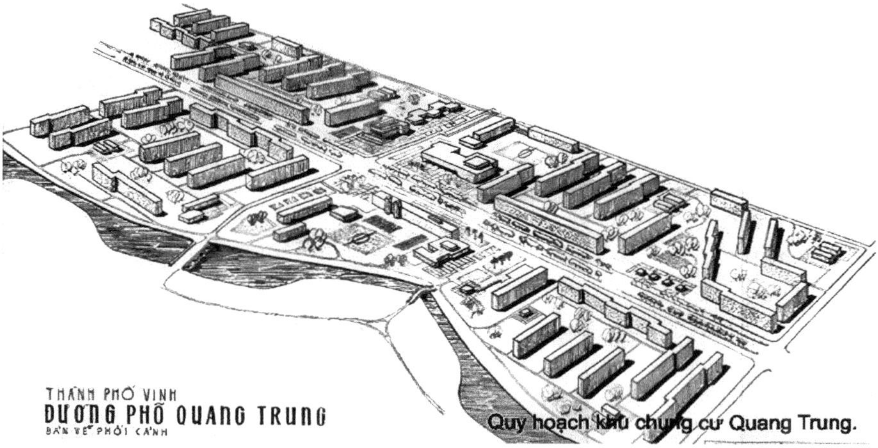

Fig. 1: The original plan for Quang Trung housing estate, Vinh City. Only the right side would be built by 1980 owing to material scarcities and longer construction times than planned.
Source: Nghệ An News.

The housing estate, in particular, would bring the city national recognition for its rational planning and ecological design at a scale that was unprecedented at the time. Images released by the Vietnamese and East German press tried to capture the magnificence of the project through wide-angle shots of the buildings that resembled townscapes in socialist Europe. Curious spectators flocked to the construction site to witness the dramatic conversion of the cratered landscape into a modernist city with staggered rows of multistory housing blocks stretching into the horizon, and paused to have their picture taken against this backdrop (Fig. 2). The Ministry of Construction also considered the housing estate as a prototype for future projects, organising a conference in Vinh in 1978 for a delegation of planners from northern provinces to visit the model design. Delegates gazed upon the high-rise buildings like "palaces that had dropped from the moon", as one participant described to me in an interview, capturing the spectacle of infrastructure at the time.[40]

But this enchantment was short-lived and underpinned by certain ambivalences – from conception and implementation to use and inhabitation, as I show in the next section. The original "Conceptual Design for the Construction of Quang Trung [Housing Estate]" – named after an eighteenth-century emperor and military hero from Nghệ An – emphasised a balance between tradition and modernity, or

40 Schwenkel, *Building Socialism*, 183.

Fig. 2: Vietnamese women dressed in *áo dài* for the lunar new year (Tết) pose in front of the GDR-built water fountain across from the housing estate in 1978 for the Tết issue of the newspaper. Source: Nghệ An News.

socialist internationalism and Vietnamese national identity. The high-rises should be built in the style of modernist architecture in conjunction with a national aesthetic or motif. They should have vibrant accents with "the possibility to incorporate artistic works, flower gardens, and water fountains". Destroyed heritage, like pagodas, and sites of social gatherings, like the cinema, "should be restored in their original locations".[41] This concern with balance and harmony, and with the spirit of international solidarity framed as co-production, allowed Vietnamese actors to intervene at multiple scales to change the architectural plan and the distinctive form of social organisation it disseminated through design.

41 *Konzeption für die Bebauung Quang Trung* [*Conceptual Design for the Construction of Quang Trung*] (15 May 1974), Bundesarchiv Deutschland, File DH1 28549.

Architectural translations

In his provocative book, *Spaces of Hope*, geographer David Harvey identifies the creative work of twentieth-century architects and urban planners, whose utopian schemes for a just society conjoined "an intense imaginary of some alternative world (both physical and social) with a practical concern for engineering and re-engineering urban and regional spaces according to radically new designs".[42] In Vinh, the dream of a model socialist city found material expression in the creation of a mass residential development as an outcome of architectural aid to Vietnam. Place annihilation had turned the city into an urban lab for modernist experimentation, which extended to housing and its infrastructure to enable dense urban living in self-contained units based on the European ideal of nuclear families, which was in tension with the more typical three-generation living arrangement found in Vietnam and marked a shift from the workplace as the locus of social organisation.[43] The original design called for 36 five-story buildings that could house more than 15,000 workers and government employees, although the 22 blocks erected offered accommodation to nearly 9,000 residents only in a total of 1,800 units (Fig. 1). Private family apartments with modern amenities, such as indoor kitchens and plumbing, marked a shift away from communal living in cramped spaces with shared, outdoor facilities, which were the norm at the time. The sudden appearance across Vinh of German experts and imported technologies – bulldozers, lorries, cranes, cars, hoists, excavators, pumps, and pipes – suggested that socialism was indeed the best path to modernity, prosperity and well-being.

Scholars have shown how citizens of the Eastern Bloc, including architects and urban planners themselves, tended to be ambivalent about the standardised housing complex, or microrayon, and its emphasis on function over form. For example, Kimberly Zarecor has argued that Czechoslovakians saw such architecture and planning practises as Soviet impositions.[44] For Vietnamese, socialist urban forms, like their colonial predecessors, were the latest in a long history of non-indigenous architectures and foreign styles of "tropical" modernist dwellings. In my interviews with residents in Quang Trung housing during my residency in the complex, some waxed nostalgically about the settlement as having once been the pride of the city and a symbol of postwar recovery, while others expressed

42 David Harvey, *Spaces of Hope* (Berkeley: University of California Press, 2000), 164.

43 For a discussion of how postcolonial housing policy mirrored the collectivist, workplace-based model of the *danwei* in a period of Chinese architectural aid before the US war and the Sino-Soviet split, see Schwenkel, *Building Socialism*, 174.

44 Kimberly Elman Zarecor, *Manufacturing a Socialist Modernity: Housing in Czechoslovakia, 1945–1960* (Pittsburgh: University of Pittsburgh Press, 2011).

ambivalence about the very form of dwelling – high-rise apartments – that they were "forced" (*bị bắt buộc*) to live in. Travellers passing through Vinh often mistook the housing blocks as uniform Soviet prefabricated housing, even though the buildings were designed by the GDR, built with brick – by women who went on to live in the complex – and were remarkably diverse.

I saw this diversity firsthand when I lived in block C2 in 2010 to 2011 to carry out anthropological fieldwork on urban transformation and privatisation of the units: the variable configurations of the blocks, each with a different ventilation design; the ample green spaces between the buildings that residents appropriated and made into gardens and spaces of commerce; and the unique interiors that had been redesigned by officials who desired two families per unit, and then "rebuilt" by residents as I describe below. Looking closely, as Boym dared her readers, I could see that no window, balcony, door, or façade was alike. "People in these anonymous dwelling places develop the most nuanced language of minor variations", she noted of housing in the Soviet Union, and which my experience in Quang Trung confirmed, though these spaces were far from anonymous in Vinh.[45] On the contrary, the housing complex functioned as a "vertical village", my respondents, who knew intimate details about their neighbours and workplace colleagues, joked with me. In what follows I focus on two types of modifications to architectural "imports" that were translated to better fit with urban cultural practises and the socioeconomic realities of postwar Vietnam at the time. My goal is to show the distributive agency among state and non-state actors who insisted on shaping their living environments according to their own needs and in so doing, challenged the disciplinary power envisioned of buildings.

Architectural re-designs

Like other forms of development assistance, architecture-as-aid raises important questions about the circulation of foreign ideas and their local adaptation. As Stephen Ward asks of urban planning practices that travelled to postcolonial countries, where does the locus of power and control reside?[46] When I asked German architects who had worked in Vinh City this question, they reflected on their anti-war activism and political support for the mass solidarity with Vietnam movement. In putting their politics into action, solidarity on the ground through rebuilding cities allowed these experts to circumvent racial and cultural difference by positioning

45 Boym, *Architecture of the Off-Modern*, 77.
46 Ward, "Transitional Planners," 63.

their work in Vietnam as a co-production within a cohesive moral community of common interest, thus downplaying power asymmetries.

Likewise, Vietnamese architects and planners framed urban reconstruction as a productive collaboration, suggesting equal contributions from all sides. And yet, over the course of my research, a more complex picture of negotiation and tensions over cultural translation began to emerge that showed contested ideas about social organisation to be the norm rather than the exception. Many of these deliberations centred on the spatial design of apartment units, explained to me as disparities between "foreign" and "Vietnamese" approaches to housing. For example, while the East Germans took a functionalist approach – calculating the greatest number of families that could be housed in self-contained units with the lowest output of resources, for example – the Vietnamese took a more practical approach that sought to house the greatest number of unhoused people possible – beyond GDR calculations of maximum occupancy – by allocating each unit to two families. This risked an increase in the building's structural load beyond intended capacity, one German expert recalled. It would also undermine the project of producing modern socialist families based on the German notion of private space for nuclear families. Different visions of socialism and its spatio-material realisation were thus at play in architecture-as-aid.

Cultural incongruities also emerged in the design of the units: In Vietnamese architecture, dwellings are typically divided into an auxiliary or "wet" area of sanitation and food preparation, and a main living or "dry" area that includes rooms for sleeping and receiving guests. Traditionally, these areas were kept separate, with the auxiliary area typically located outside the home owing to its association with pollution (sewage and smoke). They are also gendered: the former female spaces for women's domestic work, and the latter male spaces for men's socio-political work. Western-style housing blocks with self-contained units for nuclear families positioned these two areas in close proximity. Of particular concern was the linear layout of the toilet, washroom, and kitchen opposite a large communal living room. East German experts had carefully calculated this design to take the seasonal winds into account, which would ventilate the flat and blow kitchen smoke from burning embers out the back window and balcony, rather than through the house.

Vietnamese architects did not reject this layout, which brought plumbing indoors to reduce the daily drudgery of household labour. In fact, they praised the eco-socialist design of the housing estate and the staggered arrangement of the buildings to channel the sun and wind for natural light and ventilation. On the one hand, the spatial design of the complex as a whole corresponded with Vietnamese architectural concerns with *phong thủy*, or *feng shui*, which emphasises harmony between the built and natural environments. On the other hand, the design of the individual flats was at odds with geomantic principles of propitious location and suitable spatialisation in human-environment relations, to ensure healthy and harmonious living. The ideal solution would have been to lay out the apartment with the "wet" area with its threat of contamination to the back of the dwelling. Yet, in the East German design, one encountered the toilet immediately upon entering the unit, which was a source of anxiety for Vietnamese residents, who saw its placement as indecorous. Thus, while East German architects saw indoor plumbing as central to the creation of a modern hygienic order, Vietnamese tenants saw it as unsanitary and indiscreet.[47] Alas, given the small sizes of the units (with an average 40 square metres), there were few design alternatives, both GDR and Vietnamese architects lamented to me.

These attempts at architectural translation were not driven by economics alone: efficient construction of inexpensive mass housing in keeping with a steady *Bautempo*, or construction speed. There were other cultural logics at work in the spatial design of the units and the housing complex more broadly, such as cultivating a certain lifestyle that GDR experts deemed desirable, and Vietnamese officials viewed with suspicion. In the words of one German chief architect: "We asked ourselves what kind of urban lifestyle did we want to develop in Vinh?" The shift from the work unit (cooperative model) as the basis of social organisation to the nuclear family as an economic unit and basis for social reproduction was promoted through architecture – for example, the addition of walls to create rooms with a specific user-purpose (like bedroom for sleeping) rather than leave spaces open for multifunctional use, as in conventional Vietnamese housing. East German publicity images also promoted a new lifestyle: with harmonious (heteronormative) families in their furnished apartments with household fixtures that people could only dream of owning at a time of food and material insecurity. This emphasis on consumption – and of the socialist good life through things – concerned Vietnamese authorities. Architecture-as-aid thus revealed deep ideological differences among stakeholders involved in the reconstruction of Vinh as conflicts arose over which path to socialism – and which kind of Socialist Person – was desirable.

Residential re-assemblages

Vietnamese architects and officials were not the only ones to question East German urban designs. Residents did as well. Although many were optimistic about high-rise housing and the modernisation of infrastructure that enabled the transition

47 Schwenkel, *Building Socialism*, 267–268.

from outdoor to indoor plumbing, others expressed concern about their lack of familiarity with apartment living in self-contained units detached from land. Modernist urban forms offered an entirely new spatial and sensory experience of the city for inhabitants, a majority of whom were female rural migrants who had come to the city to work in factories. They expressed their perplexing cultural experiences with incommensurability through the media and art, including examples that were published in the local press. In the poem, "High Rise in Vinh", for example, the author conveys the bewilderment of residents as they struggled to make sense of their new material and sensory world around them through more familiar cultural frameworks and practices: "Raised among the rice seedlings, in homes of myrtle and thatch; still following our old ways of life, under the same roof of a five-story flat",[48] The emphasis on "following of the old ways of life" rather than on becoming modern urban citizens, it should be noted, was at odds with the forward-looking project of building socialism. Translated architecture thus became a site and object of indiscipline and even opposition to the state's (and the GDR's) civilising mission to forge an urban proletariat lifestyle.

Like the architects and urban planners, residents commended the ecological design and *phong thủy* of the complex and its surrounding green environs, which offered shade, wind, and natural light. This had been especially important in the postwar years when the supply of electricity was limited due to damaged power stations. The small, self-contained flats, however, violated a key principle of *phong thủy* by locating the entrances to the living room and bathroom directly across from one another, allowing for bad winds to flow through the units, thereby affecting health. More critically, the layout meant that the ancestral altar, typically placed in the center of the all-purpose room across from the main entrance, would directly face the wet area of the bathroom, which threatened the well-being and harmony of the family (Fig. 3). Surely, this would insult ancestors and bring bad luck to the household, my neighbour, a geomancer and war veteran, explained to me.

Residents engaged in a range of design interventions to "improve" their apartments by maximising the flow of good energy and creating balance in the home. Their reassemblages of living spaces violated the building code, which most people ignored but officials generally tolerated, sometimes with a small penalty for the infringement. The geomancer, for example, renovated his apartment to better align space with his idea of the traditional Vietnamese home. First, he moved the toilet to the washroom and opened up the front space as a small guestroom where visitors would sit and drink tea upon their entry into the flat. He then sealed the door

48 Xuân Hoài, *Nghệ An News* (14 November 1978): 3. Also discussed in *Schwenkel, Building Socialism*, 159.

Fig. 3: Living room in Quang Trung housing complex with altar placed between doorways. Soot marks on the ceiling from burning incense sticks at the front of the room (position of the photographer) show that the altar has been moved to create better *phong thủy*.
Source: author.

to bathroom and made it accessible only via the kitchen, where he opened up a connecting wall. This common redesign made it easier for women to access water, as there were no lines to the kitchen originally. It also solved the issue of the placement of the altar, which he erected against the main wall, which no longer faced the restroom. Such renovations, which I observed in the majority of flats – each reassemblage distinct from the next – shows how inhabitants became active designers of their living spaces and translated architecture-as-aid to better correspond with their own cultural and spatial logics of modern life in the city.

Other renovations were more utilitarian; for example, to undo obsolescence as material needs and ideas about "modern life" changed, particularly after the collapse of the Soviet Union. While tenants altered walls and doors to harmonise living space at the front of their homes, in the back, they renovated balconies to enlarge their units for social and economic purposes. I have described elsewhere some of the early modifications to the apartments after residents moved in and enclosed their balconies to create stalls for livestock in order to survive a period of food insecurity.[49] Over the years, these enclosures, often called "tiger cages," expanded to larger, room-size attachments onto the backs of buildings to address the need for more space in now-multigenerational families (Fig. 4). The geomancer, for example, turned his attachment into a functioning kitchen with eating area, large enough for a dining table, which was rare in the complex. These planned renovations reconciled socialist obsolescence with capitalist aspirations and desires for middle class lives. Their variability in size and construction materials applied revealed growing socioeconomic inequalities across the complex. While outsiders disparaged the attachments as dangerous and contributing to urban blight, within the complex, they were visual markers of a family's upward mobility.

Fig. 4: The back of the housing blocks each display a different history of renovations to balconies from simple brick enclosures to expensive corrugated steel attachments.
Source: author.

49 Christina Schwenkel, "Post/Socialist Affect: Ruination and Reconstruction of the Nation in Urban Vietnam." *Cultural Anthropology* 28 (2013): 252–277, 264.

Conclusion: The afterlife of architecture as development

The cosmic era of socialist architectural experimentation may be over, but the materiality of this history remains visible around the world and continues to shape post-socialist urban life – at least for the moment. In Vinh, architecture-as-aid to build socialism and advance industrialisation now speaks to the "failures" of the socialist past to secure the good life for citizens in the city, according to critics. The presence of modernist "ruins" has become fodder for the next generation of development experts, who have advocated demolition and market liberalisation as the means to urban development. Yet, for many, the housing complex with its soccer field, parks, cinema, trade centre, schools, daycares, youth house, and multistory buildings with public utilities, remained a celebrated achievement for its technological and ecological innovation at a time of bare life. More than once I heard the response: "It was the best available housing in the city – at the time"; it gave people who had lost their homes permanent shelter. And in so doing, the state took liberties to try and use architecture as a tool of disciplinary power to shape people's behaviours and subjectivities as urban socialist moderns. Yet as I have argued, Vietnamese stakeholders did not unconditionally accept the GDR's model of architectural modernism and the particular culture of individualism it promoted. Rather, they translated concepts and forms into more culturally familiar norms of social and spatial organisation, and in so doing they showed competing understandings and visions of what the future of socialism might look like.

For the global South, modernity is often treated as fragmentary if not ephemeral, as a status or sensibility that a nation or a population can aspire to, achieve, and then suddenly lose. Catching up only to lag behind again. After the collapse of the Soviet Union, the widespread transformations that swept the world seemed to affirm the backwardness of forward-looking socialisms. What was once a symbol of progress, that stirred collective optimism among many, now signifies that which is not-quite-modern: public built forms, for example, that need privatisation – and private investment – to create responsible homeowners as the latest urban moderns.

The GDR-built housing complex in Vinh had a similar trajectory but for different reasons given its construction as a solidarity aid project. By the mid 1990s, after a decade of economic reforms, the image of the housing blocks had changed from a symbol of urban progress – and popular photo backdrop – to that of decay and underdevelopment, an unplanned obsolescence to be sure. Like other places around the world, revitalisation projects have radically altered the built environment and lives of its residents, as the housing blocks have been demolished incrementally and replaced by condominiums – but only partially. To this day (2022), one entire area remains, though its fate will surely follow the same path.

Vinh is no shrinking model socialist city, however.[50] On the contrary, it has grown rapidly as a centre of industry, though it has been less successful at attracting international investors than other provincial capitals. Its growth is not a story of neoliberal conquest of the city, either. The original residents of the housing complex organised successfully to retain their rights to live in the centre of the city and to control the direction of redevelopment, which they stalled for ten years.[51] As profit-driven restructuring threatens to increase vulnerability and the spatialisation of urban inequality (by relocating the poor to urban margins), the approach taken by municipal authorities in Vinh – on-site resettlement to maintain communities – might offer a new model of architecture for future urban development.

50 See Felix Ringel, *Back to the Postindustrial Future: An Ethnography of Germany's Fastest-Shrinking City* (New York: Berghahn Books, 2018).
51 Details are provided in Chapter 10 of Schwenkel, *Building Socialism.*

About the Authors

Christoph Bernhardt, PhD, is a historian, deputy director at the Leibniz Institute for Research on Society and Space (IRS) in Erkner/Berlin and adjunct Professor for Modern and Contemporary History at Humboldt University Berlin. His main fields of research are European urban and environmental history. For more details, see: https://leibniz-irs.de/en/people-careers/staff/person/christoph-bernhardt-0508

Andreas Butter, PhD, has worked as an author and exhibition curator, freelance monument conservation expert and lecturer, including at the IES Berlin. His main fields of research are the urban and architectural history of the 20th century. He was involved in the implementation of projects at the Bauhaus Dessau Foundation, the Institute for Foreign Cultural Relations and the Berlinische Galerie. Since 2010 he has been a research associate at Leibniz Institute for Research on Society and Space (IRS) Erkner. In 2012 he conceived a research project on East German architecture abroad.

Nikolay Erofeev is a Postdoctoral Fellow at the University of Kassel working on the history of socialist architecture and urban planning. Erofeev received his D.Phil (PhD) in History from the University of Oxford in 2020 and his specialist degree in the History of Art from Moscow State University in 2014. Erofeev had fellowships at the Department of Urban Studies at the University of Basel and at the Jordan Center for the Advanced Study of Russia at New York University. Erofeev's current fellowship is funded by the Alexander von Humboldt Foundation.

Jasna Galjer is an art historian, professor in the Department of the History of Art and Architecture at the University of Zagreb. Her research interests focus on 20th and early 21st century history, theory and criticism of architecture and design. She is especially interested in transfers and mediations of ideas, ideologies and discourses in the context of cultural history from the early 1950s to the end of 1970s. For more details, see https://www.bib.irb.hr/pregled/profil/14470

Anne-Kristin Hartmetz, having studied African studies and history with a focus on Eastern European and global history, is currently finishing her PhD project on relations between Ghana and the Soviet Union during the Cold War. Her research interests include South-East relations during the Cold War, transnational history, global aspects of socialism, and economic aspects of Cold War history. She is a doctoral candidate at the Chair of Eastern European History at the Humboldt University in Berlin.

Franziska Klemstein is art historian and since 2019 research associate for Digital Humanities at the Bauhaus-Universität Weimar/Germany. Her research focuses on architectural history and historic preservation as well as on visual studies and digital humanities. Recently, her dissertation was published: Denkmalpflege zwischen System und Gesellschaft. Vielfalt denkmalpflegerischer Prozesse in der DDR (1952-1975), Bielefeld (transcript) 2021. For more details see: https://www.uni-weimar.de/de/medien/professuren/medienwissenschaft/medientheorie-und-wissenschaftsgeschichte/personen/klemstein/

Rachel Lee is an assistant professor at the History of Architecture and Urban Planning Chair, TU Delft. Her research explores the histories of colonial and postcolonial architecture and urbanism at their intersections with migration and exile, transnational practice, heritage, mobility, and gender,

https://doi.org/10.1515/9783110658491-013

particularly in South Asia and East Africa. She is currently also a Mellon Fellow with the Canadian Centre for Architecture's "Centring Africa" project. Amongst her publications count: Rachel Lee and Anooradha Iyer Siddiqi, eds. "On Collaborations: Feminist Architectural Histories of Migration." *Aggregate*, no. Plots (November 14, 2022). http://we-aggregate.org/project/on-collaborations-feminist-architectural-histories-of-migration.

Monika Motylińska is an architectural historian and head of the junior research group "Histories of the Built Environment" at the Leibniz Institute for Research on Society and Space (IRS) in Erkner. Her main fields of research are the architectural and urban history of the 20th century, with a particular focus on global flows of construction materials, labour and capital. For more details, see https://leibniz-irs.de/en/people-careers/staff/person/monika-motylinska-0820.

Mariya Petrova is a doctoral researcher at the Leibniz Institute for Regional Geography (IfL) in Leipzig, Germany. Her PhD project explores public transportation infrastructures and policies in post-Soviet Uzbekistan. Prior to this, she conducted research on the history of building and housing in Soviet Uzbekistan and worked in the project "A Global History of Technology, 1850 – 2000" at the Technical University of Darmstadt. Recent publications: Nah am Boden. Privater Hausbau zwischen Wohnungsnot und Landkonflikt im Samarkand der 50er- und 60er-Jahre, Berlin, Boston: De Gruyter. 2021 (open access).

Christina Schwenkel is Professor of Anthropology and Southeast Asian Studies at the University of California, Riverside, USA. Her work examines urban infrastructure and the legacies of Cold War-era circulations of people, objects, technologies, and knowledge between Vietnam and East Germany. She is the author of The American War in Contemporary Vietnam: Transnational Remembrance and Representation (Indiana University Press, 2009) and, most recently the award-winning book, Building Socialism: The Afterlife of East German Architecture in Urban Vietnam, published in 2020 with Duke University Press. For more information, see: https://christinaschwenkel.com

Paul Sprute is a research associate in the junior research group Histories of the Built Environment at the Leibniz Institute for Research on Society and Space. His contribution expands on his Master's thesis in Global History at Freie Universität and Humboldt-Universität in Berlin on the institutional history of SODI. After completing both projects written independently of SODI, Paul Sprute joined SODI's board. His dissertation research at the Bauhaus-Universität Weimar deals with different modes of port constructions by German companies in post-colonial West Africa.

Łukasz Stanek is professor of architectural history at A. Alfred Taubman College of Architecture and Urban Planning, University of Michigan, Ann Arbor, USA. His research focuses on architectural exchanges between the socialist countries and the newly independent countries during the Cold War, which was the topic of his latest book "Architecture in Global Socialism. Eastern Europe, West Africa and the Middle East in the Cold War" (Princeton University Press, 2020). https://taubmancollege.umich.edu/architecture/faculty/directory/lukasz-stanek

Susanne Stein, PhD, is project coordinator for the Higher Education Alliance Ruhr (HAR) in Herne and adjunct lecturer at the Center for Cultural Studies on Science and Technology in China, TU Berlin, Germany. Her research and writing focus on urban planning and environmental history in twentieth-century China. For more details, see: https://www.china.tu-berlin.de/menue/home/team/gastwissenschaftlerinnen_und_lehrbeauftragte/susanne_stein/

Jonas van der Straeten is Assistant Professor at the Technology, Innovation and Society Group of Eindhoven University of Technology. In his research, he studies processes of technological change in Africa and Asia from a systemic, transdisciplinary, and global perspective. Prior to this, he worked as a postdoctoral researcher for the project "A Global History of Technology, 1850 – 2000" at the Technical University of Darmstadt where he focused on the temporality of technology in Central Asia. Recent publications: van der Straeten, J., & Obertreis, J. (2022). Technology, temporality, and the study of Central Asia: an introduction. Central Asian Survey, 41(2), 211-222. https://doi.org/10.1080/02634937.2022.2063795.

www.ingramcontent.com/pod-product-compliance
Ingram Content Group UK Ltd.
Pitfield, Milton Keynes, MK11 3LW, UK
UKHW022226051026
15624UKWH00002B/377

9 783110 654066